S0-FBV-477

REPRINTS OF ECONOMIC CLASSICS

THEORIES OF PRODUCTION & DISTRIBUTION

Also Published in

REPRINTS OF ECONOMIC CLASSICS

By Edwin Cannan

A Review of Economic Theory [1929]

Edited by Edwin Cannan

The Paper Pound of 1797-1821 [1925]

Adam Smith, Lectures on Justice, Police, Revenue & Arms [1896]

A HISTORY OF THE

THEORIES OF PRODUCTION & DISTRIBUTION

IN ENGLISH POLITICAL ECONOMY

from

1776 *to* 1848

EDWIN CANNAN

M.A., LL.D.

Late Professor of Political Economy in the University of London

Reprints of Economic Classics

Augustus M. Kelley · Publishers

NEW YORK · 1967

First Edition 1893
(London: Percival & Co., 1893)
Third Edition 1917

Reprinted 1967 by
AUGUSTUS M. KELLEY PUBLISHERS

Library of Congress Catalogue Card Number
– 66 - 22618 –

PRINTED IN THE UNITED STATES OF AMERICA
by SENTRY PRESS, NEW YORK, N. Y. 10019

PREFACE TO THE THIRD EDITION

Alterations in this edition are confined to half-a-dozen small corrections, none of them affecting the substance, which escaped being made when the second edition was prepared, and the addition at p. 408 of a table designed for the assistance of any critical reader who desires to pursue a quotation from Adam Smith in my own edition of the *Wealth of Nations* published in 1904 rather than in M'Culloch's edition. In present circumstances it is hoped that such a reader will be content to accept this expedient instead of the more obvious but costly plan of altering the 160 references in footnotes which occur on seventy-five pages.

If any time were suitable for bringing out a thoroughly revised version of the book it would not be the middle of 1917. But even if the practical difficulties caused by the war were removed, I think it would be undesirable to attempt such a revision. Twenty-four years is a long time in the life of a man, and I no longer feel any acute sense of identity with the rather youthful author who published in 1893. For me to add here, to omit there, and to alter somewhere else, all from the point of view of 1917, would most probably have the unsatisfactory results which usually follow an attempt to improve work done by another man at a much earlier date.

I hope, however, that within the next few years I may be able to supplement the present work by the production of an independent book in which the period 1776–1848 may be put in its proper relation both with what preceded it and with what followed it.

LONDON SCHOOL OF ECONOMICS
July 9th, 1917

PREFACE TO THE SECOND EDITION

The history of the theories dealt with in this book has not been much affected by the researches of the last ten years. The publication of the student's notes of Adam Smith's lectures and Dr W. R. Scott's study of the philosophy of Francis Hutcheson, have indeed thrown much additional light upon the origin of the *Wealth of Nations*, but that subject lies outside the limits laid down, and can be conveniently treated by itself. The new information contradicts nothing in the present work, and confirms the conjecture of Chapter VI, §1, as to the manner in which the Smithian scheme of Distribution was evolved.

Certain critics of the first edition complained of its tone, but I have great hope that what appeared to be ill-tempered blasphemy in 1893 will now be seen to be the calm statement of undoubted fact. No suggestion of actual misrepresentation or mistake in the history has reached me. Substantial changes therefore do not appear to be called for, and my experience in collating different editions of some of the greatest economic works does not incline me to regard extensive changes of an unimportant character with favour. Such changes generally add unnecessarily to the bulk of a book, almost always destroy its consistency, and invariably confuse and annoy the serious student. I have consequently resisted all temptations to strengthen or modify arguments, and to add new quotations.

The only changes in the text are the correction of a few misprints and grammatical blunders, the conversion of 'Mr Giffen' into 'Sir Robert Giffen', and the modification of one or two references to time which might have been confusing to the readers of a book dated 1903. In the references in the footnotes several alterations have been made necessary by the reprinting of Ricardo's letters to the *Morning Chronicle*, and by Professor Marshall's revision of successive editions of the first volume of his *Principles;* it has also been made clear that the tripartite division of Say's *Traité* occurs first in his second edition.

But while thus confining the alterations within the narrowest possible limits, I have not thought myself precluded from adding at the end of the last chapter two entirely new sections, in which I have attempted to indicate the relation of the theories of today to those of the period under review, and to show that the old theories have been replaced by others stronger from a scientific point of view, and equally for the practical needs of their own time.

London School of Economics
June 1903

PREFACE TO THE FIRST EDITION

As no one any longer believes that political economy was invented by Adam Smith and perfected by John Stuart Mill, it has become necessary almost to apologize for taking the dates of the publication of the *Wealth of Nations* and Mill's *Principles of Political Economy* for the limits of a history of a portion of economic theory.

I have chosen to begin with 1776 because what may be called the framework of the theories of Production and Distribution which have been taught in English economic works for the last hundred years, appears to owe its origin entirely to that peculiar combination of indigenous economics with the system of Quesnay which is to be found in the *Wealth of Nations*. I have ended with 1848 because it is yet too early to treat in an historical spirit the twenty-five years which have elapsed since 1868, and the period of stagnation which followed the publication of Mill's work is not a profitable subject of study except in connexion with the outburst of new ideas which ended it.

I have been able to obtain surprisingly little assistance from previous writers. Sir Travers Twiss' *View of the progress of Political Economy* is forty-six years old. Professor Ingram's *History of Political Economy*, and Mr Price's *Short History of Political Economy in England from Adam Smith to Arnold Toynbee* are both excellent, but the present work is so much more detailed within its own limits that opportunities for making use of them scarcely occurred. Much the same may be said of M. Block's *Progrés de la Science Economique* and some other histories. Of more service was the First Part of Dr Eugen von Bohm-Bawerk's *Kapital und Kapitalzins*, perhaps the most brilliant work extant on the history of any part of economic theory. To the valuable fragment which Adolf Held left behind him, when, by the fatality which hung over the economists of the last generation, he was cut off in his prime, *Zwei Bucher zur socialen Geschichte Englands*, I am indebted for first making me aware of that close connexion between the economics and the politics of the Ricardian period which provides the key to many riddles.

In the ordinary critical and constructive books on political economy there are frequent statements respecting the history of economic doctrines. But these statements are seldom of much value to the historian. They are often based on inaccurate quotations from memory, and the reader is scarcely ever given the reference which would enable him to check them. So far as they relate to the early nineteenth century period they are especially unsatisfactory and untrustworthy. It has been constantly supposed that 'abstract theory' must be defended at almost any cost against the attacks of the 'historical school', and the result has been the creation of a mythical Ricardo and Malthus, who never wrote anything which cannot be 'limited and explained' till it ceases to be in conflict either with recognized fact or accepted modern opinion. With such idealization I have no sympathy, and I fear I shall disappoint any one who expects me to hold up a few chosen economists as exempt from human error, and to exhibit all their opponents as persons of feeble intellect, who entirely failed to understand them. It is no part of my plan to recommend any particular method of economic inquiry, or to praise or decry any particular authors. My object is simply to show what the various theories concerning production and distribution were, and to explain how and why they grew up, and then either flourished or decayed.

To all my quotations I have given exact references. The pages of the *Wealth of Nations* referred to are those of M'Culloch's edition in one volume, which has been very frequently reprinted with the same paging. As there is no even tolerably good edition, I have thought it best to refer to that of which most copies are in existence. In a couple of cases where I have detected small inaccuracies in the text I have restored the true reading. Where any doubt arises as to the name or date of any other book referred to, it will be resolved by looking out the author's name in the index. In quotations I have often taken the liberty of omitting a word such as 'then' or 'therefore', when it occurs near the beginning, and merely connects the proposition with unquoted matter which precedes it. With this exception they will always, I hope, be found to be identical with the original.

OXFORD, *April* 1893

CONTENTS

CHAPTER V

The Third Requisite of Production – Land

CHAPTER VI

The Idea of Distribution

CHAPTER VII

Pseudo-Distribution

CHAPTER VIII

Distribution Proper

CHAPTER IX

General Review: Politics and Economics

CHAPTER I

THE WEALTH OF A NATION

§ 1. *Originally a State or Condition*

'Production' and 'distribution' in political economy have always meant the production and distribution of wealth. The first problem that confronts us is therefore the question of the nature of this 'wealth' which is the subject of production and distribution.

Etymologically nothing but a longer form of the word 'weal',[1] 'wealth' originally meant a particular state of body and mind. In the Litany it is opposed to 'tribulation', and in the prayer for the Queen's Majesty it is obviously intended to cover as much of welfare in general as is not already included in 'health'. In the words of the Authorized Version of the Bible, Mordecai seeks 'the wealth of his people';[2] the wicked, according to Job's complaint, 'spend their days in wealth';[3] and St Paul exhorts the Corinthians to 'let no man seek his own, but every man another's wealth'.[4]

The kind of welfare denoted by 'wealth' in this older sense is so dependent on the possession or periodical receipt of certain external objects, such as bread, meat, clothes, or money, that the word came to be applied to those objects themselves as well as to the state of body and mind produced by access to them. Before Adam Smith adopted the phrase, *An Inquiry into the Nature and Causes of the Wealth of Nations*, as the title of his work, the use of the word to indicate the objects which were supposed to make a man wealthy had become so common that lexicographers forgot to mention the older sense. In the dictionary compiled by Dyche and Pardon (1735) 'wealth' is made to signify only 'all sorts of riches, whether money, sheep, horses, merchandise, land, etc.' Johnson in 1755 explained it as 'riches, money or precious goods', and gave examples of its use in this sense alone from Spenser, Shakespeare, Bishop Corbet, and Dryden.

§ 2. *Supposed Identification with Gold and Silver*

Though Adam Smith says that 'it would be too ridiculous to go about seriously to prove that wealth does not consist in money or in gold and silver, but in what money purchases and is valuable only for purchasing',[b] he certainly seems to try to give his readers the impression

[1] Skeat, *Etymological Dictionary*, s.v. Wealth: 'An extended form of *weal* (ME *wele*), by help of the suffix *-th*, denoting condition or state; cf. *heal-th* from *heal*, *dear-th* from *dear*', etc.

[2] Esther x, 3. [3] Job xxi, 13. [4] 1 Cor. x, 24.

[5] Bk. IV, ch. i, M'Culloch's ed., p. 191 *b*.

that the groundless opinion that wealth consists exclusively in money was firmly held by the mercantilistwriters of the seventeenth and eighteenth centuries. Now it is quite possible to quote from these writers passages in which bullion and wealth are identified, and the riches or poverty of a nation made to depend upon the quantity of bullion it possesses.[1] But whether this is absurd or not entirely depends on the meaning given to the words wealth, riches, and poverty. A writer may use a word in a sense which is not given to it in ordinary conversation without being ridiculous. It would be ridiculous, indeed, to contend that a nation could be well fed and comfortably clothed and housed by gold alone; but there is no reason to suppose that the wildest mercantilist ever suffered from this delusion. The mere existence of the fable of Midas was a sufficient safeguard. The mercantilists may be justly accused of exaggerating the importance of having a hoard of bullion and of recommending a number of useless regulations for the purpose of securing such a hoard, but none of them ever imagined gold and silver to be the only economic good. They were, indeed, rather inclined to represent the acquisition of gold and silver as the only economic good which could be obtained by one single department of industry, foreign trade;[2] but in this they were not, considering

[1] *E.g.*: 'The general measures of the trade of Europe at present are gold and silver, which, though they are sometimes commodities, yet are the ultimate objects of trade; and the more or less of those metals a nation retains it is denominated rich or poor.' – William Richardson, *Essay on the Cause of the Decline of the Foreign Trade*, 1744, in Overstone's *Select Tracts on Commerce*, p. 157. 'So mistaken are many people that they cannot see the difference between having a vast treasure of silver and gold in the kingdom, and the mint employed in coining money, the only true token of treasure and riches, and having it carried away; but they say money is a commodity, like other things, and think themselves never the poorer for what the nation daily exports.' – Joshua Gee, *The Trade and Navigation of Great Britain considered, showing that the surest way for a nation to increase in riches is to prevent the importation of such foreign commodities as may be raised at home, etc.*, 1729, 6th ed. 1755, p. 8. 'That which is commonly meant by the balance of trade is the equal importing of foreign commodities with the exporting of the native. And it is reckoned that nation has the advantage in the balance of trade that exports more of the native commodities and imports less of the foreign. The reason of this is, that if the native commodities be of a greater value that are exported, the balance of that account must be made up in bullion or money; and the nation grows so much richer as the balance of that account amounts to.' – Postlethwayt, *Universal Dictionary of Trade and Commerce*, 2nd ed., 1757, vol. i, p. 184 *a*, s.v. Balance of Trade. Cf. vol. ii, p. 283 top.

[2] 'The balance of trade is commonly understood two ways: (1) Generally, something whereby it may be known whether this kingdom gains or loses by foreign trade; (2) Particularly, something whereby we may know by what trades this kingdom gains, and by what trade it loses. For the first of these it is the most general received opinion, and that not ill-grounded, that this balance is to be taken by a strict scrutiny of what proportion the value of the commodities exported out of this kingdom bear to those imported; and if the exports exceed the imports, it is concluded the nation gets by the general course of its trade, it being supposed that the overplus is imported bullion, and so adds to the treasure of the kingdom, gold and silver being taken for the measure and standard of riches.' – Josiah Child, *A New Discourse of Trade*, 4th ed., p. 164.

the nature of European and especially English foreign trade at the time they wrote, so very ridiculously wrong. Exchange between nation and nation of the bulky articles which constitute the necessaries of life is a thing which has grown up with modern facilities of transport. In the seventeenth century the articles other than bullion imported into England were mostly of a somewhat insignificant character. Most of them were superfluous, and many deleterious. Writers of that time may well be excused for having imagined that the chief use of foreign trade to England was to introduce gold and silver rather than nutmeg.[1]

Petty's *Verbum Sapienti* shows what was understood by the wealth of a nation in 1691. It contains a 'computation' of the 'wealth of the kingdom', of which the following is a summary:[2]

Land (24,000,000 acres yielding £8,000,000 rent)	£144,000,000
Houses	30,000,000
Ships (500,000 tons)	3,000,000
Cattle, horses, etc.	36,000,000
Gold and silver coin	6,000,000
Merchandise, plate, and furniture ..	31,000,000
	£250,000,000

It does not appear that any one ever quarrelled with this 'computation' on the ground that the gold and silver should alone have been reckoned, and the 'wealth of the kingdom' consequently valued at £6 million instead of £250 million.

About the middle of the eighteenth century some writers seem to have imagined that the coin of a country must always bear the same proportion to the rest of its wealth, so that the increase of coin would measure the increase of wealth.[3] But Steuart, the last and most systematic of the school to which Adam Smith was so hostile, disapproved of 'the modern way of estimating wealth by the quantity of

[1] Davenant urged that Europe sustained a loss by the trade with India on this ground: 'Europe draws from thence nothing of solid use; materials to supply luxury and only perishable commodities, and sends thither gold and silver, which is there buried and never returns.' – *East India Trade*, 1696, p. 12. Even Sir Theodore Janssen, the author of *General Maxims in Trade*, 1713, reprinted in the *British Merchant*, 1721, only claimed that 'the importing of commodities of mere luxury is so much real loss as they amount to', and admitted 'that the imports of things of absolute necessity cannot be esteemed bad', vol. i, p. 6.

[2] Chap. i, pp. 3–7.

[3] See *An Essay on the National Debt and National Capital, or the Account truly stated, Debtor and Creditor*, by Andrew Hooke, 1750. A summary of Hooke's conclusions will be found in R. Giffen, *Growth of Capital*, pp. 87, 88.

coin in circulation'.[1] Adam Smith's predecessors really knew as well as he did that the money of a nation was not its only wealth, and the emphasis with which some writers have insisted on the fact[2] is to be regarded merely as the consequence of a desire to make a good point against protectionism, which has almost always been associated with fallacies about 'carrying money out of the country'.

§ 3. *Restriction to Objects with Exchange Value*

But while no one really considered the wealth of a nation to consist exclusively of its money, every one took it for granted that it consisted exclusively of objects which possessed a money value. The physiocrats, from whom Adam Smith derived many of the ideas which he introduced into English political economy, expressly excluded *biens gratuits* from *richesses*:

> 'Les biens', says Quesnay, 'sont ou gratuits ou commerçables. Les biens gratuits sont ceux qui sont surabondants et dont les hommes peuvent jouir partout et gratuitement, tel est l'air que nous respirons, la lumière du soleil qui nous éclaire, etc. Les biens commerçables sont ceux que les hommes acquièrent par le travail et par échange: c'est ce genre de biens que nous appelons richesses, parce qu'ils ont une valeur vénale, relative et réciproque les uns aux autres, et en particulier à une espèce de richesse que l'on appelle monnaie, qui est destinée à représenter et à payer la valeur vénale de toutes les autres richesses.'[3]

Though he does not say so, there is no doubt that Adam Smith shared Quesnay's opinion. It is implied in his making the wealth of a nation consist exclusively of the produce of labour, and in his attaching great importance to the 'exchangeable value' of the whole of this produce.[4] It is indeed quite natural where private property is established to omit all things which possess no money value from the catalogue of the things which constitute an individual's wealth, because however useful or agreeable they may be to him, their possession does not make him any better off than his fellows. But national wealth is on a somewhat different footing. This was perceived in 1804 by Lauderdale, who was desirous of showing that the Sinking Fund was about to ruin the nation, not because it paid off little or no debt, but because it paid off too much. With this purpose in view, he endeavoured to prove that public wealth and private riches are not increased in the same way, and that value, though necessary to private riches,

[1] *An Inquiry into the Principles of Political Economy*, 1767, vol. i, p. 177; vol. ii, p. 42 (in *Works*, vol. i, p. 238; vol. iii, pp. 56, 57).

[2] *E.g.* M'Culloch, Introductory Discourse to *Wealth of Nations*, p. xix. J. S. Mill, *Principles*, Preliminary Remarks, [illegible], pp. 2–4, People's ed., pp. 1, 2.

[3] *Œuvres*, ed. Oncken, p. 289 note.

[4] See *e.g.* Bk. I, ch. vi, p. 24 *a*; Bk. II, ch. ii, p. 123 *b* and ch. iii, pp. 149 *b*, 150 *b*, 216 *a*.

is not necessary to public wealth. Value, he says, is dependent on scarcity, while national wealth is dependent on abundance. For instance, a bad harvest is certainly inimical to national wealth, although the smaller quantity of grain produced may be worth more than the greater quantity produced in a good year. So public wealth must be defined 'to consist of all that man desires as useful or delightful to him', and 'individual riches' must be defined 'to consist of all that man desires as useful or delightful to him which exists in a degree of scarcity'.[1] The absurdity of Lauderdale's conclusions about the Sinking Fund blinded his contemporaries to much of what was acute and valuable in his arguments. They seem to have considered that he was sufficiently answered by the assertion that if there is a rise in the value of grain there is a fall in the value of other things,[2] a statement which leads to nothing. If the whole year's produce be valued in grain it will appear much smaller than in an ordinary year; if it be valued in any other commodity it will appear larger, and this is the fact of which Lauderdale complains. In *Commerce Defended* (1808) James Mill remarks that 'wealth is relative to the term value', and says, 'The term wealth will always be employed in the following pages as denoting objects which have a value in exchange, or at least notice will be given if we have ever occasion to use it in another sense'.[3] The author of the article 'Political Economy' in the fourth edition of the *Encyclopædia Britannica*, writing in 1810, is equally unhesitating:

> 'External accommodations which are in complete and universal abundance, the air we breathe, the light of heaven, are not wealth. To constitute this, the article must exist in some degree of scarcity. It is then only that it can possess exchangeable value, that its possessor can procure other commodities in exchange for it.'[4]

J.-B. Say gave, in 1814, the following definition of national wealth: '*La richesse d'une nation est la somme des valeurs possédées par les particuliers dont se compose cette nation et de celles qu'ils possèdent en commun.*'[5] But what is the meaning of '*la somme des valeurs*'?

> 'VALEUR ou VALEURS (au pluriel) se prend quelquefois pour la chose ou les choses évaluables dont on peut disposer, mais en faisant abstraction de la chose et en ne considérant que sa valeur. C'est ainsi qu'on dit: *Il a déposé des valeurs pour gage de sa dette.*'[6]

These definitions suggest that it is possible to get an idea of national wealth by considering only the value of the things which constitute it. Against this theory Ricardo wrote a whole chapter, which he entitled,

[1] *Nature and Origin of Public Wealth*, 1804, pp. 56, 57.
[2] *Edinburgh Review*, July 1804, pp. 351, 352.
[3] P. 22.
[4] Vol. xvii, p. 107 *b*.
[5] *Traité*, 2nd ed., 1814, vol. ii, p. 472.
[6] *Ibid.*, p. 478.

'Value and Riches, their Distinctive Properties'. If he had had the literary education which, according to M'Culloch, some of his contemporaries thought he had been fortunate in escaping,[1] he would have known that it was unnecessary in English to explain that value 'essentially differs from riches'.[2] No one ever imagined that 'value' and 'riches' were synonymous. What Ricardo really wished to show was simply the fact that the wealth of a nation does not vary with the value of its produce (reckoning the value of the produce in his peculiar method by the amount of labour necessary for its production), but with the abundance of the produce.[3] Malthus, seldom blessed with a clear-cut opinion on any subject, thought that 'in making an estimate of wealth, it must be allowed to be as grave an error to consider quantity without reference to value as to consider value without reference to quantity'.[4] He saw that though a country continued to have the same quantity of produce, or rather of products, a change might take place in its wealth owing to events which affected the value of the products, and rashly assumed that the alteration in wealth was caused by the change of value, instead of directly by the events which caused the change of value.[5] However, in his *Definitions* (1827) he did not assert that in order to be 'wealth' an article must possess value, but only that it must 'have required some portion of human exertion to appropriate or produce'.[6] M'Culloch thought it necessary to make 'exchangeable value' an indispensable condition of wealth, in order to exclude 'atmospheric air and the heat of the sun', and similar 'necessary, useful, and agreeable products'.[7] J. S. Mill says: 'Things for which nothing could be obtained in exchange, however useful or necessary they may be, are not wealth in the sense in which the term is used in Political Economy'. In answer to the objection that this would make the wealth of mankind increase if air 'became too scanty for the consumption', he reproduces the argument which had already done duty in 1804:

> 'The error', he says, 'would lie in not considering that however rich the possessor of air might become at the expense of the rest of the community, all persons else would be poorer by all that they were compelled to pay for what they had before obtained without payment.'[8]

But to the theory that nothing which does not possess value can constitute part of the wealth of a community there is the fatal objection that it makes the existence of wealth dependent on the existence

[1] *The Works of David Ricardo*, ed. M'Culloch, pp. xv, xvi.
[2] 1st ed., p. 377; 3rd ed. in *Works*, p. 165.
[3] Cf. with the chapt. quoted, *Letters of Ricardo to Malthus*, ed. Bonar, pp. 211, 212.
[4] *Political Economy*, 1820, p. 344. [5] *Ibid.*, p. 340. [6] P. 234.
[7] *Principles*, 1825, p. 5.
[8] *Principles*, Preliminary Remarks, People's ed., pp. 4–5. See above, p. 6.

of separate property. Long before J. S. Mill wrote, Torrens had pointed this out. Conditions, he showed, can easily be conceived in which human beings would have wealth, but nothing with exchange value. Nothing could be said to have any value where there were no exchanges; and so it appears that an isolated man or an isolated communist society could not possibly have any wealth, if wealth be confined to things with exchange value.[1] Some years later this conclusion was boldly accepted by Whately and Senior. Whately, after remarking that 'Catallactics, or the Science of Exchanges', would be the 'most descriptive, and on the whole least objectionable', name for what is commonly called political economy, observes that a man like 'Robinson Crusoe is in a situation of which Political Economy takes no cognizance', and will only grant that he might be 'figuratively' rich.[2] Senior says:

> 'Colonel Torrens supposes a solitary family, or a nation in which each person should consume only his own productions, or one in which there should be a community of goods, and urges, as a *reductio ad absurdum*, that in these cases, though there might be an abundance of commodities, as there would be no exchanges, there would, in our sense of the term, be no wealth. The answer is, that for the purposes of Political Economy there would be no wealth; for, in fact, in such a state of things, supposing it possible, the Science of Political Economy would have no application. In such a state of society, Agriculture, Mechanics, or any other of the arts which are subservient to the production of the commodities which are, with us, the subjects of exchange, might be studied, but the Science of Political Economy would not exist.'[3]

Now it is doubtless true that a very great deal – we might almost, perhaps, say much the greater part – of what has been written on political economy relates only to a state of things where private property is established and exchange is practised. It probably never occurred to Adam Smith to speculate as to the possibility of society existing and enjoying necessaries, conveniences, and amusements without separate property. Separate property was to him a 'natural' institution, which existed in much the same form among savage tribes of hunters and fishermen as in eighteenth century England. Malthus thought separate property a necessary institution which would soon be re-established if its abolition were ever accomplished by followers of Godwin.[4] Ricardo, as became a stockbroker, took it for granted without any consideration. Consequently, in almost the whole of the doctrines of these writers, the existence of private property and the practice of exchange is assumed. Obviously their theories of exchange and distribu-

[1] *Production of Wealth*, 1821, pp. 7–17.

[2] *Introductory Lectures on Political Economy*, 1831, 3rd ed., 1847, pp. 5, 6.

[3] *Political Economy*, 8vo ed., p. 25.

[4] *Essay on the Principles of Population*, 1798, pp. 194–198.

tion could have no application to a communist society, and the key-note of their theory of production is to be found in a conception of 'capital' which is entirely dependent on the existence of private property.

But by the time of Senior and J. S. Mill universality was claimed for at least a part of the teachings of political economy. Senior himself declares that those inferences of the political economist 'which relate to the Nature and the Production of Wealth are universally true';[1] and J. S. Mill asserts that 'the laws and conditions of the production of wealth partake of the character of physical truths'.[2] If this is so, it is clear that there must be a certain amount of political economy which would remain true, and possibly useful, even if the institution of private property or the practice of exchange ceased to exist.

§ 4. *The Nation a Collection of Individuals*

As to the meaning of the word 'nation' in his phrase 'the wealth of nations', Adam Smith evidently felt no difficulty. By a nation at any particular time he understood a number of individuals who at that time constitute the whole population of a given territory under one government. Now a nation does not die with the individuals who happen to be members of it at any particular time. Every one who belonged to the English nation in 1776 is dead, but the nation still exists. Consequently it has been urged that political economy should consider the wealth of a nation in some way or other apart from the wealth of the individuals of whom it is composed. The interests of the individuals who compose the nation at one particular moment may, it is said, sometimes conflict with the permanent interests of the nation. If this had been put before Adam Smith he would doubtless have answered that the future interests of the nation are only the interests of the individuals who will at various future times constitute the nation, just as its present interests are the interests of the individuals who constitute it at present, so that there is nothing in the plan of considering a nation to be at any given time an aggregate of individuals which in any way precludes an economist from taking account of the future as well as of the present. No change in this method of regarding the question was made by his followers.

§ 5. *Aggregate and Average Wealth*

Granting that a nation is only a collection of individuals, we are immediately confronted by the question whether the wealth of this collection of individuals, when considered as an amount susceptible of

[1] *Political Economy*, 8vo ed., p. 3.

[2] *Principles*, Bk. II, ch. i, § 1, 1st ed., vol. i, p. 239; People's ed., p. 123 *a*.

increase and decrease, is their aggregate or their average wealth. Are we to say that the German nation has much more wealth than the Dutch because the wealth of all Germans taken together is much larger than that of all Dutchmen taken together? or are we to say that the Dutch nation is richer or has more wealth than the German, because the aggregate of Dutchmen's wealth divided by the number of Dutchmen is greater than the aggregate of German's wealth divided by the number of Germans? In 'computations' like that of Petty[1] the national wealth was always understood to be the aggregate and not the average wealth, and to general opinion in the first half of the eighteenth century the plan of creating an imaginary average individual as the representative of the nation would have appeared strange and almost incomprehensible. But in the second paragraph of the *Wealth of Nations* Adam Smith speaks as if the wealth of a nation should be measured by its average and not by its aggregate wealth. According as the produce of labour, he tells us, 'bears a greater or smaller proportion to the number of those who are to consume it, the nation will be better or worse supplied with all the necessaries and conveniences for which it has occasion'. A nation well supplied with all the necessaries and conveniences for which it has occasion is presumably considered by Adam Smith to be a wealthy nation, and so we have the wealth of nations measured by the proportion which their produce bears to their populations. But in most cases Adam Smith forgets, so to speak, to divide by the population. He has, for example, a theory that the wealth of a country may be very great in spite of wages being very low,[2] although he very properly insists on the fact that 'servants, labourers, and workmen of different kinds make up the far greater part of every great political society'.[3] Now if the great majority are very poor, the average cannot be rich unless the small minority are enormously rich, and about this Adam Smith says nothing. He was obviously thinking of the aggregate and not of the average. Very probably he allowed himself to be slightly misled by the substitution of the word 'country' for 'nation'. A rich or wealthy 'country', no doubt, suggested to him, as it does to us, not flourishing inhabitants so much as a large produce from a given area of land. When he speaks of Holland as being, 'in proportion to the extent of the land and the number of its inhabitants, by far the richest country in Europe',[4] he is evidently calculating richness by the produce per acre as well as by the produce per inhabitant. When he says 'China has been long one of the richest, that is, one of the most fertile, best cultivated, most industrious, and most populous countries in the world',[5] he calculates riches by the produce per acre

[1] Above, p. 4. [2] Bk. I, ch. viii, p. 32. [3] *Ibid.*, p. 36 *a*.
[4] Bk. II, ch. v, p. 167 *a*.
[5] Bk. I, ch. viii, p. 32 *b*. In Adam Smith's time, '*La Chine était à la mode*'

only. But the produce per acre, depending as it does not only on the productiveness of industry, but also on the density of population, though it may indicate the riches of a 'country', or of a certain area of land, has nothing to do with the riches of the people of the country or the 'nation'. Bentham, in his *Manual of Political Economy*, distinguishes wealth from 'opulence', or 'relative opulence', meaning by 'wealth' aggregate wealth, and by 'relative opulence' having increased between two periods when 'an average individual of the posterior period has been richer than an average individual at an anterior period'.[1] In *Commerce Defended* James Mill says: 'A nation is poor or is rich according as the quantity of property she annually creates in proportion to the number of her people is great or is small',[2] and Malthus, in his *Political Economy*, distinguishes between the wealth of a country and that of its people in these terms: 'A country will be rich or poor according to the abundance or scarcity with which' the objects which constitute wealth 'are supplied compared with the extent of territory; and the people will be rich or poor according to the abundance with which they are supplied compared with the population',[3] but in spite of all this, the early nineteenth century economists generally used the terms an increase of wealth and a decrease of wealth to indicate increases and decreases of the aggregate wealth of a nation irrespective of 'the number of those who are to consume it'. In Malthus, Ricardo, and J. S. Mill the increase or 'progress' of wealth is always treated as quite compatible with a decreasing productiveness of industry.[4] Now it is scarcely possible for the productiveness of industry to decrease without occasioning a decrease of the average produce, the produce per head, and therefore, according to Adam Smith's second paragraph, of the wealth of the nation. One of the most curious results of the later economists' want of appreciation of Adam Smith's attempt to consider average rather than aggregate wealth is to be found in Malthus's complaint, or, at any rate, allegation, that he 'occasionally mixes' an 'inquiry into the causes which affect the happiness and comfort of the lower orders of society' with 'the professed

(Schelle, *Du Pont de Nemours et l'école physiocratique*, 1888, p. 93). He frequently represents China as enormously rich; see, besides the passage quote above, Bk. I, ch. xi, p. 87 *a*; Bk. II, ch. v, p. 163 *b*; Bk. IV, ch. iii, p. 219 *b*, and ch. vii, p. 251 *a*. Buchanan, in his edition of the *Wealth of Nations*, evidently thinking of average and not aggregate riches, observes in a note to the first of these passages, 'If Dr Smith means that China is richer in food than any part of Europe, this is certainly a mistake; as all travellers represent that country to be more fully supplied with people than with food' (vol. i, p. 315). But Adam Smith knew the facts: he only attributes a different sense to 'riches'.

[1] *Works*, vol. iii, p. 36 *b*, note 1, p. 82 *a*.

[2] P. 105.

[3] P. 29.

[4] See Malthus, *Political Economy*, pp. 236, *note* 2, 351, 472; Ricardo, *passim*; J. S. Mill, *Principles*, Bk. IV, ch. i, title, and ch. ii, § 2.

object' of his inquiry, 'the nature and causes of the wealth of nations'.[1]

§ 6. *Capital Wealth and Income Wealth*

At the present time the wealth of an individual may mean either his possessions at a given point of time or his net receipts for a given length of time; it may, in short, be either his capital or his income. When we say that Smith is richer than Jones, we may always be asked to explain whether we mean that Smith has more capital or more income, or more of both. By the 'wealth of the kingdom' Petty evidently understood the capital wealth, and not the income wealth of the nation. His 'computation' is the lineal ancestor of the tables in Sir R. Giffen's *Growth of Capital.* He speaks of 'the annual proceed of the stock or wealth of the nation', which, as we have seen, he reckoned at £250 million, yielding but £15 million, while the total 'expense' was £40 million, and concludes that 'the labour of the people must furnish the other twenty-five'.[2] Thus the income-wealth of the nation is clearly conceived and set out as well as the capital-wealth, and 'the wealth of the nation' is certainly taken to be the capital and not the income. The same identification of the wealth of the nation with its accumulated possessions or capital is obviously made in Gregory King's table of 'the income and expense of the several families of England', in which 'temporal lords' appear as 'increasing the wealth of the kingdom' by £10 a year each, and 'labouring people and out-servants' as 'decreasing the wealth of the kingdom' by 2*s* a year each.[3]

The importance which the French physiocrats and their forerunners attached to agriculture, which produces commodities of great utility and little durability, had the effect of drawing away their attention

[1] 'The professed object of Adam Smith's "Inquiry" is "The Nature and Causes of the Wealth of Nations". There is another, however, still more interesting, which he occasionally mixes with it – the causes which affect the happiness and comfort of the lower orders of society, which in every nation form the most numerous class. These two subjects are no doubt nearly connected; but the nature and extent of this connexion, and the mode in which increasing wealth operates on the condition of the poor, have not been stated with sufficient correctness and precision.' – *Essay*, 8th ed., pp. 367, 368, slightly altered from 1st ed., p. 303; 2d, p. 420. A minor writer said in 1921: 'It is a great object that every such increase of wealth, as I have been speaking of, should not be less in proportion than the increase of numbers during the same period. For, in this case, though the world or nation may be said, if you please, to have more wealth than it had before, yet it would consist of individuals, each of whom, one with another, would have less.' – *An Inquiry into those Principles respecting the Nature of Demand and the Necessity of Consumption lately advocated by Mr Malthus*, etc., 1821, p. 4.

[2] *Verbum Sapienti*, p. 7.

[3] Gregory King's *Natural and Political Observations and Conclusions upon the State and Condition of England*, 1696, was first fully prinetd in 1802 at the end of the second edition of George Chalmer's *Estimate of the Comparative Strength of Great Britain.* The table, however, appeared in Davenant's *Balance of Trade*, 1699, p. 23.

from accumulated goods and concentrating it on the periodical production of goods. Vauban wrote in 1699:

> 'Ce n'est pas la grande quantité d'or et d'argent qui font les grandes et veritables richesses d'un état, puisqu'il y a de très grands pays dans le monde qui abondent en or et en argent, et qui n'en sont pas plus à leur aise, ni plus heureux. Tels sont le Pérou et plusieurs Etats de l'Amérique, et des Indes orientales et occidentales, qui abondent en or et en pierreries, et qui manquent de pain. La vraie richesse d'un royaume consiste dans l'abondance des denrées, dont l'usage est si nécessaire au soutien de la vie des hommes, qui ne sauraient s'en passer.'[1]

Abundance of the commodities which sustain human life, such as bread, is obviously secured, not by accumulation, but by continual production. So Quesnay says:

> 'L'argent en tant que monnaie, n'est point du genre des richesses que les hommes recherchent pour satisfaire à leurs besoins; celles-ci ne sont qu'un flux de productions continuellement détruites par la consommation, et continuellement renouvelées par les travaux des hommes.'[2]

And in his famous economical table he takes the '*richesses annuelles*' of the nation for his subject-matter.

Adam Smith adopted[3] Quesnay's 'annual riches' as the subject of his inquiry regarding the wealth of nations without seeing very clearly that he was thereby breaking with the traditional meaning of the phrase. He begins his introduction with two paragraphs which imply that the wealth of a nation consists of the annual produce of its labour, which supplies 'the necessaries and conveniences of life which it annually consumes', and he ends it with a sentence in which 'the real wealth' and the annual produce of the land and labour of the society' are treated as synonymous. In Book II, chap. iii he says that 'plain reason seems to dictate' that 'the real wealth and revenue of a country' consists not 'in the quantity of the precious metals which circulate within it as vulgar prejudices suppose', but 'in the value of the annual produce of its land and labour'.[4] In Book I, chap. xi, he treats 'the increased wealth of the people' as the same thing as 'the increased produce of their annual labour'.[5] But he never mentions the fact that his practice is different from the common one or draws attention to the matter in any way, and sometimes he uses phrases like

[1] *Dime Royale*, Petite Bibliothèque Economique, pp. 21, 22.

[2] *Œuvres*, ed. Oncken, p. 289 *note*.

[3] That the word 'adopted' may fairly be used here is shown by the following passage, from Adam Smith's account of the physiocratic system, in Book IV, chapter ix, p. 307 *a*: 'In representing the wealth of nations as consisting not in the unconsumable riches of money, but in the consumable goods annually reproduced by the labour of the society; and in representing perfect liberty as the only effectual expedient for rendering this annual reproduction the greatest possible, its doctrine seems to be in every respect as just as it is generous and liberal'.

[4] Pp. 150, 151.

[5] P. 86 *b*. Cp. Bk. II, ch. ii, p. 124 *a*, ch. iii, p. 150 *a*; Bk. V, ch. i, p. 314 *b*.

'the real wealth of the society',[1] or 'the wealth of the world',[2] in the sense of accumulations and not of annual produce. A certain amount of confusion naturally followed. When considered from the statistician's point of view the wealth of the country continued to be identified with its capital or possessions at a point of time. Pulteney, for instance, though he had read and admired Adam Smith,[3] says, in his *Considerations on the Present State of Public Affairs* (1779):

> 'The total wealth of Great Britain . . . I may safely venture to affirm, now exceeds very much one thousand millions. In this I comprehend the value of the land, the value of the houses, the value of the stock of all kinds, and materials of manufacture, shipping, cash, money in the funds due to inhabitants, and debts due to us by persons out of the kingdom, but deducting the like debts due by us to other countries; in short, I comprehend everything which can be denominated wealth or property.'[4]

Colquhoun in his *Treatise on the Wealth, Power, and Resources of the British Empire* (1814), made estimates of the value both of the existing property and the 'new property acquired annually', and speaks of the first of these, the capital, and not the second, the produce, as 'the wealth of the British Empire'.[5] Even in our own day statisticians seem to regard the wealth of a country as its capital and not its income. But economists, as a rule, at any rate in the greater part of their demonstrations, have followed Adam Smith. Godwin, in *Political Justice* (1793), remarks:

> 'The wealth of any state may intelligibly enough be considered as the aggregate of all the incomes which are annually consumed within that state without destroying the materials of an equal consumption in the ensuing year.'[6]

Malthus, indeed, in the *Essay on Population*, uses the word wealth in such a vague way that it is quite impossible to say whether, if the question had been put to him, he would have explained the wealth of a country to be its capital or its income; he had no very clear conception of the difference between the two things.[7] Lauderdale also, in his *Inquiry into the Nature and Origin of Public Wealth*, entirely failed to separate the idea of capital and income. But in his reply to Spence's *Britain Independent of Commerce*, James Mill expressed plainly the opinion that the wealth of a country is its annual produce and not its capital:

> 'Mr Spence', he says, 'has an extremely indistinct and wavering notion of national wealth. He seems on the present occasion to regard it as consisting in the actual accumulation of the money and goods which at any time exists in the nation. But this is a most imperfect and

[1] Bk. IV, ch. ix, p. 306 *a*.
[2] Bk. I, ch. v, p. 14 *a*.
[3] See p. 21 of the work cited.
[4] P. 28.
[5] 2nd ed., 1815, p. 102.
[6] Pp. 791, 792.
[7] See especially 1st ed. ch. xvi, 2nd ed. Bk. III, ch. vii.

erroneous conception. The wealth of a country consists in her powers of annual production, not in the mere collection of articles which may at any instant of time be found in existence.'[1]

Subsequent writers generally allowed themselves to be diverted from the task of explaining what they understood by the wealth of a nation into an attempt to define the mere word 'wealth' in such a way as to make it applicable to every single thing which might constitute a part of the wealth of a nation or individual, and to nothing else. Such definitions do not advance the question. A definition of wealth as, for instance, 'things which have value in exchange', does not help us in the least. By substituting the definition of the word for the word itself, we should only get the result that 'the wealth of a nation' consists of 'the things which have value in exchange of a nation'. Other words must be substituted for the preposition 'of', and the question turns on what these should be. But if we disregard the economists' definitions and look at the general drift of their works, it becomes obvious that the wealth of the nation is understood to be its income and not its capital. 'Production' and 'the production of wealth', which are always treated as being the same thing, are, primarily, at any rate, the production of income, because capital is never considered as directly produced, but as being saved or accumulated from produce or income. 'Distribution' and 'the distribution of wealth' are still more plainly the distribution of the income and not of the capital of the nation; it is not the capital but the income that is distributed into rent, wages, and profits.[2] It must be admitted, however, that very often the economists use the expression 'the wealth of a nation' in its older sense, and make a country 'richer' when it has larger accumulations rather than when it has a larger income. J. S. Mill, in his *Essays on some Unsettled Questions of Political Economy*, declares distinctly that 'the wealth of a country consists of the sum-total of the permanent sources of enjoyment, whether material or immaterial, contained in it'.[3]

§ 7. *Restriction to Material Objects*

Adam Smith's failure to perceive that the wealth of a nation may mean either its capital or its income had a great deal to do with the

[1] *Commerce Defended*, pp. 51, 52. Cp. p. 72.

[2] Sometimes we come very near a definite statement that the wealth of a country is its income and not its capital; *e.g.* 'We want to know, then, by what causes mankind, or the inhabitants of a particular country, are led to increase their wealth; that is, to produce every year a greater quantity of the "necessaries, comforts, and conveniences of life" (to use a phrase which I know is somewhat vague), than they did the year before'. – *An Inquiry into those Principles respecting the Nature of Demand and the Necessity of Consumption, lately advocated by Mr Malthus*, etc., 1821, p. 2.

[3] P. 82.

length to which the controversy about productive and unproductive labour was drawn out.

In the first paragraph of his 'Introduction', he seems to imply that the income-wealth of a nation consists of 'necessaries and conveniences of life', and at the beginning of Book I, chap. v, he says: 'Every man is rich or poor according to the degree in which he can afford to enjoy the necessaries, conveniences, and amusements of human life',[1] a phrase which may have been suggested by unconscious reminiscence of Cantillon's proposition that '*la richesse en elle-meme n'est autre chose que la nourriture, les commodités et les agrémens de la vie*'.[2] Now if the wealth of a man or nation consists of necessaries, conveniences, and amusements, it clearly does not consist entirely of material objects, such as bread and meat, clothes and houses, chairs and tables. The surgeon and the policeman supply necessaries, the cab-driver and the hairdresser supply conveniences, the actor and the musician supply amusements, which cannot, without straining the accepted meaning of words, be called material objects. Throughout the First Book Adam Smith discloses no design of excluding the products of these labourers from the annual produce, and appears to have no idea that their produce is of a fundamentally different character from that of other labourers. In the chapters 'Of the wages of labour', and 'Of wages and profit in the different employments of labour and stock', there is no hint of any such difference. The office of the physician and the lawyer is exalted; 'the price of their labour is enhanced by the expense of their education and the large income they must have to prevent them being 'of a very mean or low condition'.[3] The last paragraph of the chapter 'Of the principle which gives occasion to the division of labour' even goes so far as to imply that the 'philosopher' is a useful labourer.[4]

Before he wrote the Second and Fourth Books, however, Adam Smith had come under the influence of the French physiocrats. In their revolt against Colbertism, the physiocrats were led to deny that commerce is a creation of wealth; they represented it as consisting merely of exchanges of things of equal value. Now, of course, exchange in itself is not creation of wealth, and the things which are exchanged for each other are for the moment of equal value, but this does not prove that persons engaged in facilitating exchanges do not create wealth, for, where private property is established, exchange is necessary in order to secure the advantages of division of employments and the localization of industries in the places best fitted for them. The physiocrats not only failed to see this, but endeavoured to show that

[1] P. 13 *b*.
[2] *Essai sue le Commerce en général*, 1755, repr. Boston, 1892, pp. 1, 2.
[3] P. 46 *a*, 47 *b*. [4] P. 8 *a*.

all workers who do not happen to be engaged in growing crops or cattle or in obtaining raw produce in some other way directly from the earth, are exchangers and not producers. The extra value added to raw produce by the labour of the artisan was, they said, only the equivalent of the earnings of the artisan, and these earnings they seem to have supposed to consist entirely of raw produce. Manufactures are thus, like commerce, merely exchanges of equal values, and produce no wealth. The point involved is made very clear in one of Quensay's dialogues:

> 'M. N. [Quesnay]. Mes réponses, mon ami, ne vous paraissent abstraites que parce que vous n'avez pas encore vu bien clairement que la valeur vénale de ces marchandises n'est que la valeur même de la matière première et de la subsistance que l'ouvrier a consommée pendant son travail, et que le débit de cette valeur vénale, répété par l'ouvrier, n'est au fond qu'un commerce de revendeur. Avez-vous donc dessein de me faire croire que *revendre* est *produire*? Je pourrais vous rétorquer à mon tour que votre intention serait fort captieuse.
>
> M. H. [antiphysiocrat]. Mon intention n'est point captieuse, car je pense bien sincèrement que REVENDRE AVEC PROFIT EST PRODUIRE.
>
> M. N. Vous m'accuserez donc encore de ne répondre que par des maximes générales, si je vous répète que le *commerce n'est qu'un échange de valeur pour valeur égale* et que relativement à ces valeurs il n'y a ni perte ni gain entre les contractants.'[1]

Agriculture, on the other hand, not only provides the subsistence of the labourer, but also the rent of the land and the taxes levied from the land. It is therefore, Quesnay thought, something more than an exchange of equal values; it is productive, while commerce and manufactures are sterile. So in the *Tableau Economique*, the *productions* and the *reproduction totale* consist of raw produce only.[2] Classes which do not produce raw produce are conceived as being 'paid out of' the raw produce. 'This system', as Adam Smith himself says, 'seems to suppose' that 'the revenue of the inhabitants of every country' consists altogether 'in the quantity of subsistence which their industry could procure to them'.[3]

Adam Smith was not prepared to go as far as this. The epithet *stérile*, which he translates 'barren and unproductive', applied to the labour of 'artificers, manufacturers, and merchants', appeared to him, as it did to most other people, 'improper'.[4] But instead of falling back on his 'necessaries, conveniences, and amusements of human life', and saying that no labour which produced any of them was barren or unproductive, he seems to have begun looking about him to see where the division between productive and barren or unproductive labour ought to be drawn. To his frugal mind there was one form of labour

[1] *Œuvres de Quesnay*, ed. Oncken, pp. 537, 538.
[2] *Ib.*, pp. 305 ff.
[3] Book IV, ch. ix, p. 306 *b*.
[4] *Ibid.* p. 305 *a*.

which was obviously barren or unproductive, that of the menial servant. 'A man grows rich by employing a multitude of manufacturers; he grows poor by maintaining a multitude of menial servants'.[1] The observation bears a sort of semblance of truth because it is so very much more likely that a man will ruin himself by employing too many menial servants than by employing too many factory hands, just as it is more likely that he will ruin himself by buying too much wine than by buying too many spades. Adam Smith, however, thought he had detected a difference between the labour of the 'manufacturer' and that of the 'menial servant', in the fact that the manufacturer produces a tangible article which can be sold, a 'vendible commodity', while the work done by the menial servant adds to the value of nothing, 'and does not fix or realise itself in any permanent subject or vendible commodity which endures after that labour is past'. Finding that the sovereign, the officers of justice and war, churchmen, lawyers, physicians, men of letters of all kinds (even economists), players, buffoons, musicians, opera-singers, dancers, resemble in this respect menial servants, he sets them all down as 'unproductive'.[2] But unproductive or not productive of what? It does not seem as if he meant that the labour in question is productive of nothing. That it produces something seems to be implied in his remark that 'the noblest and most useful' unproductive labour 'produces nothing which could afterwards purchase or procure an equal quantity of labour', and also in his observation that 'the work of all' unproductive labourers 'perishes in the very instant of its production'. When he could say, 'Like the declamation of the actor, the harangue of the orator, or the tune of the musician, the work of all of them perishes in the very instant of its production', it is clear that he did not mean to deny that the actor, the orator, and the musician produce[3] declamations, harangues, and tunes. He even admits that the labour of producing declamations, harangues, or tunes 'has a certain value regulated by the very same principles which regulate that of every other sort of labour', and as he could scarcely have maintained that any sort of labour has a value except for what it produces, he would probably, if pressed, have admitted that the declamations, harangues, and tunes, have a value. Evidently what really impressed him was not the valuelessness of the

[1] Book II, ch. iii, p. 146 *a*. [2] *Ibid.* pp. 145, 146.

[3] Quesnay sometimes speaks of 'sterile' classes 'producing', *e.g.*: 'Par exemple, deux millions d'hommes peuvent faire naître par la culture des terres la valeur d'un milliard en productions: au lieu que trois millions d'hommes ne produiront que la valeur de 700 millions en marchandises de main d'œuvre'. – *Œuvres*, ed. Oncken, p. 289 *note*. In one of his dialogues he says: 'On n'a point entrepris de faire disparaître la production des ouvrages formés par le travail des artisans'. The only 'production' which he has endeavoured to disprove is, 'une production *réelle* de richesses; je dis *réelle*, car je ne veux pas nier qu'il n'y ait addition de richesses â la matière première des ouvrages formés par les artisans'. – *Ibid*, p. 529.

produce of 'unproductive labour', but its want of duration. 'Unproductive labour' does not fix and realize itself in any permanent subject or vendible commodity which endures after the 'labour is past, and for which an equal quantity of labour could afterwards be procured'. Now as regards the capital wealth of a community, this distinction between labour which produces permanent subjects or vendible commodities, and labour which produces things which perish in the very instant of their production, is by no means absurd. The things which perish in the very instant of their production can never form a part of the capital wealth of a country. The declamation of the actor, the harangue of the orator, and the tune of the musician find no place in Sir R. Giffen's *Growth of Capital.* So the 'unproductive' labour, though it may often assist men to produce things which will, while they last, form a part of the capital of the country, does not directly and immediately produce such things. And it must be remembered that it is in the Second Book, 'Of the Nature, Accumulation, and Employment of Stock', that the distinction between productive and unproductive labour occurs.

But, unfortunately, being far from clear as to the difference between capital-wealth and income-wealth, Adam Smith allowed the fact that some labour is unproductive of 'stock' to affect his conception of the annual produce, the 'real wealth' of the nation, with regard to which the durability of the things produced by labour is in reality of no significance. The declamations, harangues, and tunes are just as much a part of the annual produce as champagne or boots; but Adam Smith, in his Second Book, excludes them all from the annual produce, which is, he declares, produced entirely by the 'productive labourers',[1] who thus 'maintain' not only themselves but all other classes, including the unproductive labourers.[2]

People have always been rather apt to imagine that the class which they happen to think the most important 'maintains' all the other classes with which it exchanges commodities. The landowner, for instance, considers, or used to consider, his tenants as his 'dependants'. All consumers easily fall into the idea that they are doing a charitable act in maintaining a multitude of shopkeepers. Employers of all kinds everywhere believe that the employed ought to be grateful for their

[1] 'The whole annual produce, if we except the spontaneous productions of the earth, being the effect of productive labour.' – Bk. II, ch. iii, p. 147 *a*.

[2] 'Both productive and unproductive labourers and those who do not labour at all are all equally maintained by the annual produce of the land and labour of the country.' – Bk. II, ch. iii, p. 146 *b*. Hume apparently shared these opinions: – 'Lawyers and physicians beget no industry; and it is even at the expense of others they acquire their riches; so that they are sure to diminish the possessions of some of their fellow-citizens as fast as they increase their own. Merchants, on the contrary, beget industry by serving as canals to convey it through every corner of the State'. – *Essay of Interest*, vol. ii, p. 71 in 1770 ed. of *Essays.*

wages, while the employed firmly hold that the employer is maintained entirely at their expense. So the physiocrats alleged that the husbandman maintained himself and all other classes; and Adam Smith alleged that the husbandman, the manufacturer, and the merchant maintained themselves and all other classes. The physiocrats did not see that the husbandman was maintained by the manufacturing industries of threshing, milling, and baking, just as much as the millers or the tailors are maintained by the agricultural industries of ploughing and reaping. Adam Smith did not see that the manufacturer and merchant are maintained by the menial services of cooking and washing just as much as the cooks and laundresses are maintained by the manufacture of bonnets and the import of tea.

The annual produce or 'real wealth' of a nation, in the later part of Adam Smith's work, thus comes to consist exclusively of material objects. The total annual produce ceases to be equal to the total annual income or revenue of the community; the annual revenue is divided into two parts – original revenue and derived revenue, and the total 'produce' is equal to the original revenue alone. The original revenue is equal to the wages of productive labour, the rent of land, and the profits of stock, and the derivative revenue is equal to the wages of unproductive labour and the rent of houses. A house 'is no doubt extremely useful' to its owner when he lives in it, but it 'contributes nothing to the revenue of its inhabitant'. 'If it is to be let to a tenant for rent, as the house itself can produce nothing, the tenant must always pay the rent out of some other revenue which he derives either from labour, or stock, or land.'[1] It did not occur to Adam Smith to reflect that if a plough is let for rent, as the plough itself can produce nothing, the tenant must always pay the rent out of some other revenue. He concludes that 'the revenue of the whole body of the people can never be in the smallest degree increased' by the existence of houses, so that a people living in palaces have no more original revenue, produce, or 'real wealth' than if they were housed in mud hovels.[2]

This very narrow conception of the annual produce or wealth of a nation, though perhaps it is generally considered the 'orthodox' conception, was by no means readily accepted by Adam Smith's followers.

[1] Bk. II, ch. i, p. 121 *a*.

[2] The unproductiveness of houses was a physiocratic tenet. Cp. Mercier de la Rivière, *L'Ordre Naturel et Essentiel*, 12mo ed., 1767, vol. ii, p. 123, in Daire's *Physiocrates*, p. 487. 'Ce n'est pas cette maison qui produit elle même ces mille francs. . . . Le loyer d'une maison n'est point pour la société une augmentation de revenu, une création de richesses noubelles, il n'est au contraire qu'un changement de main.' The canonist Pontas, on the other hand, writing a little before the physiocratic period, says: 'La maison qu'Aristide a vendue est un fonds qui lui produiroit un revenu dont il se prive par la vente.' – *Dictionaire*, 1736, s.v. Interêt, vol. ii, p. 786.

In France, where familiarity with the physiocratic system had bred contempt, it never obtained any hold. Sismondi accepted it,[1] but Garnier and J.-B. Say set the example, which has been followed by subsequent French writers, of rejecting it. Garnier acutely points out that Adam Smith's assertion in the Second Book that a large proportion of wage-paid labour does not 'produce' is in contradiction with the doctrine of the First Book that 'the produce of labour constitutes the natural recompense or wages of labour'.[2] J.-B. Say has a chapter,[3] '*Des produits immatérials, ou des valeurs qui sont consommées au moment de leur production*', in which he entirely declines to accept Adam Smith's restriction to wealth to durable objects. In England Lauderdale exposed Adam Smith's inconsistency as follows:

> 'There is no one who has criticized the distinction which rests the value of commodities on their durability with greater acrimony than the person who wishes to make the distinction betwixt productive and unproductive labour depend merely upon the duration of its produce. "We do not", says he, "reckon that trade disadvantageous which consists in the exchange of the hardware of England for the wines of France, and yet hardware is a very durable commodity, and were it not for this continual exportation, might, too, be accumulated for ages together, to the incredible augmentation of the pots and pans of the country." '[4]

Wealth 'regarded in its true light' is, according to Lauderdale, 'the abundance of the objects of man's desire', whether durable or perishable. The able criticism of Lauderdale's book in the *Edinburgh Review* for July 1804, though it found many faults with Lauderdale's theories, followed him on this question. When Adam Smith spoke of unproductive labourers he did not mean, says the reviewer, to undervalue their work,[5] but merely to assert that 'they do not augment the *wealth* of the community:

> 'But it may be observed in general that there is no solid distinction between the effective powers of the two classes whom Dr Smith denominates productive and unproductive labourers. The end of all labour is to augment the wealth of the community; that is to say, the fund from which the members of that community derive their subsistence, their comforts, and enjoyments. To confine the definition of wealth to mere subsistence is absurd. Those who argue thus admit butcher's meat and manufactured liquors to be subsistence; yet neither

[1] *De la Richesse Commerciale*, 1803, vol. i, pp. xxxiii, 29, 84.

[2] *Recherches sur la nature et les causes de la richesse des nations par Adam Smith*, vol. v, p. 171.

[3] *Traité*, Livre I, ch. xiii.

[4] *Public Wealth*, 1804, pp. 152, 153; *Wealth of Nations*, p. 192 *a*.

[5] If Adam Smith did not undervalue their work, why did he say of the physiocrats that 'they honour' farmers and labourers 'with the peculiar appellation of the productive class', and 'endeavour to degrade' artificers, manufacturers, and merchants 'by the humiliating appellation of the barren or unproductive class'? (Bk. IV, ch. ix, p. 300 *a*).

of them are necessary; for if all comfort and enjoyment be kept out of view, vegetables and water would suffice for the support of life; and by this mode of reasoning the epithet of *productive* would be limited to the sort of employment that raises the species of food which each climate and soil is fitted to yield in greatest abundance with the least labour; . . . and in no country would any *variation* of employment whatever be consistent with the definition. According to this view of the question, therefore, the menial servant, the judge, the soldier, and the buffoon are to be ranked in the same class with the husbandmen and manufacturers of every civilized community. The produce of the labour is, in all these cases, calculated to supply either the necessities, the comforts, or the luxuries of society; and that nation has more real wealth than another which possesses more of *all* those commodities.'[1]

The writer of the article 'Political Economy' in the fourth edition of the *Encyclopædia Britannica* (1810), though himself 'rather disposed to adhere to the doctrine of Smith', says of the distinction between productive and unproductive labour:

> 'The most eminent writers on this subject in the present age seem disposed to treat this distinction as nugatory. They urge that wealth consists merely in the abundance of conveniences and pleasures of life, and that whoever contributes to augment these is a productive labourer, though he may not present us with any tangible commodity.'[2]

We might expect to find some discussion of Adam Smith's theory in James Mill's *Commerce Defended*, since William Spence, against whom Mill was writing, was a thorough-going physiocrat, and maintained that agriculture alone is productive. But neither in *Commerce Defended* nor in his *Elements* (1821) does James Mill enter into the question. Doubtless he accepted Adam Smith's doctrine. In one place he says 'the dogs, the horses of pleasure, and the menial servants produce nothing'.[3] Ricardo quotes with approval Adam Smith's dictum that a man is rich or poor according to the degree in which he can afford to enjoy the necessaries, conveniences, and amusements of human life,[4] but is otherwise quite silent on the subject.[5] Malthus, desirous as usual of supporting Adam Smith, says: 'I should define wealth to be those *material* objects which are necessary, useful, or agreeable to mankind'.[6] But he was not, apparently, altogether satisfied with this definition, for he thought it worth while to put forward a plan for calling all labour productive, but productive in different degrees, 'if we do not confine wealth to tangible and material objects'.[7] Agricultural labour would be the most productive labour because it produces rent and profits as well as wages; next would come other

[1] P. 355. [2] Vol. xvii, p. 112. [3] *Commerce Defended*, p. 69.

[4] *Principles*, 1st ed., p. 377; 3rd ed. in *Works*, p. 165.

[5] In one of his *Letters to Malthus*, p. 153, he says: 'If by wealth you mean, as I do, all those things which are desirable to man'; but this only means 'if you think manufacturing labour productive'.

[6] *Political Economy*, p. 28. [7] *Ibid.* p. 38.

labour assisted by capital, which produces profits as well as wages; and last would come Adam Smith's 'unproductive' labour, which produces wages only. Malthus rejects his own suggestion, because 'it makes the circumstance of the payment made for any particular kind of exertion, instead of the quality of the produce, the criterion of its being productive';[1] but it is far from clear what he means by this. M'Culloch, in his article, 'Political Economy', in the Supplement to the fourth edition of the *Encyclopædia Britannica* (1823), said that political economy treats of wealth, 'if by wealth be meant those material products which possess exchangeable value and which are necessary, useful, or agreeable to man',[2] but in the enlarged edition of this article, published as *Principles of Political Economy* in 1825, 'material products' are replaced by 'articles or products',[3] the word material being thus omitted; and towards the end of the work there occurs a vigorous attack on Adam Smith's theory of productive and unproductive labour. 'To begin', says M'Culloch, 'with his strongest case, that of the menial servant:

> 'Dr Smith says that his labour is *unproductive* because it is not realized in a vendible commodity, while the labour of the manufacturer is *productive* because it is so realized. But of what is the labour of the manufacturer really productive? Does it not consist exclusively of comforts and conveniences required for the use and accommodation of society? The manufacturer is *not* a producer of matter but of *utility* only. And is it not obvious that the labour of the menial servant is also productive of utility? It is universally allowed that the labour of the husbandman who raises corn, beef, and other articles of provision is productive; but if so, why is the labour of the menial servant, who performs the *necessary* and *indispensable* task of preparing and dressing these articles, and fitting them to be used, to be set down as unproductive? It is clear to demonstration that there is no difference whatever between the two species of industry – that they are either both productive or both unproductive. To produce a fire, it is just as necessary that coals should be carried from the cellar to the grate as that they should be carried from the bottom of the mine to the surface of the earth; and if it is said that the miner is a productive labourer, must we not also say the same of the servant who is employed to make and mend the fire? . . . The end of all human exertion is the same – that is, to increase the sum of necessaries, comforts, and enjoyments; and it must be left to the judgment of every one to determine what proportion of these comforts he will have in the shape of menial services, and what in the shape of material products.'[4]

If this was not enough, the question ought to have been settled finally by the remarks of Senior in his treatise on Political Economy in the *Encyclopædia Metropolitana* (1836). Senior declined to confine wealth to material objects,[5] and explained, with some skill, that the

[1] *Ibid.* p. 41.
[2] Supplement, vol. vi, p. 217 *a*.
[3] P. 5. See also p. 1, where the same alteration is made.
[4] Pp. 406, 407.
[5] 8vo ed., p. 22.

difference between the products of Adam Smith's productive labourers and those of his unproductive labourers is, for the most part, merely verbal:

> 'It appears to us that the distinctions that have been attempted to be drawn between productive and unproductive labourers, or between the producers of material and immaterial products, or between commodities and services, rest on differences existing not in the things themselves which are the objects considered, but in the modes in which they attract our attention. In those cases in which our attention is principally called, not to the act of occasioning the alteration but to the result of that act, to the thing altered, economists have termed the person who occasioned that alteration a productive labourer, or the producer of a *commodity* or material product. Where, on the other hand, our attention is principally called, not to the thing altered, but to the act of occasioning that alteration, economists have termed the person occasioning that alteration an unproductive labourer, and his exertions *services* or immaterial products. A shoemaker alters leather, and thread, and wax into a pair of shoes. A shoeblack alters a dirty pair into a clean pair. In the first case our attention is called principally to the things as altered. The shoemaker, therefore, is said to make or produce shoes. In the case of the shoeblack, our attention is called principally to the act as performed. He is not said to make or produce the commodity – clean shoes, but to perform the service of cleaning them. In each case there is, of course, an act and a result; but in the one case our attention is called principally to the act, in the other to the result.'[1]

Whether our attention is called chiefly to the act or the result depends principally, Senior adds, on the question whether the thing altered still retains the same name, and also on the mode in which the payment is made:

> 'In some cases the producer is accustomed to sell, and we are accustomed to purchase, not his labour, but the subject on which that labour has been employed; as when we purchase a wig or a chest of medicine. In other cases, what we buy is not the thing altered but the labour of altering it, as when we employ a haircutter or a physician. Our attention in all these cases naturally fixes itself on the thing which we are accustomed to purchase; and, according as we are accustomed to buy the labour, or the thing on which that labour has been expended – as we are, in fact, accustomed to purchase a commodity or a service, we consider a commodity or a service as the thing produced.'

Borrowing, without acknowledgment, M'Culloch's comparison of the labour of the coal-miner and of the servant who carries coal to the drawing-room, he concludes:

> 'The consumer pays for the coals themselves when raised and received into his cellar, and pays the servant for the act of bringing them up. The miner, therefore, is said to produce the material commodity, coals; the servant the immaterial product, or service. Both, in fact, produce the same thing, an alteration in the condition of the existing

[1] 8vo ed., pp. 51, 52.

particles of matter; but the attention is fixed in the one case on the act, in the other on the result of that act.'[1]

Probably no more would now have been heard of attempts to exclude from the annual produce, 'the real wealth' of a nation, an important part of its income, if J. S. Mill had not put forward in 1844 and 1848 views of the subject which he had acquired in his early youth many years before. After the success of his *Logic*, he published the *Essays on some Unsettled Questions of Political Economy* (1844), which he had written fourteen or fifteen years earlier, at the age of 23, and before Senior's work was published. In Essay III, 'On the words Productive and Unproductive', he declares that all labour should be considered unproductive if it does not produce 'permanent sources of enjoyment'. It is, he says, 'subversive of the ends of language' to say that 'the labour of Madame Pasta was as well entitled to be called productive labour as that of a cotton spinner'.[2] 'The wealth of a country consists of the sum-total of the permanent sources of enjoyment, whether material or immaterial, contained in it; and labour or expenditure which tends to augment or to keep up these permanent sources should, we conceive, be termed productive.'[3] It is clear that these remarks have no bearing on the question of what constitutes the annual produce, 'the real wealth', of the country. Mill is thinking exclusively of the capital-wealth. Indeed at the end of the essay he uses the term, 'the permanent sources of enjoyment', which is said, in the passage just quoted, to be equivalent to 'the wealth of the country', as an alternative expression for 'the national capital'.[4] But in the *Principles*, instead of profiting by Senior's observations, he excludes, not only from capital but also from produce, all 'utilities not fixed or embodied in any object, but consisting in a mere service rendered; a pleasure given, an inconvenience or a pain averted during a longer or a shorter time, but without leaving a permanent acquisition in the improved qualities of any person or thing':[5]

> 'The three requisites of production, as has been so often repeated, are labour, capital, and land. . . . Since each of these elements of production may be separately appropriated, the industrial community may be considered as divided into landowners, capitalists, and productive labourers. Each of these classes, as such, obtains a share of the produce; no other person or class obtains anything, except by concession from them. The remainder of the community is, in fact, supported at their expense, giving, if any equivalent, one consisting of unproductive services.'[6]

This implies, of course, that in adding up the national income we must exclude all wages of unproductive labour. The author of an ele-

[1] 8vo ed., pp. 52, 53. [2] P. 76. [3] P. 82. [4] P. 89.
[5] Book I, ch. iii, § 2, 1st ed., vol. i, pp. 57, 58; People's ed. p. 29 *b*.
[6] Book II, ch. iii, § 1, 1st ed., vol. i, p. 279; People's ed., p. 145 *a*.

mentary manual, writing 40 years after J. S. Mill, actually accepted this doctrine, saying that if we include in the national income the incomes both of a landowner and his butler, 'we have counted twice over what the butler receives'. We have, of course, done nothing of the kind. The butler has an income consisting of the necessaries, conveniences, and amusements, which he obtains by means of the board, lodging, and money furnished him by his employer, and his employer has an income consisting of the necessaries and conveniences produced for him by the butler. Fortunately few or none of the economists who have expressed themselves in favour of excluding the produce of 'unproductive' labour from the annual produce have attempted to adhere consistently to the exclusion. When they divide the annual produce into wages, profits, and rent, they mean, and their readers understand them to mean, all rent, all profits, and all wages.

CHAPTER II

THE IDEA OF PRODUCTION

§ 1. *Production as a Division of Political Economy*

English economic treatises have long been so commonly divided into several 'Books' or other divisions, two of which are entitled 'Production' and 'Distribution', that we are almost apt to regard these two titles as obvious ones which must have occurred at once to the very first person who attempted any systematic treatment of political economy. 'Production' and 'Distribution' do not seem, however, to have been used in England before 1821 as titles of divisions of political economy; and, before Adam Smith wrote, they were not in any sense technical economic terms. Steuart, whose *Principles of Political Economy* appeared only nine years before the *Wealth of Nations*, knew nothing of them. He divided his work into five Books:

i. Of Population and Agriculture.
ii. Of Trade and Industry.
iii. Of Money and Coin.
iv. Of Credit and Debts.
v. Of Taxes and of the proper application of their amount.

The *Wealth of Nations* is likewise divided into five Books:

i. Of the Causes of Improvement in the productive Powers of Labour, and of the Order according to which its Produce is naturally distributed among the different Ranks of the People.
ii. Of the Nature, Accumulation, and Employment of Stock.
iii. Of the different Progress of Opulence in different Nations.
iv. Of systems of Political Economy.
vi. Of the Revenue of the Sovereign or Commonwealth.

Both production and distribution are suggested by the use of the words 'productive', 'produce', and 'distributed', in the title of the first of these Books. The article, 'Political Economy', in the fourth edition of the *Encyclopædia Britannica* (1810), is divided into five chapters:

i. Of the Nature and different Species of Wealth.
ii. Of the Sources of Wealth.
iii. Of the manner in which Wealth is produced and distributed.
iv. Of the Mercantile and Economical Systems.
v. Of Public Revenue.

The approach towards the familiar arrangement is here not quite so great as it seems. This can be sufficiently shown by quoting the headings of the seven sections into which the chapter on 'the manner in which wealth is produced and distributed' is divided. They are:

1. The Division of Labour.
2. Machinery.
3. Of the different Employments of Labour and Stock.
4. Agriculture.
5. Manufactures.
6. Commerce.
7. The Retail Trade.
8. On the Coincidence between Public and Private Interest.

Further advance is evident in D. Boileau's *Introduction to the Study of Political Economy, or Elementary View of the Manner in which the Wealth of Nations is Produced, Increased, Distributed, and Consumed* (1811). This work is divided into four books:

i. Nature and Origin of the Wealth of Nations.
ii. Increase of the Wealth of Nations.
iii. Of the Distribution of the Wealth of Nations.
iv. Consumption of the Wealth of Nations.

'Origin' in the title of Book I is merely a synonym of 'production'. Ricardo's *Principles of Political Economy and Taxation* (1817) never made any pretence to logical or systematic arrangement. The chapters followed each other almost at random, and in the first edition, from which the following list is taken, they were not even correctly numbered:

1. On Value.
2. On Rent.
3. On the Rent of Mines.
4. On Natural and Market Price.
5. On Wages.
*5. On Profits.
6. On Foreign Trade.
7. On Taxes.
8. Taxes on Raw Produce.
*8. Taxes on Rent.
9. Tithes.
10. Land Tax.
11. Taxes on Gold.
12. Taxes on Houses.
13. Taxes on Profits.
14. Taxes on Wages.
15. Taxes on other Commodities than Raw Produce.
16. Poor Rates.
17. On Sudden Changes in the Channels of Trade.
18. Value and Riches, their Distinctive Properties.
19. Effects of accumulation on Profits and Interest.
20. Bounties on Exportation and Prohibitions of Importation.
21. On Bounties on Production.
22. Doctrine of Adam Smith concerning the Rent of Land.
23. On Colonial Trade.
24. On Gross and Net Revenue.
25. On Currency and Banks.
26. On the comparative Value of Gold, Corn, and Labour in Rich and in Poor Countries.
27. Taxes paid by the Producer.
28. On the Influence of Demand and Supply on Prices.
29. Mr Malthus's Opinions on Rent.[1]

We might hunt in vain among these chapters for any trace of production and distribution as divisions of political economy.

[1] The chapter 'On Machinery' was added in the third edition.

Malthus divided his *Political Economy* (1820) into seven chapters:

i. On the Definitions of Wealth and Productive Labour.
ii. On the Nature and Measures of Value.
iii. Of the Rent of Land.
iv. Of the Wages of Labour.
v. Of the Profits of Capital.
vi. Of the distinction between Wealth and Value.
vii. On the Immediate Causes of the Progress of Wealth.

At last, in James Mill's *Elements of Political Economy* (1821), we find the divisions to which the next generation became accustomed. James Mill's four chapters are entitled:

i. Production.
ii. Distribution.
iii. Interchange.
iv. Consumption.

In the same year Torrens published his *Essay on the Production of Wealth*, and talked of completing 'the task by remodelling and extending the disquisitions respecting the distribution of wealth' which he had 'already laid before the public',[1] in the *Essay on the Corn Trade*. Since that time, though James Mill's 'consumption' has often been omitted, and his 'interchange', which other people call 'exchange', has often been put in the first or second place instead of in the third, 'production' and 'distribution' have seldom failed to appear in English economic treatises as two of the great divisions of political economy. They probably came, along with 'consumption', immediately from J.-B. Say's *Traité d'Economie Politique*, which is divided into three Books:

i. De la Production des Richesses.
ii. De la Distribution des Richesses.
iii. De la Consommation des Richesses.[2]

The occurrence of the word *forment* in the second title of the *Traité*, '*Simple Exposition de la Manière dont se forment, se distribuent, et se consomment les Richesses*', seems to show that Say obtained the idea of his division of the subject as much from Turgot's *Réflexions sur la Formation et la Distribution des Richesses*, as from Book I of the *Wealth of Nations*.

§ 2. *General Conception of the Theory of Production*

Before the middle of the eighteenth century a theory of production can scarcely be said to have existed. Durable objects being looked upon as the sole or chief kind of wealth, the functions of industry and trade seemed to be the 'circulation' of wealth.[3] When the physiocratic

[1] P. v.

[2] 2nd ed., 1814; 1st ed. (1803) is differently divided.

[3] Even so acute a man as Franklin wrote in 1768: 'It may seem a paradox if I should assert that our labouring poor do in every year receive *the whole revenue of the nation*.' – *Memoirs*, 1833, vol. vi, p. 46.

school turned the attention of economists to the consumable goods obtained by means of agriculture, the idea of circulation gave way to the idea of an annual reproduction, which gradually grew into the modern conception of production and consumption. The transition is very obvious in Adam Smith's chapter 'Of money considered as a particular branch of the general stock of the society, or of the expense of maintaining the national capital', in which the whole annual produce of the country is supposed to be annually circulated by money, 'the great wheel of circulation'.[1]

In his 'Introduction and Plan', however, no doubt the latest portion of his work, Adam Smith seems to have looked at the matter quite from the modern standpoint. He says that the proportion which the annual produce bears to the number of those who are to consume it

> 'must in every nation be regulated by two different circumstances; first, by the skill, dexterity, and judgment with which its labour is generally applied; and secondly, by the proportion between the number of those who are employed in useful labour and that of those who are not so employed.'[2]

A discussion of the different circumstances which regulate the amount of *per capita* produce is exactly what we should expect to find in a theory of production. But neither of the 'two different circumstances' which regulate it are systematically discussed in the *Wealth of Nations*. As to the first circumstance, we are told at the beginning of the first chapter of Book I, that

> 'the greatest improvement in the productive powers of labour, and the greater part of the skill, dexterity, and judgment with which it is everywhere directed or applied, seem to have been the effects of the division of labour',[3]

but we hear nothing of the minor causes of improvement and the smaller part of the skill, dexterity, and judgment. The first four chapters of Book I remain what they were in all probability originally intended to be, an essay on the causes and consequences of the division of labour. They thus contain only a fragment, though, doubtless, in Adam Smith's opinion a large fragment, of a theory as to the skill, dexterity, and judgment with which labour is generally applied.

The second of the 'two different circumstances' fares even worse than the first. The fourth paragraph of the Introduction and Plan gives some warning of its approaching fate, by depreciating its importance compared with that of the first circumstance. Savage nations, it seems, are miserably poor, though among them 'every individual who is able to work is more or less employed in useful labour', while civilized nations are well off, 'though a great number of people do not

[1] Bk. II, ch. ii, pp. 125 *a*, 127 *a*, etc. [2] P. 1 *a*. [3] P. 2 *b*.

labour at all, many of whom consume the produce of ten times, frequently of a hundred times, more labour than the greater part of those who work'. The fifth and sixth paragraphs are obviously intended to suggest that the first circumstance will be dealt with in Book I, and the second in Book II, but the sixth paragraph in reality substitutes something entirely different:

> 'Whatever be the actual state of the skill, dexterity, and judgment with which labour is applied in any nation, the abundance or scantiness of its annual supply must depend, during the continuance of that state, upon the proportion between the number of those who are annually employed in useful labour, and that of those who are not so employed. The number of useful and productive labourers, it will hereafter appear, is everywhere in proportion to the quantity of capital stock which is employed in setting them to work, and to the particular way in which it is so employed. The Second Book, therefore, treats of the nature of capital stock, of the manner in which it is gradually accumulated, and of the different quantities of labour which it puts into motion, according to the different ways in which it is employed.'

To give us a real theory of production, the Second Book ought, according to this arrangement of the matter, to show what regulates, not 'the number of useful and productive labourers', but 'the proportion between the number of those who are annually employed in useful labour, and that of those who are not so employed'. This it does not do. Most of it deals only with the absolute number of useful labourers, a 'circumstance' which has nothing to do with *per capita* produce, and chapter iii deals not with the proportion between the number of those who are employed in *useful* labour, and that of those who are not so employed, which is the second circumstance according to the third paragraph of the 'Introduction and Plan', but with the proportion between the number of those who are employed in *productive* labour, and those who are not so employed, and it is expressly admitted that 'unproductive' labour may be, and often is, in the highest degree 'useful'.[1] The lame attempt in the sixth paragraph of the 'Introduction and Plan' to gloss over the discrepancy between the third paragraph and Book II, by first speaking of 'useful' labour alone, and then of 'useful and productive' labourers, as if 'productive' were a mere synonym of 'useful', could scarcely, one would suppose, succeed except in the case of the most careless readers.

So, instead of a full discussion of the causes which affect the skill, dexterity, and judgment with which labour is applied, we are put off with an essay on the division of labour, and instead of a discussion of the causes which regulate 'the proportion between the number of those who are employed in useful labour and that of those who are not

[1] Bk. II, ch. iii, p. 146 *b*.

so employed', we are given a treatise on 'the proportion between the productive and unproductive hands',[1] 'productive' meaning something quite different from useful.

If Ricardo had been asked where his theory of production was to be looked for in his *Principles of Political Economy and Taxation*, he would have answered with perfect justice, that in spite of the generality of its title,[2] his work did not profess to deal with the production of wealth. It was merely an attempt to offer a solution of 'the principal problem in political economy', which is, he thought, 'to determine the laws which regulate' the distribution of the produce of a country between rent, profit, and wages.[3] He certainly had much to do with the addition to nineteenth-century political cconomy of the 'law of diminishing returns', but he and Malthus and West seem always to have been more concerned with the effects of that law on distribution than with its effects on production.

Malthus's theory of production lies hidden in the confused tangle of the seventh chapter of his *Political Economy*, 'On the immediate causes of the progress of wealth'. Its chief feature seems to have been an insistence on the necessity of consumption in order to cause or stimulate production.

In the first edition of James Mill's *Elements* (1821), the inquiry as to 'What are the laws which regulate the production of commodities'[4] fills less than four sparsely printed pages. These merely explain that man 'can do nothing more than produce motion', that capital is a requisite of production, that capitalists and labourers are separate classes, and that division of labour and great manufactories are advantageous. It was Torrens who set the example of writing a considerable quantity about production. His *Essay on the Production of Wealth* (1821) contains 430 pages and is about the same length as the Book on Production in J. S. Mill's *Principles*. A considerable portion of it, however, deals with questions of value, trade, currency, and demand and supply, which by most later writers have been relegated to the separate division of political economy entitled 'Exchange'. The main body of the work consists of four chapters on the different kinds of industry – appropriative, manufacturing, agricultural, and mercantile.

Stimulated perhaps by the appearance of Torrens's book, James Mill, in the second edition of his *Elements*, added a dozen new pages to his chapter on production, dividing them into two sections, of which the first is on 'Labour', and consists chiefly of an exposition of the advantages of division of labour, more expanded than that contained in the first edition, and the second is on 'Capital', and consists chiefly of an explanation of the nature of capital.

[1] *Ibid*, p. 147 *b*. [2] *On the Principles of Political Economy and Taxation*.
[3] Preface, pp. iii, iv. [4] P. 4.

M'Culloch considered that with regard to production, the business of the economist is 'an investigation of the means by which labour in general may be rendered most productive'.[1] Accordingly the bulk of his discussion of production falls in the section which treats of the 'Means by which the Productive Powers of Labour are increased'.[2]

Senior and J. S. Mill conceived the treatment of production as properly consisting of a collection of observations about the three requisites of production.

§ 3. *The Three Requisites of Production*

One of the most familiar and striking features of the theory of production, as taught in the text-books of the second half of the nineteenth century, is the practice of ascribing production to the co-operation or concurrence or joint use of three great agents, instruments, or requisites of production, Labour, Land, and Capital. This triad of productive requisites did not very early become an integral part of English political economy. Its origin is apparently to be found in Adam Smith's division of the component parts of prices into wages, profit, and rent. When Adam Smith had divided the prices of commodities and afterwards the revenue of the community into the wages of labour, the profits of stock, and the rent of land, it was to be expected that some one would say that the revenue of the community is produced by labour, capital, and land, and proceed to arrange the theory of production under the three headings, labour, capital, and land. This was done by J.-B. Say. The first chapter of Book I of his *Traité* explains what is meant by 'production', the second deals with 'the different sorts of industry and the manner in which they co-operate in production', the third explains 'what a productive capital is and how capitals co-operate in production', the fourth discusses 'the natural agents, especially land, which are of service in the production of wealth', and the fifth, on 'how industry, capitals, and natural agents join in production', begins:

> 'Nous avons vu de quelle manière l'industrie, les capitaux et les agens naturels concourent, chacun en ce qui les concerne, à la production; nous avons vu que ces trois élémens de la production sont indispensables pour qu'il y ait des produits créés.'[3]

D. Boileau, in his *Introduction to the Study of Political Economy*, adopts an arrangement similar to that of Say, having chapters on land, labour, capital, and the 'conjoint operation of land, labour, and capital'. But the familiar triad of productive requisites can scarcely have been present in the mind of Ricardo, when, in the first words of

[1] *Principles*, 1825, p. 72. [2] *Principles*, Pt. II, § 2.
[3] 2nd ed., 1814, vol. i, p. 35.

his Preface, he spoke of 'the produce of the earth – all that is derived from its surface by the united application of labour, machinery, and capital'.[1] Malthus and M'Culloch make no use of it. James Mill says 'the requisites to production are two – Labour and Capital'.[2] Torrens, however, teaches the doctrine of the triad very clearly:

> 'In the language of political economy', he says, 'the original acquisition of wealth is called production; and those things by means of which this acquisition is made are termed instruments of production. Thus the land which supplies the primary materials of wealth, the labour by which these materials are appropriated, prepared, augmented, or transferred, and the capital that aids these several operations, are all instruments of production.'[3]

But he does not divide his exposition of production into divisions on labour, capital, and land. Senior and J. S. Mill make labour and land which Senior, like Say, calls 'natural agents') the 'primary' requisites of production, and capital (which Senior calls 'abstinence') only a secondary requisite. Senior says:

> 'We now proceed to consider the agents by whose intervention production takes place.
>
> 'I. *Labour.* – The primary instruments of production are Labour and those Agents of which Nature, unaided by man, affords us the assistance. . . .
>
> 'II. *Natural Agents.* – Under the term "the agents afforded to us by Nature", or, to use a shorter expression, " Natural Agents", we include every productive agent so far as it does not derive its powers from the art of man. . . .
>
> 'III. *Abstinence.* – But although human labour and the agency of Nature, independently of that of man, are the primary productive powers, they require the concurrence of a third productive principle to give them complete efficiency. . . .
>
> 'To the third principle . . . we shall give the name of Abstinence.'[4]

J. S. Mill at first says 'the requisites of production are two – labour, and appropriate natural objects',[5] and only adds subsequently that

> 'besides the primary and universal requisites of production, labour and natural agents, there is another requisite without which no productive operations beyond the rude and scanty beginnings of primitive industry are possible; namely, a stock, previously accumulated, of the products of former labour.'[6]

Thus even in 1848 the triad of requisites of production was not quite firmly established.

[1] For a further reference to this passage, see below, ch. iv, § 5.

[2] *Elements*, 1st ed., p. 7.

[3] *Production of Wealth*, p. 66.

[4] *Political Economy*, 8vo ed., pp. 57, 58.

[5] *Principles*, Bk. I, ch. i, § 1, 1st ed., vol. i, p. 29; People's ed., p. 15 *a*.

[6] *Ibid.*, Bk. I, ch. iv, § 1, 1st ed., vol. i, p. 67; People's ed., p. 34 *a*.

CHAPTER III

THE FIRST REQUISITE OF PRODUCTION – LABOUR

§ 1. *The Requisiteness of Labour*

Hume in his essay *Of Commerce* says: 'Everything in the world is purchased by labour';[1] and in Book I, chapter V, of the *Wealth of Nations*, Adam Smith, using the same phrase, says: 'All the wealth of the world was originally purchased by labour', and speaks of labour as 'the original purchase-money that was paid for all things'.[2] These propositions are obviously far too general. It cannot reasonably be contended that an acre of land from which all traces of man's labour have been carefully removed has been originally purchased by labour; and yet such land, if favourably situated, often constitutes a part of the capital wealth of the world.

But to make labour a requisite of production it is only necessary that it should be requisite for the production of income-wealth, and Adam Smith claims no more for it in the opening paragraph of his work, which asserts that' all the necessaries, and conveniencies of life' which a nation 'annually consumes' are originally supplied by its annual labour. He puts the assertion forward as a self-evident proposition which requires no proof, and, in fact, its truth is implied in the very conception of production. No question was raised on the subject, and we may proceed at once to the discussion of the causes which make the productiveness of labour greater at one time than another.

§ 2. *The Productiveness of Labour*

As we have already had occasion to observe,[3] Adam Smith enumerated no 'causes of improvement in the productive powers of labour', except the increase of division of labour.

By the division of labour he did not, of course, understand merely the division of labour which takes place within the walls of a single factory, or within the limits of a single business. The celebrated example of the pin factory, with which he begins his exposition of the subject, was only an endeavour to make 'the effects of the division of labour in the general business of society' 'more easily understood by considering in what manner it operates in some particular manufactures'.[4] He includes in the division of labour all that is sometimes called the separation of employments; it is not over the manufacture

[1] *Essays*, ed. of 1770, vol. ii, p. 13. [2] P. 14 *a*. [3] Above, p. 36.
[4] Bk. I, ch. i, p. 2 *b*.

of pins' heads that he waxes eloquent, but in the paragraph at the end of Chapter i, where he shows how each article of 'the accommodation of the most common artificer or day labourer in a civilised and thriving country' 'is the produce of the joint labour of a great multitude of workmen'.[1]

The maintenance and extension of division of labour in this large sense he attributes to the belief of each individual that he will serve his own interests best by devoting himself entirely to one or two occupations, but its first origin he seems inclined to attribute to a sort of instinct which he calls 'a trucking disposition',[2] 'a propensity to truck, barter, and exchange'.[3] He rejects the idea that its first origin can have been caused by a sense of the advantage which results from it, because he thinks that the advantage is due, not to the difference of natural talents between different individuals, but to the difference of acquired talents. 'The difference of natural talents in different men is, in reality, much less than we are aware of; and the very different genius which appears to distinguish men of different professions when grown up to maturity is not, upon many occasions, so much the cause as the effect of the division of labour'. Without the disposition to truck, barter, or exchange, the great philosopher would have been no better than a street porter.[4]

As every one knows, Adam Smith says that the great increase in the productiveness of industry which results from the division of labour,

> 'is owing to three different circumstances; first, to the increase of dexterity in every particular workman; secondly, to the saving of the time which is commonly lost in passing from one species of work to another; and lastly, to the invention of a great number of machines which facilitate and abridge labour, and enable one man to do the work of many.'[5]

It was not necessary for his followers to add anything to his doctrine as to the increased dexterity of the workman. It is obvious that no men can learn all trades, and that very few men are capable of learning to execute efficiently more than a small number of different operations. The popular recognition of the fact is sufficiently attested by the proverbial phrase, 'Jackof all trades and master of none'. But against the increased dexterity of the workman at his particular business there may be set a certain disadvantage arising from too exclusive an attention to that business. Though Adam Smith does not mention this in Book I, he has some strong remarks on the subject in Book V, Chapter i, Article 2, 'Of the expense of the institutions for the educa-

[1] *Ibid.*, p. 6 *a*. The passage very probably owes something to Locke on *Government*, Bk. II, § 43.

[2] Bk. I, ch. ii, p. 7 *b*.

[3] *Ibid.*, p. 6 *b*.

[4] *Ibid.*, pp. 7, 8.

[5] Bk. I, ch. i, p. 4.

tion of youth'. He there says that the increased dexterity of the workman seems 'to be acquired at the expense of his intellectual, social, and martial virtues':

> 'The man whose whole life is spent in performing a few simple operations, of which the effects too are perhaps always the same, or very nearly the same, has no occasion to exert his understanding, or to exercise his invention in finding out expedients for removing difficulties which never occur. He naturally loses, therefore, the habit of such exertion, and generally becomes as stupid and ignorant as it is possible for a human creature to become. The torpor of his mind renders him not only incapable of relishing or bearing a part in any rational conversation, but of conceiving any generous, noble, or tender sentiment, and consequently of forming any just judgment concerning many even of the ordinary duties of private life.'[1]

This is perhaps too severe. But we can scarcely agree with M'Culloch that 'the statements in this paragraph are as unfounded as can well be imagined'.[2] Specialization has its disadvantages, and they ought to be recognised. Adam Smith may have omitted mention of them in Book I, owing to an impression that they had not much to do with the productive powers of labour. J.-B. Say, himself a versatile genius,[3] had no such scruples, and treats of the advantages and disadvantages of the separation of industries in the same chapter of his *Traité* (Book I, chapter viii). 'It is', he says, 'a sad thing for a man to have to testify that he has never made more than the eighteenth part of a pin'. A clever lawyer, he remarks, 'if obliged to mend some trifling article of his furniture, would not know how to begin; he could not even knock in a nail without making the most mediocre apprentice laugh'.[4]

The second of the three circumstances which, according to Adam Smith, cause division of labour to increase the productiveness of industry, 'the saving of the time which is commonly lost in passing from one species of work to another', is also a very simple matter. It is generally agreed that, at any rate after childhood has been passed, it is a waste of time to be always passing from one occupation to another. J. S. Mill quarrelled with Adam Smith's dictum that a man who has often to change his occupation becomes 'slothful and lazy'; but he certainly does not carry conviction to the ordinary mind by saying: 'Few workmen change their work and their tools oftener than a gardener; is he usually incapable of vigorous application?'[5] for

[1] P. 350 *b*. [2] In a note on the passage quote.

[3] J.-B. Say was successively a commercial clerk, a journalist, a civil servant, a writer on political economy, a cotton spinner, a professor of political economy, and failed in none of these capacities.

[4] 2nd ed., vol. i, p. 76.

[5] *Principles*, Bk. I, ch. viii, § 5, 1st ed. vol. i, p. 151; People's ed., p. 78 *a*.

Adam Smith, and most owners of gardens, would answer in the affirmative.

With regard to the third 'circumstance', the invention of machinery, Senior very justly observed that Adam Smith had attributed too much to the division of labour:

> 'His remark, "that the invention of all those machines by which labour is so much facilitated and abridged, seems to have been originally owing to the division of labour", is too general. Many of our most useful implements have been invented by persons neither mechanics by profession, nor themselves employed in the operations which those implements facilitate. Arkwright was, as is well-known, a barber; the inventor of the power-loom is a clergyman. Perhaps it would be a nearer approach to truth if we were to say that the division of labour has been occasioned by the use of implements. In a rude state of society every man possesses, and every man can manage, every sort of instrument. In an advanced state, when expensive machinery and an almost infinite variety of tools have superseded the few and simple implements of savage life, those only can profitably employ themselves in any branch of manufacture who can obtain the aid of machinery, and have been trained to use the tools by which its processes are facilitated; and the division of labour is a necessary consequence. But, in fact, the use of tools and the division of labour so act and react on one another that their effects can seldom be separated in practice.'[1]

There is no justification for denying to isolated man all inventive power, and it is clear that in many cases the division of labour acts rather as a check than as a stimulus to the inventive faculty. We may well doubt whether it is really 'natural'[2] for a workman to be so attracted by the possibility of obtaining a lucrative patent as to turn his attention to the discovery of a means for superseding his own labour. Moreover, as J. S. Mill remarks, 'whatever may be the cause of making inventions, when they are once made, the increased efficiency of labour is owing to the invention itself, and not to the division of labour'.[3] It is a mistake to cram the whole effects of the invention of machinery under the head of division of labour.

It is rather curious that Adam Smith, in spite of his apparent willingness to multiply as much as possible the advantages of division of labour, should not have included among them the possibility of executing different kinds of work in the places best suited for them, which, as he fully recognised,[4] is created by trade between different countries. Without division of labour it would obviously be impossible, for example, for tea to be raised in China for English consumption; we should have to grow our tea in England or go without it. Six years before the *Wealth of Nations* was published Turgot had ascribed

[1] *Political Economy*, 8vo ed., pp. 73, 74.
[2] *Wealth of Nations*, Bk. I, ch. i, p. 5 *a* bottom; 'naturally'.
[3] *Principles*, Bk. I, ch. viii, § 5, 1st ed., vol. i, p. 154; People's ed., p. 80 *a*.
[4] Bk. IV, ch. ii, pp. 200, 201.

the very origin of exchange and division of labour to the fact that 'every soil does not produce everything'.[1] James Mill, in *Commerce Defended*, said:

> 'The commerce of one country with another is, in fact, merely an extension of that division of labour by which so many benefits are conferred on the human race. . . . In the world at large, that great empire of which the different kingdoms and tribes of men may be regarded as the provinces, . . . one province is favourable to the production of one species of accommodation and another province to another: by their mutual intercourse they are enabled to sort and to distribute their labour as most peculiarly suits the genius of each particular spot. The labour of the human race thus becomes much more productive, and every species of accommodation is afforded in much greater abundance.'[2]

Ricardo was quite aware of the fact that the reason why exchanges are made between distant places is that each kind of labour may be carried on, so far as possible, in the place best fitted for it:

> 'Under a system of perfectly free commerce', he says, 'each country naturally devotes its capital and labour to such employments as are most beneficial to each. This pursuit of individual advantage is admirably connected with the universal good of the whole. By stimulating industry, by rewarding ingenuity, and by using most efficaciously the peculiar powers bestowed by nature, it distributes labour most effectively and most economically. . . . It is this principle which determines that wine shall be made in France and Portugal, that corn shall be grown in America and Poland, and that hardware and other goods shall be manufactured in England.'[3]

But, not having occasion to write systematically on production or the division of labour, he had no opportunity or occasion to represent the fact as one of the advantages which result from the division of labour. This was done by Torrens, with his usual turgidity, in his *Essay on the Production of Wealth*:

> 'It is not in mechanical operations alone that the division of employment augments the powers of industry. Nature, by giving to different districts different soils and climates, has adapted them for different productions. . . . If we sow corn on our arable land, and feed cattle on our pastures; if we cultivate the grape beneath a congenial sky, and breed sheep where their fleeces will be adundant; then shall we enjoy more corn and cattle, more wine and clothing, than if we reversed the order of nature. . . .
>
> 'The view which we have here given of the advantages resulting from the division of employment will enable us to form a just conception of

[1] *Réflexions*, § ii (in *Œuvres*, ed. Daire, vol. i, p. 7). Steuart, in his *Principles*, Book II, chap. iii (vol. i, p. 179; *Works*, vol. i, pp. 241, 242), says: 'Another advantage of trade is that industrious people in one part of the country may supply customers in another, though distant. They may establish themselves in the most commodious places for their respective business. . . .'

[2] Pp. 38, 39.

[3] *Principles*, 1st ed., pp. 156, 157; 3rd ed. in *Works*, pp. 75, 76.

gence and trustworthiness in the community generally'.[1] The first two of these had been treated by Adam Smith in so far as they are produced by division of labour, but they are obviously also the result of other causes.

In addition to all these causes of variation the productiveness of labour is also effected by changes in the magnitude of the accumulation of instruments of production, and by changes in the number of persons who have to live and work on a given area. But owing to the practice of treating land and capital as requisites, or even agents of production, co-ordinate with labour itself, these changes will be more conveniently dealt with in the next two chapters.

[1] *Ibid.*, Book I, chap. vii, §§ 3, 4, 5, headings in Contents.

CHAPTER IV

THE SECOND REQUISITE OF PRODUCTION – CAPITAL

§1. *The Word*

The word 'capital', in its economic sense, has neither more nor less to do with the French '*cheptel*' and the English 'cattle' and 'chattels'[1] than it has with the 'chapter' of a book or the 'capital' of a pillar. In Dr Murray's *New English Dictionary* the article on the word 'capital' is divided into two sections. In the first of these, which treats of the word when used as an adjective, the eighth meaning is, 'Of or pertaining to the original funds of a trader, company, or corporation; principal; *hence*, serving as a basis for financial and other operations'. In the second section, which treats of the adjective elliptically used as a substantive, the first meaning given is 'a capital letter', the second 'a capital town or city', and the third 'a capital stock or fund.' Under this head we read:

> '(*a*) *Commerce.* – The stock of a company, corporation, or individual with which they enter into business, and on which profits or dividends are calculated; in a joint-stock company it consists of the total sum of the contributions of the shareholders. (*b*) *Political Economy.* – The accumulated wealth of an individual, company, or community, used as a fund for carrying on fresh production; wealth in any form used to help in producing more wealth.'

The adjective was 'used elliptically as a substantive' in the commercial sense, at least as early as the first half of the seventeenth century;[2] but the fact that it was merely an adjective was by no means forgotten. In 1697 Parliament passed 'an Act for making good the

[1] Sir H. Maine says: 'There are some few facts both of etymology and of legal classification which point to the former importance of oxen. *Capitale* – kine reckoned by the head – cattle – has given birth to one of the most famous terms of law and to one of the most famous terms of political economy, Chattels, and Capital' (*Early History of Institutions*, p. 147); but he adduces no evidence of any historical connexion between *capitale*, kine, and capital in the economic or commercial sense. Still more groundless is the statement of Mr H. D. Macleod: 'The word capital comes to us from the Greek κεφάλαιον a capital, or principal sum placed out at interest' (*Principles of Economical Philosophy*, 2nd ed., 1879, vol. i, p. 225).

[2] *The Merchant's Mirrour; or Directions for the perfect ordering and keeping of his Accounts*, by Richard Dafforne (1635), gives among examples of book-keeping:

'No. 96. *To booke the capitall which each partner of a joint company promiseth to bring in:*

Simon Sands promiseth into the company for his stocke ..	.. gl. 11,400
And Richard Rakes for his stocke intendeth	.. gl. 7,800
	gl. 19,200.'

Deficiencies of several Funds therein mentioned, and for enlarging the Capital Stock of the Bank of England, and for raising the Public Credit'.[1] Section xx. of this Act not only shows that the adjective 'capital', applied to stock, could then be placed between two other adjectives, but also shows that the plan of issuing new capital at a premium, or at a discount, was not then understood. Before the new capital was created it was considered necessary to compute the old at the value of the actual property held:

> 'And for the better settling and adjusting the Right and Property of each Member of the present Corporation of the Governor and Company of the Bank of England, before any such Enlargement as aforesaid, be made thereunto; be it further enacted by the authority aforesaid that before the Four and Twentieth Day of July One thousand six hundred and ninety-seven, the Common, Capital, and Principal Stock of the said Governor and Company shall be computed and estimated by the Principal and Interest owing to them from the King or any others, and by Cash, or by any other Effects whereof the said Capital Stock shall then really consist over and above the Value of the Debts which they shall owe at the same Time for Principal or Interest to any other Person or Persons whatsoever.'[2]

In Dyche and Pardon's *Dictionary* (1735) the article on 'Capital' begins:

> 'CAPITAL (A). Chief, head, or principal; it relates to several things, as the *capital stock*, in trading companies, is the fund or quantity of money they are by their charter allowed to employ in trade.'[3]

§2. *Adam Smith on the Nature and Origin of the Capital of a Community*

In the First Book of the *Wealth of Nations* we hear little of 'capital' or 'capital stock'. When it is mentioned it is not distinguished from

[1] 8 and 9 W. & M. cap. 20.

[2] In Thorold Rogers' *First Nine Years of the Bank of England*, p. 89, the words, 'from the king or any others, and by cash or by any other effects', are corrupted, evidently by misreading of manuscript, into 'by the king and by each or any other effects'.

[3] Compare with this: 'The Hollanders' capital in the East India Company is worth above three millions.' – Petty, *Several Essays in Political Arithmetic* (1699), p. 165. The author of *A Discourse of Money . . . with Reflections on the present evil state of the Coin of this Kingdom* (1696) represents hoarding as 'a means of increasing the capital stock of national treasure', and says: 'You trade to loss if you buy from abroad and pay more money for what you fetch from foreigners than you receive from them for your service and your native fruits and manufactures. . . You are blowing a dead cole, and take all this pains but to diminish your capital or national stock of treasure' (p. 198). William Richardson, in his *Essay on the Causes of the Decline of the Foreign Trade* (1744), uses the word capital in its commercial sense in the plural, complaining that customs duties 'lessen the capitals of our merchants by keeping a great part of their stocks by them idle to pay the duties of the goods they import' (p. 173 in Overstone's *Tracts on Commerce*). Philip Cantillon, on the other hand, uses the singular, speaking of 'the capital of our merchants'. – *Analysis of Trade* (1759), p. 160. Richard Cantillon uses singular and plural (in French) indifferently. – *Essai sur le Commerce*, p. 376.

'stock'.[1] Now the 'stock' of a trader, so far as his trade is concerned, consists, and seems always to have consisted, of the movable goods which he holds in his possession in the way of business. The stock of a shopkeeper is the wares in his shop, the 'live and dead stock' of a farmer is his cattle, horses, and implements, and so on. Movables shade into fixtures in rather an insensible manner, and fixed property, such as factories, houses, and other buildings, can scarcely be separated from the land on which it stands; so that the meaning of the phrase, the stock of an individual trader, could easily be extended so as to make it include all the property which he holds for the purpose of his business at any one time. And when we look at the matter from a comprehensive point of view, regarding rather the things which are of importance to the community than those which are only of importance to the individual, the distinction between what is held for the purpose of a man's business and what is held for his own immediate benefit appears rather trivial. For example, ovens are ovens, and useful for baking, whether they belong to a baker or a private individual.

As to the meaning of 'stock' and its synonym 'capital' in Book I of the *Wealth of Nations*, all that can be said with complete certainty is that it is the amount upon which the profits of a business are calculated. In Book II, where Adam Smith for the first time goes into the question, the stock of an individual is the whole amount of personal property, or property other than land, which he possesses at any given point of time, and the stock of a community is the sum of the stocks of its individual members. The capital of an individual is not identical with his stock, but is only that part of it which is to afford him a revenue – that is, a revenue in money, or at any rate a revenue in commodities obtained not directly but by way of exchange. The rest of the stock is merely a reserve for 'immediate' consumption, and is not entitled to be called capital:

> 'When the stock which a man possesses is no more than sufficient to maintain him for a few days or a few weeks, he seldom thinks of deriving any revenue from it. . . . But when he possesses stock sufficient to maintain him for months or years, he naturally endeavours to derive a revenue from the greater part of it; reserving only so much for his immediate consumption as may maintain him till this revenue begins to come in. His whole stock, therefore, is distinguished into two parts. That part which he expects is to afford him this revenue is called his capital. The other is that which supplies his immediate consumption, and which consists either, first, in that portion of his whole stock which was originally reserved for this purpose; or secondly, in his revenue, from whatever source derived, as it gradually comes in; or thirdly, in such things as had been purchased by either of these in

[1] See pp. 22 *b*, 23 *b*, 43 *a*, 51 *a*.

former years, and which are not yet entirely consumed, such as a stock of clothes, household furniture, and the like.'[1]

In other words, a man's total stock or capital-wealth may be divided into the part which he invests in a business intended to bring in a money return and the part which he retains for his own use, and Adam Smith chooses to call only the first of these two parts his 'capital'. The stock of John Brown, baker, is the whole of John Brown's possessions other than land, but his 'capital' is only that part of his possessions which is employed in the bakery business. Now even as regards the individual, this definition of capital gives us rather an unsatisfactory and useless entity. In the first place, it is neither customary nor convenient to exclude land from the capital of an individual or company. A factory-owner includes in the sum of money at which he reckons his capital the cost or value of the land he has bought for his business; and it would puzzle any one to exclude land from the capital of a railway or dock company. In the second place, so long as an individual derives a benefit from the possession of his stock, it is of little importance whether he receives that benefit directly or first receives money which he exchanges for it. According to Adam Smith, if a man goes to live in his own house, which is worth £2,000, instead of continuing to let it for £120 a year and hiring some other person's house for £120 a year, he thereby reduces his capital by £2,000. If this is so, all that can be said is that the magnitude of a man's capital is not of much importance.

Not content with having made a somewhat trivial distinction in the case of the individual, Adam Smith, according to his usual practice of reasoning from the individual to the community, endeavoured to apply it, with but slight modification, to the case of the nation.

Before doing so, however, he divided an individual's capital into two parts: (1) 'circulating capital', and (2) 'fixed capital'. These terms were probably used in his time in the ordinary conversation of men of business very much as they are to-day, an individual's fixed capital being the amount of money he has invested in buildings, stationary machines, and other immovable instruments of trade, and his circulating capital being the portion of his capital which he is in the habit of laying out at regular intervals in the form of money, with the expectation of seeing it come round again to him in the same form. But when the words are used in this sense there is obviously a good deal of capital which is neither fixed nor circulating. No one who had kept himself free from the infection of political economy would classify a carrier's cart as either fixed or circulating capital.[2] So in some trades the terms might convey a useful meaning, and might between them

[1] Bk. II, ch. i, beginning, pp. 119 *b*, 120 *a*.

[2] Malthus, *Political Economy*, p. 263, speaks of horses as 'fixed capital'.

exhaust the whole of the capital; in others they would not be applicable. The efforts of Adam Smith and his followers were directed towards finding definitions of the terms which would give them a precise meaning and make them cover all kinds of capital.

Adam Smith makes the distinction turn on the question whether the individual obtains his profit on the capital by keeping and using or by selling the articles of which it is composed:

> 'There are', he says, 'two different ways in which a capital may be employed so as to yield a revenue or profit to its employer.
>
> '*First*, It may be employed in raising, manufacturing, or purchasing goods, and selling them again with a profit. . . .
>
> '*Secondly*, It may be employed in the improvement of land, in the purchase of useful machines and instruments of trade, or in such like things as yield a revenue or profit without changing masters or circulating any further.'[1]

If employed in the first way it is a circulating, and if employed in the second way it is a fixed, capital. Adam Smith proceeds to observe that different occupations require very different proportionate amounts of fixed and circulating capital. 'The capital of a merchant,' he assures us, 'is altogether a circulating capital. He has occasion for no machines or instruments of trade unless his shop or warehouse be considered as such', and why not? The needles of a master tailor are, it seems, his fixed capital ; but 'the far greater part of the capital of all such master artificers' as tailors, shoemakers, weavers, 'is circulated either in the wages of their workmen or in the price of their materials, and repaid with a profit by the price of the work'.

> 'That part of the capital of the farmer which is employed in the instruments of agriculture is a fixed, that which is employed in the wages and maintenance of his labouring servants is a circulating, capital. He makes a profit of the one by keeping it in his own possession, and of the other by parting with it. The price or value of his labouring cattle is a fixed capital in the same manner as that of the instruments of husbandry; their maintenance is a circulating capital in the same manner as that of the labouring servants. The farmer makes his profit by keeping the labouring cattle, and by parting with their maintenance. Both the price and the maintenance of the cattle which are bought in and fattened, not for labour but for sale, are a circulating capital. The farmer makes his profit by parting with them. A flock of sheep or a herd of cattle that in a breeding country is bought in neither for labour nor for sale, but in order to make a profit by their wool, by their milk, and by their increase, is a fixed capital. The profit is made by keeping them. Their maintenance is a circulating capital. The profit is made by parting with it, and it comes back with both its own profit and the profit on the whole price of the cattle, in the price of the wool, the milk, and the increase. The whole value of the seed, too, is properly a fixed capital. Though it goes backwards and forwards between

[1] P. 120 *a*.

> the ground and the granary, it never changes masters, and therefore does not properly circulate. The farmer makes his profit not by its sale but by its increase.'[1]

This is exceedingly, not to say excessively, ingenious. The cost or value of your fruit-tree is fixed capital, because you only sell the fruit and not the tree itself; but the cost or value of your growing corn, or so much of it as will not be kept for seed, is circulating capital, because you sell the stalk or straw as well as the fruit or grain. If you reserve part of your grain for seed, the value of this part is fixed capital; but if, for any reason, you sell the whole of your grain, and buy your seed from some one else, the value of the whole of your grain is circulating capital.

It is curious to notice how Adam Smith, in his account of the capital of an individual, wavers between the conception of the capital as a sum of money 'employed', as he calls it, or 'invested', as we should call it, in the purchase of some commodity, and the conception of the capital as the commodity itself. The capital is 'employed in raising, manufacturing, or purchasing goods, and selling them again with a profit', or 'in the improvement of land, in the purchase of useful machines and instruments of trade'; it is 'fixed in the instruments' of a master artificer's trade; it is 'the price or value' of a farmer's labouring cattle and 'the value of the seed' which he uses; in all these cases the capital is a sum of money laid out. In other cases is it the articles obtained by means of this money: 'the goods of the merchant' are his circulating capital, and 'a flock of sheep or a herd of cattle' is a part of the farmer's capital. The first conception – that in which the capital appears to be a sum of money – is, of course, the popular one; in ordinary conversation, if the question be asked, 'What is the capital of such and such an individual or company?' every one expects the answer to be, 'So many thousand or so many million pounds'. The capital of an individual is the number of pounds his property is supposed to be worth; the capital of a company is the sum of money which has been nominally, but not necessarily actually, invested in the business by the shareholders. The second conception, that in which the capital appears as the actual property possessed by the individual, is the more appropriate to the purposes of economic inquiry, and when Adam Smith proceeds to consider the capital of the community he keeps it very steadily before him.

In discussing the division of the stock of a community Adam Smith does not, as in the case of the individual, first divide it into the reserve for consumption and the capital, and then subdivide the capital into the fixed and the circulating capital, but divides the whole stock at

[1] Pp. 120 *b*, 121 *a*.

once into three portions: (i) the reserve for consumption, (ii) the fixed capital, and (iii) the circulating capital.[1]

(i) The reserve for consumption consists of the 'stock of food, clothes, household furniture, etc., which have been purchased by their proper consumers, but which are not yet entirely consumed', and also of 'the whole stock of mere dwelling-houses' 'subsisting at any one time'.

(ii) The fixed capital consists chiefly of (1) 'useful machines and instruments of trade'; (2) 'profitable buildings which are the means of procuring a revenue, not only to their proprietor who lets them for a rent, but to the person who possesses them and pays that rent for them'; (3) 'improvements of land'; and (4) 'the acquired and useful abilities of all the inhabitants or members of the society'.

(iii) The circulating capital consists of (1) money; (2) provisions in the possession of sellers; (3) materials and unfinished goods in the possession of makers; and (4) finished goods in the possession of makers, merchants, or retailers.[2]

Adam Smith had begun by assuming that *prima facie*, or as he expresses it, 'naturally', the community's stock might be expected to divide itself into the same three portions as an individual's stock, each part doubtless consisting of the sum of the corresponding parts of individual's capitals. The characteristic of the first part is, he says, that it affords no revenue or profit, the characteristic of the second part is that it affords a revenue without circulating or changing masters, and the characteristic of the third part is that it affords a revenue only by circulating or changing masters. Now, as regards the community, the distinction between stock which brings in a revenue in money to its owner, and stock which brings in immediate benefits, is even more trivial than it is as regards the individual. There may be some slight reason for distinguishing the stock of John Brown, baker, into stock invested in the bakery business and other stock, since, in all probability, the stock invested in the business is the only part of which John Brown keeps any accurate accounts; the rest of the stock will be cared for on rule of thumb principles by Mrs Brown. But to the community in general the distinction can in itself be of no importance. Whether a thing brings in a money revenue to its owner or not, depends on the prevalence of exchange. Thus, where people live in their own houses and bake their own bread, ovens bring in no money revenue to their owners; when division of labour and exchange is carried so far that people buy their bread from a baker, some ovens begin to yield a money revenue. The advantage which the community obtains from the possession of ovens, is of exactly the same nature as

[1] P. 121 *a* [2] Pp. 121, 122.

before. Having some inkling of this, Adam Smith, while he says that the general stock of any country or society is the same with that of all its inhabitants, is not prepared in Book II, chapter i to assert that the capital of a country is exactly the same with that of all of its inhabitants.[1] In order that a thing may form part of the capital of a country, it must, he thinks, not only bring in a money revenue to its owner, but also bring in a real revenue to the community. The real revenue of the community he always, at least in the Second Book, as we have already seen,[2] imagines to consist solely of tangible objects. Consequently he excludes from the capital of the community everything which does not appear to him to yield a revenue consisting of such objects. It is nothing to him that houses, clothes, and furniture yield shelter, warmth, and comfort; they yield no tangible objects and no real revenue. If the owners of such things receive a money revenue from them, that money revenue is 'paid out of some other revenue',[3] and therefore they are not part of the capital of the country.

Innumerable fallacies have lurked under propositions to the effect that the incomes of one set of persons are 'paid out of' those of another set. The truth is that the real incomes consist of what is bought with money. The 'money' which a man pays as the rent of his house is not his real income or revenue; his real income or revenue is the comfort of living in the house. This is not paid out of any other revenue; the money he pays is doubtless derived from some other source, but this is the case with all his payments. The man's house rent is paid out of the money he derives from his labour or from his property, but so is his butcher's bill. His landlord's income is as real an income as that of his butcher.[4] 'The house itself,' says Adam Smith, by way of clinching his argument, 'can produce nothing.'[5] If this is to prove his case, the things which do constitute the capital and bring in a real revenue, ought all to produce something, but how a shop or a warehouse can be any more capable of producing something than a house, it is impossible to conceive; Adam Smith does no more than suggest that they do so because 'they are a sort of instruments of trade', and instruments of trade 'facilitate and abridge labour'.[6] In order to show that money, provisions, and materials produce something, he is reduced to insinuating that they do so because the most

[1] In chap. iii, however (p. 149 *b*), he speaks of 'the capital of a society' as being 'the same with that of all the individuals who compose it'.

[2] Above, p. 24.

[3] P. 121 *a*.

[4] Of course the total received by the landlord is not entirely his money income any more than the total received by the butcher is entirely his money income; in both cases the money income is only the profits, the amounts which the landlord and the butcher could, if they chose, spend upon the comforts, conveniences, and amusements of life without reducing their property, and the real income is what they actually do buy with these amounts of money.

[5] P. 121 *a*.

[6] P. 121 *b*.

useful machines and instruments of trade will produce nothing without them.[1] That the revenue which the owners of all the articles comprised in the capital of the country derive from them is not, just as much as the rent of houses, 'paid out of some other revenue', he makes no attempt to show, except in the case of 'profitable buildings', and, with regard to them, he only says that they are a means of procuring a revenue to their tenants as well as to their owners.[2] His meaning probably is that the tenants pay the rent out of their gross receipts, and not out of their net receipts or income. This, no doubt, is true, but it only carries the matter one step further back: the rent of a grocer's shop does not come out of the grocer's money revenue or income, but it does come out of the money revenues or incomes of his customers, just as much as the rent of a dwelling-house comes out of the money income of the occupier. If whether a thing is part of the capital of a country or not is to be decided by the answer to the question whether the payments made for the use of it are drawn immediately from the payer's gross receipts or from his income, a dwelling-house let to a lodging-house keeper would form part of the capital of the country, in spite of its inability to produce anything, and in spite of its exact similarity to another house let to a private individual.

Adam Smith's division of the stock of a society into the part from which it derives a revenue and the part from which it does not derive a revenue is, in short, perfectly indefensible. The society derives a real revenue consisting of 'necessaries, conveniences, and amusements' from the whole of its stock. According to Book II, chap. i, of the *Wealth of Nations*, the commodities stored in the shop of a dealer yield a revenue to the community, while the very same commodities, when sold to their final user or consumer, yield no revenue; a carriage, for instance, yields a revenue, and perhaps even 'produces something', so long as it is standing idle in the coachmaker's shop, but ceases to yield a revenue the moment it is sold and taken into use. A house yields a revenue so long as it remains in the hands of the builder, finished or unfinished, but when it is sold and inhabited, it ceases to yield a revenue. It would even appear that if the builder built the house with the intention of letting it, it would yield a revenue so long as he failed to find a tenant, and cease to yield a revenue when he found a tenant and began to receive a rent.

Statisticians, who have to do with concrete things, have never attempted to divide the nation's property at a given point of time into its land, its capital, and it stock for immediate consumption. Andrew Hooke, in his *Essay on the National Debt and National Capital* (1750), takes the national capital to consist of (1) 'cash, stock, or coin',

[1] P. 122 *b*.

[2] P. 121 *b*.

(2) 'personal stock', or 'wrought plate and bullion, jewels, rings, furniture, apparel, shipping, stock in trade, stock for consumption, and live stock of cattle,' and (3) 'land stock' or land capital, 'the value of all the lands in the kingdom'.[1] Sir R. Giffen, in his *Growth of Capital* (1889), a hundred and forty years later, understands the national capital in the same sense.

But not content with excluding a part of the stock of the nation from its capital, Adam Smith very frequently forgets that the nation's capital is at least a part of its stock. Travers Twiss thought that he did not very clearly conceive the stock of an individual or community as an accumulation or amount existing at a given moment, since he includes in a man's stock reserved for immediate consumption, 'his revenue, from whatever source derived, as it gradually comes in'. As Twiss observes, 'Revenue as it gradually comes in is incoming produce; stock is accumulated produce'.[2] A man's stock is x pounds at a given point of time, while his revenue or income is x pounds *per annum*. An income of £1,000 a year cannot possibly be added into a man's stock. But it is quite possible and surely far more probable, that Adam Smith meant by his 'revenue as it gradually comes in', merely so much of his revenue – money revenue – as he happens to have in hand at any given moment. A man's income cannot be part of his stock, but his last half-year's dividends lying unspent, certainly are for the time being a part of his stock. It is, accordingly, justifiable to assume that the capital of a country, being a part of its stock, should always in Adam Smith, as in ordinary language, be an accumulated amount, and not a periodical or recurrent receipt or expense. It should be so much at such and such a day and hour, and not so much a week, or so much a month, or so much a year.

It is not, however, always so conceived by Adam Smith. In the sixth paragraph of the 'Introduction and Plan', as we have seen,[3] he says that the Second Book shows that 'the number of useful and productive labourers is everywhere in proportion to the quantity of capital stock which is employed in setting them to work, and to the particular way in which it is so employed.' A part of what is intended as the proof of this proposition is contained in the third chapter, 'Of the accumulation of capital, or of productive and unproductive labour', and in that chapter the capital which determines the number of productive labourers is looked on as a part of the annual produce instead of, or as well as, a part of the accumulated stock:

'Though', says Adam Smith, 'the whole annual produce of the land

[1] Pp. 4, 5, 13, *et passim*.
[2] *View of the Progress of Political Economy in Europe since the Sixteenth Century* 1847, p. 186.
[3] Above, p. 37.

and labour of every country is, no doubt, ultimately destined for supplying the consumption of its inhabitants and for procuring a revenue to them, yet when it first comes either from the ground or from the hands of the productive labourers, it naturally divides itself into two parts. One of them, and frequently the largest, is, in the first place, destined for replacing a capital, or for renewing the provisions, materials, and finished work which had been withdrawn from a capital; the other for constituting a revenue either to the owner of this capital, as the profit of his stock, or to some other person as the rent of his land. Thus, of the produce of land, one part replaces the capital of the farmer; the other pays his profit and the rent of the landlord, and thus constitutes a revenue both to the owner of this capital as the profits of his stock and to some other person as the rent of his land. Of the produce of a great manufactory, in the same manner, one part, and that part always the largest, replaces the capital of the undertaker of the work; the other pays his profit, and thus constitutes a revenue to the owner of this capital.'[1]

The first part, that which is destined for replacing a capital, 'never is immediately employed to maintain any but productive hands', since

> 'Whatever part of his stock a man employs as a capital, he always expects it to be replaced to him with a profit. He employs it, therefore, in maintaining productive hands only; and after having served in the function of a capital to him, it constitutes a revenue to them.'

The second part of the produce, 'that which is immediately destined for constituting a revenue either as profits or as rent, may maintain indifferently either productive or unproductive hands'. It seems, 'however, to have some predilection for the latter':

> 'The proportion, therefore, between the productive and unproductive hands depends very much in every country upon the proportion between that part of the annual produce which, as soon as it comes either from the ground or from the hands of the productive labourers, is destined for replacing a capital, and that which is destined for constituting a revenue either as rent or as profit.'[2]

In this passage, instead of the absolute number of productive hands, we find ourselves investigating the proportion between the number of productive and the number of unproductive hands. But here, as in the 'Introduction and Plan', Adam Smith mixes up proportion and absolute magnitude, as well as 'unproductive' labour and idleness, in the most inextricable confusion. After giving some most unconvincing historical examples of the way in which the proportion between the two parts of the produce 'necessarily determines in every country the general character of the inhabitants as to industry or idleness',[3] he concludes:

> 'The proportion between capital and revenue, therefore, seems everywhere to regulate the proportion between industry and idleness.

[1] P. 147 *a*. [2] P. 147 *b*. [3] P. 148 *b*.

Wherever capital predominates, industry prevails; wherever revenue, idleness. Every increase or diminution of capital, therefore, naturally tends to increase or diminish the real quantity of industry, the number of productive hands.'[1]

Here he not only confuses the proportion which the first part of produce bears to the second with its absolute magnitude,[2] but identifies that part of the annual produce 'which is destined for replacing a capital' with the capital itself. He thus makes the capital of the country a part of its annual produce instead of a part of its stock; it becomes a thing which must be said to be worth so much *per annum* instead of so much at a point of time. As a matter of fact, the capital of England, even understood in the restricted sense attributed to it by Adam Smith in Book II, Chapter i, must be three times as great as the whole annual produce, and a part can scarcely be three times greater than the whole.

The confusion which prevailed on this subject in Adam Smith's mind was probably increased by some imperfect understanding or partial adoption of the physiocrat theory of *avances primitives* (original capital) and *avances annuelles* (annual working expenses), but its origin is to be found in the fact that the capital of a business is commonly conceived as the amount on which profits are earned, and profits are in some cases calculated as a percentage on two entirely different things. When a man 'makes a profit' of ten per cent in any business, this means that he makes an annual gain equal in value to one-tenth of the sum which is invested in his business, that is to say, the value of his plant, machinery, and other stock-in-trade at any one time. But when a man makes a profit of ten per cent on any given transaction, this merely means that he has made a gain equal to one-tenth of the sum he expended with an immediate view to that particular transaction.[3] It is difficult to express the distinction in a manner free from all objection, but an example will make it perfectly clear. The same shopkeeper may be said to make a profit of 20 per cent, and also to make a profit of 50 per cent. In the first case, what is meant is that he makes 20 per cent on the amount he has spent in setting up shop and getting together a stock of goods; in the second case, what

[1] P. 149 *a*.

[2] That the proportion between part i and part ii determines the proportion between industry and idleness does not prove that increase of part i will necessarily increase industry, because (*a*) part ii may increase still more than part i, so that the proportion which part i bears to part ii, will diminish, and (*b*) the number of persons among whom industry and idleness is to be shared may diminish.

[3] As an example, the following extract from a prospectus may be given: 'We have examined the accounts relating to the Consigments of Bacon from Russia in February last, and find that the profit on the sale thereof amounts to 42 per cent upon the cost price, after deducting cost of freight, commission, and incidental charges. – HERMAN LESCHER AND CO.'

is meant is merely that he sells his goods for 50 per cent more than he gives for them. If the amount of his annual gain is £200, and the expense of setting up shop £1,000, this is 'a profit of 20 per cent' [on his capital]. If the amount of his annual gain is still £200, and the amount he has expended in buying goods in the year is £400, this is also a profit of 50 per cent [on his annual outlay in purchases]. The two sums on which these profits are calculated have nothing to do with each other. The £1,000 is the capital invested in the business, and the £400 is merely a part of the annual working expenses. Adam Smith, however, was in the habit of confounding the two. Considering the origin of the term 'capital', and the signification which it now bears in ordinary language, no one can doubt that the 'capital' of our imaginary shopkeeper must always have meant to persons versed in accounts the £1,000, and not the £400. But in the very first place in Book I[1] of the *Wealth of Nations* where he uses the word 'capital', Adam Smith calculates the 'annual profits of manufacturing stock' as a percentage on a sum called by him 'the capital annually employed', which corresponds to our shopkeeper's £400, and not to his £1,000:

> 'Let us suppose', he says, 'for example, that in some particular place where the common annual profits of manufacturing stock are 10 per cent, there are two different manufactures, in each of which 20 workmen are employed at the rate of £15 a year, or at the expense of £300 a year in each manufactory. Let us suppose, too, that the coarse materials annually wrought up in the one cost only £700, while the finer materials in the other cost £7,000. The capital annually employed in the one will in this case amount only to £1,000, whereas that employed in the other will amount to £7,300. At the rate of 10 per cent, therefore, the undertaker of the one will expect a yearly profit of about £100 only; while that of the other will expect about £730.'[2]

Here the real capital of the undertakers, their factories, their machinery, and the stocks of goods and materials in their hands at one time, is left out of account altogether, and 'the common annual profits of manufacturing stock' are calculated on what Adam Smith calls 'the capital annually employed', which would now in most cases be called the annual working expenses.[3]

[1] 'Capital stock' is spoken of in the 'Introduction and Plan', but that was doubtless written after Book I.

[2] Bk. I, ch. vi, p. 22 *b*.

[3] The example is the more striking because the confusion between working expenses and capital leads Adam Smith to make a statement which is obviously contrary to fact. It is not true that 'the undertaker of the one will expect a yearly profit of about £100 only; while that of the other will expect about £730', unless, of course, the true capital invested in the one business is £1,000 and the true capital invested in the other £7,300, which is not said by Adam Smith to be the case, and, considering the facts stated by him, seems wildly improbable. Unless the circumstances of the two undertakers are very exceptional, the probability is that their true capitals (and consequently their true profits) will not be nearly so different in magnitude as £1,000 and £7,300.

Immediately afterwards Adam Smith remarks that, in the progress of the manufacture of an article,

> 'every subsequent profit is greater than the foregoing; because the capital from which it is derived must always be greater. The capital which employs the weavers, for example, must be greater than that which employs the spinners, because it not only replaces that capital with its profits but pays, besides, the wages of the weavers.'[1]

He evidently imagines that 'the capital which employs the weavers must be greater than that which employs the spinners' because thread is worth more than the material out of which it is spun. But this fact could not possibly be supposed to prove that the true capital invested in weaving, the machinery and stock-in-trade of the master-weavers, is greater than the true capital invested in spinning, the machinery and stock-in-trade of the master-spinners, while it might very well be supposed to prove that the amount annually spent in employing one weaver (that is, in paying his wages and supplying him with thread) is greater than the amount annually spent in employing one spinner (that is, in paying his wages and supplying him with his material).

These instances, it may be objected, are removed by a considerable distance from Book II, Chapter iii. But in that very chapter Adam Smith calculates the current rate of interest as a percentage on a part of the annual produce or expenditure, instead of on the true capital. Being desirous of showing that

> 'that part of the annual produce, therefore, which, as soon as it comes either from the ground or from the hands of the productive labourers, is destined for replacing a capital, is not only much greater in rich than in poor countries, but bears a much greater proportion to that which is immediately destined for constituting a revenue either as rent or as profit',[2]

he first proves, or rather alleges, that 'in the progress of improvement, rent, though it increases in proportion to the extent, diminishes in proportion to the produce, of the land', and then, in order to show that profit similarly diminishes in proportion to the produce, says:

> 'In the opulent countries of Europe, great capitals are at present employed in trade and manufactures. In the ancient state, the little trade that was stirring, and the few homely and coarse manufactures that were carried on, required but very small capitals. These, however, must have yielded very large profits. The rate of interest was nowhere less than ten per cent, and their profits must have been sufficient to afford this great interest. At present, the rate of interest in the improved parts of Europe is nowhere higher than six per cent, and in some of the most improved it is so low as four, three and two per cent.

[1] P. 23 *b*. [2] P. 148.

Though that part of the revenue of the inhabitants which is derived from the profits of stock is always much greater in rich than in poor countries, it is because the stock is much greater; in proportion to the stock, the profits are generally much less.'[2]

Here it is obviously assumed that a decline in the rate of interest or profit, though of course consistent with an increase in the total or aggregate absolute amount of profits, is necessarily accompanied by (or identical with) a decline in the proportion which the total of profits bears to the total of produce. But as a matter of fact, the rate of profit on the true capital of a country tells nothing about the proportion of the produce which falls to the share of profit, unless both the amount of the capital and the amount of the produce are given quantities, which is not here the case. Three per cent on a capital of *a* may be a greater or less proportion of produce *b* than ten per cent on a capital of *c* was of a produce *d*. Three per cent on a capital of £10,000 million may even be a greater proportion of a produce *x* than ten per cent on a capital of £2,000 million was of a produce *y*. We must conclude, then, that Adam Smith was calculating the rate of interest, not as a rate on the true capital, but as a rate on the capital considered as that portion of the annual produce which is neither rent nor profit.

'But,' it may be urged, 'Adam Smith immediately goes on to teach that capitals are increased by parsimony, and that "whatever industry might acquire, if parsimony did not save and store up, the capital would never be the greater".[1] This surely shows that he considered the capital to be not a part of incoming produce, so much a week, or so much a year, but stored up produce, so much on January 1st, or September 30th, 1772, for instance.' Unfortunately for this objection, Adam Smith's notion of the manner in which parsimony saves and stores up is quite consistent with what is saved and stored up being a part of incoming produce, and quite inconsistent with its being in reality accumulated. Not only the part of a community's stock to which Adam Smith in Book II, Chapter i, gave the name of capital, but the whole of its stock is saved and stored up. The existence of a stock of the produce of past labour in a country is clearly due, not only to the things having been produced, but also to their not having been consumed. If consumption had always equalled production, no such stock could exist. If at the end of any given period, all that had been produced during that period had been consumed, the stock could not have been increased during that period. The existing stock of houses, furniture and clothes, to which Adam Smith denies the name of capital, is just as much a part of the surplus of production over consumption, and, therefore, the result of saving, as the stock of warehouses, machinery, and provisions, to which he grants the name of

[1] P. 148 *a*. [2] P. 149 *b*.

capital. It is true that an individual does not usually regard what he spends upon books and clothes as saved and added to his capital. In the case of clothes he is right, because when he has once acquired a stock of clothes, which probably happened when he was a minor, all he had to do is to keep up that stock, and the maintenance of a stock is not the same as the increase of a stock. But when a man accumulates a library of books, he is obviously saving and investing money; the investment may be a good or a bad one, but so may any investment. In regard to the accumulation of houses, which, according to Adam Smith, are not part of the community's capital, no one ever thinks of doubting the necessity of saving, and houses only differ from furniture, books, and such like things, because they constitute so large a portion of the value of men's property that definite accounts are kept in relation to them. When, then, we find Adam Smith only teaching that the 'capital' of a country is the result of saving,[1] we naturally begin to suspect that he must mean by saving, something different from what we now mean by it, and this is indeed the case. When we say a thing has been 'saved', we mean that it has been produced, and not (yet, at any rate) consumed. The things the British nation has saved are its whole present stock of goods acquired by industry. But according to Adam Smith, what is saved is consumed:

> 'What is annually saved is as regularly consumed as what is annually spent, and nearly in the same time too; but it is consumed by a different set of people. That portion of his revenue which a rich man annually spends, is in most cases consumed by idle guests and menial servants, who leave nothing behind them in return for their consumption. That portion which he annually saves, as, for the sake of the profit, it is immediately employed as a capital, is consumed in the same manner, and nearly in the same time too, but by a different set of people; by labourers, manufacturers, and artificers, who reproduce with a profit the value of their annual consumption. His revenue, we shall suppose, is paid to him in money. Had he spent the whole, the food, clothing, and lodging, which the whole could have purchased, would have been distributed among the former set of people. By saving a part of it, as that part is, for the sake of the profit, immediately employed as a capital, either by himself or by some other person, the food, clothing, and lodging, which may be purchased with it, are necessarily reserved for the latter. The consumption is the same, but the consumers are different.'[2]

In the chapter 'Of Money', Adam Smith had explained clearly enough that the real revenue of individuals and societies consists not of the money or metal pieces at which it is valued, but of the things which are bought with those metal pieces. In accordance with this view of the subject, if we were asked, what was the difference between

[1] 'Whatever a person saves from his revenue he adds to his capital', p. 149 *b*.
[2] P. 149 *b*.

the part of the rich man's revenue represented by the £800 which he 'spent' last year, and that represented by the £200 which he 'saved', we should say that the £800 which he spent, represents certain things, such as the food, the fuel, the shelter, the maintenance of furniture and clothes, and the menial service, which he consumed or gave to his friends to consume; and the £200 represents certain other things, such as a few feet of the Manchester Ship Canal, or a portion of waterworks in Argentina, which he has acquired, and which neither he nor any one else has consumed. But in Adam Smith's argument just quoted, it is not the new canal or the new waterworks[1] which are said to be saved, but 'the food, clothing, and lodging',[2] consumed by the productive labourers who produce them. 'What is annually saved', is thus made to signify, not the annual additions to the stock of the community, the surplus of production over consumption, but the wages of productive labourers.[3] Whether it means the wages of all productive labourers or only the wages of those who are employed in producing the additions to the capital, it is not necessary to decide. In either case, it is plain that Adam Smith does not mean by 'saving' what we mean by it. His 'savings', instead of being accumulations or stores of the produce of past labour, are a part of the annual produce and annual consumption. When he wishes to show that in spite of all prodigality and misconduct the capital of England has increased, does he take the course which would be obvious to any one who understood the capital to be an accumulation of goods? Does he say the land of England has been improved, the farm-houses and other buildings have increased and grown better in quality, the cattle, sheep, and horses are more numerous and finer? By no means. He says that increase of capital is 'almost always' necessary for increase of produce,[4] and sets himself to prove that the annual produce has increased, and even then he does not exactly arrive at the conclusion that the capital has increased, but only that 'the capital annually employed' has increased:

[1] Of course it frequently happens that the 'rich man' does not invest in new enterprises, but buys shares in old ones. The annual savings of the community in any particular year, consequently, do not altogether belong to the persons who have saved during that year, but partly to others who have exchanged old property for new. The savers determine the amount of the annual addition to the community's capital, but they have abdicated, to a great extent, the office of determining what form the addition shall take.

[2] How does the inclusion of 'lodging' in 'what is employed as a capital' fit in with Adam Smith's theory that houses are not part of a country's capital, and produce nothing?

[3] Adam Smith imagined that labour employed for a money profit is all 'productive' labour, labour which 'fixes and realizes itself in a particular subject or vendible commodity'. He forgot entirely that an employer's profit can be made by employing labourers whose work 'perishes in the very instant of its performance', just as well as by employing productive labourers. The profits, for example, of the hotel-keeper and the hairdresser are obtained by employing 'menial servants'.

[4] P. 152 *a*.

'Though the profusion of government must undoubtedly have retarded the natural progress of England towards wealth and improvement, it has not been able to stop it. The annual produce of its land and labour is undoubtedly much greater at present than it was either at the restoration or the revolution. The capital, therefore, annually employed in cultivating this land, and in maintaining this labour, must likewise be much greater.'[1]

Now, if the capital of a country, or what seems in Book II, Chapter iii, of the *Wealth of Nations* to be much the same thing, 'the capital annually employed', is to be, sometimes at any rate, considered as a part of its periodical produce, the question naturally arises, what part? In Book II, Chapter iii, it is apparently that part of produce which is not 'revenue', and for the purpose in hand 'revenue' seems to consist entirely of rent and profit. The 'capital', then, or the part of produce which in the course of a year 'replaces a capital', is that part of the annual produce which is neither rent nor profit. But in Book I, and indeed at the beginning of Chapter ii of Book II, that part of the annual produce which is neither rent nor profit is wages. The 'capital', then, of Book II, Chapter iii, and the wages paid in a year ought to be identical. But if this were so, it could scarcely have escaped the attention of Adam Smith himself; moreover, there seem to be included in the capital of Book II, Chapter iii, things which are evidently not thought of as constituting wages, namely, 'materials'. The explanation of the discrepancy must lie in an ambiguity of the word 'produce'. When following his earlier or British train of thought, Adam Smith makes 'produce' exactly the same thing as 'revenue', or what we call 'income'; it is the necessaries, conveniences, and amusements which men actually enjoy *plus* any objects which they may add to their accumulated stock or capital. But when following his later or physiocrat train of thought, as in Book II, Chapter iii, he looks on the produce of a country as a mass of material objects. We have already observed that the income or revenue of a community includes many things which are not material objects.[2] It is also the case that many of the material objects which are produced cannot possibly be regarded as parts of the income of the community. Nothing strikes the ordinary mind as better entitled to be called produce than wheat. But it is not wheat but bread and other things made of flour that reach the consumer and constitute a part of his revenue or income. The amount spent by the consumers on bread is supposed to be about double the value of the wheat after it has been harvested and threshed. If, then, we were making up a computation of national income by adding together products, instead of by the usual and simple method of adding individual incomes, we should have to leave wheat out of account alto-

[1] P. 153 *b*.

[2] Above, pp. 18–31.

gether. If we took wheat alone as the income, we should under-estimate the item in question by 50 per cent; if we took both wheat and bread as the income, we should over-estimate the item by 50 per cent. So when 'produce' is taken as equivalent to revenue or income, we must understand by it only ultimate produce, no intermediate products being taken into account. Adam Smith was probably groping for this truth when he made the distinction between gross and net revenue, which is to be found in the opening paragraphs of the second chapter of Book II:

> 'The gross revenue of all the inhabitants of a great country comprehends the whole annual produce of their land and labour; the net revenue, what remains free to them after deducting the expense of maintaining, first, their fixed, and secondly, their circulating, capital, or what, without encroaching upon their capital, they can place in their stock reserved for immediate consumption, or spend upon their subsistence, conveniencies, or amusements.
>
> 'The whole expense of maintaining the fixed capital must evidently be excluded from the net revenue of the society. Neither the materials necessary for supporting their useful machines and instruments of trade, their profitable buildings, etc., nor the produce of the labour necessary for fashioning those materials into the proper form, can ever make any part of it.'[1]

The materials fashioned into proper form which 'support' useful machines and instruments of trade are clearly intermediate, not ultimate, products. Such things as new tyres for wheels, machine-oil, and coal used in steam-engines form part of nobody's income.

Very possibly when Adam Smith divided the total produce into wages, profits, and rent, he was thinking of his 'net produce', and when he divided produce into profits, rent, and the part of produce destined for replacing a capital, he was thinking of his 'gross produce'. But this does not make it much easier to say what the part of produce destined for replacing a capital is, for Adam Smith's gross revenue or gross produce is a mere chimæra. It is impossible to form any conception of the aggregate of products, intermediate and ultimate, all jumbled together. We cannot think of a country's annual produce as consisting of x qrs. of wheat $+ y$ sacks of flour $+$ z lbs. of bread. We cannot make an aggregate of the coal, iron, oil, cotton, and other things used to make a calico shirt, and add them to the shirt itself. Adam Smith was misled by the fact that an individual carrying on a business has a gross revenue, or, as we should say, gross receipts, consisting of two parts, one of which 'replaces his capital', or, as we should say, pays his working expenses, while the other constitutes his profits. This, of course, does not show that the world in general has similar gross receipts divisible into what replaces a capital on the one

[1] P. 124 *a*.

hand and what constitutes profit on the other. To add together the gross receipts of every separate business would bring out a ridiculous total the amount of which would depend chiefly on the number of different owners into whose possession products pass successively on their way to the consumer. Of what use could it be to add together the gross receipts of the tailor, the weaver, and the spinner, or those of the baker, the miller, and the farmer?

On the whole, the probability seems to be that the part of produce which is called 'capital' in Book II, Chapter iii, is much the same thing as the last three parts – 'provisions, materials, and finished work' – of the 'circulating capital' of Chapter i.

But how can a particular part of the year's produce be the same thing as a particular part of the accumulated stock? The answer is that Adam Smith had evidently imbued himself with the physiocratic idea of 'reproduction', and that the difference between the daily or annual produce and the stock of articles which are supposed to be daily or annually reproduced is, if the time when the stock is largest be selected, *nil.* If a reservoir be filled every night and emptied every day, the stock of water in that reservoir at 6 a.m. will obviously be also the amount of daily supply. Similarly if wheat were all harvested on August 31st, and no less than the previous year's supply were ever consumed in the year, the stock on the evening of August 31st would be the same thing as the year's supply of wheat. So, if the whole stock of provisions, materials, and finished work be supposed to be consumed and reproduced, or to be 'turned over' or 'circulated', in a given period, it becomes much the same thing as the part of the produce which during that period replaces the stock; the produce of one period becomes the stock out of which the wants of the next period are supplied. Adam Smith says that of the four parts of which the circulating capital consists,

> 'three, provisions, materials, and finished work, are either annually or in a longer or shorter period regularly withdrawn from it, and placed either in the fixed capital or in the stock reserved for immediate consumption. . . .
>
> 'So great a part of the circulating capital being continually withdrawn from it in order to be placed in the other two branches of the general stock of the society, it must in its turn require continual supplies, without which it would soon cease to exist. These supplies are principally drawn from three sources, the produce of land, of mines, and of fisheries. . . .
>
> 'Land, mines, and fisheries require all both a fixed and circulating capital to cultivate them; and their produce replaces with a profit, not only those capitals, but all the others in the society. Thus the farmer annually replaces to the manufacturer the provisions which he had consumed and the materials which he had wrought up the year before; and the manufacturer replaces to the farmer the finished work which

he had wasted and worn out in the same time. This is the real exchange that is annually made between those two orders of people.'[1]

Though the passage begins with the admission that some of the provisions, materials, and finished work are consumed and reproduced in a longer and others in a shorter period than a year, the tendency of the whole is to suggest that, at any rate roughly speaking, the whole stock of provisions, materials, and finished goods is turned over or circulated once a year, so that the annual produce of them and the stock of them are equal. The evidence afforded by the tone of the passage that this was the idea latent in Adam Smith's mind receives strong corroboration from the second reason he gives for treating the stock of money as a sort of fixed capital:

> 'As the machines and instruments of trade, etc., which compose the fixed capital either of an individual or of a society make no part either of the gross or of the net revenue of either, so money, by means of which the whole revenue of the society is regularly distributed among all its different members, makes itself no part of that revenue.'

By this he implies, of course, that the other three parts of the circulating capital do make a part of the society's revenue.

> 'The great wheel of circulation', he proceeds, 'is altogether different from the goods which are circulated by means of it. The revenue of the society consists altogether in those goods, and not in the wheel which circulates them. In computing either the gross or the net revenue of any society, we must always, from their whole annual circulation of money and goods, deduct the whole value of the money, of which not a single farthing can ever make any part of either.'[2]

If he had quite clearly conceived the revenue as a periodical produce, and not as a 'circulation', he would surely have had no need of this proposition, which he expects to appear 'doubtful or paradoxical'. The stock of money is perfectly obviously not part of the annual produce of the labour of a nation. Moreover, it is quite impossible to give any intelligible meaning to the process of deducting the whole value of the money from 'the whole annual circulation of money and goods', unless 'the whole annual circulation of money and goods' means the stock of provisions, materials, and finished goods considered as an annual produce, together with the stock of money. It cannot mean the aggregate price of all the things bought and sold in the year, for, if the whole stock of money were deducted from this total, the amount remaining would still have nothing to do with the gross or net revenue; and if the whole amount of money paid for all the things sold were deducted, the amount left would obviously be *nil*. It cannot mean the aggregate annual produce, because there is no reason for subtracting the stock of money from the annual produce;

[1] Pp. 122, 123 *a*.

[2] Bk. II, ch. ii, p. 125.

and if the money paid for the produce, or its money value, were deducted from it, the remainder would again be *nil.* We are driven, therefore, to conclude that 'the whole annual circulation of money and goods' means nothing more or less than the whole circulating capital, of which the last three parts, the stocks of provisions, materials, and finished goods, are taken to be annually consumed and reproduced, so that their 'annual circulation', or the amount of them annually circulated, is equal to the amount of them annually produced.

§ 3. *Adam Smith on the Functions of the Capital of a Community*

If Adam Smith had been asked what is the function or use of 'capital', he would probably have answered in the first place, 'To yield a profit'; and, doubtless, to each individual capitalist this appears to be the principal use of his capital. But the yielding of a profit is a distributive, and not a productive function. The capital of the community would still be useful if there were no private property, and consequently no profits. A bridge has its uses when the toll for passing over is abolished just as much as before when it yielded a profit. And so we find that besides the yielding of a profit, Adam Smith ascribes various other functions to the capital or to its different parts.

In the Introduction to Book II, he endeavours to show that the accumulation of capital is necessary in order to enable exchange and division of labour to flourish:

> 'In that rude state of society in which there is no division of labour, in which exchanges are seldom made, and in which every man provides everything for himself, it is not necessary that any stock should be accumulated or stored up beforehand in order to carry on the business of the society. Every man endeavours to supply by his own industry his own occasional wants as they occur. . . .
>
> 'But when the division of labour has once been thoroughly introduced, the produce of a man's own labour can supply but a very small part of his occasional wants. The far greater part of them are supplied by the produce of other men's labour, which he purchases with the produce, or, what is the same thing, with the price of the produce, of his own. But this purchase cannot be made till such time as the produce of his own labour has not only been completed, but sold. A stock of goods of different kinds, therefore, must be stored up somewhere sufficient to maintain him, and to supply him with the materials and tools of his work till such time, at least, as both these events can be brought about. A weaver cannot apply himself entirely to his peculiar business, unless there is beforehand stored up somewhere, either in his own possession or in that of some other person, a stock sufficient to maintain him and to supply him with the materials and tools of his work till he has not only completed, but sold, his web. This accumulation must, evidently, be previous to his applying his industry for so long a time to such a peculiar business.

'As the accumulation of stock must, in the nature of things, be previous to the division of labour, so labour can be more and more subdivided in proportion only as stock is previously more and more accumulated. The quantity of materials which the same number of people can work up increases in a great proportion as labour comes to be more and more subdivided; and as the operations of each workman are gradually reduced to a greater degree of simplicity, a variety of new machines come to be invented for facilitating and abridging those operations. As the division of labour advances, therefore, in order to give constant employment to an equal number of workmen, an equal stock of provisions, and a greater stock of materials and tools than what would have been necessary in a ruder state of things must be accumulated beforehand.'[1]

It is not easy to understand how Adam Smith came to commit himself to the statements he made about the weaver. 'Beforehand' must mean before the weaver begins his web, and what possible justification can there be for saying that before a weaver begins his web there must be stored up somewhere a stock sufficient to maintain him and supply him with materials till he has completed or sold the web? The bread and meat which maintain the weaver certainly cannot have been stored up before he began, or they would be uneatable before he finished, and there is no reason why all the materials should have been stored up before he began. Maintenance and materials must be supplied to him as the work proceeds, not stored up beforehand. In return or exchange for this gradual supply of the produce of other men's labour he gradually creates cloth.

The whole of Adam Smith's argument is most delusive. Division of labour, far from necessitating a greater provision of stock or capital, rather economizes it. The isolated man is not less, but more, in need of a stock of the produce of past labour than men who live in society. If a hundred men on board ship, instead of dividing their labour in the usual manner, all tried to turn their hand to everything, they would very soon be wrecked, but they would not require less stores than a crew of the same number who behaved more sensibly. If the same hundred men, when establishing themselves on the desert island on which we may suppose them to wreck their ship, proceeded to divide their labour, they certainly would not be any more in need of a stock than if they attempted to live in isolation. If, for example, 30 went to hunt, 20 to fish, 10 to gather sticks for fires, 10 to find water, and 30 to build huts, no greater accumulation would be required before they could devote themselves to these peculiar businesses than if each man hunted for 3 hours, fished for 2, looked for water for 1, and built himself a hut for 3 hours. On the contrary, they would require a smaller stock of provisions, tools, and materials.

[1] Pp. 118 *b*, 119 *a*.

Whether the division of labour takes place as in this case, by conscious arrangement, or as in an ordinary individualist society, by way of exchange, makes no difference. In a later passage Adam Smith himself shows with some vigour that if there were no such trade as that of a butcher, every man would be obliged to purchase a whole ox or a whole sheep every time he wanted beef or mutton.[1] If there were not only no butcher, but no cattle-breeders and sheep-breeders, every man would be obliged to keep his own stock of cattle and sheep. So if men lived in isolation instead of practising exchange, the stock of cattle and sheep would have to be enormously increased in order to give an equal result. Even the stock of wheat would have to be greater in order to provide equally well against the risk of starvation, since each man, having to grow his own wheat, would be obliged to keep in hand a stock sufficient to maintain him for a year or two in case of some accident happening to his own particular crop. It is equally clear that tools and machinery are economized by division of labour. With division of labour a smaller, not a greater stock of tools and machinery is required. It is true that the differentiation of occupations and trades allows more elaborate machinery to be used, but this is not the same thing as necessitating its use. In consequence of division of labour, some of us can use steam-ploughs, but if there were no division of labour, every one of us would be obliged to have his spade, unless indeed some cumbrous system of using spades by rotation were devised. Materials also are economized by division of labour; a smaller, and not a larger stock of them is required in consequence of division of labour. If 'every man provided everything for himself', he would have to keep the materials of many articles on his hands for years before he could hope to complete the process of manufacture, whereas at present the same materials are worked up in two or three days. The very fact on which Adam Smith relies, that with division of labour 'the quantity of materials which the same number of people can work up' in a given time increases, is conclusive against himself; in that case a less stock of materials will be required to be kept in hand.

As usual, we must here trace Adam Smith's error to his habit of reasoning too hastily from the individual to the community. Seeing that the capital of an employer should be greater, if he is to be successful, when the division of labour is far advanced and the processes of production are more effective and elaborate, he promptly assumes that the community is subject to the same need; whereas, though the increase of capital and the increase of division of labour may, as a matter of fact, advance together, the increase of capital is not the cause or indispensable preliminary of the increase of division of labour.

[1] Book II, chap. V, p. 160.

Proceeding from the Introduction to the description of the capital of a country in the first chapter of Book II, we find Adam Smith practically ascribing different functions to the fixed and the circulating capital. Machines are his great type of fixed capital, and the function of machines is obvious. The machines which constitute part of the capital of a nation are useful, because (after making allowance for the labour necessary to keep them in repair) they enable labour to produce more easily. Some things can be done by the aid of machinery which could not be done at all in any length of time by any amount of machineless labour, and other things can be done by the aid of machinery quicker, better, or with less labour than without it. In short, the use of machinery is to make labour more productive. So Adam Smith teaches that fixed capital 'facilitates and abridges labour'. Useful machines and instruments of trade, he says, 'facilitate and abridge labour', and 'shops, warehouses, work-houses, and farm-houses, with all their necessary buildings', 'are a sort of instruments of trade'. 'An improved farm may also be very justly regarded in the same light as those useful machines which facilitate and abridge labour'.[1] But to discover the function or use ascribed by Adam Smith to that part of the capital which he calls the circulating capital is more difficult than to discover the function which he attributes to the fixed capital:

> 'Every fixed capital', he says, 'is both originally derived from, and requires to be continually supported by, a circulating capital. All useful machines and instruments of trade are originally derived from a circulating capital which furnishes the materials of which they are made, and the maintenance of the workmen who make them. They require, too, a capital of the same kind to keep them in constant repair.'[2]

He here makes the function of the circulating capital, indirectly, the same as that of the fixed capital, namely, the facilitation and abridgment of labour. Directly, he makes the function of the circulating capital the furnishing of materials and maintenance for persons engaged in constructing things which facilitate the abridge labour. In the next chapter he says 'it is the circulating capital which furnishes the materials and wages of labour, and puts industry into motion', and seems to imply that this function is not shared by the fixed capital:

> 'The whole capital of the undertaker of every work is necessarily divided between his fixed and his circulating capital. While his whole capital remains the same, the smaller the one part, the greater must necessarily be the other. It is the circulating capital which furnishes the materials and wages of labour, and puts industry into motion.'[3]

This is exactly the function attributed to the peculiar 'capital', of Chapter iii. That 'capital' 'maintains productive hands', 'pays the

[1] P. 121 *b*. [2] P. 122 *b*. [3] P. 126 *b*.

wages of productive labour', and puts 'into motion its full complement of productive labour'.[1]

When Adam Smith says that it is the circulating capital which puts industry into motion, he is using the term in its narrowest sense, to indicate only the last three parts of the circulating capital of Chapter i:

> 'When we compute the quantity of industry which the circulating capital of any society can employ, we must always have regard to those parts of it only which consist in provisions, materials, and finished work; the other, which consists in money, and which serves only to circulate those three, must always be deducted.'[2]

But so far from never forgetting to always have regard to those parts only of the circulating capital which consist in provisions, materials, and finished work, he constantly speaks as if it was not only the whole of the circulating capital, but the whole of the circulating and fixed capital together which puts industry into motion, and regulates the quantity of industry which can be exerted in a country. The amount of industry must, he says, remain the same, if the capital remains the same:

> 'The general industry of the society never can exceed what the capital of the society can employ. As the number of workmen that can be kept in the employment of any particular person must bear a certain proportion to his capital, so the number of those that can be continually employed by all the members of a great society must bear a certain proportion to the whole capital of that society, and never can exceed that proportion.'[3]
>
> 'The capital of the country remaining the same, the demand for labour will likewise be the same or very nearly the same.'[4]

An increase of the capital of a country increases the quantity of industry, and a decrease of the capital of a country decreases the quantity of industry exerted in it:

> 'The quantity of industry . . . increases in every country with the increase of the stock which employs it.'[5]

And lastly, the quantity of industry can only be increased when the capital increases:

> 'The industry of the society can augment only in proportion as its capital augments.'[6]
>
> 'The increase in the quantity of useful labour actually employed within any society must depend altogether upon the increase of the capital which employs it.'[7]

Certainly all these statements are to be understood subject to the qualification contained in the fifth chapter, to the effect that the pro-

[1] P. 147.
[2] P. 128 *a*.
[3] Bk. IV, chap. ii, p. 198 *b*.
[4] *Ibid.*, p. 207 *a*.
[5] Bk. II, Introduction, p. 119 *b*.
[6] Bk. IV, chap. ii, p. 200 *b*.
[7] Bk. IV, chap. ix, p. 306 *a*.

portions in which the capital is divided between four different classes of employment must remain the same,[1] and if Adam Smith had attempted to divide all the different employments of capital into four great classes in each of which it was divided in a particular proportion between fixed and circulating capital, he would have been consistent even if incorrect. But he did not attempt anything of the kind.

The four different ways in which, according to Chapter v, capital may be employed are:

1. In procuring raw produce from the ground.
2. In preparing that produce for consumption.
3. In transporting either the raw produce or the commodities into which it has been fashioned, from the places where they abound, to the places where they are wanted.
4. In dividing particular portions of either the raw produce or the finished commodities into small parcels to suit the convenience of those who want them.[2]

To put the matter shortly, capital may be invested in agriculture and mining, in manufactures, in commerce, or in retail trade.

> 'Equal capitals employed in each of those four different ways, will immediately put into motion very different quantities of productive labour.'[3]

A given capital will put into motion more labour when it is invested in commerce than when it is invested in retail trade, still more when it is invested in manufacture, and most of all when it is invested in agriculture. Adam Smith does not attempt to prove this by asserting that in agriculture the greatest, and in retail dealing the least proportion of the capital will be circulating capital, which, according to Book II, Chapter ii, is the part of capital which puts industry into motion, but launches forth into what is perhaps the most illogical argument he ever employed.

The retailer's capital, he says, puts into motion the least labour, because the retailer himself is the only productive labourer whom it immediately employs'.[4] The wholesale merchant's capital puts 'a good deal' more labour into motion, because it 'employs the sailors and carriers who transport his goods from one place to another'. The manufacturer's capital 'puts immediately into motion a much greater quantity of productive labour . . . than an equal capital in the hands of any wholesale merchant', becasue 'a great part of it is always either

[1] 'Though all capitals are destined for the maintenance of productive labour only, yet the quantity of that labour which equal capitals are capable of putting into motion varies extremely according to the diversity of their employment' (P. 159 *b*).

[2] Bk. II, chap. v, pp. 159, 160.

[3] *Ibid.*, p. 161 *a*.

[4] P. 161 *a*.

annually, or in a much shorter period, distributed among the different workmen whom he employs'.[1] Lastly, the farmer's capital puts into motion a greater quantity of labour[2] than even the manufacturer's, because not only the farmer's 'labouring servants, but his labouring cattle are productive labourers', and in agriculture 'nature labours along with man'. Adam Smith seems to have entirely forgotten that the question is not whether one retailer, one merchant, one manufacturer, or one farmer employs many or few persons (to say nothing of cattle and nature), but whether a given amount of capital in the hands of a retailer, a merchant, a manufacturer, employs many or few persons. Even if it were true that shopkeepers employed no assistants – and it was not true even in Adam Smith's time – the fact that each shopkeeper's capital only employed one labourer, while each manufacturer's capital employed twenty, would prove nothing to the purpose, unless we knew that each manufacturer's capital was less than twenty times as great as each shopkeeper's.

The chief use of examining Adam Smith's arguments on the different amounts of industry put into motion by capital invested in the four different employments, is to show how excessively vague was his idea of the connexion between the magnitude of the capital of a country and the amount of industry exerted in it. He seems to have had no better basis for his theory that the magnitude of the capital regulates the number of useful and productive labourers, than the observation of the facts that in every business, as a rule, the large capitalists are the large employers, and that the power of an individual to employ labourers in any particular business depends to a great extent on the amount of his capital. From these facts he deduced the proposition that in each of four great employments, a man's ability to employ depends on the amount of his capital, and in turn from this proposition, reasoning in his usual manner from the individual to the society, he deduced the further proposition that the ability of a nation to employ useful and productive labourers depends on the amount of its capital, and the proportions in which it is divided between the four employments. There is more than one weak link in this chain of reasoning.

First, though it may be said, roughly speaking, that at the same time and place an individual's power to employ labourers in some one particular business depends, at any rate very greatly, on the amount of his capital, it cannot be said with any approach to accuracy that even at the same time and place an individual's power to employ labour in (1) agriculture, (2) manufactures, (3) commerce, and (4)

[1] P. 161 *b*.

[2] At first Adam Smith only says, 'No equal capital puts into motion a greater quantity of productive labour than that of the farmer', but he clearly means, 'No equal capital puts into motion *so much* productive labour as that of the farmer'.

retail trade, depends on the amount of his capital. It is only true that all farmers farming the same kind of land and producing the same kind of produce, will (if they are all farming in the most profitable manner), employ much the same number of labourers to each £100 of their capital. It is not true that all farmers employ the same number of labourers to each £100 of their capital. To give an obvious illustration, the number of labourers employed to each £100 will be much less on a grazing than on an arable farm. Again, it is only true that all manufacturers using the same kind of machinery and producing the same kind of goods will employ much the same number of hands to each £100 of their capital. It is not true that all manufacturers of whatever kind employ the same number of labourers to each £100 of their capital.

Secondly, the fact that in exactly similar businesses, and at the same time and place, an individual's power to employ labour depends greatly on the magnitude of his capital, does not prove, even excluding changes and differences in the proportions in which the whole capital is divided between different businesses, that the capacity of a whole community to employ labour is regulated at all by the magnitude of its capital. Whether a particular individual has much or little capital will seldom have any appreciable effect on the profitableness of different methods of production. Consequently in order to produce any particular commodity profitably, an employer must generally conform pretty closely to the methods in use at the time. It would be possible, physically possible, for a man to employ people to spin wool by hand with a distaff at present in Bradford, but it certainly would not be profitable, and so no one does it. No one employs people to spin unless he can command the usual machinery. If he gets much machinery he employs many people; if he gets little, he employs few. But the whole community is in no way bound by these limitations. If the community had no means of providing expensive spinning mills, it would not follow that no one would be employed in spinning. On the contrary, if thread were considered a great necessary of life, more hands would be employed in spinning than are employed under present conditions; labour would be diverted to spinning from less necessary occupations.

It can scarcely be denied that Adam Smith left the whole subject of 'capital' in the most unsatisfactory state. He makes unscientific distinctions between the stock which is capital and the stock which is not capital; he makes trivial distinctions between fixed and circulating capital; he confuses the capital of a country with a particular part of its annual produce; and with regard to the functions of the capital he completely fails to prove his most important proposition, namely, that the amount of the capital determines the amount of industry.

§ 4. *Adam Smith's successors on the Nature and Origin of the Capital of a Community*

The critic of Lauderdale's *Public Wealth* in the *Edinburgh Review* for July 1804, rejected Adam Smith's distinction between the capital of a country and its stock reserved for consumption:

> 'A difference is established by some, especially by Dr Smith, between capital and the other parts of stock; capital being, according to them, that part which brings in a revenue. This idea clearly appears, by the whole of the illustrations given of it, to have arisen from the fundamental error of considering nothing as productive which does not yield a tangible return, and of confounding use with exchange. For may not a man live upon his stock, that is, enjoy his capital, without either diminishing or exchanging any part of it? In what does the value, and the real nature of stock reserved for immediate consumption, differ from stock that yields what Dr Smith calls a revenue or profit? Merely in this – that the former is wanted and used itself by the owner; the latter is not wanted by him, and therefore is exchanged for something which he does want.'[1]

Subsequent writers scarcely discussed the division of the community's stock into capital and reserve for consumption, because they did not conceive the capital of a country as a part of its accumulated stock. They succumbed completely to Adam Smith's tendency to regard the capital of the country as a particular part of its annual produce, and the misunderstood as completely as he did the process of adding to the capital by saving. In *Commerce Defended*, James Mill remarks:

> 'The whole annual produce of every country is distributed into two great parts; that which is destined to be employed for the purpose of reproduction, and that which is destined to be consumed.'[2]

Though he does not actually say that the first of these is the capital of the country, he shows that he thought so by using 'the augmentation of capital', and 'the augmentation of that part of the annual produce which is consumed in the way of reproduction',[3] as synonymous phrases. That he did not understand that all that a nation saves is simply the additions which it makes to its accumulated stock is shown by his bold assertion that 'every country will infallibly consume to the full amount of its production'.[4] The writer of the article 'Political Economy' in the fourth edition of the *Encyclopædia Britannica* understood that the capital is an accumulated stock as little as James Mill in *Commerce Defended*:

> 'Every man's wealth', he says, 'is of two kinds; the one which he lays aside for immediate consumption; the other which he reserves for the

[1] Vol. iv, p. 366. [2] P. 70. [3] Pp. 86,87.
[4] P. 79; see also pp. 71, 76.

> supply of future wants, or employs in such a manner as to make it produce new wealth. The former is called his income, the latter his capital.'[1]

This is like dividing a water company's water into the water in its reservoir and its supply, into x gallons collected at one time in its reservoir and y gallons supplied *per diem* or *per annum*.

Ricardo says: 'Capital is that part of the wealth of a country which is employed in production, and consists of food, clothing, tools, raw materials, machinery, etc., necessary to give effect to labour.'[2] This is rather vague, for we do not know exactly what Ricardo meant by 'the wealth of a country', or by 'employed in production'. In his chapter 'On Taxes', he distinctly implies that the houses, clothes, and furniture used by labourers are part of the capital of the country,[3] a fact which is difficult to harmonize with Adam Smith's conception of the stock reserved for immediate consumption not being part of the capital of the country.

In the first and second editions of his *Principles* he gives a fairly clear account of the process of saving or adding to the capital or stock:

> 'When the annual productions of a country', he said, 'exceed its annual consumption, it is said to increase its capital; when its annual consumption at least is not replaced by its annual production, it is said to diminish its capital. Capital may therefore be increased by an increased production, or by a diminished consumption.
>
> 'If the consumption of the government, when increased by the levy of additional taxes, be met either by an increased production, or by a diminished consumption on the part of the people, the taxes will fall upon revenue, and the national capital will remain unimpaired; but if there be no increased production or diminished consumption on the part of the people, the taxes will necessarily fall on capital.'[4]

It is not quite logical, because if the production already exceeds the consumption, the capital will be increased without either 'an increased production' or a 'diminished consumption', and if the consumption already exceeds the production, the capital will be diminished without either a decreased production or an increased consumption. Instead of saying that 'the national capital will remain unimpaired', Ricardo ought to have said, 'the rate at which the capital is increasing or decreasing may remain unaltered'. Doubtless, however, it was only his want of command of language that prevented him saying this, and the taxes may, perhaps, without any great impropriety, be said to 'fall on capital', if they diminish its increase or accelerate its decrease.

In the third edition of his work (1821), however, Ricardo altered

[1] Vol. xvii, p. 108 *a*.
[2] 1st ed., pp. 93, 94; 3rd ed. in *Works*, p. 51.
[3] 1st ed., pp. 186, 187; 3rd ed. in *Works*, p. 87.
[4] 1st ed., p. 187; 2nd ed., p. 170.

the passage by inserting the word 'unproductive' before 'consumption', both in the fifth and tenth lines, and adding at the end, 'That is to say, they will impair the fund allotted to productive consumption'. He also added a note which runs as follows:

> 'It must be understood that all the productions of a country are consumed; but it makes the greatest difference imaginable whether they are consumed by those who reproduce, or by those who do not reproduce another value. When we say that revenue is saved and added to capital, what we mean is, that the portion of revenue so said to be added to capital is consumed by productive instead of unproductive labourers. There can be no greater error than in supposing that capital is increased by non-consumption. If the price of labour should rise so high, that, notwithstanding the increase of capital, no more could be employed, I should say that such increase of capital would be still unproductively consumed.'[1]

By these alterations and additions the picture of the capital of a country as a store or stock of produce increased in any given period by the excess of production over consumption, is smeared over by the hand that painted it. In the first edition we were told that the addition to the capital consists of such productions as are over and above what replaces the annual consumption. In the third we are told that the whole produce is consumed, so that there cannot be any such thing as an excess of production over consumption. Ricardo had evidently, in the meanwhile, allowed himself to get confused by some of his tangled discussions with Malthus.[2]

The distinction between fixed and circulating capital is formally made by Ricardo to depend simply on the degree of durability of the things of which they are constituted. He says:

> 'According as capital is rapidly perishable, and requires to be frequently reproduced, or is of slow consumption, it is classed under the heads of circulating or of fixed capital. A brewer, whose buildings and machinery are valuable and durable, is said to employ a large portion of fixed capital: on the contrary, a shoemaker, whose capital is chiefly employed in the payment of wages, which are expended on food and clothing, commodities more perishable than buildings and machinery, is said to employ a large proportion of his capital as circulating capital.'[3]

In the second edition (1819) he added a note:

> 'A division not essential, and in which the line of demarcation cannot be accurately drawn.'[4]

Substantially, however, the distinction between Ricardo's fixed and circulating capital is simply that the fixed capital is conceived as consisting entirely of machinery, implements, and buildings, while the

[1] 3rd ed. in *Works*, p. 87, note.

[2] See below, p. 100, note 2.

[3] 1st ed., p. 22, note; 3rd ed. in *Works*, p. 21, note.

[4] 2nd ed., p. 20; 3rd ed. in *Works*, p. 21.

circulating capital is conceived as consisting entirely of amounts paid by employers in wages.

> 'In one trade very little capital may be employed as circulating capital, that is to say, in the support of labour – it may be principally invested in machinery, implements, buildings, etc., capital of a comparatively fixed and durable character.'[1]

He has numerous examples in which the circulating capital of an employer is the amount he pays in wages in a year. The fixed capital of a fisherman is his 'canoe and implements', and his circulating capital is the £100 which he pays in wages in the course of a year; the fixed capital of the hunter is his weapons, and his circulating capital is also the £100 a year which he pays in wages.[2] This is so because, although in the second and third editions Ricardo allows that 'the circulating capital may circulate or be returned to its employer, in very unequal times',[3] he usually assumes that the capital employed in paying wages circulates once a year. In the first edition, for example, he describes what will happen if an 'amount of capital, viz. £20,000, be employed in supporting productive labour, and be annually consumed and reproduced, as it is when employed in paying wages'.[4] In the third edition he says that if a machine which would do the work of 100 men in some trade for a year, and then be worn out and worthless, cost £5,000, and the wages annually paid to 100 men were likewise £5,000, 'it is evident that it would be a matter of indifference to the manufacturer whether he bought the machine or employed the men'.[5] It obviously could not be said to be 'a matter of indifference' to the manufacturer unless the amount he pays in wages 'circulates', or goes away from him and returns to him, once a year. If it circulates once a week he would lose greatly by buying the machine, since he would have £5,000 'locked up in machinery' throughout the year, instead of about £100 locked up at the end of each week in payment of his wages' bill.[6]

James Mill, in the formal discussion of the nature of capital which appeared first in the second edition (1824) if his *Elements of Political Economy*,[7] after some remarks on the usefulness of instruments, says: 'The provision made of these is denominated capital.'[8] Now he might

[1] Only in 3rd ed. in *Works*, p. 21. [2] 1st ed., pp. 23–33.

[3] 2nd ed., p. 21; 3rd ed. in *Works*, p. 21. [4] P. 35. [5] *Works*, p. 26.

[6] Of course if we were to look at the transaction more closely, and apply the principles of arithmetic more accurately than Ricardo was in the habit of doing, it would appear that the manufacturer would lose by buying the machine, even if he sold none of his goods till the 31st of December. The £5,000 for the machine would have to be laid out in a lump at the beginning of the year, whereas the £5,000 for wages would be gradually disbursed during the year. The manufacturer would consequently lose one year's interest on £2,500, or, which is the same thing, six months' interest on £5,000, if he bought the machine. Ricardo's arguments always require the absurd assumption, not only that no goods are sold till the end of a year, but also that all the wages are paid at the beginning of the year.

[7] Chap. i, § 2. [8] 2nd and 3rd eds., p. 16.

have been understood to mean by 'the provision made' the stock, or the number or quantity accumulated and existing at one time, if he had not gone on to say that 'the materials', not 'the provision made of materials', 'upon which labour is to be employed, where they have . . . been the result of previous labour, are also denominated capital'.[1] Thus he practically defines 'capital' as 'instruments and materials', whether accumulated into a stock or not, and accordingly 'the capital of England' would mean the instruments and materials of England, that is to say, all the instruments and materials which have existed, do exist, or will exist in England from the time when the first man set foot in the country to the time when the last shall leave it. No reference to time is included in the definition, so that the amount of the capital of England might be the instruments and materials produced in a given period just as well as the number existing at a given point of time.

With regard to the origin of the capital, James Mill says:

> 'As capital, from its simplest to its most complicated state, means something produced for the purpose of being employed as the means towards a further production, it is evidently a result of what is called saving. The meaning of this term is so well understood and so little liable to abuse, that not many words will be necessary to explain this particular relating to capital, though it is a law of great importance to remark.
>
> 'It is sufficiently evident that without saving there could be no capital. If all labour were employed upon objects of immediate consumption, which were all immediately consumed, such as the fruit for which the savage climbs the tree, no article of capital, no article to be employed as a means to further production, would ever exist. To this end something must be produced which is not immediately consumed, which is saved and set apart for another purpose.
>
> 'All the consequences of this fact, to which it is necessary here to advert, are sufficiently obvious.
>
> 'Every article which is thus saved becomes an article of capital. The augmentation of capital, therefore, is everywhere exactly in proportion to the degree of saving; in fact, the amount of that augmentation annually is the same thing with the amount of the savings which are annually made.'[2]

Here the capital does appear to be conceived as a stock or accumulation which consists of the surplus of past production over past consumption, and is augmented by saving. But James Mill did not keep this conception steadily before him, since in Chapter iv, § ii, he adhered to the old proposition, 'That which is annually produced is annually consumed'.[3] If it is true 'that the whole of what is annually produced is annually consumed; or that what is produced in one year

[1] 2nd and 3rd eds., p. 17. [2] 2nd ed., pp. 19, 20.

[3] Title of section in all editions. The next section is entitled 'That consumption is co-extensive with production'.

is consumed in the next',[1] it is difficult to see how there can exist any considerable surplus of past production over past consumption. James Mill seems to have fallen into Adam Smith's mistake of overlooking the actual articles saved and added to the capital of the community, and imagining that what is saved is the wages of the persons who make these things – wages which are of course, at any rate for the most part, consumed:

> 'Whatever', he says, 'is saved from the annual produce in order to be converted into capital is necessarily consumed; because to make it answer the purpose of capital it must be employed in the payment of wages, in the purchase of raw material to be worked into a finished commodity, or lastly, in the making of machines, effected in like manner by the payment of wages and the working up of raw materials.'[2]

He endeavours to draw a rather more definite line between fixed and circulating capital than Ricardo had done, by saying that fixed capital consists of the instruments of production, such as tools, machines, and buildings, which 'are of a durable nature, and contribute to production without being destroyed', or 'do not perish in the using', while circulating capital consists of 'the articles subservient to production which do perish in the using', such as 'all the tools worn out in one set of operations, all the articles which contribute to production only by their consumption, as coals, oil, the dye-stuffs of the dyer, the seed of the farmer', and the raw materials worked up in the finished manufacture.[3] Like his predecessors, he assumes that the circulating capital of a country, or perhaps the whole capital, circulates or is consumed and reproduced once a year. Unlike them, he gives almost definite expression to the assumption:

> 'A year', he says, 'is assumed in political economy as the period which includes a revolving circle of production and consumption. No period does so exactly. Some articles are produced and consumed in a period much less than a year. In others the circle is greater than a year. It is necessary for the ends of discourse that some period should be assumed as including this circle. The period of a year is the most convenient. It corresponds with one great class of productions, those derived from the cultivation of the ground. And it is easy when we have obtained forms of expression which correspond accurately to this assumption, to modify them in practice to the case of those commodities, the circle of whose production and consumption is either greater or less than the standard to which our general propositions are conformed.'[4]

Here he both minimizes the falsity of the assumption and exaggerates the facility of modifying the 'forms of expression which correspond accurately to the assumption' in such a way as to make them applicable to the whole mass of 'articles'. A great many 'articles',

[1] 1st ed., p. 184; 3rd ed., p. 226.
[2] 2nd ed., pp. 220, 221; 3rd ed., pp. 226, 227.
[3] 2nd and 3rd eds., pp. 22, 23. [4] 1st ed., p. 185; 3rd ed., p. 227.

such as the Koh-i-noor diamond and the East India Docks, are never consumed at all, and the assumption that many of the other things are consumed and reproduced in a year is far too violent a one to be in any sense 'convenient'. It has the great inconvenience of fostering the confusion between the capital and the annual productive expenditure.

M'Culloch, in the italics for which he had an extraordinary affection, says:

> 'The capital of a country may be defined to be *that portion of the produce of industry existing in it, which can be made* DIRECTLY *available, either to the support of human existence or to the facilitating of production.*'[1]

If 'existing in it' meant 'existing in it at any one point of time', the capital of a country would be here plainly conceived as an accumulated stock, and when M'Culloch goes on to object to the division of the whole stock into the capital and the not-capital, the capital would be the whole accumulated or saved produce of past industry. But he seems to have attached no particular force to the words 'existing in it':

> 'This definition', he says, 'differs from that given by Dr Smith, and which has been adopted by most other economists. The whole produce of industry belonging to a country is said to form its *stock*; and its capital is supposed to consist of that portion only of its stock which is employed in the view of producing some species of commodities. The other portion of the stock of a country, or that which is employed to maintain its inhabitants without any immediate view to production, has been denominated its *revenue*, and is not supposed to contribute anything to the increase of its wealth. These distinctions seem to rest on no good foundation.'[2]

It does not occur to him to object that the revenue cannot possibly be a part of the 'stock' of a country, and in his edition of the *Wealth of Nations* he had nothing to say against the fallacious paradox that what is saved is consumed.[3] Nevertheless he sometimes approached the conception of the capital of a country as its accumulated stock a little more nearly than James Mill:

> 'Capital of all descriptions', he says, 'is nothing more . . . than the accumulated or hoarded produce of previous industry. When a savage kills more game in a day than is required for his own consumption, he preserves the surplus, either in the view of consuming it directly himself on some future occasion, or of exchanging it with his fellow-savages for some article belonging to them. Now this surplus is capital, and it is from such small beginnings as this that all the accumulated riches of the world have taken their rise. . . . If men had always lived up to their incomes, that is, if they had always consumed the whole produce of their industry in the gratification of their immediate wants or desires, there could have been no such thing as capital in the world.'[4]

[1] *Principles*, p. 92.
[2] *Principles*, pp. 92, 93.
[3] *Wealth of Nations*, p. 149 *b*.
[4] *Principles*, p. 102.

In distinguishing circulating and fixed capital, he follows neither Adam Smith, nor James Mill, nor Ricardo, but says that circulating capital 'comprises all the food and other articles applicable to the subsistence of man', while fixed capital 'comprises all the lower animals, and all the instruments and machines which either are, or may be, made to assist in production'.[1]

Malthus, in his *Definitions*, attacked M'Culloch's views of the nature of capital with considerable asperity, but he was perhaps himself even more confused on the subject than any of his contemporaries. No one confounded capital and produce more hopelessly than he did:

> 'Both in the language of common conversation and of the best writers,' he says, 'revenue and capital have always been distinguished; by revenue being understood that which is expended with a view to immediate support and enjoyment, and by capital, that which is expended with a view to profit.'[2]

Obviously he here takes the capital of a country to be merely a part of its annual produce. It is true that in complaining that some writers had used the word 'stock' as if it were synonymous with 'capital', he says incidentally that the capital of a country is a part of its 'accumulated wealth',[3] but he understood accumulation in the extraordinary sense attached to it by Adam Smith, and not in its ordinary meaning of heaping or storing up. This is shown by a passage in the second edition of his *Political Economy*, where he says the 'advances necessary to produce' a commodity consist of 'accumulations generally made up of wages, rents, taxes, interest, and profits',[4] and gives an example in which these 'accumulations' appear as the amount expended by a farmer in a year, on 'seed, keep of horses, wear and tear of his fixed capital, interest upon his fixed and circulating capitals, rent, tithes, taxes, etc., and . . . immediate labour'.[5] Obviously, whatever may be said of the other times, the farmer's interest cannot possibly be an 'accumulation' in any ordinary sense. So too in his *Definitions* Malthus defines 'the accumulation of capital' as 'the employment of a portion of revenue as capital', and adds, 'capital may therefore increase without an increase of stock or wealth',[6] whereas, if a portion of revenue be really accumulated, there must necessarily be an increase of stock. Consequently, his admission that the capital is a part of the accumulated wealth of a country, is not inconsistent with a belief that the capital is merely a part of the periodical produce used in a particular way. In the section 'On productive and unproductive labour' in his *Political Economy*, he upholds Adam Smith's distinction between these two kinds of labour, because first,

[1] *Ibid.*, p. 94. [2] P. 86. [3] *Political Economy*, p. 293; 2nd ed., p. 262
[4] *Ibid.*, 2nd ed., p. 262.
[5] *Ibid.*, p. 268. The figures in this example are quoted below, p. 101.
[6] P. 238.

> 'in tracing the cause of the different effects of produce employed as capital, and of produce consumed as revenue, we shall find that it arises from the different kinds of labour maintained by each';

and secondly,

> 'it is stated by Adam Smith, and it must be allowed to be stated justly, that the produce which is annually saved is as regularly consumed as that which is annually spent, but that it is consumed by a different set of people. If this be the case, and if saving be allowed to be the immediate cause of the increase of capital, it must be absolutely necessary, in all discussions relating to the progress of wealth, to distinguish by some particular title, a set of people who appear to act so important a part in accelerating this progress. Almost all the lower classes of people of every society are employed in some way or other, and if there were no grounds of distinction in their employments, with reference to their effects on the national wealth, it is difficult to conceive what would be the use of saving from revenue to add to capital, as it would be merely employing one set of people in preference to another, when, according to the hypothesis, there is no essential difference between them. How then are we to explain the nature of saving, and the different effects of parsimony and extravagance upon the national capital? No political economist of the present day can by saving mean mere hoarding; and beyond this contracted and inefficient proceeding, no use of the term, in reference to national wealth, can well be imagined, but that which must arise from a different application of what is saved, founded upon a real distinction between the different kinds of labour which may be maintained by it.'[1]

In the whole of this passage the capital seems to be nothing except the amount annually paid for productive labour, and it seems as if everything which is paid for productive labour is supposed by Malthus to be 'saved'.[2] The idea of the capital as a stock is entirely absent. In the chapter 'Of the wages of labour', 'the capital and revenue of the country' are treated as being together equal to 'the annual produce':

> 'A great and continued demand for labour . . . is occasioned by, and proportioned to, the rate at which the whole value of the capital

[1] *Political Economy*, pp. 31, 32.

[2] In a letter written by Ricardo to Malthus soon after the publication of the third edition of the *Principles*, there occurs a passage in which the word saving appears to be used in the same peculiar sense. 'A master manufacturer might be so extravagant in his expenditure, or might pay so much in taxes, that his capital might be deteriorated for many years together; his situation would be the same if, from his own will or from the inadequacy of the population, he paid so much to his labourers as to leave himself without adequate profits, or without any profits whatever. From taxation he might not be able to escape, but from this last most unnecessary *unproductive* expenditure he could and would escape, for he could have the same quantity of labour with less pay, if he only saved less; his saving would be without an end, and would therefore be absurd.' – *Letters of Ricardo to Malthus*, ed. Bonar, pp. 186, 187. This manufacturer is obviously saving nothing in the modern sense of the word. His capital, by hypothesis, is 'deteriorating', not increasing.

and revenue of the country increases annually; because, the faster the value of the annual produce increases, the greater will be the power of purchasing fresh labour, and the more will be wanted every year.'[1]

Like Adam Smith, Malthus is apt to calculate the rate of profit as a percentage, not on the true capital, but on the annual working expenses of a business, and he goes beyond Adam Smith by including interest (on the true capital) among these working expenses. He supposes, as an illustration, that

> 'a farmer employs in the cultivation of a certain portion of land £2,000, £1,500 of which he expends in seed, keep of horses, wear and tear of his fixed capital, interest upon his fixed and circulating capitals, rent, tithes, taxes, etc., and £500 on immediate labour; and that the returns obtained at the end of the year are worth £2,400. It is obvious that the value required to replace the advances being £2,000, the farmer's profits will be £400, or twenty per cent.'[2]

He has another example of a similar kind taken from 'the first Report of the Factory Commissioners (p. 34)':

'Capital sunk in building and machinery	£10,000
Floating capital	7,000

£500 interest at 5 per cent on £10,000 fixed capital.
350 ditto on floating capital.
150 rents, taxes and rates.
650 sinking fund of $6\frac{1}{2}$ per cent for wear and tear of the fixed capital.
1,100 contingencies, carriage, coal, oil, etc.
———
£2,750
2,600 wages and salaries.
———
£5,350

Spun 363,000 lb twist, value £16,000.
Raw cotton required, about 400,000 at 6*d*
Equal to £10,000
Expenses 5,350
———
£15,350 Value when sold, £16,000.

Profit, £650, or about 4.2 on the advance of £15,350.'[3]

[1] *Political Economy*, p. 261. On the next page the proposition quoted is referred to as 'the principle that the demand for labour depends upon the rate at which the value of the general produce, or of the capital and revenue taken together, increases'.

[2] *Political Economy*, 2nd ed., p. 268.

[3] *Political Economy*, 2nd ed., pp. 269, 270. The reference is, doubtless, to Parl. Papers 1833, No. 450, 'Examinations' D.2, p. 34 (vol. XX, p. 784 in the House of Commons collection). It is curious, however, that the particulars given in the last five lines, beginning with 'raw cotton', though printed by Malthus as if they were taken from the Factory Commissioners' Report, are not to be found in it. Instead there is a statement that 'the raw material is purposely omitted throughout' – no doubt in order to prevent a too public disclosure of the profits made by the mill-owners, Messrs. Samuel Greg and Co.

The form in which we should naturally expect to find these figures would now, at any rate, be:

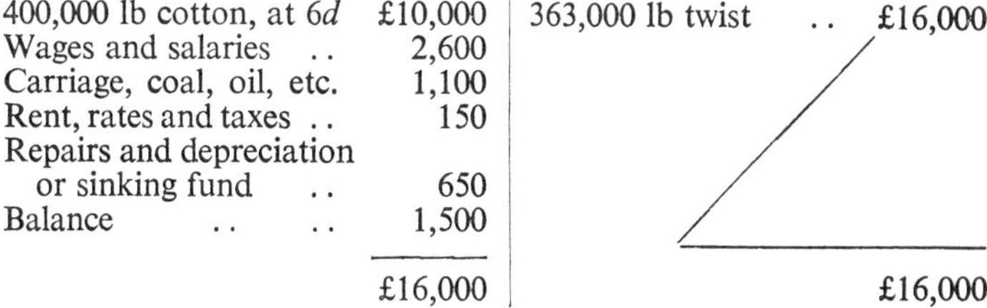

400,000 lb cotton, at 6*d*	£10,000	363,000 lb twist ..	£16,000
Wages and salaries ..	2,600		
Carriage, coal, oil, etc.	1,100		
Rent, rates and taxes ..	150		
Repairs and depreciation or sinking fund ..	650		
Balance	1,500		
	£16,000		£16,000

The balance of £1,500 is the year's profits $8\frac{14}{17}$ per cent on the capital, fixed and floating, of £17,000. To Malthus the capitalist seems to have had two capitals – one his real capital of £17,000, on which 'interest' is calculated, and the other his annual working expenses, on which his 'profit' is calculated. The 'interest' rate is a rate per annum, but the rate of profit, 4·2 per cent, cannot be a rate per annum, since it is obvious that the expenses are not all incurred at the beginning of the year.

Senior says:

> 'The term Capital has been so variously defined that it may be doubtful whether it have any generally received meaning. We think, however, that in popular acceptation, and in that of economists themselves, when they are not reminded of their definitions, that word signifies an article of wealth, the result of human exertion, employed in the production or distribution of wealth.'[1]

This is a mere verbal definition like James Mill's, and tells us very little about the capital of a country. Is the capital the whole of these 'articles' existing at one time, or the quantity used in a given length of time? We must suppose that Senior meant the quantity used in a given length of time when he implies that 'the gas which lights a manufactory' is capital.[2] Doubtless the stock of gas in a gas company's gasometer is a part, though a small part, of the company's real capital, but 'the gas which lights a manufactory' is a supply, and not a stock, of gas; the cost of it is a part of the periodical working expenses, not a part of the capital of the manufacturer.

The remark of Sir Travers Twiss that 'revenue as it gradually comes in is incoming produce; stock is accumulated produce',[3] does not appear to have attracted the attention of J. S. Mill, who, though he begins by speaking of capital as an 'accumulated stock of the produce of labour',[4] and puts forward as his second 'fundamental theorem respecting capital' that 'it is the result of saving', seems to have agreed

[1] *Political Economy*, 8vo ed., p. 59. [2] *Ibid.*, p. 65.
[3] *Progress of Political Economy*, p. 186. See above, p. 64.
[4] *Principles*, Bk. I, ch. iv, § 1; 1st ed., vol. i, p. 67; People's ed. p. 34 *a*.

with Adam Smith as to the nature of accumulation and saving. After saying that capital is the result of saving, he adds that there is a 'trifling exception'

> 'because a person who labours on his own account may spend on his own account all he produces, without becoming destitute; and the provision of necessaries on which he subsists until he has reaped his harvest or sold his commodity, though a real capital, cannot be said to have been saved, since it is all used for the supply of his own wants, and perhaps as speedily as if it had been consumed in idleness.'[1]

Whether a thing has been saved or not is thus settled, not by whether it is actually in existence, and therefore constitutes for the time a part of the excess of produce over consumption, but by what ultimately becomes of it. A little lower down, however, an increase of saving is treated as equivalent to the existence of 'a greater excess of production over consumption', and we are told that 'to consume less than is produced is saving'. But although saving is consuming less than is produced, and capital is the result of saving,

> 'a third fundamental theorem respecting capital, closely connected with the one last discussed, is that, although saved, and the result of saving, it is nevertheless consumed. The word saving does not imply that what is saved is not consumed [nor even necessarily that its consumption is deferred], but only that [if consumed immediately] it is not consumed by the person who saves it.'[2]

And in the next section it is alleged that 'everything which is produced is consumed; both what is saved and what is said to be spent; and the former quite as rapidly as the latter'.[3] This is a mere paraphrase of Adam Smith's 'what is annually saved is as regularly consumed as what is annually spent, and nearly in the same time too.'[4] But instead of here falling into Adam Smith's confusion between what is actually saved and the income of the persons who produce the things saved, J. S. Mill supports the proposition by asserting that all the things of which the stock or capital of a country at any time consists are in the course of time worn out and consumed. That is not quite true; but even if it were true it would not justify the statement that 'what is saved' (by which Mill seems to mean the whole capital) 'is consumed':

> 'The growth of capital', he says, 'is similar to the growth of population. Every individual who is born dies, but in each year the number born exceeds the number who die; the population, therefore, always

[1] *Principles*, Bk. I, ch. v, § 4; People's ed., p. 43 *a*. The 1st ed., vol. i, p. 85, reads, 'no abstinence has been practised' in place of 'perhaps' and the following words.

[2] *Ibid.*, Bk. I, ch. v, § 5, 1st ed., vol. i, p. 87; People's ed., p. 44 *a*. The words in brackets were not in the 1st ed.

[3] *Ibid.*, Bk. I, ch. v, § 6, 1st ed., vol. i, p. 91; People's ed., p. 46 *a*.

[4] Above, p. 72.

increases, though not one person of those composing it was alive until a very recent date.'[1]

Exactly; and so we cannot properly say 'capital is consumed' any more than we can say 'population dies'. The persons of whom the population is composed at any given time die, and the things of which the capital is composed at any given time, or some of them, are consumed, but the population and the capital remain. In a later section, however, J. S. Mill admits that some of the things which constitute fixed capital never require entire renewal, and completely adopts Adam Smith's view of the matter, supporting the proposition that 'the capital, like all other capital, has been consumed', by saying 'it was consumed in maintaining the labourers who executed the improvement, and in the wear and tear of the tools by which they were assisted'.[2] Here the capital is first treated as consisting of the things themselves, 'a dock or canal', for example, and then as consisting of the maintenance and tools which were consumed in producing these things. On the whole, it cannot be said that J. S. Mill in 1848 was one whit less confused as to the nature and origin of the capital of a community than Adam Smith in 1776.

As to the division of the capital into fixed and circulating capital, J. S. Mill speaks as if the distinctions drawn by Adam Smith, Ricardo, and James Mill were identical. He says: 'Capital which . . . fulfils the whole of its office in the production in which it is engaged, by a single use, is called Circulating Capital': this is from James Mill. 'The term, which is not very appropriate, is derived from the circumstance that this portion of capital requires to be constantly renewed by the sale of the finished product, and, when renewed, is perpetually parted with in buying materials and paying wages; so that it does its work, not by being kept, but by changing hands': this is from Adam Smith. 'Another large portion of capital, however, consists in instruments of a more or less permanent character' – this is from Ricardo – 'which produce their effect, not by being parted with, but by being kept' – Adam Smith again – 'and the efficacy of which is not exhausted by a single use': James Mill again. 'Capital which exists in any of these durable shapes, and the return to which is spread over a period of corresponding duration' – Ricardo again – 'is called Fixed Capital'.[3] But as Senior had already shown with regard to two of them,[4] the three distinctions are by no means identical. According to Adam Smith, the seed corn of a farmer is fixed capital, because he will not sell it. According to Ricardo, it is fixed if a year be considered a long period,

[1] Bk. I, ch. v, § 6, *ad fin.* 1st ed., vol. i, p. 92; People's ed., p. 47 *a*.
[2] Bk. I, ch. vi, § 1, 1st ed., vol. i, pp. 109, 110; People's ed., p. 58.
[3] Bk. I, ch. vi, § 1, 1st ed., vol. i, pp. 107, 108; People's ed., p. 57.
[4] *Political Economy*, 8vo ed., pp. 61–66.

and circulating if a year be considered a short period. According to James Mill, it is circulating capital because it is consumed in one set of operations.

J. S. Mill admits that some of the capital connot properly be described as either fixed or circulating:

> 'Since all wealth which is destined to be employed for reproduction comes within the designation of capital, there are parts of capital which do not agree with the definition of either species of it; for instance, the stock of finished goods which a manufacturer or dealer at any time possesses unsold in his warehouses.'

But instead of concluding that fixed and circulating are not exhaustive divisions of the capital, and that the capital must be divided into (1) fixed, (2) circulating, and (3) another kind of capital, he proceeds:

> 'But this, though capital as to its destination, is not yet capital in actual exercise; it is not engaged in production, but has first to be sold or exchanged, that is, converted into an equivalent value of some other commodities; and therefore is not yet either fixed or circulating capital; but will become either the one or the other, or be eventually divided between them.'[1]

If, however, whether the thing is capital at all or not is settled, not by its actual exercise, but by its ultimate destination, it is difficult to see why the question whether it is fixed or circulating capital should not be settled by the same criterion. Equally difficult is it to see how the straightforward term 'exchanged' is explained by the metaphorical 'converted'.[2]

§ 5. *Adam Smith's successors on the Functions of the Capital of a Community*

With regard to the functions of the capital of a community, Lauderdale's *Nature and Origin of Public Wealth* shows a great advance upon the *Wealth of Nations*. Lauderdale denied that the function of the capital is to set labour in motion or to support industry, and saw that the functions ascribed to the fixed capital belong also to the circulating capital.

Capital may be employed, he says, in five different ways:

(1) In obtaining buildings and machinery.

(2) 'In procuring and conveying to the manufacturer the raw materials in advance of wages, or conveying the manufactured commodity to the market, and furnishing it to the consumer; that is, in the home trade'.

[1] Bk. I, ch. vi, § 3, 1st ed., vol. i, p. 117; People's ed., p. 62 *a*.

[2] In another place (Bk. I, ch. iv, § 1, *ad fin*; People's ed., 35 *b*) Mill says the 'shape' of the 'values' destined for productive reinvestment, 'whatever it may be, is a temporary accident; but, once destined for production, they do not fail to find a way of transforming themselves into things capable of being applied to it'. The mystic process is not explained.

(3) In importation and exportation.

(4) In agriculture.

(5) In circulation (as money).[1]

In all cases where capital is so employed as to produce a profit, that profit arises from the capital 'supplanting a portion of labour which would otherwise be performed by the hand of man, or from its performing a portion of labour which is beyond the reach of the personal exertion of man to accomplish'.[2]

In the case of buildings and machinery, he thought Adam Smith showed 'a strange confusion of ideas' when he said that machinery facilitates labour or increases its productive powers.[3] 'The same process of reasoning', he says, 'would lead a man to describe the effect of shortening a circuitous road between any two given places from ten miles to five miles *as doubling the velocity of the walker*.' He wished to say that machinery 'supplants labour'. The force of this lies entirely in the illustration, which is not very fairly chosen. Had Adam Smith lived at the present time he might have retorted that it is surely better to say that a pneumatic-tyred ball-bearing safety bicycle increases the productive (locomotive) power of the cyclist's labour as compared with the time when he rode an old-fashioned 'bone-shaker', than to say that it 'supplants his labour'. Lauderdale's 'walker' apparently stops when he has got to the second of the two given places, but the world in general behaves more like the cyclist, who with his improved machine exerts the same labour as before, but travels double the distance.

In the cases of the home and foreign trade he teaches that capital supplants labour because less labour is required to produce a given result when there are middlemen like shopkeepers, manufacturers, and merchants, than if the consumers had always to deal directly with the producers. The fact that the middleman saves more labour to the consumer than he himself expends, 'proves that it is his capital, and not himself', that supplants the consumer's labour:

> 'Though the proprietor of capital so employed saves, by the use of it, the labour of the consumer, he by no means substitutes in its place an equal portion of his own; which proves that it is his capital, and not himself, that performs it. He, by means of his capital, perhaps, does the business of three hundred consumers by one journey; and carts, boats, and a variety of other machinery, all tending to supplant labour, are applicable to the large scale in which he deals, from which a consumer could derive no benefit in procuring for himself the small quantity adapted to the satisfaction of his individual desires.'[4]

[1] *Public Wealth*, p. 159.

[2] *Ibid.*, p. 161.

[3] *Public Wealth*, p. 185, note. The reference is to *Wealth of Nations*, Bk. II, ch. ii, p. 124 *a*.

[4] *Ibid.*, p. 179.

The case of capital employed in agriculture is identical with that of capital employed in buildings and machinery. The 'circulating' capital or money supplants labour by doing away with the necessity of the laborious processes involved in barter.

> 'From this short examination it appears that capital, whether fixed or circulating, whether embarked in the home or in foreign trade, far from being employed in putting labour into motion, or in adding to the productive powers of labour, is, on the contrary, alone useful or profitable to mankind from the circumstance of its either *supplanting the necessity of a portion of labour that would otherwise be performed by the hand of man, or of its executing a portion of labour beyond the reach of the powers of man to accomplish*: and this is not a mere criticism on words, but a distinction in itself most important.'[1]

In general, however, the economists of the first half of the nineteenth century seem to have been very well satisfied with Adam Smith's account of the functions of the capital of a country.

Many of them seem to have adopted his doctrine that the great use of the capital is to make division of labour possible. Lauderdale's critic in the *Edinburgh Review* says:

> 'The remaining part of Lord Lauderdale's theory – his assertion that the capital employed in commerce supplants a labour otherwise unavoidable – appears to have proceeded from an oversight of a different nature, and to have been indebted for all its novelty to a mistake of the remote for the proximate cause. The accumulation of capital is necessary to that division of labour by which its productive powers are increased, and its total amount diminished. . . . All Lord Lauderdale's explanation of the manner in which mercantile and manufacturing capital supplants the labour of the purchaser resolves itself into this doctrine of the division of employments. The accumulation of stock enables one class of men to work in any line cheaper for the rest of the community than if each class worked in every line for itself. The immediate saving of labour is here occasioned by its subdivision. It is a consequence of the same accumulation of stock, that one class of men collects the articles necessary for the others all at once, and thus saves each the necessity of collecting for itself, which would be a repetition of the same toil for every transaction. This saving, too, is occasioned by the division of labour; and all writers have agreed in giving the same account of the connexion between the division of labour and the accumulation of stock. Lord Lauderdale's discovery consists in dropping the intermediate link of the chain, and ascribing the effect directly to what the schoolmen used to call the *causa causæ*.'[2]

Doubtless Lauderdale was wrong when he ignored the division of labour, but that scarcely proves that the account given by 'all writers' of 'the connexion between the division of labour and the accumulation of stock' is correct. The fact that the division of labour makes labour more productive does not prove that the accumulation of capital em-

[1] *Public Wealth*, pp. 203, 204.

[2] Vol. iv, p. 370.

ployed in commerce only makes labour more productive by facilitating the division of labour. Malthus, Ricardo, and James Mill pay little attention to the subject. Senior, however, expressed an approval of Adam Smith's view which was so qualified as to amount to a condemnation. Quoting the passage from the Introduction to Book II of the *Wealth of Nations* in which Adam Smith endeavours to explain the connexion between the accumulation of capital and the division of labour, he says:

> 'Perhaps this is inaccurately expressed; there are numerous cases in which production and sale are contemporaneous. The most important divisions of labour are those which allot to a few members of the community the task of protecting and instructing the remainder. But their services are sold as they are performed. And the same remark applies to almost all those products to which we give the name of services. Nor it is absolutely necessary in any case, though, if Adam Smith's words were taken literally, such a necessity might be inferred, that, before a man dedicates himself to a peculiar branch of production, a stock of goods should be stored up to supply him with subsistence, materials, and tools, till his own product has been completed and sold. That he must be kept supplied with those articles is true; but they need not have been stored up before he first sets to work, they may have been produced while his work was in progress. Years must often elapse between the commencement and sale of a picture. But the painter's subsistence, tools, and materials for those years are not stored up before he sets to work: they are produced from time to time during the course of his labour. It is probable, however, that Adam Smith's real meaning was, not that the identical supplies which will be wanted in a course of progressive industry must be already collected when the process which they are to assist or remunerate is about to be begun, but that a fund or source must then exist from which they may be drawn as they are required. That fund must comprise in specie some of the things wanted. The painter must have his canvas, the weaver his loom, and materials – not enough perhaps to complete his web, but to commence it. As to those commodities, however, which the workman subsequently requires, it is enough if the fund on which he relies is a productive fund, keeping pace with his wants, and virtually set apart to answer them.'[1]

The criticism is sound, but the apology is lame. It is not in the least probable that when Adam Smith said that 'a weaver cannot apply himself entirely to his peculiar business unless there is beforehand stored up somewhere . . . a stock sufficient to maintain him, and to supply him with the materials and tools of his work, till he has not only completed but sold his web', his 'real meaning' was that the maintenance and materials used by the weaver must be forthcoming from some source when they are required. Moreover, the real meaning, obligingly invented for Adam Smith by Senior, does not prove the case. The facts that the painter must have his canvas, the weaver

[1] *Political Economy*, 8vo ed., pp. 78, 79.

his loom, and materials, not enough, perhaps, to complete his web, but to commence it, and that a productive fund, keeping pace with the workman's wants, and virtually set apart to answer them, is necessary for the supply of those commodities which the workman subsequently requires, have nothing to do with the division of labour. Every one who paints must have his canvas, whether he devotes himself principally to painting or not, every one who weaves must have his loom and materials, whether he is only a weaver, or also a tinker, tailor, and apothecary. And the 'productive fund' which the workman subsequently requires is not formed by 'abstinence', and so is not, even according to Senior himself, 'capital'. The baker does not abstain when he supplies the wants of the weaver by giving him bread in exchange for cloth, nor does the weaver abstain when he supplies the wants of the baker by giving him cloth in exchange for bread.

Of course, no economist could fail to see that the function of the 'fixed capital', the stock of machinery, and instruments of production, is to enable men to produce wealth more easily. This was looked upon as an obvious fact, which needed at the most a cursory mention.[1] But at the end of the eighteenth and the beginning of the next century the high price of corn cause attention to be concentrated on subsistence and the capital of the corn-growing farmer, instead of on produce and capital in general. Now the capital of the corn-growing farmer consists more largely of what Adam Smith called circulating capital than the whole capital of the country. It is true that on every corn-growing area a considerable fixed capital is used, but in England this belonged, for the most part, to the landlord, and being let with the land was easily confounded with the land. Moreover, much of the capital in money with which a corn-growing farmer was supposed to begin business was expended in wages. Owing to these facts the economists of the period came to look upon circulating capital as the most important part of 'capital', and on 'the funds for the maintenance of labour' as almost the only component of the circulating capital. Fixed capital was sometimes so completely forgotten that 'capital' could be used to indicate the funds for the maintenance of labour only, 'machinery'

[1] The fact is implied rather than plainly expressed in Ricardo and Malthus. It is mentioned by Torrens, *Production of Wealth*, pp. 69–71; James Mill, *Elements*, 2nd and 3rd eds., p. 16; M'Culloch, *Principles*, pp. 96, 97. Senior deals with it at greater length, *Political Economy*, 8vo ed., pp. 67–73, and remarks that 'to give anything like an adequate account of it, however concise, would far exceed the limits' of his treatise (p. 69). J. S. Mill ignores it almost entirely in his three chapters on capital. In the next chapter, 'On what depends the degree of Productiveness of Productive Agents', he makes a few observations upon it, and refers his readers to Babbage's *Economy of Machinery and Manufactures*, but this is only in a section (§ 4) on the effects of superior skill and knowledge on the productiveness of land, labour, and capital (1st ed., vol. i, p. 127; People's ed., p. 66*b*).

being put in a separate category. Ricardo, as we have seen,[1] in his Preface, makes 'machinery' a requisite of production, in addition to 'capital'. This might be set down as mere tautology, if we had not the evidence of one of his letters to Malthus to show how entirely he separated machinery and capital:

> 'I do not clearly see', he says, 'the distinction which you think important between productiveness of industry and productiveness of capital. Every machine which abridges labour adds to the productiveness of industry, but it adds also to the productiveness of capital. England with machinery and with a given capital will obtain a greater real net produce than Otaheite with the same capital without machinery, whether it be in manufactures or in the produce of the soil. It will do so because it employs much fewer hands to obtain the same produce. Industry is more productive; so is capital. It appears to me that one is a necessary consequence of the other, and that the opinion which I have advanced and which you are combating is that in the progress of society, independently of all improvements in skill and machinery, the produce of industry constantly diminishes, as far as the land is concerned, and consequently capital becomes less productive.'[2]

In consequence of their habit of regarding the 'funds for the maintenance of labour' as the most important component of the capital, the early nineteenth-century economists attached themselves with fervour to Adam Smith's idea that the maintenance of productive labour is the principal function of the capital of a country. Adam Smith seems to have had in his mind the picture of a 'capitalist' arriving in a village with his capital, and turning 'idle' menials and beggars into 'industrious' labourers. But in the next generation, Malthus, with his doctrine that the increase or decrease of the population of a country follows the increase or decrease of the amount of subsistence produced in it, put the theory on a new basis. The tendency of his work was to identify 'population' with number of labourers, and 'subsistence' with 'capital', and thus to make capital a thing which must be provided before labourers can exist, rather than a vivifying influence which makes idle men become industrious. Once at least, however, an attempt was made to recall attention to the existence of capital other than funds for the maintenance of labour, and to represent that the amount of industry employed must be dependent on the magnitude of these funds alone, instead of on the magnitude of the whole capital. A Committee of the House of Commons on the Poor Laws, which reported in 1817, declared that:

> 'What number of persons can be employed in labour must depend absolutely upon the amount of the funds which alone are applicable to the maintenance of labour. In whatever way these funds may be applied or expended, the quantity of labour maintained by them in the first instance would be very nearly the same. The immediate effect of a com-

[1] Above, p. 41.

[2] *Letters to Malthus*, ed. Bonar, p. 95.

pulsory application of the whole or a part of these funds it to change the application, not to alter the amount of them. Whatever portion is applied under the provisions of the law would have been applied to some other object had the money been left to the distribution of the original owner; whoever therefore is maintained by the law as a labouring pauper is maintained only instead of some other individual, who would otherwise have earned by his own industry the money bestowed on the pauper.'[1]

Perusal of this passage suggested to John Barton, the author of *Observations on the Circumstances which influence the Condition of the Labouring Classes of Society*, a pamphlet praised by Ricardo as containing 'much valuable information',[2] and by Malthus as 'ingenious',[3] the following remarks, which seem to be the original source of all the later discussions about the effects of a somewhat imaginary process known as 'the conversion of circulating capital into fixed':

'It does not seem that every accumulation of capital necessarily sets in motion an additional quantity of labour. Let us suppose a case. A manufacturer possesses a capital of £1,000, which he employs in maintaining twenty weavers, paying them £50 per annum each. His capital is suddenly increased to £2,000. With double means he does [not], however, hire double the number of workmen, but lays out £1,500 in erecting machinery, by the help of which five men are enabled to perform the same quantity of work as twenty did before. Are there not then fifteen men discharged in consequence of the manufacturer having increased his capital?

'But does not the construction and repair of machinery employ a number of labourers? Undoubtedly. As in this case a sum of £1,500 was expended, it may be supposed to have given employment to thirty men for a year at £50 each. If calculated to last fifteen years (and machinery seldom wears out sooner), then thirty workmen might always supply fifteen manufacturers with these machines; therefore each manufacturer may be said constantly to employ two. Imagine also that one man is always employed in the necessary repairs. We have then five weavers and three machine-makers where there were before twenty weavers.'[4]

It may also be allowed, he thinks, that the manufacturer may employ two more domestic servants, as his revenue will have increased from £100 to £200, but even then we have only a total of 10 persons employed in place of the 20 weavers. He infers that 'the demand for labour depends on the increase of circulating and not of fixed capital':

'Were it true that the proportion between these two sorts of capital is the same at all times and in all countries, then, indeed, it follows that the number of labourers employed is in proportion to the wealth of

[1] *Report from the Select Committee on the Poor Laws*, 1817, No. 462, p. 17 (vol. vi, p. 17, in the House of Commons collection).

[2] *Principles*, 3rd ed. in *Works*, p. 241 note.

[3] *Political Economy*, p. 261 note.

[4] P. 15.

the state. But such a position has not the semblance of probability. As arts are cultivated and civilization is extended, fixed capital bears a larger and larger proportion to circulating capital. The amount of fixed capital employed in the production of a piece of British muslin is at least a hundred, probably a thousand, times greater than that employed in the production of a similar piece of Indian muslin. And the proportion of circulating capital employed is a hundred or a thousand times less. It is easy to conceive that under certain circumstances the whole of the annual savings of an industrious people might be added to fixed capital, in which case they would have no effect in increasing the demand for labour.'[1]

Ricardo, commenting on this passage in the chapter 'On machinery', which he added in the third section of his *Principles*, objects to the last sentence, but practically concedes all that Barton was contending for:

> 'It is not easy, I think', he says, 'to conceive that under any circumstances an increase of capital should not be followed by an increased demand for labour; the most that can be said is that the demand will be in a diminishing ratio.'[2]

This clearly admits that the amount of labour does not vary in the same proportion as the whole capital, though it varies always in the same direction, and when Ricardo continues to teach that every increase of the whole capital increases (though it may be 'in a diminishing ratio') the demand for labour, we are to understand him as teaching this, not because he thinks the whole capital regulates the demand for labour, but because he thinks every increase of the whole capital is necessarily accompanied by an increase of the circulating capital. He agrees with Barton in believing that if the fixed capital is increased at the expense of the circulating capital the funds for the maintenance of labour will be diminished.[3] Malthus, however, thought the new theory unnecessary, because 'where the substitution of fixed capital saves a great quantity of labour which cannot be employed elsewhere, it diminishes the value of the annual produce, and retards the increase of the capital and revenue taken together'.[4] To unravel the tangled skein of thought in this sentence would require a whole book to itself.

James Mill does not seem to have paid any attention to the distinction made by Barton and admitted by Ricardo:

> 'It follows necessarily', he says, 'if the instruments of labour, the materials on which it is employed, and the subsistence of the labourer are all included under the name of capital, that the productive industry of every country is in proportion to its capital; increases when its capital increases, and declines when its capital declines. It is obvious that when there is (*sic*) more instruments of labour, more materials to work upon, and more pay for workmen, there will be more work, provided more

[1] P. 16, quoted by Ricardo, *Works*, p. 241 note.
[2] 3rd ed. in *Works*, p. 241, note. [3] 3rd ed. in *Works*, p. 238.
[4] *Political Economy*, p. 261.

workmen can be obtained. If they cannot, two things will happen: wages will be raised, which, giving an impulse to population, will increase the number of labourers; while the immediate scarcity of hands will whet the ingenuity of capitalists to supply the deficiency by new inventions in machinery and by distributing and dividing labour to greater advantage.'[1]

The first part of this message seems a restatement of the theory of Adam Smith, but the last part makes it somewhat doubtful what James Mill means by 'industry'.

From the fact that M'Culloch treats of the 'accumulation and employment of capital' only as one of the 'means by which the productive powers of labour are increased', a reader might be tempted to infer that he had abandoned the theory that the chief function of the capital of a country is to maintain its labourers, but this would be a mistake. After treating of the way in which the capital increases the productive powers of labour, he adds as a sort of appendix:

> 'There are other considerations which equally illustrate the extreme importance of the accumulation and employment of capital. The produce of the labour of a nation cannot be increased otherwise than by an increase in the number of its labourers or in their productive powers. But without an increase of capital it is in most cases impossible to employ another workman with advantage. If the food and clothes destined for the support of the labourers, and the tools and machines with which they are to operate, be all required for the maintenance and efficient employment of those already in existence, there can be no additional demand for others.'[2]

The theory, however, finds no place in Senior's *Political Economy*, and was gradually losing its hold on men's minds, when it re-appeared in J. S. Mill's work. The first of Mill's fundamental propositions respecting capital is 'that industry is limited by capital'. 'This is so obvious', he says, 'as to be taken for granted in many common forms of speech'. For instance:

> 'The act of directing industry to a particular employment is described by the phrase "applying capital" to the employment. To employ industry on the land is to apply capital to the land. To employ labour in a manufacture is to invest capital in the manufacture. This implies that industry cannot be employed to any greater extent than there is capital to invest.'[3]

It is difficult to attach any meaning to this last statement. If Mill had proved that 'to employ one labourer in a manufacture is to invest £100 of capital in the manufacture', he might have intelligibly said that this implies that labourers cannot be employed in any greater number than one to every hundred pounds of capital. Seeking some more

[1] *Elements*, 2nd ed., pp. 24, 25; 3rd (slightly altered), pp. 24, 25.
[2] *Principles*, p. 100.
[3] *Principles*, Book I, chap. v, § 1, 1st ed., vol. i, p. 78; People's ed. pp. 39, 40.

secure basis for the proposition that capital limits industry, he falls back on the necessity, for the existence of labourers, of a store of food:

> 'There can be no more industry than is supplied with materials to work up and food to eat. Self-evident as the thing is, it is often forgotten that the people of a country are maintained and have their wants supplied, not by the produce of present labour, but of past. They consume what has been produced, not what is about to be produced. Now, of what has been produced, a part only is allotted to the support of productive labour; and there will not and cannot be more of that labour than the portion so allotted (which is the capital of the country) can feed and provide with the materials and instruments of production.'[1]

It is perfectly obvious that industry or labour can never be brought to a stand by the inaccessibility of materials or the absence of instruments of production so long as food, drink, and, in some situations, clothing and fuel are obtainable. The inaccessibility of materials and the absence of instruments of production will make production a more laborious process, but will not stop labour. So Mill's argument really depends entirely on the necessity of food for labourers, though he has perfunctorily introduce the materials and instruments of production. He first tells us that 'the people of a country' are maintained by the produce of past labour, and that only a part of this is 'allotted' to the productive labourers, and then invites us to conclude that the number of productive labourers cannot be more than the part of the produce of past labour (periodically?) allotted to them will support. Exactly the same thing might, of course, be said of any class; for instance, it might be said, with equal truth, that there cannot be more landlords than the produce of past labour allotted to landlords will maintain. There may, of course, be fewer landlords than the produce allotted them would maintain; but so also, Mill proceeds to admit, may there be fewer labourers than the produce allotted them would maintain.[2] So that, granting the truth of the parenthetical statement that the produce allotted to productive labourers is the capital of the country, it would be just as correct to say 'landholding is limited by rent', as 'industry is limited by capital'.

Mill's only reason for writing the paragraph seems to have been that he considered 'industry is limited by capital' a useful catchword with which to attack the protectionist fallacy of giving employment or 'creating an industry':

> 'A government would', he says, 'by prohibitory laws, put a stop to the importation of some commodity; and when by this it had caused

[1] *Principles*, Book I, chap. v, § 1, 1st ed., vol. i, p. 79; People's ed., p. 40 *a*.

[2] Book I, chap. v, § 2, begins, 'Because industry is limited by capital we are not, however, to infer that it always reaches that limit. There may not be as many labourers obtainable as the capital would maintain and employ'. – 1st ed., vol. i, p. 80; People's ed., p. 41 *a*.

the commodity to be produced at home, it would plume itself upon having enriched the country with a new branch of industry. . . . Had legislators been aware that industry is limited by capital, they would have seen that the aggregate capital of a country not having been increased, any portion of it which they by their laws had caused to be embarked in the newly acquired branch of industry must have been withdrawn or withheld from some other, in which it gave or would have given employment to probably about the same quantity of labour which it employs in its new occupation.'[1]

This argument is, of course, entirely destroyed by his admission that industry does not always reach the exterior limit imposed by the amount of capital. Whenever it does not reach this supposed limit (and who can say when it does?) a new industry might, according to his own theory, be created without additional capital. He gives away his case when he admits that 'where industry has not come up to the limit imposed by capital, governments may in various ways, for example, by importing additional labourers' ['or', the protectionist would naturally interpolate, 'by imposing protective duties on the products of foreign industry'], 'bring it nearer to that limit'.[2]

Under the arrangements to which we in English-speaking countries are accustomed, it may possibly be said with truth that it is the capitalists or owners of the capital who for the most part take the initiative in industrial enterprise, and so in a way 'put labour into motion'. But it certainly is not the capital itself, a mere mute mass of objects, which puts industry into motion. Nor does the magnitude of the capital decide how much labour shall be put into motion. Every one knows that neither the number of workers in each of the different countries of the world, nor the length of time they work, nor the energy they show, is regulated by the magnitude of the different national capitals. A country which is poor in aggregate capital may be more populous and more industrious than one which is richer in capital; the destruction of a part of the capital of a country, while it would certainly diminish the produce of industry, would not seriously[3] diminish the quantity of industry unless the destruction was so great as to lead to starvation or ill-health; and, finally, an increase of the capital of a country may, and often does cause, not an increase, but a diminution of industry by allowing more people to 'live on their means'.

The capital of a country cannot even properly be said to 'support' its labourers. To support the labourers, as well as to support the landlords, the capitalists, and their families, is the office, not of the accumulated stock of produce, but of the supply of produce. The utility

[1] Book I, chap. v, § 1, 1st ed., vol. i, pp. 79, 80; People's ed., p. 40 *b*.

[2] Book I, chap. v, § 2, 1st ed., vol. i, p. 81; People's ed., p. 41 *a*.

[3] Of course, like any other disaster, it would probably cause some dislocation of business arrangements and consequent slackness of work in some departments of industry.

of things as periodical produce, must be kept entirely separate from the utility of an accumulated stock of them. If a discovery were made by which we could reap corn all the year round instead of only in the autumn, the utility of grain would not be affected; we should require every year the same quantity of bread in order to be equally well provided for in that respect. But the utility of a great stock of grain would be entirely destroyed; it would be of no use whatever to accumulate a year's crop of grain and store it up. It is the annual produce of grain, or rather the daily produce of bread, which supports the population, and the year's stock of grain stored up in barns and elevators in October only exists in order to enable that daily bread to be supplied with the required regularity.

If, then, the capital of a country consisted entirely of stocks of cereal crops, its office would not be directly to support labourers, but only to facilitate the support of the whole population by increasing the utility of the produce of labour. But, as a matter of fact, the stocks of cereal crops form a very small portion of the whole capital of a country, and no one ever seriously imagined that the office of the stocks of 'improved land', ships, railways, mills, warehouses, shops, tools, and such like is to support labour. And if the capital of a country is a useful and convenient term, we should naturally expect that it would be possible to ascribe some general function to the whole of it. Adam Smith was on the right track when he discovered that a part of the 'circulating capital', the stock of money, in many respects, resembled the 'fixed capital'. He was able to discover this because he was obliged, by the necessity of the case, to contemplate the money as a stock and not as an annual supply of produce. Had he clearly conceived the other components of the circulating capital as accumulated stocks, he would have seen that the points of resemblance which he saw between the money and the fixed capital were also to be found between the rest of the circulating capital and the fixed capital. He says that the stock of money resembles the fixed capital, first, because the cost of maintaining it is not part of the net revenue of the society; secondly, because the stock itself does not form a part of the net revenue; and thirdly, because every saving in the expense of maintaining it is an advantage to the society. All this may be said of any of the stocks, whether of 'circulating capital' or reserves for consumption. The cost, which, so far as the community is concerned, means the labour, of keeping the stock of houses in good repair and keeping the stock of wheat dry and in good condition is obviously not part of the income of the community. The stocks of machine oil, wheat, and houses are no part of the income of the country; the income for any year consists of the 'necessaries, conveniences, and amusements' produced and enjoyed during the year, *plus* any additions to the stock existing at the beginning of it. And finally, every saving in the expense of maintaining the stocks of houses, machine oil, and wheat are of obvious advantage to the community.

So far from its being a good plan, as James Mill imagined, to assimilate the fixed capital by an assumption[1] to the circulating capital, the true solution should have been looked for in the direction suggested by Adam Smith's chapter 'Of Money', and by Lauderdale's 'supplanting labour' theory. Instead of either forgetting the fixed capital or assimilating it to the circulating capital, Adam Smith's successors should have shown that the function of the 'circulating capital' is the same as that which has always been ascribed to the fixed, namely, to enable an equal amount of labour to produce more necessaries, conveniences, and amusements than could be produced without it.

[1] 'There is a mode of viewing the gross return to the capitalist, which has a tendency to simplify our language, and so far, has a great advantage to recommend it. The case of fixed and of circulating capital may be treated as the same, by merely considering the fixed capital as a product which is regularly consumed and replaced by every course of productive operations. The capital not consumed may always be taken as an additional commodity, the result of the productive process.

'According to this supposition, the share of the capitalist is always equal to the whole of his capital together with its profits.' – *Elements*, 3rd ed., pp. 80, 81.

CHAPTER V

THE THIRD REQUISITE OF PRODUCTION – LAND

§ 1. *Land in General and Amount of Land* per capita

'Everything useful to the life of man', says Hume, 'arises from the ground.'[1] The magniloquent Torrens observes:

> 'The earth supplies, spontaneously, productions calculated to supply the wants and gratify the desires of the sensitive beings which dwell upon her surface. The surrounding atmosphere, the depths of the waters, the bowels of the earth, and above all, the exterior soil, abound with materials adapted to our use. Hence the air, the waters, and the earth, and even the physical laws which determine their combinations, may be considered as the primary instruments in the formation of wealth. To avoid unnecessary circumlocution, however, the natural agents which constitute the primary instruments of production are usually included under the term land; because land is the most important of the class, and because the possession of it generally gives the command of all the others.'[2]

That 'land' in this extended sense is a requisite of production has always been recognised. So also has the fact that the productiveness of industry must depend partly on the original quality of the 'land', that is to say, on the natural fertility of the soil, the accessibility of the minerals, the richness of the fisheries, and so on. About this there has never been any doubt.

But economic theory as to the way in which the productiveness of industry may be affected by the quantity of land available *per capita*, or, to express the same thing in other words, by the density of population, had only just begun to develop at the close of the eighteenth century.

§ 2. *Eighteenth-Century Views of Population*

General opinion in the seventeenth and eighteenth centuries seems to have regarded every increase of population with approval. In France, Vauban wrote in 1698:

> 'Il est constant que la grandeur des rois se mesure par le nombre de leurs sujets; c'est en quoi consiste leur bien, leur bonheur, leurs richesses, leurs forces, leur fortune, et toute la considération qu'ils ont dans le monde.'[3]

In England, Joshua Gee wrote in 1729: 'Numbers of people have always been esteemed the riches of a state.'[4]

[1] *Essay of Interest* in *Essays* (ed. of 1770), vol. ii, p. 68.
[2] *Production of Wealth*, p. 67.
[3] *Dîme Royale* (Petite Bibliothèque Économique), p. 18.
[4] *Trade and Navigation of Great Britain considered*, Preface.

The worthy Vicar of Wakefield 'was ever of opinion that the honest man who married and brought up a large family did more service than he who continued single and only talked of population'.[1] Hume speaks of 'the general rule that the happiness of any society and its populousness are necessary attendants'.[2] Adam Smith says 'the most decisive mark of the prosperity of any country is the increase of the number of its inhabitants'.[3] As late as 1796, Pitt thought that a man had 'enriched his country' by producing a number of children, even if the whole family were paupers. He opposed Whitbread's bill for regulating the wages of labourers in husbandry, partly on the ground that it would make no difference in favour of fathers of large families, and proposed as an alternative to amend the Poor Law:

> 'Let us', he said, 'make relief in cases where there are a number of children a matter of right and an honour, instead of a ground for opprobium and contempt. This will make a large family a blessing and not a curse; and this will draw a proper line of distinction between those who are able to provide for themselves by their labour, and those who, after having enriched their country with a number of children, have a claim upon its assistance for their support.'[4]

The 'powerful, affluent, and luxurious' were ready to agree with Paley that

> 'It may and ought to be assumed in all political deliberations that a larger portion of happiness is enjoyed amongst *ten* persons possessing the means of healthy subsistence, than can be produced by *five* persons under every advantage of power, affluence, and luxury';

and that consequently,

> 'the decay of population is the greatest evil a state can suffer; and the improvement of it the object which ought in all countries to be aimed at in preference to every other political purpose whatsoever.'[5]

If the common herd had a healthy subsistence, that was enough. Cantillon seems to have felt that he was not quite in sympathy with his age when he remarked:

> 'C'est aussi une question qui n'est pas de mon sujet de savoir s'il vaut mieux avoir une grande multitude d'Habitans pauvres et mal entre-

[1] Goldsmith, *Vicar of Wakefield*, 1776, vol. i, p. 1.

[2] *Essay of the Populousness of Ancient Nations in Essays* (ed. of 1770), vol. ii, p. 179, note.

[3] Bk. I, ch. viii, p. 32 *a*.

[4] Hansard, vol. xxxii, pp. 709, 710 (Feb. 12, 1796). Whitbread was not to be outbid; he replied: 'As to the particular case of labourers who have to provide for a number of children, the wisest thing for government, instead of putting the relief afforded to such on the footing of a charity, supplied perhaps from a precarious fund, and dealt with a reluctant, hand, would be at once to institute a liberal premium for the encouragement of large families' (p. 714).

[5] *Moral and Political Philosophy*, 1785, Bk. VI, ch. xi, third and fourth paragraphs.

tenus, qu'un nombre moins considérable, mais bien plus à leur aise; un million d'Habitans qui consomment le produit de six arpents par tête, ou quatre millions qui vivent de celui d'un arpent et demi.'[1]

It was, of course, quite recognised that there are 'checks' to the growth of population, or that the population of a country does not commonly increase as fast as it would increase if everybody married at sixteen and lived to be seventy. It was also recognised that the actual 'checks' consist principally of vicious, corrupt, and violent manners, and of simple inability to procure a 'healthy subsistence'. An Italian writer, Giovanni Botero, whose treatise *Of the causes of the Magnicence and Greatness of Cities* was translated into English in 1606, and quoted in Anderson's *Origin of Commerce*, says:

'Great cities are more subject to dearths than are small ones, and plagues afflict them more grievously and frequently and with a greater loss of people: so that although men were as apt to generation in the height of old Roman greatness, as in the first beginning thereof, yet for all that, the peop le increased not proportionably, because the virtue nutritive of that city had no power to go further; and in succession of time, the inhabitants finding much want, and less means to supply the same, either forebore to marry, or else fled their country; and for the same reasons, mankind, grown to a certain complete number, hath grown no further. And it is three thousand years or more, that the earth was as full of people as at present; for the fruits of the earth, and the plenty of victuals do not suffice to feed a greater number. Man first propagated in the east, and thence spread far and near; and having peopled the continent, they next peopled the islands; thence they passed into Europe, and last of all to the new world. The barrenness of soils, scarcity of necessaries, inundations, earthquakes, pestilences, famines, wars, etc., have occasioned numberless migrations, and even the very driving out by force of the younger people, and in many countries the selling of them for slaves, in order to make room for such as remained; all which are the let and stay that the number of men cannot increase and grow immoderately.'[2]

Robert Wallace, one of those who contended, in opposition to Hume, that the world was more oppulous in ancient than in modern times, inserted in his *Dissertation on the Numbers of Mankind* (1753), a table which shows by numerical examples how enormously rapid the growth of population would be, if it depended merely on the fecundity of mankind.[3]

'It is not', he declared, 'owing to the want of prolific virtue, but to the distressed circumstances of mankind, that every generation does not more than double themselves.'[4]

'Through various causes there has never been such a number of inhabitants on the earth at any one point of time as might have been easily raised by the prolific virtue of mankind. The causes of this paucity of inhabitants and irregularity of increase are manifold. Some of them may be called physical, as they depend entirely on the course

[1] *Essai sur le commerce*, p. 113.
[2] *Origin of Commerce*, 1787, vol. ii, p. 178. [3] P. 4. [4] P. 8, note.

of nature, and are independent of mankind. Others of them are moral, and depend on the affections, passions, and institutions of men. . . . To this last article we may refer so many destructive wars which men have waged against one another; great poverty, corrupt institutions, either of a civil or religious kind, intemperance, debauchery, irregular amours, idleness, luxury, and whatever either prevents marriage, weakens the generating faculties of men, or renders them negligent or incapable of educating their children, and cultivating the earth to advantage. 'Tis chiefly to such destructive causes we must ascribe the small number of men.'[1]

'In every country there shall always be found a greater number of inhabitants, *ceterus paribus*, in proportion to the plenty of provisions if affords, as plenty will always encourage the generality of the people to marry.'[2]

Adam Smith, who as an observer of the facts of everyday life was seldom at fault, believed the chief 'check' to be infant mortality caused by poverty:

'Every species of animals naturally mutliplies in proportion to the means of their subsistence, and no species can ever multiply beyond it. But in civilized society it is only among the inferior ranks of people that the scantiness of subsistence can set limits to the further multiplication of the human species; and it can do so in no other way than by destroying a great part of the children which their fruitful marriages produce.'[3]

He arrived at this conclusion because he believed that any discouragement which poverty gives to marriage is amply counterbalanced by the greater fruitfulness of the marriages which take place in spite of it.[4]

Paley says that in the fecundity of the human race 'nature has provided for an indefinite multiplication', and that in 'circumstances favourable to subsistence' population has doubled in twenty years. To the question, therefore, 'what are the causes which confine or check the natural progress of this multiplication', he answers that it is not the incapacity of the soil to support more inhabitants, but licentiousness and the difficulty and uncertainty of being able to provide 'for that mode of subsisting which custom hath in each country established':

'It is in vain to allege that a more simple diet, ruder habitations, or coarser apparel, would be sufficient for the purposes of life and health, or even of physical ease and pleasure. Men will not marry with this encouragement. For instance, when the common people of a country are accustomed to eat a large proportion of animal food, to drink wine, spirits, or beer, to wear shoes and stockings, to dwell in stone houses, they will not marry to live in clay cottages upon roots and milk, with no other clothing than skins, or what is necessary to defend the trunk of the body from the effects of cold.'[5]

[1] Pp. 12, 13.
[2] P. 15.
[3] Bk. I, ch. viii, p. 36 *b*.
[4] Bk. I, ch. viii, p. 36 *a*.
[5] *Moral and Political Philosophy*, Bk. VI, ch. xi.

The difficulty which would eventually arise, if the existing checks to the growth of population were removed for any considerable length of time, was used by Wallace, in his *Various Prospects of Mankind, Nature, and Providence* (1761), as an argument to show that 'a perfect government', which he practically identifies with a communist society, 'though consistent with the human passions and appetites is, upon the whole, inconsistent with the circumstances of mankind'.[1]

> 'Under a perfect government,' he says, 'the inconveniences of having a family would be so entirely removed, children would be so well taken care of, and everything become so favourable to populousness, that though some sickly seasons or dreadful plagues in particular climates might cut off multitudes, yet, in general, mankind would increase so prodigiously that the earth would at last be overstocked, and become unable to support its numerous inhabitants. . . .
>
> 'Now, since philosophers may as soon attempt to make mankind immortal as to support the animal frame without food; it is equally certain that limits are set to the fertility of the earth, and that its bulk, so far as is hitherto known, hath continued always the same, and probably could not be much altered without making considerable changes in the solar system. It would be impossible, therefore, to support the great numbers to men who would be raised up under a perfect government; the earth would be overstocked at last, and the greatest admirers of such fanciful schemes must foresee the fatal period when they would come to an end, as they are altogether inconsistent with the limits of that earth in which they must exist.'[2]

After discussing various expedients, he concludes that artificial regulations

> 'could never answer the end, but would give rise to violence and war. For mankind would never agree about such regulations. Force and arms must at last decide their quarrels, and the deaths of such as fall in battle leave sufficient provisions for the survivors, and make room for others to be born.'[3]

Joseph Townsend, a writer who, unlike Wallace, was not known to Malthus in 1798,[4] used what he called the 'principles of population'[5] in an argument against the English poor law. He treated the poor law as a partial establishment of a community of goods, and maintained that it was harmful because it weakened what long afterwards became known as the 'prudential check'.

> 'There is', he says, 'an appetite which is, and should be, urgent, but which, if left to operate without restraint, would multiply the human species before provision could be made for their support. Some check, some balance, is therefore absolutely needful, and hunger is the proper balance; hunger, not as directly felt or feared by the individual for himself, but as foreseen and feared for his immediate offspring. Were it not

[1] Chap. iv, Title. [2] Pp. 114, 116. [3] P. 119.

[4] Malthus, *Essay on the Principle of Population*, 2nd ed., Preface.

[5] *Journey through Spain*, 2nd ed., 1792, *passim*. See the index at the end of each of the three volumes, s.v. 'Population'.

for this, the equilibrium would not be preserved so near as it is at present in the world, between the numbers of people and the quantity of food. Various are the circumstances to be observed in different nations which tend to blunt the shafts of Cupid, or at least to quench the torch of Hymen.'[1]

Quite in the style of Mr Herbert Spencer, he objected to 'furthering the survival of the unfittest':[2]

> 'By establishing a community of goods, or rather by giving to the idle and vicious the *first* claim upon the produce of the earth, many of the more prudent, careful, and industrious citizens are straitened in their circumstances and restrained from marriage. The farmer breeds only from the best of all his cattle; but our laws choose rather to preserve the worst, and seem to be anxious lest the breed should fail! The cry is, Population, population! population at all events!'[3]

Mercifully, he thought, the poor law, while it removed the fear of starvation, imposed some check on marriages by causing the number of cottages to be restricted:

> 'In every village will be found plenty of young men and women, who only wait for habitations to lay the foundations of new families, and who with joy would hasten to the altar, if they could be certain of a roof to shelter them at night. If has been chiefly from the want of houses that the poor have not more rapidly increased.'[4]

[1] *Dissertation on the Poor Laws*, 1786, reprinted 1817, pp. 57, 58.

[2] Spencer, *The Man versus the State*, p. 69.

[3] *Dissertation*, repr. 1817, p. 62.

[4] *Dissertation*, repr. 1817, p. 68. As a remedy, he desired to reduce state poor relief to a minimum, or rather to abolish it altogether:

'Unless the degree of pressure be increased, the labouring poor will never acquire habits of diligent application, and of severe frugality. To increase this pressure, the poor's tax must be gradually reduced in certain proportions annually, the sum to be raised in each parish being fixed and certain, not boundless and obliged to answer unlimited demands. This enormous tax might easily in the space of nine years be reduced nine-tenths; and the remainder being reserved as a permanent supply, the poor might safely be left to the free bounty of the rich, without the interposition of any other law. But if the whole system of compulsive charity were abolished, it would be still better for the State.' – *Ibid.*, pp. 96, 97. As substitutes for the poor law, he recommended public parish workshops, compulsory insurance, reduction of the number of alehouses, taxation of farm-horses in order to force a return to the use of oxen, division of common fields without imposing the obligation of making hedges and ditches, and above all, voluntary charity. – *Ibid.*, § xiv; see also *Journey through Spain*, places referred to under 'Population, principles of', in the index at the end of each volume.

Townsend was a son of Chauncey Townsend, a London merchant, M.P. for Westbury, 1747–68, and took his B.A. degree in 1762 at Clare College, of which he became a fellow. He studied physic, attended Dr Cullen's lectures, preached among Calvinistic Methodists, and at Lady Huntingdon's chapel at Bath, was satirized as 'the spiritual Quixote', and became rector of Pewsey, Wilts. Besides the works already mentioned and several theological treatises, he wrote *Observations on various Plans for the Relief of the Poor*, 1788, *Free thoughts on Despotic and Free Governments*, 1791, *The Physician's Vade Mecum*, 1794, 10th ed., 1807, *A Guide to Health*, 2 vols. 'He stood pre-eminent' as a scholar, a mineralogist, a fossilist, and conchologist, and he was a principal projector and large shareholder of the Kennet and Avon Canal. He died Nov. 9, 1816. See *Gentleman's Magazine*, 1816, Pt. II, pp. 477, 606.

§ 3. *Malthus's Essay on the Principle of Population*[1]

Malthus, however, was the first to write a book in which the causes which regulate the increase of population are the main subject. Even he did not strike out this new line all at once. The title of the first edition[2] of his great work (1798) was:

AN

ESSAY

ON THE

PRINCIPLE OF POPULATION,

AS IT EFFECTS

THE FUTURE IMPROVEMENT OF SOCIETY.

WITH REMARKS

ON THE SPECULATIONS OF MR GODWIN,
M. CONDORCET,
AND OTHER WRITERS

He had been disputing with his father[3] on 'the general question of the improvement of society', and had discovered that the necessity of checks to the growth of population could be used as an argument against the possibility of society ever arriving at the state of perfection dreamt of by Godwin and Condorcet. All checks, he held, are necessarily productive of misery or vice, and therefore, if checks are and always will be necessary, vice or misery, or both, must always continue to exist, so that perfectibility is impossible.[4]

In the first edition the bulk of his work consisted of an attempt to show that the necessary checks all produce vice or misery, and therefore offer an invincible obstacle to indefinite improvement. He had, of course, no difficulty in showing that the growth of population was actually, and always had been, checked by misery and vice, that is to say, by poverty, pestilence, war, and such like misfortunes and calamities (chapters iii, iv, v, vi, vii). He was not so successful in showing that these checks are the only actual and the only possible checks. Persons who have been born can scarcely be got rid of without misery or vice, and births may be kept down by vice. But births may also be kept down by mere abstention from marriage, or postponement of

[1] Parts of this section have already appeared in an article on 'The Malthusian anti-socialist argument', in the *Economic Review* for January 1892, in which the subject is treated from another point of view.

[2] It was a very loosely printed small octavo volume of 396 pages, containing about 50,000 words. The 2nd edition was a quarto of 604 pages, and contained about 200,000 words. The 6th edition contains about 250,000 words.

[3] Bonar, *Malthus and his Work*, pp. 6, 8; Malthus, *Essay*, 1st ed. Preface.

[4] *Essay*, 1st ed., pp. 14, 37, 100, 141.

the time of marriage. Malthus realised this, but contended that such abstention from marriage or postponement of marriage led to vice and constituted misery.[1] There have been, however, many very virtuous and very happy old bachelors and old maids, and a somewhat prolonged period of courtship is not always looked back upon as the most miserable period of life. So in the second edition (1803), which he regarded as a new work,[2] Malthus abandoned the attempt to show that vice and misery are the only possible checks to the growth of population:

> 'Throughout the whole of the present work,' he says in the preface, 'I have so far differed in principle from the former, as to suppose another check to population possible which does not come under the head either of vice or misery.'[3]

This check is 'moral restraint' or virtuous abstention from marriage, either temporary or permanent, and not accompanied by 'misery'.

When he had admitted this check, Malthus could, of course, no longer use 'the principle of population' as an argument against the ultimate perfectibility of mankind. But he could still argue, as Wallace and Townsend had done before him, that an anarchist or communist organisation of society must necessarily fail because the only check which is not productive of vice or misery – moral restraint – is dependent for its very existence upon the maintenance of private property:

> 'The last check which Mr Godwin mentions, and which, I am persuaded, is the only one which he would seriously recommend, is "that sentiment, whether virtue, prudence, or pride, which continually restrains the universality and frequent repetition of the marriage contract." . . . Of this check . . . I entirely approve; but I do not think that Mr Godwin's system of political justice is by any means favourable to its prevalence. The tendency to early marriages is so strong, that we want every possible help that we can get to counteract it; and a system which in any way whatever tends to weaken the foundation of private property, and to lessen in any degree the full advantage and superiority which each individual may derive from his prudence, must remove the only counteracting weight to the passion of love that can be depended on for any essential effect. Mr Godwin acknowledges that in his system "the ill consequences of a numerous family will not come so coarsely home to each man's individual interest as they do at present". But I am sorry to say, that from what we know hitherto of the human character, we can have no rational hopes of success without this coarse application to individual interest which Mr Godwin rejects.'[4]

[1] P. 108.

[2] It was four times as large as the first edition (see above, p. 130, note 3), and much of the first new edition did not reappear in it. Malthus, indeed, says he had retained 'few parts' of the former work (2nd ed., Preface), but this is rather an exaggeration.

[3] P. vii.

[4] *Essay*, 2nd ed., pp. 385, 386. The references are to Godwin's *Thoughts occasioned by the perusal of Dr Parr's Spital Sermon*, etc., 1801.

But before the second edition appeared Malthus had evidently lost most of his interest in the argument against the perfectibilists. He changed the title of the book to

AN ESSAY
ON THE
PRINCIPLE OF POPULATION;
OR,
A VIEW OF ITS PAST AND PRESENT EFFECTS
ON
HUMAN HAPPINESS
WITH AN INQUIRY INTO OUR PROSPECTS RESPECTING THE FUTURE REMOVAL OR MITIGATION OF THE EVILS WHICH IT OCCASIONS.
A NEW EDITION VERY MUCH ENLARGED.

Originally he had used the principle of population merely as a weapon in his argument with his father about perfectibility; now he studied it for its own sake. He ransacked histories and descriptions of foreign countries, and travelled on the Continent to discover what checks to population were chiefly operative in different countries at different times.[1] The old argument against perfectibility and systems of equality at last sank so far into the background, that it was suggested to him by persons for whose judgment he had a high respect, 'that it might be advisable in a new edition to throw out the matter relative to systems of equality, to Wallace, Condorcet, and Godwin, as having in a considerable degree lost its interest, and as not being strictly connected with the main subject of the Essay, which is an explanation and illustration of the theory of population', and he only defended the retention of the matter in question on the grounds that it treated of one of the illustrations and applications of the principle of population, and that he had 'some little partiality for that part of the work which led to those inquiries on which the main subject rests'.[2]

It is in great measure the result of this change between the first and the later editions that the soundest economists will hesitate if asked directly, 'What is the principle of population as understood by Malthus?' or 'What is the Malthusian theory of population?'

Very probably Malthus obtained the phrase 'the principle of population' from the following passage in Godwin's *Political Justice*:

> 'There is a principle in human society by which population is perpetually kept down to the level of the means of subsistence. Thus among the wandering tribes of America and Asia we never find through the lapse of ages that population has so increased as to render necessary the cultivation of the earth. Thus among the civilized nations of Europe, by means of territorial monopoly, the sources of subsistence are kept

[1] Bonar, *Malthus and his Work*, pp. 48, 49. [2] 8th ed., p. 281.

within a certain limit, and if the population became overstocked, the lower ranks of the inhabitants would be still more incapable of procuring for themselves the necessaries of life. There are no doubt extraordinary concurrences of circumstances, by means of which changes are occasionally introduced in this respect; but in ordinary cases the standard of population is held in a manner stationary for centuries. Thus the established system of property may be considered as strangling a considerable portion of our children in their cradle. Whatever may be the value of the life of man, or rather whatever would be his capability of happiness in a free and equal state of society, the system we are here opposing may be considered as arresting upon the threshold four-fifths of that value and that happiness.'[1]

Malthus quotes the first part of this passage near the beginning of the tenth chapter of the first edition of his *Essay*, and remarks on it:

> 'This principle, which Mr Godwin thus mentions as some mysterious and occult cause, and which he does not attempt to investigate, will be found to be the grinding law of necessity; misery, and the fear of misery.'[2]

Later in the chapter he recurs to it:

> 'It is a perfectly just observation of Mr Godwin, that "there is a principle in human society, by which population is perpetually kept down to the level of the means of subsistence". The sole question is, what is this principle? Is it some obscure and occult cause? Is it some mysterious interference of heaven, which at a certain period strikes the men with impotence, and the women with barrenness? Or is it a cause, open to our researches, within our view, a cause which has constantly been observed to operate, though with varied force, in every state in which man has been placed? Is it not a degree of misery, the necessary and inevitable result of the laws of nature, which human institutions, so far from aggravating, have tended considerably to mitigate though they can never remove?'[3]

Here the 'principle' by which population is kept down to the level of the means of subsistence is said to be 'a degree of misery'. Turning to the contents or heading of the chapter, we find:

> 'Mr Godwin's system of equality.–Error of attributing all the vices of mankind to human institutions. – Mr Godwin's first answer to the difficulty arising from population totally insufficient. – Mr. Godwin's beautiful system of equality supposed to be realized. – Its utter destruction simply from the principle of population in so short a time as thirty years.'[4]

It is difficult not to suppose that 'the principle of population' in the heading is much the same thing as 'the principle by which population is kept down to the level of the means of subsistence'. Consequently

[1] *Political Justice*, 1793, p. 813, Bk. VIII, chap. ii.
[2] 1st ed., p. 176; slightly altered, 2nd ed., p. 367; 8th ed., p. 272.
[3] 1st ed., pp. 193, 194; 2nd ed., pp. 373, 374; 8th ed., p. 277.
[4] 1st ed., p. 173.

it seems probable, it would be rash to say more, that in the first edition of the *Essay* 'the principle of population' is that the growth of population must necessarily be checked by misery, and in the second edition it is that the growth of population must necessarily be checked by misery or prudential motives.

But to the question why the growth of population must necessarily be checked, Malthus seems to have no better answer than the assertion that 'the power of population is indefinitely greater than the power in the earth to produce subsistence for man',[1] or that there is a 'constant tendency in all animated life to increase beyond the nourishment prepared for it'.[2] If he had merely desired to prove, like Wallace, that the growth of population must eventually be checked, he would have been on firm ground here. The earth is limited in size, and obviously there must be some limit to the population which can exist upon it. But he constantly rejects with contempt any such interpretation of his doctrine.[3] He meant to prove that checks to the growth of population are always necessary, and when he says 'the power of population is indefinitely greater than the power in the earth to produce subsistence for man', he is thinking of the present and not of a remote future. Expressing 'astonishment' at the fact that writers have treated 'the difficulty arising from population' as 'at a great distance',[4] he says:

> 'Even Mr Wallace, who thought the argument itself of so much weight as to destroy his whole system of equality, did not seem to be aware that any difficulty would occur from this cause till the whole earth had been cultivated like a garden, and was incapable of any further increase of produce. Were this really the case, and were a beautiful system of equality in other respects practicable, I cannot think that our ardour in the pursuit of such a scheme ought to be damped by the contemplation of so remote a difficulty. An event at such a distance might fairly be left to providence; but the truth is, that if the view of the argument given in this essay be just, the difficulty, so far from being remote, would be imminent and immediate. At every period during the progress of cultivation, from the present moment, to the time when the whole earth was become like a garden, the distress for want of food would be constantly pressing on all mankind if they were equal. Though the produce of the earth might be increasing every year, population would be increasing much faster, and the redundancy must necessarily be repressed by the periodical or constant action of misery or vice.'[5]

'The period when the number of men surpass their means of subsistence', Malthus believed, 'has long since arrived.'[6] Now this does not mean that he thought the country or the earth already what we call 'over-populated'. When we say that a country is over-populated,

[1] 1st ed., p. 13.
[2] 2nd ed., p. 2; 8th ed., p. 2.
[3] See esp. Appendix to 3rd ed., p. 10; in 8th ed., p. 489.
[4] 1st ed., ch. viii, title, p. 142.
[5] 1st ed., pp. 142–144; 2nd ed., pp. 353, 354.
[6] 1st ed., p. 153; 2nd ed., p. 357

we mean that the productiveness of industry in that country is not so great as it would be if the population had not grown so big: we thus admit the idea that there may be too many people. Malthus, on the contrary, was so far infected with the prevalent opinions of his age, that the idea of there being too many people was quite strange to him. If there are too many people the checks to the growth of population cannot have been as strong as it is desirable they should have been – they must have been inefficient. But Malthus denied the possibility, and even the conceivability of the checks to population being inefficient:

> 'It has been said by some', he says, 'that the natural checks to population will always be sufficient to keep it within bounds, without resorting to any other aids; and one ingenious writer has remarked that I have not deduced a single original fact from real observation to prove the inefficiency of the checks which already prevail. These remarks are correctly true, and are truisms exactly of the same kind as the assertion that man cannot live without food. For undoubtedly as long as this continues to be a law of his nature, what are here called the natural checks cannot possibly fail of being effectual.'[1]

And in a note to the first sentence of this passage, he adds:

> 'I should like much to know what description of facts this gentleman had in view when he made this observation. If I could have found one of the kind which seems here to be alluded to, it would indeed have been truly original.'[2]

The question of population with Malthus was not, as it is with us, a question of density of population and productiveness of industry, but a question about the comparative rapidity of the increase of population and of the increase of the annual produce of food. He did not think that the checks upon the growth of population were made necessary by the population having approached or exceeded some economic limit, but simply by the impossibility of increasing the annual produce of food as fast as an 'unchecked' population would increase. His reason for believing it impossible to increase the production of

[1] Appendix to 3rd ed., p. 9; 8th ed., p. 488.

[2] It may perhaps be remarked that the belief that the checks cannot be inefficient, and so that over-population is impossible, is scarcely consistent with the passages quoted above, p. 136, 'though the produce of the earth might be increasing every year, population would be increasing much faster; and the redundancy must necessarily be repressed', and 'the period when the number of men surpass their means of subsistence has long since arrived'. Malthus saw this himself, and altered these passages to 'though the produce of the earth would be increasing every year, population would have the power of increasing much faster, and this superior power must necessarily be checked', and 'the period when the number of men surpasses their means of easy subsistence has long since arrived', 8th ed., pp. 263 and 266. These alterations, together with the substitution of 'the argument of the principle of population', in the 2nd ed., p. 353, for 'the argument of an overcharged population', in the 1st ed., p. 142, show that it was only by inadvertence that Malthus occasionally seems to admit that over-population is possible.

food as fast as the unchecked population was that 'population, when unchecked, increases in a geometrical ratio. Subsistence increases only in an arithmetical ratio'.[1]

If this were true, the constant necessity of checks would be proved at once. A quantity increasing like terms in geometrical progression,[2] however small originally, and however small the common ratio by which it is multiplied, must, of given time enough, overtake a quantity which is increasing like terms in arithmetical progression,[3] however large originally, and however large the common difference. To put the same thing into commercial language, the smallest sum accumulating at the smallest rate of compound interest must eventually grow bigger than the largest sum accumulating at the highest rate of simple interest. So, if population increased geometrically and subsistence only arithmetically, the increase of population would eventually be checked by want of food, even if there had at first been an enormous surplus annual produce of food. But as a matter of fact there never is any appreciable surplus produce of food in an average year, and so population and subsistence must be supposed, so to speak, to start from the same line. In this case the necessity of checks becomes immediately obvious. The annual addition to the population 'when unchecked' would be greater every year, but the annual addition to the food could never exceed what it was in the first year.

Now Malthus was, of course, quite right in saying that an increasing population, if the checks on its increase do not alter in force, increases in a geometrical ratio. But he was completely wrong in saying that subsistence 'increases', or can be increased, only in an arithmetical ratio. His attempt to prove this proposition is extremely feeble:

'Let us now', he says, 'take any spot of earth, this Island, for instance,

[1] 1st ed., p. 14. 'It may safely be pronounced, therefore, that population, when unchecked, goes on doubling itself every twenty-five years, or increases in a geometrical ratio' (2nd ed., p. 5; 8th ed., p. 4). 'It may be fairly pronounced, therefore, that, considering the present average state of the earth, the means of subsistence, under circumstances the most favourable to human industry, could not possibly be made to increase faster than in an arithmetical ratio' (2nd ed., p. 7; 8th ed., p. 6).

[2] 'Quantities are said to be in geometrical progression when each is equal to the product of the preceding and some constant factor. The constant factor is called the *common ratio* of the series, or more shortly, the *ratio*. Thus the following series are in geometrical progression:

1, 2, 4, 8, 16, . . .
1, ⅓, à, *rr*, *rr*, . . .
a, ar, ar^2, ar^3, ar^4, . . .' – Todhunter's *Algebra*.

[3] 'Quantities are said to be in arithmetical progression when they increase or decrease by a common difference. Thus the following series are in arithmetical progression:

1, 3, 5, 7, 9, . . .
40, 36, 32, 28, 24, . . .
a, $a+b$, $a+2\,b$, $a+3\,b$, . . .' – *Ibid.*

and see in what ratio the subsistence it affords can be supposed to increase. We will begin with it under its present state of cultivation.

'If I allow that by the best possible policy, by breaking up more land, and by great encouragments to agriculture, the produce of this Island may be doubled in the first twenty-five years, I think it will be allowing as much as any person can well demand.

'In the next twenty-five years it is impossible to suppose that the produce could be quadrupled.[1] It would be contrary to all our knowledge of the qualities of land. The very utmost we can conceive is that the increase in the second twenty-five years might equal the present produce. Let us, then, take this for our rule, though certainly far beyond the truth; and allow that, by great exertion, the whole produce of the Island might be increased every twenty-five years by a quantity of subsistence equal to what it at present produces. The most enthusiastic speculator cannot suppose a greater increase than this. In a few centuries it would make every acre of land in the Island like a garden.

'Yet this ratio of increase is evidently arithmetical.

'It may be fairly said, therefore, that the means of subsistence increase in an arithmetical ratio.'[2]

He seems to have overlooked the fact that to increase in a geometrical ratio is not necessarily the same thing as doubling every twenty-five years. It was no doubt impossible that the subsistence annually produced in Great Britain could be doubled every twenty-five years for an indefinite period. It was improbable that it could be increased every twenty-five years by an amount equal to the amount produced in 1798. But this does not prove that it could not increase in a geometrical ratio, or that it could only increase in an arithmetical ratio. If the amount produced increase only $\frac{1}{10000000}$ per annum, or if it doubled itself every fifty thousand years, it would be increasing in geometrical progression. Malthus prided himself on relying upon experience, but in this case experience was entirely against him. He admits – indeed, he bases his whole work on the fact, that in the North American colonies the population had increased for a long period in a geometrical ratio.[3] This population must have been fed, and consequently the annual produce of food must also have increased in a geometrical ratio. By the time he got to his sixth chapter, Malthus seems to have had some inkling of this objection to his argument, and he endeavours to answer it in a note:

'In instances of this kind', he says, 'the powers of the earth appear to be fully equal to answer all the demands for food that can be made upon it by man. But we should be led into an error, if we were thence to suppose that population and food ever really increase in the same ratio.'

[1] He means 'again doubled'. The original produce is 'quadrupled', but the quadrupling takes place in the whole fifty years, not in the second twenty-five.

[2] *Essay*, 1st ed., pp. 21–23.

[3] *Ibid.*, 1st ed., p. 20; cp. Appendix to 3rd ed., p. 12, note (in 8th ed., p. 491, note), quoted below, p. 143.

It is certainly difficult to see how we could be led into an error by supposing what is an admitted fact. However,

> 'The one', Malthus continues, 'is still a geometrical and the other an arithmetical ratio; that is, one increases by multiplication and the other by addition.'

But if the population and food increased *pari passu*, it is impossible that the one could have increased in a geometrical and the other in an arithmetical ratio; so Malthus, instead of attempting to prove or explain directly his extraordinary proposition, resorts to his favourite device, and takes refuge in a simile:

> 'Where there are few people and a great quantity of fertile land, the power of the earth to afford a yearly increase of food may be compared to a great reservoir of water supplied by a moderate stream. The faster population increases, the more help will be got to draw off the water, and consequently an increasing quantity will be taken every year. But the sooner, undoubtedly, will the reservoir be exhausted, and the streams only remain. When acre has been added to acre till all the fertile land is occupied, the yearly increase of food will depend upon the amelioration of the land already in possession; and even this moderate stream will be gradually diminishing. But population, could it be supplied with food, would go on with unexhausted vigour, and the increase of one period would furnish the power of a greater increase the next, and this without any limit.'[1]

It is doubtless true that if more water runs out of a reservoir than runs in, the reservoir will in time be exhausted, but this does not prevent the outflow from being increased in geometrical ratio until the reservoir is empty; and if it did, that would not disprove Malthus's own fact – that the annual supply of subsistence had doubled every twenty-five years in New Jersey.

In 1803 Malthus bowed to the inevitable, and abandoned the attempt to show, in spite of his own facts, that subsistence never increases in a geometrical ratio. The note just quoted did not appear in its place in the second edition,[2] and only its last three sentences were preserved and introduced into the discussion of 'the rate according to which the productions of the earth may be supposed to increase'[3] in Book I, Chapter i. In that discussion Malthus treads far more gingerly than he did in the first edition. He does not assert that subsistence never has increased in geometrical ratio, and practically admits that it has done so 'sometimes in new colonies'. He merely asserts that subsistence cannot in the future be made to increase over the whole earth faster than in an arithmetical ratio. He arrived at this

[1] *Essay*, 1st ed., p. 106, note. [2] See p. 338.

[3] 2nd ed., p. 5. Though he had struck out the 'reservoir', Malthus continued to talk of the 'stream', an oversight which has a curious effect. Eventually he substituted the word 'fund' (8th ed., p. 4).

conclusion because he chose to take Great Britain as fairly typical of the whole earth, and refused to believe that subsistence in Great Britain could be made to increase faster than in an arithmetical ratio. This was leaving experience, and soaring into prophecy, and, like most prophets, Malthus turned out to be wrong. He lived long enough to record the falsification of his prophecies, though he seems to have been blind to the fact that they were falsified. When he prepared his sixth edition for the press, he had before him the results of the censuses of 1801, 1811, and 1821. On account of the uncertainty introduced into the statistics relating to males by the movements of the army and navy during the war, he preferred to estimate the growth of population by the numbers of females alone; and, after making all corrections and allowances, he gave the female population of England and Wales as, 'in 1801, 4,687,867; in 1811, 5,313,219; and in 1821, 6,144,709'.[1] These three terms are not in geometrical progression, but this is not because the rate of increase fell, but because it rose. As Malthus himself observes, the increase is 13·3 per cent in the first decade and 15·6 in the second.[2] Had the population multiplied itself only by $1\frac{625352}{4687867}$ in the second as well as in the first decade, the female population in 1821 would have been only 6,021,991 instead of 6,144,709. Now, if Malthus had been right in saying that subsistence could only increase in an arithmetical ratio in this island (and *a fortiori* in England and Wales as being more 'improved' and fully peopled than Scotland) the absolute increase of subsistence between 1811 and 1821 would have been no greater than the increase between 1801 and 1811, so that England and Wales would have been in 1821 only able to support a population (females only being reckoned, as before) of 5,313,219 + 625,352 = 5,938,571; and 206,138 females or 400,000 persons must have been 'totally unprovided for'.[3] The census of 1831, taken some years before Malthus's death, showed that the female population had then increased to 7,125,601; whereas, on the arithmetical-ratio basis of an addition of 625,352 each decade, it should have been only 6,563,923. Over half a million females, or about a million persons 'totally unprovided for' in England and Wales alone! The theory, then, that subsistence could only at the outside be increased in an arithmetical ratio – that 'the yearly additions which might be made to the former average produce' could only at the very utmost be supposed 'to remain the same', 'instead of decreasing, which they certainly would do'[4] – was quite untenable.

It is sometimes alleged that Malthus attached little or no impor-

[1] 8th ed., p. 216.

[2] He says, 'in the period from 1800 to 1821', but this is a mere slip of the pen or misprint for '1811 to 1821'.

[3] *Essay*, 1st ed., p. 24; 8th ed., p. 6.

[4] 2nd ed., p. 7; 8th ed., p. 5.

tance to his geometrical and arithmetical ratios.[1] There is no foundation whatever for this statement. Malthus himself, in the appendix to the third edition (1806), after mentioning 'the comparison of the increase of population and food at the beginning of the Essay', goes on to speak of 'the different ratios of increase on which all' his 'principal conclusions are founded',[2] and in a note a little further on he says:

> 'It has been said that I have written a quarto volume to prove that population increases in a geometrical, and food in an arithmetical ratio; but this is not quite true. The first of these propositions I considered as proved the moment the American increase was related, and the second proposition as soon as it was enunciated. The chief object of my work was to inquire what effects these laws, which I considered as established in the first six pages, had produced and were likely to produce on society; a subject not very readily exhausted. The principal fault of my details is that they are not sufficiently particular; but this was a fault which it was not in my power to remedy. It would be a most curious, and to every philosophical mind a most interesting, piece of information to know the exact share of the full power of increase which each existing check prevents; but at present I see no mode of obtaining such information.'[3]

Deprived of the theory that the periodical additions to the average annual produce cannot possibly be increased or, as Malthus preferred to put it, that subsistence can increase only in an arithmetical ratio, the *Essay on the Principle of Population* falls to the ground as an argument, and remains only a chaos of facts collected to illustrate the effect of laws which do not exist. Beyond the arithmetical ratio theory, there is nothing whatever in the *Essay* to show why subsistence for man should not increase is fast as an 'unchecked' population. 'With every mouth God sends a pair of hands', so why should not the larger population be able to maintain itself as well as the smaller?

In our own day, of course, the merest tyro in political economy promptly replies, 'Because of the law of diminishing returns'. But that law remained practically unknown till near the close of the Great War. Malthus may, perhaps, display some inkling of it here and there in the first edition. In the second he certainly uses one of the principal ideas on which it is based as an incidental and subsidiary argument. In the later editions its existence is frequently recognised. But to imagine that the *Essay on the Principle of Population* was ever based on the law of diminishing returns is to confuse Malthusianism as expounded by

[1] J. S. Mill says Malthus 'hazarded' them 'chiefly by way of illustration' and 'laid no stress' on them. – *Principles*, Bk. II, ch. xi, § 6, 1st ed., vol. i, p. 421; People's ed., p. 217 *a*. See also for a more careful defence of Malthus, Marshall, *Principles of Economics*, Bk. IV, ch. iv, § 3, 4th ed., p. 256, note.

[2] Appendix, p. 10; reprinted in 8th ed., p. 489.

[3] Appendix to 3rd ed., p. 12, note; 8th ed., p. 491, note.

J. S. Mill with Malthusianism as expounded by Malthus.[1] Those who were convinced by Malthus that food cannot be increased so fast as an 'unchecked' population were convinced simply because he succeeded in giving them a vague general impression that this is usually true, not because he deduced the proposition from any ascertained facts. In his second edition he appealed especially to 'those who have the slightest acquaintance with agricultural subjects'[2] in support of his doctrine that the addition which can be made in a year to the former annual produce can not only not increase, but 'must be gradually and regularly diminishing'; but, of course, no such law was known to the agriculturists of the time. James Anderson, the writer who is commonly imagined to have anticipated the Ricardian theory of rent, and who certainly had been a farmer, and was a very able man, had already expressed a completely contrary opinion. Writing in January 1801, he says:

> 'Man, when he once betook himself to the cultivation of the soil became an agriculturist; and in process of time he made discoveries that were of infinite consequence to him as an inhabitant of this globe. Instead of finding his subsistence, as before, limited to a certain extent which it was beyond the reach of his power to exceed, he found himself encowed with faculties that enabled him to augment the quantity of subsistence for man to an extent to which he hath never been able as yet to assign any limits. At the first, he no doubt conceived that it was only those spots which were naturally of the most fertile kind that could afford him abundant crops of corn; but experience taught him, that if the dung of the animals that were fed by the native produce of the soil were preserved and laid upon those parts of the ground that were cultivated, and properly dug into it, and judiciously managed, even barren fields could be rendered productive, and not only for a time but even for a perpetuity; for the forage that was produced by these crops enabled him to sustain more cattle, which, of course, afforded a greater quantity of manure; and this extra manure, when conjoined with others that he found in the bowels of the earth itself in inexhaustible quantities, if blended with the earth in a proper manner by labour under the guidance of skill, tended still to add more and more to the fertility of the soil the longer it was continued; so that thus he saw it was in his power to form at will, as it were, a new creation. He could not, indeed, add to the extent of his fields, but he could add to their productiveness from year to year, so as to make it keep pace with his population, what-

[1] Careless readers of Malthus are apt to imagine that the law of diminishing returns is stated or implied in 'The improvement of the barren parts would be a work of time and labour; and it must be evident to those who have the slightest acquaintance with agricultural subjects, that in proportion as cultivation extended, the additions that could yearly be made to the former average produce must be gradually and regularly diminishing' (2nd ed., p. 7; 8th ed., p. 5). But this says nothing about the produce per head of producers, and the real law of diminishing returns says nothing about the annual increments of produce.

[2] 2nd ed., p. 7; 8th ed., p. 5.

> ever that might be; allowing him still to enjoy plenty to an inconceivable amount.'[1]

'Let not man, then', says Anderson, 'complain of Heaven if he suffers want at any time'. He only requires 'to exert himself in order to avoid that afflictive calamity':

> 'The melioration of the soil must ever be proportioned to the means that are made use of to augment its productiveness; and this will ever depend upon the quantity of *labour* and manure that is judiciously bestowed upon it. I mean to say that no permanent or general melioration to any considerable extent can ever be effected but by labour; and that, under skilful management, the degree of melioration will be proportioned to the *labour* that is bestowed upon the soil, and the attention that is paid to the proper use of manures, those especially which arise from the soil itself. In other words, the productiveness of the soil will be proportioned to the number of persons who are employed in active labour upon the soil, and the economy with which they conduct their operations.'[2]

Malthus was aware of Anderson's opinion. When he prepared his second edition he had read Anderson's *Calm Investigation of the Circumstances which have led to the present Scarcity of Grain in Britain* (1801), and found, as he says himself, that Anderson maintained 'that every increase of population tends to increase relative plenty and *vice versa*'. Commenting on this, he remarks:

> 'When an accidental depopulation takes place in a country which was before populous and industrious, and in the habit of exporting corn, if the remaining inhabitants be left at liberty to exert, and do exert, their industry in the same direction as before, it is a strange idea to entertain that they would then be unable to supply themselves with corn in the same plenty; particularly as the diminished numbers would, of course, cultivate principally the more fertile parts of their territory, and not be obliged, as in their more populous state, to apply to ungrateful soils.'[3]

In the last sentence of this passage Malthus introduces quite casually, and as a merely subsidiary argument, the theory that a smaller population has an advantage over a greater one in the fact that it need only cultivate the more fertile land. This theory is the 'law of diminishing returns' in a rudimentary form. Malthus little dreamt in 1803 that in less than three-quarters of a century a casual argument which he introduced with the word 'particularly' would have become accepted as the foundation of the 'Malthusian' theory of population, to the entire exclusion of the geometrical and arithmetical ratios on which he himself declared all his principal conclusions to have been founded.[4]

[1] *Recreations in Agriculture, Natural History, Arts, and Miscellaneous Literature*, 1801, vol. iv, pp. 373, 374.

[2] *Recreations*, vol. iv, pp. 375, 376.

[3] *Essay*, 2nd ed., p. 472; 8th ed., p. 380.

[4] Above, p. 143.

§ 4. *Origin of the Theory that Increasing Density of Population is connected with Diminishing Returns to Industry*[1]

It must always have been known to every practical agriculturist that it does not 'pay' to expend more than a certain amount of labour in the cultivation of a particular acre. If asked why this is so, the ordinary agriculturist would probably always have answered, 'Because after a certain amount of labour has been expended no more produce is obtainable'. But this is because the practical agriculturist thinks only of the particular methods of cultivation which he sees commonly practised around him. By adopting a different system of cultivation, it is generally the case that by extra labour the produce might be somewhat increased. The scientific statement of the truth which underlies the broad assertion of the agriculturist is merely that, at any particular time, an increase of the labour employed on an acre of land beyond a certain amount causes a diminution of the returns to the average unit of labour.

Turgot put the matter very well in some remarks which he wrote on a prize essay submitted to him. He says:

> 'Granting to the writer of the essay that, where ordinary good cultivation prevails, the annual advances bring in 250 to the hundred, it is more than probable that if the advances were increased by degrees from this point up to that at which they would bring in nothing, each increment would be less and less fruitful. In this case the fertility of the earth would be like a spring which is forced to bend by being loaded with a number of equal weights in succession. If the weight is light and the spring not very flexible, the effect of the first load might be almost *nil*. When the weight becomes sufficient to overcome the first resistance, the spring will be seen to yield perceptibly and to bend; but, when it has bent to a certain point, it will offer greater resistance to the force brought to bear on it, and a weight which would have made it bend an inch will no longer bend it more than half a line. This comparison is not perfectly exact; but it is sufficient to show how, when the soil approaches near to returning all that it can produce, a very great expense may augment the production very little. . . .
>
> 'Seed thrown on a soil naturally fertile but totally unprepared would be an advance almost entirely lost. If it were once tilled the produce will be greater; tilling it a second, a third time, might not merely double and triple, but quadruple or decuple the produce, which will thus augment in a much larger proportion than the advances increase, and that up to a certain point, at which the produce will be as great as possible compared with the advances.
>
> 'Past this point, if the advances be still increased, the produce will still increase, but less, and always less and less until the fecundity of the earth being exhausted, and art unable to add anything further, an addition to the advances will add nothing whatever to the produce.'[2]

[1] A large portion of this section has already appeared in the *Economic Journal* for March 1892.

[2] *Observations sur le mémoire de M. de Saint-Peravy en faveur de limpôt indirect, couronné par la Société royale d'agriculture de Limoges*, written about 1768; in *Œuvres*, ed. Daire, vol. i, pp. 420, 421. See also p. 436.

There is, of course, no reason to suppose that this passage had any influence on English political economy. The early nineteenth-century English economists deduced their doctrines, not from study of the works of their predecessors, but from the actual experience of England during the war.

About the year 1813 there were two features in the economic condition of the country which could not fail to strike the most superficial observer – the high prices of corn and the improvement and extension of cultivation. From 1711 to 1794 neither the Ladyday nor the Michaelmas price of the Winchester quarter of wheat at Windsor had ever been more than 60*s* 5¼*d*. But at Michaelmas 1795 it was 92*s*; at Ladyday 1801 it was 177*s*; and from Michaelmas 1808 to Michaelmas 1813 neither the Michaelmas nor the Ladyday price ever fell below 96*s*.[1] The rise was not only great but progressive. The average of the yearly prices of wheat for the decade 1770–1779 was 45*s*; for the decade 1780–1789, 45*s* 9*d*; for the decade 1790–1799, 55*s* 11*d*; for the decade 1800–1809, 82*s* 2*d*; and for the four years, 1810–1813, 106*s* 2*d*.[2] The improvement and extension of cultivation is more difficult to represent in statistical form, but at the time it was obvious to every traveller. Not only were the remaining common fields divided and brought under the better cultivation of several property, but immense quantities of waste lands, such as the great heaths in a corner of which Bournemouth has since grown up, were distributed in 'allotments' among the neighbouring proprietors, enclosed, and to a greater or less extent brought into cultivation. We have, unfortunately, no means of telling how much waste was enclosed, to say nothing of how much was brought into cultivation.[3] We can, however, roughly compare the progress of the movement at one period with its progress during the preceding period by the variations in the number of Enclosure Acts. How closely the two things, the improvement and extension of agriculture and the price of corn were connected will be seen by the diagram on the next page. When the price of corn went up, up went also the number of Enclosure Acts.

The corn laws had, at any rate directly and immediately, very little to do with producing the high prices. The law of 1791 (31 Geo. III, chap. 30) subjected foreign wheat to what was called the 'high' duty

[1] See the table of Windsor prices in Tooke's *History of Prices*, 1838, vol. ii, pp. 388, 389.

[2] See the table in Porter's *Progress of the Nation*, 1836, vol. i, pp. 155, 156.

[3] It is a great mistake to assume that all the land that was enclosed was brought into cultivation. The particular heaths referred to in the text are a case in point, as there is no reason to suppose they were even temporarily cultivated. The end of the war and the collapse of prices probably arrived before the preliminary steps were accomplished. A few of the allotments (of several hundred acres each) were planted with Scotch firs, and all the rest long remained, as some of them still remain, much as they were in 1790.

MONTHLY AVERAGE PRICE OF WHEAT AND ANNUAL NUMBER OF ENCLOSURE ACTS, 1793–1815

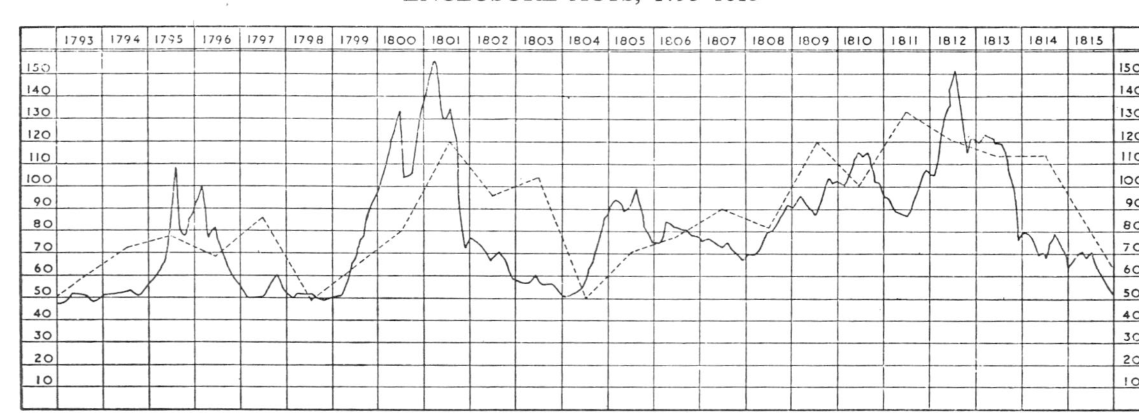

——— PRICE OF WHEAT. .... NUMBER OF ENCLOSURE ACTS.

The figures at the sides of the diagram stand both for the number of shillings in the price of a quarter of wheat and for the number of Enclosure Acts passed in each year of George III (October 26 to October 26). It is assumed that all the Acts of a year were passed on July 1 of that year.

The price of wheat is taken from the table in Tooke's *History of Prices*, 1838, vol. ii, p. 390. The number of Enclosure Acts has been found by counting the titles in the Statute Book. There are three parliamentary returns on the subject which agree neither with the Statute Book nor with one another – (1) *Reports by the Lords' Committees on the Resumption of Cash Payments*, 1819, sess. vol. iii, p. 430; (2) *Third Report from the Commons' Committee on Agriculture*, 1836, sess. vol. viii, Part II, p. 501; (3) *Waste Lands Enclosure Acts*, 1843, sess. vol. xlviii, pp. 467–479. The table in Porter's *Progress of the Nation*, sect. II, ch. i, vol. i, p. 156, agrees with the second, which is by far the most incorrect of the three. From 1800 to 1813 it seems to attribute to each year the number which really belongs to the previous year.

of 24*s* 3*d* per quarter only when the English price was below 50*s*. When the English price was between 50*s* and 54*s* the duty was 2*s* 6*d*, and when it was over 54*s* the duty was only 6*d*. Now from 1795 to 1802 the price was usually much above 50*s*, and importation consequently almost free. In 1804 the agricultural interest persuaded the legislature to raise the price limit. Henceforward foreign wheat was made subject to the prohibitive duty whenever the English price was below 63*s* (44 Geo. III, chap. 109). This change, however, made no practical difference. The English price remained above the new limit, so that freedom of importation was no more interfered with than before.

It was perhaps only natural that landlords and farmers should deduce from these facts the conclusion that free importation was no remedy for high prices, and that the high prices would eventually reduce themselves, by causing such an extension of cultivation that a full supply of food would be produced at home. They immediately did so, and accordingly urged that in order ultimately to obtain low prices, or rather 'steady and moderate' prices,[1] all that was required was to maintain for the present the high prices.[2] A select committee of the House of Commons, appointed to inquire into the corn trade, gravely alleged in May 1813 that prices had been low till 1765 because till that time exportation was encouraged[3] and importation practically prohibited,[4] and that they had since been high becauseimportation had been encouraged and exportation restrained.[5] They recommended, therefore, that until February 1814, the 'high duty' of 24*s* 3*d* should be charged on imported wheat whenever the home price was below 105*s* 2*d*, and after that date it should be charged whenever the home price was not 33⅓ per cent above the average price of the twenty years immediately preceding.[6] Sir Henry Parnell, the chairman of the committee, in drawing attention to its report in the House of Commons on June 15th, 1813, began by asserting in emphatic terms that 'it was not the object of the report of the committee to increase the profits of any particular set of dealers, either of farmers or of land-

[1] *Report from the Select Committee appointed to inquire into the Corn Trade*, 1812–12, No. 184 (vol. iii, pp. 479–530, in the House of Commons collection), p. 7. This Report is reprinted in *Hansard*, vol. xxv, Appendix.

[2] See *Hansard*, 1813–15, *passim*.

[3] By a bounty of 5*s* when the price did not exceed 48*s*.

[4] By a duty of 16*s* when the price did not exceed 53*s* 4*d*, and of 8*s* when it was between 53*s* 4*d* and 80*s*.

[5] From 1765 to 1772, inclusive, temporary laws were passed prohibiting exportation and allowing importation free of duty. In 1773, by 13 Geo. III, chap. 43, the bounty ceased to be paid whenever the price was above 44*s*, instead of 48*s*, and the 'high duty' ceased to be charged on imports whenever the price rose to 48*s*, instead of 53*s* 4*d*.

[6] *Report* (see note 1 above), p. 9. The 105*s* 2*d* fixed for 1813 was arrived at by this method (*Hansard*, June 15, 1813, p. 654).

lords'. 'Their affairs', he added, 'had long been and still were in a very prosperous condition', and they required no aid from the legislature. The committee had, he declared,

> 'been influenced by no other motive than that of a strong sense of the danger of continuing to depend upon our enemies for a sufficient supply of food, and of the impolicy of sending our money to improve other countries, while we have so much of our own lands that stand in need of the same kind of improvement. The whole object of their report is merely to prove the evils which belong to this system as it now exists, and to obtain such an alteration in the law as shall draw forth our own means into operation of growing more corn, by increasing the capital that is now vested in agriculture. If they succeed in this they will secure a greater production of grain, at the same time with diminished expenses in producing it, and at reduced prices to the consumer. For if the agricultural capital is considerably increased, its effects on the quantity produced and the expense of production, and also in lowering prices, will be just the same as when employed in manufactures. Every one knows how it operates in increasing the quantity of manufactures; and that those who employ it in manufactures can afford to sell them at very reduced prices, in consequence of the reduced expenses at which, with its help, they can make them. In the same way the farmer, by being able to render his land more productive in proportion as he improves it, and at a small expense, according as he makes use of good implements, will be able to afford to sell his corn at reduced prices; and in this manner the increase of agricultural capital will secure us a sufficiency of food independent of foreign supply, and at the same time at a reduced price to the consumer.'[1]

Here we have a distinct denial of the law of diminishing returns.

Nothing was accomplished in the session of 1813, but before the next the energies of the landed interest were thoroughly aroused by the fact that the end of the war was seen to be approaching. The stoutest advocates of the theory that encouraging importation made corn dear did not maintain that this was its immediate effect. Peace, it was argued, would bring great imports, prices would fall, farmers would be ruined, rents would be reduced or swept away, the extension of cultivation would cease, land lately reclaimed would return to a state of nature, and then prices would be again as high as ever. These disasters must be prevented by a great restriction if not an entire prohibition of imports. Sir Henry Parnell's supporters no longer repudiated the idea that they required aid from Parliament, but they still asked that it should be granted in the interest not of themselves but of the country in general.

Malthus, though a protectionist himself, was not imposed upon by the protectionist argument that restriction of importation would eventually produce steady and moderate prices. In the *Observations on the effects of the Corn Laws and of a rise or fall in the Price of Corn on the*

[1] *Hansard*, vol. xxvi, pp. 644, 645. June 15, 1813.

agricultural and general wealth of the country, which he published in the spring of 1814[1] and intended as an impartial exposition and comparison of the advantages and disadvantages of protection and free trade, he asserted strongly that the effect of restricting imports must necessarily be to raise the price of corn.[2] To grow at home all the corn required would involve, he pointed out, 'a certain waste of the national resources by the employment of a greater quantity of capital than is necessary for procuring the quantity of corn required'.[3] This seems to imply that he saw it would be easier, would involve less labour, for the population of England to buy some of their corn from abroad than to grow it all at home. Exactly why it should be easier he does not immediately explain, but he says, rather incidentally, later on, that the whole difference between the expense of raising corn in England and in the corn countries of Europe

> 'does not by any means arise solely from taxation. A part of it, and I should think no inconsiderable part, is occasioned by the necessity of yearly cultivating and improving more poor land to provide for the demands of an increasing population; which land must, of course, require more labour and dressing and expense of all kinds in its cultivation. The growing price of corn, therefore, independently of all taxation, is probably higher than in the rest of Europe; and this circumstance not only increases the sacrifice that must be made for an independent supply, but enhances the difficulty of framing a legislative provision to secure it.'[4]

During the session of 1813–14 there were long and acrimonious debates in the House of Commons on a proposal of the ministry to impose a sliding-scale duty of 24*s* on the quarter of wheat when the home price was not more than 64*s*, and one shilling less for every shilling by which the home price exceeded 64*s* till it reached 86*s*. Petitions against this proposal poured in from the towns, and its opponents demanded delay and further inquiry with such pertinacity that the ministry at last agreed to appoint a committee, and the question was shelved for the year, so far as actual legislation was concerned.[5]

The committee's report[6] began with a eulogy of the 'very rapid and extensive progress' which had taken place in the last twenty years, and a suggestion that it would be an unparalleled disaster if many of the improvements should be abandoned in an unfinished state, from want of sufficient encouragement to continue them. The cause of these improvements was in the judgment of the committee chiefly 'to be traced to the increasing population and growing opulence of the United Kingdom':

> 'But it is also not to be concealed that these causes, which they trust

[1] Malthus, *Grounds of an Opinion*, p. 1. [2] P. 25. [3] P. 34.
[4] Pp. 40. 41. [5] *Hansard*, vol. xxvii, p. 1102. June 6, 1814.
[6] *On petitions relating to the Corn Laws*, 1813–14; No. 339. In the House of Commons collections, vol. iii, pp. 195–342.

will be of a permanent and progressive nature, have been incidentally but considerably aided by those events which during the continuance of the war operated to check the importation of foreign corn. The sudden removal of these impediments seems to have created among the occupiers of land a certain degree of alarm which, if not allayed, would tend in the opinion of the witnesses . . . not only to prevent the enclosure and cultivation of great tracts of land still lying waste and unproductive, but also to counteract the spirit of improvement in other quarters, and to check its progress upon lands already under tillage.'[1]

Doubtless thinking that this was sufficient to show that something must be done in the way of maintaining the impediments to importation, the committee proceeded to consider 'the expense of cultivation including the rent'. Money rent, they said, had been doubled within twenty years. Other expenses of cultivation had also been doubled, and so they concluded that at least 80*s* per quarter was required to remunerate the grower of British wheat. Some witnesses, they added, thought a much higher price would be necessary.

> 'It may be proper to observe', they remarked, 'that these latter calculations appear in most instances to be furnished by witnesses whose attention and experience have been principally directed to districts consisting chiefly of cold clay or waste and inferior lands, on which wheat cannot be grown but at an expense exceeding the average charge of its cultivation on better soils. On lands of this description, however, a very considerable proportion of wheat is now raised, and it appears by the evidence that if such lands were withdrawn from tillage they would for many years be of very little use as pasture; and that the loss from such a change, as well to the occupier as to the general stock of national subsistence, would be very great.'[2]

Either with the object of showing that the rise of prices had not been caused by the rise of rents, or in order to show that a great reduction of prices could not be met by a fall of rents, the committee collected evidence to show that the proportion which the rent bore to the whole produce had diminished during the last twenty years, and now formed about a fourth or a fifth of the whole instead of a third.[3]

A committee of the Lords, appointed at the same time as the Commons' committee, followed much the same lines. They too collected evidence to show that where high farming was practised, and on poor lands, the landlord received a smaller proportion of the produce. They too assumed that to interrupt what they called 'the progress of improvement'[4] would be ruinous. Two examples will suffice to illustrate the drift of their investigation.

A land surveyor was asked:

> 'What has been the cause of the great increase of enclosures of late years?'

[1] P. 4. [2] P. 5. [3] P. 4, and Minutes of Evidence, *passim*.

[4] *Reports respecting Grain and the Corn Laws*, 1814–15; No. 26 (in the House of Commons collection, vol. v, pp. 1035–1335), p. 89.

'The high price of corn.'

'What has been the effect of that?'

'A great quantity of land has been cultivated that would not otherwise have been.'

'Has the produce been increased or decreased?'

'Increased very considerably.'

'If the prices were considerably reduced, would the number of enclosures continue?'

'Certainly not.'

'Has a great quantity of produce from farming land the effect of lowering or raising the price of grain and butchers' meat?'

'Of lowering the price.'[1]

A Wiltshire landowner, with some experience as an agriculturist, was asked:

> 'If wheat should be at 80*s* and other grains at a proportionate price, do you believe the farmers would continue in the cultivation of their land at the expense of the present mode of culture?'
>
> 'Certainly not. I think less wheat would be sown and less money would be expended in the cultivation of land.'
>
> 'Would not those prices affect inferior soils much more than the superior quality of land?'
>
> 'Certainly, because the expenses are greater on inferior soils.'
>
> 'Would not the consequence of those prices then be that the farmers in general would withdraw their capital from the cultivation of the inferior soils?'
>
> 'Certainly.'[2]

These reports were widely read, and considering how distinctly they connect 'the progress of improvement', the increase of the population and wealth of the country, with the cultivation of poorer soils and a diminished proportion of the produce for the landlord, it would have been surprising if no economist had generalized from the twenty years under review, and declared that the increase of population and wealth always necessitates recourse to more expensive, or, what is the same thing, less productive agriculture. More than one economist immediately did so. Edward West enunciated a general rule of diminishing returns at the very beginning of his *Essay on the Application of Capital to Land; with observations showing the impolicy of any great restriction of the importation of corn, and that the bounty of* 1688 *did not lower the price of it*, which he published in 1815:

> 'The chief object of this essay is the publication of a principle in political economy which occurred to me some years ago, and which appears to me to solve many difficulties in the science which I am at a loss otherwise to explain. On reading lately the reports of the corn committees, I found my opinion respecting the existence of this principle confirmed by many of the witnesses whose evidence is there detailed. This circumstance, and the importance of the principle to a correct

[1] *Report*, p. 31. [2] *Ibid.*, p. 39.

understanding of many parts of the corn question, have induced me to hazard this publication before the meeting of Parliament.... The principle is simply this, that in the progress of the improvement of cultivation, the raising of rude produce becomes progressively more expensive, or, in other words, the ratio of the net produce of land to its gross produce is continually diminishing.'[1]

Adam Smith, West explains, saw the principle 'that the quantity of work which can be done by the same number of hands increases in the progress of improvement comparatively less rapidly in agriculture than in manufactures',[2] but did not see another principle which may retard or stop such improvement in agriculture, 'or even render the powers of labour actually less productive as cultivation advances':

'The additional principle to which I allude is that each equal additional quantity of work bestowed on agriculture yields an actually diminished return, and, of course, if each equal additional quantity of work yields an actually diminished return, the whole of the work bestowed on agriculture in the progress of improvement yields an actually diminished proportionate return. Whereas is is obvious that an equal quantity of work will always fabricate the same quantity of manufactures....

'Consider the case of a new colony; the first occupiers have their choice of the land, and of course cultivate the richest spots in the country: the next comers must take the second in quality, which will return less to their labour, and so each successive additional set of cultivators must necessarily produce less than their predecessors.'[3]

And throughout the general course of history, when population increases,

'The additional work bestowed upon land must be expended either in bringing fresh land into cultivation, or in cultivating more highly that already in tillage. In every country the gradations between the richest land and the poorest must be innumerable. The richest land, or that most conveniently situated for a market, or, in a word, that which, on account of its situation and quality combined, produces the largest return to the expense bestowed on it, will of course be cultivated first, and when in the progress of improvement new land is brought into cultivation, recourse is necessarily had to poor land, or to that, at least, which is second in quality to what is already cultivated. It is clear that the additional work bestowed in this case will bring a less return than the work bestowed before. And the very fact that in the progress of society new land is brought into cultivation, proves that additional work cannot be bestowed with the same advantage as before on the old land. For 100 acres of the rich land will, of course, yield a larger return to the work of 10 men than 100 acres of inferior land will do, and if this same rich land would continue to yield the same proportionate return to the work of 20 and 30 and 100 as it did to that of 10 labourers, the inferior land would never be cultivated at all.'[4]

[1] Pp. 1, 2.
[2] P. 6. See *Wealth of Nations*, Bk. I, ch. i, p. 3 *b*.
[3] Pp. 6–8. Compare with the second paragraph *Wealth of Nations*, Bk. I, ch. ix, p. 42 *a*.
[4] Pp. 9, 10.

By 'work' West means the immediate effects of labour, as, for example, the ploughing of an acre of land in a certain way, or the digging of a ditch of a certain size. The question whether the returns to labour as well as the returns to work diminish is a further one:

> 'The quantity of work which can be done by a given number of hands is increased in the progress of improvement by means of the subdivision of labour and machinery, even in agriculture. Such increase, then, of the quantity of work which can be performed by the same number of hands in agriculture may either more than compensate, or just compensate, or fall short of compensating, the diminution of the return of the same quantity of work. In the first of which cases labour in agriculture would become absolutely more productive; in the second would remain always equally productive; in the last would become absolutely less productive.'[1]

Here, instead of inquiring directly whether agricultural labour has become less or more productive in the course of history – whether the labour of one man working on an average soil will now feed fewer or more persons than in previous ages, West endeavours to settle the question by a deduction from the 'acknowledged fact that the profits of stock are always lower in a rich than in a poor country, and that they gradually fall as a nation becomes more wealthy'.[2] He very hastily assumes that an increase in the productiveness of labour necessarily means an increase of profits,[3] and from this he infers that the increase in the productiveness of manufacturing industry would cause a rise of profits if the productiveness of agriculture did not decrease. As profits do not rise but fall, he concludes that the productiveness of agricultural industry diminishes more than enough to counter-balance the increase in the productiveness of manufacturing industry. The passage in which he recapitulates his propositions is noteworthy as containing probably the earliest instance in economic literature of the word 'tend' used in its more scientific sense.[4] West himself italicizes it:

> 'The division of labour and application of machinery render labour more and more productive in manufactures, in the progress of improvement; the same causes *tend* also to make labour more and more productive in agriculture in the progress of improvement. But another cause, namely, the necessity of having recourse to land inferior to that already in tillage, or of cultivating the same land more expensively, *tends* to make labour in agriculture less productive in the progress of improvement. And the latter cause more than counteracts the effects of machinery and the division of labour in agriculture.'[5]

He adds that this conclusion which he has endeavoured 'to prove

[1] P. 12. [2] P. 18. [3] P. 14.

[4] For this sense see Whately, *Introductory Lectures on Political Economy*, 1831, 3rd ed. 1847, pp. 231, 232, and J. S. Mill, *Essays on some Unsettled Questions*, pp. 161, 162. [5] P. 25.

theoretically'[1] is supported by the 'commonly observed fact' which 'appears in almost every page of the reports of the corn committees',[2] and in 'the evidence of practical men',[3] that the ratio of the rent to the gross produce has been diminishing in consequence of the introduction of more expensive methods of cultivation.

His object in bringing out his pamphlet in time for the parliamentary session was to prevent the adoption of what he considered an immoderately high protective price in the coming corn law[4]. If importation were totally abolished, he thought the price of wheat would immediately stand at something like 90*s* as this was, in his opinion, about the price at which an amount of corn sufficient for the existing population could be grown within the country, and this price would gradually rise as population increased, because 'the increased produce would be raised at a greater proportionate expense'.[5] And if importation were prohibited whenever the home price was less than 80*s*, the average price would never be below 80*s*.

> 'For', he says, 'it is the competition of the foreigner alone which could keep down wheat even to 80*s*; and when that competition were withdrawn, as it must be, as soon as the price fell below 80*s*, our price would again rise as far as that competition would permit, viz. to 80*s* the quarter.'[6]

It is impossible to read West's pamphlet without seeing that the form in which the 'law of diminishing returns' was subsequently taught, and the phraseology in which it was expressed, are far more due to him than is imagined by those who only know him as the subject of a civil reference in Ricardo's preface. But for securing the 'law of diminishing returns' the prominent place which it has occupied in English political economy, not West but Malthus and Ricardo are responsible. While West was writing his essay, Malthus was engaged upon his *Grounds of an opinion on the policy of restricting the importation of foreign corn, intended as an appendix to 'Observations on the Corn Laws'*, and also *An Inquiry into the Nature and Progress of Rent, and the principles by which it is regulated.*[7] The *Grounds* an-

[1] P. 26. [2] P. 27. [3] P. 30. [4] P. 55. [5] P. 34.

[6] P. 34. West had no doubt that 'the whole wealth and comfort of the community is diminished, the command of each individual over all the necessaries and luxuries, both domestic and foreign, lessened', by 'the increasing expense of raising rude produce' (p. 43), and that consequently, in principle, free importations is the best policy; but he admitted that there were 'many considerations, such as taxes, poor-rates, and the distress of individuals arising from a rapid shifting of capital from one employment to another, which 'would demand a much longer inquiry'. Taking them all into account, his personal opinion was that 70*s*, or at the most 75*s*, would be a reasonable limit or price for the importation of wheat (p. 55).

[7] These were published at some time between Jan. 13 and Feb. 6, 1815 (see Ricardo, *Letters to Malthus*, ed. Bonar, pp. 56, 58). Ricardo's *Essay on the Influence of a Low Price of Corn*, to be mentioned presently, was published after Feb. 10 (Ricardo, *Letters to Malthus*, p. 60) and before Jacob's *Letter to Whitbread*,

nounced his definite adhesion to the protectionist side,[1] chiefly, or at any rate firstly, because the evidence taken by the corn committees showed that protection was necessary to prevent a great loss of agricultural capital.[2] Here he had no occasion to draw attention to the diminishing returns which he had noticed in his *Observations*. It was, on the contrary, rather his cue to point out that the quantity of corn produced in the United Kingdom could be greatly increased without much difficulty. After adopting this line, he went so far as to suggest that there was even a chance 'of a diminution in the real price of corn owing to the extension of those great improvements, and that great economy and good management of labour of which we have such intelligent accounts from Scotland'.[3] In a note, however, he explains that this would only be due to a partial counteraction of a tendency towards diminishing returns:

> 'By the real growing price of corn I mean the real quantity of labour and capital which has been employed to obtain the last additions which have been made to the national produce. In every rich and improving country there is a natural and strong tendency to a constantly increasing price of raw produce, owing to the necessity of employing, progressively, land of an inferior quality. But this tendency may be partially counteracted by great improvements in cultivation and economy of labour.'[4]

For further treatment of the subject he refers his readers to the pamphlet on the *Nature and Progress of Rent*. This work contains the substance of some notes on rent which he had collected in the course of his duties at Haileybury, and which he had intended eventually to appear as part of a considerable book.[5] He seems to have been induced to publish the tract at that particular moment by a desire to lessen the odium into which high rents were falling among those who wished for cheap bread. This desire, however, though it led him to insist strongly on the proposition that high rents are 'one of the most certain proofs of the prosperous condition of a country',[6] did not prevent him from explaining that one of the conditions of the rise is 'the comparative scarcity of the most fertile land.'[7] Comparing the 'machinery of the land' with the machinery employed in manufactures, he says:

> 'The machines which produce corn and raw materials . . . are the gifts of nature, not the works of man; and we find, by experience, that these gifts have very different qualities and powers. The most fertile

which is dated Feb. 25, had got through the press (Appendix, p. 34). Arthur Young (*Inquiry into the Rise of Prices*, Pamphleteer, vol. vi, pp. 187, 188), speaks of West's pamphlet as having preceded that of Ricardo, and Ricardo himself, in the preface to his *Principles*, says it was published almost at the same moment as Malthus's *Nature and Progress of Rent*.

[1] P. 20. [2] P. 4. [3] P. 21. [4] P. 21, note.
[5] See the 'advertisement' or preface. [6] P. 47. [7] P. 8.

lands of a country, those which, like the best machinery in manufactures, yield the greatest products with the least labour and capital, are never found sufficient to supply the effective demand of an increasing population. The price of raw produce, therefore, naturally rises till it becomes sufficiently high to pay the cost of raising it with inferior machines and by a more expensive process; and as there cannot be two prices for corn of the same quality, all the other machines, the working of which requires less capital compared with the produce, must yield rents in proportion to their goodness.

'Every extensive country may thus be considered as possessing a gradation of machines for the production of corn and raw materials, including in this gradation not only all the various qualities of poor land, of which every large territory has generally an abundance, but the inferior machinery which may be said to be employed when good land is further and further forced for additional produce. As the price of raw produce continues to rise, these inferior machines are successively called into action; and as the price of raw produce continues to fall, they are successively thrown out of action.'[1]

So 'the high price' of raw produce which enables it to yield a large rent in rich and prosperous countries is due to the diminution of returns:

'I have no hesitation in stating that independently of irregularities in the currency of a country, and other temporary and accidental circumstances, the cause of the high comparative money price of corn is its high comparative real price, or the greater quantity of capital and labour which must be employed to produce it; and that the reason why the real price of corn is higher and continually rising in countries which are already rich and still advancing in prosperity and population is to be found in the necessity of resorting constantly to poorer land – to machines which require a greater expenditure to work them – and which consequently occasion each fresh addition to the raw produce of the country to be purchased at a greater cost – in short, it is to be found in the important truth that corn, in a *progressive country*, is sold at the price necessary to yield the actual supply; and that as this supply becomes more and more difficult, the price rises in proportion.'[2]

Improved methods of cultivation may retard for a time, but cannot permanently hold in check, the diminution of returns:

'With regard to improvements in agriculture which in similar soils is [*sic*] the great cause which retards the advance of price compared with the advance of produce, although they are sometimes very powerful, they are rarely found sufficient to balance the necessity of applying to poorer land or inferior machines. In this respect, raw produce is essentially different from manufactures.

'The real price of manufactures, the quantity of labour and capital necessary to produce a given quantity of them, is almost constantly diminishing; while the quantity of labour and capital necessary to procure the last addition that has been made to the raw produce of a rich and advancing country is almost constantly increasing. We see, in consequence, that in spite of continued improvements in agriculture the

[1] Pp. 38, 39. [2] Pp. 40, 41.

money price of corn is *cæteris paribus* the highest in the richest countries, while in spite of this high price of corn, and consequent high price of labour, the money price of manufactures still continues lower than in poorer countries.'[1]

When Malthus's pamphlets reached Ricardo, instead of making him a protectionist, they convinced him, he says 'of the policy of leaving the importation of corn unrestricted by law'.[2]

This statement, however, is only to be understood as an ironical, though quite good-humoured, compliment to an opponent. There is no reason to doubt that Ricardo had always been a convinced free-trader. For a long time he had been endeavouring in conversation and correspondence to persuade Malthus that restrictions on the importation of corn tend to lower the rate of interest. Of one of his efforts in this direction he wrote on June 26th 1814:

> 'This is a repetition, you will say, of the old story, and I might have spared you the trouble of reading at 200 miles distance what I had so often stated to you as my opinion before; but you have set me off, and must now abide the consequences. I never was more convinced of any proposition in political economy than that restrictions on importation of corn in an importing country have a tendency to lower profits.'[3]

He probably began with the simple belief, common enough among the commercial class of his time, that restrictions on importation raised the price of food, that the price of food regulated the wages of labour, and that cheap labour was necessary for high profits.[4] From this point he seems to have been gradually advancing. On August 30th 1814, he remarked that the report of the Lords' Committee 'discloses some important facts'.[5] On October 23rd, he began to connect profits directly with the causes of high or low price of food, as well as indirectly through the medium of the cost of labour:

> 'A rise in the price of raw produce may be occasioned by a gradual accumulation of capital, which, by creating new demands for labour, may give a stimulus to population and consequently promote the cultivation or improvement of inferior lands; but this will not cause profits to rise but to fall, because not only will the rate of wages rise, but more labourers will be employed without a proportional return of raw produce. The whole value of the wages paid will be greater compared with the whole value of the raw produce obtained.'[6]

On December 18th, he expressed the same theory in more emphatic terms:

> 'Accumulation of capital has a tendency to lower profits. Why? Because every accumulation is attended with increased difficulty in

[1] P. 45.
[2] *Essay on the Influence of a Low Price of Corn*, Introduction; in *Works*, p. 369.
[3] *Letters to Malthus*, ed. Bonar, p. 35.
[4] See the whole of the letter just quoted.
[5] *Letters to Malthus*, p. 42. [6] *Ibid.*, pp. 47, 48.

obtaining food, unless it is accompanied with improvements in agriculture; in which case it has no tendency[1] to diminish profits. If there were no increased difficulty, profits would never fall, because there are no other limits to the profitable production of manufactures but the rise of wages. If with every accumulation of capital we could tack a piece of fresh fertile land to our island, profits would never fall.'[2]

When he read Malthus's *Nature and Progress of Rent*, the whole subject seemed to become clearer to him, and in the course of a few weeks[3] he wrote and published *An Essay on the Influence of a Low Price of Corn on the Profits of Stock, showing the inexpediency of restrictions on importation: with remarks on Mr Malthus's two last publications, 'An inquiry into the nature and progress of rent' and 'The grounds of an opinion on the policy of restricting the importation of foreign corn'*, in which, by way of proving his contention that restrictions would tend to lower the rate of profit, he enunciated a complete theory of the changes which take place in the distribution of the whole produce between rent, profit, and wages, as a country progresses in wealth and population. This theory was based on the very propositions already put forward in West's pamphlet,[4] namely, (1) that increasing density of population tends to force recourse to inferior land and more expensive methods of cultivation, and thus to diminish the productiveness of agricultural industry; (2) that it would always actually force recourse to poorer land and more expensive cultivation, and thus actually diminish the productiveness of agricultural industry if there were no improvements in agriculture; and (3) that, as a general rule, or in the long run, in spite of the improvements which take place in agriculture, it does actually force recourse to poorer land and more expensive cultivation, and thus actually diminish the productiveness of agricultural industry. In order to prove Ricardo's practical proposition that restrictions would diminish profits, the third part of the theory was unnecessary, since there was no reason to suppose that fewer improvements in agriculture or labour-saving devices would be invented if corn was cheap than if it was dear, so that if any one had said that improvements would not only temporarily but permanently prevent a fall in the productiveness of agriculture, Ricardo could have retorted: That may be so, but if there were no restrictions the same improvements would have been made, and would have caused a rise in the productiveness of agriculture instead of only preventing a fall. But there is no doubt whatever that Ricardo, like West and Malthus, believed that the returns to agricultural industry do actually diminish in the course of history in spite of all improvements. He says:

[1] Evidently Ricardo uses the word tendency in its popular sense.
[2] *Letters to Malthus*, p. 52. [3] See above, p. 161, note.
[4] When he wrote his *Low Price*, Ricardo had not seen West's pamphlet (*Letters to Malthus*, p. 63).

> 'The causes which render the acquisition of an additional quantity of corn more difficult are, in progressive countries, in constant operation, whilst marked improvements in agriculture or in the implements of husbandry are of less frequent occurrence. If these opposite causes acted with equal effect, corn would be subject only to accidental variation of price arising from bad seasons, from greater or less real wages of labour, or from an alteration in the value of the precious metals, proceeding from their abundance or scarcity.'[1]

Obviously this implies that improvements in agriculture do not actually in the long run prevent the difficulty of producing corn from increasing, though they prevent it from increasing as fast as it would do in their absence, Malthus and Ricardo had long arguments in private as to the theory of profits advanced in the *Essay on the Influence of a Low Price of Corn*,[2] but the discussion does not seem to have led either of them to modify their opinion that the diminution of returns is a general rule liable only to temporary exceptions. Ricardo in his *Principles* constantly implies that it is so,[3] and says explicitly, 'With every increase of capital and population, food will generally rise, on account of its being more difficult to produce'.[4] Malthus in his *Political Economy* does indeed complain that Ricardo had

> 'never laid any *stress* upon the influence of permanent improvements in agriculture on the profits of stock, although it is one of the most important considerations in the whole compass of political economy, as such improvements unquestionably open the largest *arena* for the employment of capital without a diminution of profits.'[5]

But he does not seem to think that even in the most favourable circumstances such improvements could prevent returns from diminishing for more than a limited, though possibly long period, such as 'hundreds of years',[6] and in another place he says outright:

> 'The cost of producing corn and labour continually increases from inevitable physical causes, while the cost of producing manufactures and articles of commerce sometimes diminishes, sometimes remains stationary, and at all events increases much slower than the cost of producing corn and labour.'[7]

By 1822, however, Ricardo seems to have been rather more inclined to leave the question open. In his pamphlet *On Protection to Agriculture*, he says:

> 'In the progress of society there are two opposite causes operating on the value of corn; one, the increase of population and the necessity of cultivating, at an increased charge, land of an inferior quality, which

[1] *Works*, ed. M'Culloch, p. 377, note. [2] *Letters to Malthus*, passim.

[3] By making the diminution of returns the only cause of the permanent fall of profits. See especially 1st ed., pp. 91, 142, 228, 229; 3rd ed. in *Works*, pp. 50, 70, 105. [4] 3rd ed. in *Works*, p. 241.

[5] *Political Economy*, 1st ed., p. 331.

[6] P. 332. [7] P. 300, *cp*. pp. 166, note, 313, 370.

always occasions a rise in the value of corn; the other, improvements in agriculture or the discovery of new and abundant foreign markets, which always tend to lower the value. Sometimes one predominates, sometimes the other, and the value of corn rises or falls accordingly.'[1]

Yet when Attwood made a long attack upon his theory in the House of Commons, and insisted that the returns to agricultural industry do not diminish but increase with the actual historical progress of society, Ricardo did not admit the fact and explain, as many of his followers would have done at a later period, that it was not incompatible with a 'tendency' to diminishing returns.[2]

Shortly after the publication of Ricardo's *Essay on the Influence of a Low Price of Corn*, Torrens brought out *An Essay on the External Corn Trade; containing an inquiry into the general principles of that important branch of traffic; an examination of the exceptions to which these principles are liable; and a comparative statement of the effects which restrictions on importation and free intercourse are calculated to produce upon subsistence, agriculture, commerce, and revenue.* This work, which, though as longwinded as its title, quite deserves the praise awarded to it by Ricardo,[3] affords another example of the way in which circumstances had impressed the idea of diminishing returns upon the minds of the economists of the time. For Torrens also, writing before he had seen Malthus's *Grounds of an opinion* and *Nature and Progress of Rent*, or West's *Application of Capital*, or Ricardo's *Influence of a Low Price of Corn*,[4] opposed restriction of imports on the ground that it must cause a diminution of returns by forcing the cultivation of inferior land:

> 'Every restriction', he says, 'on the import trade in corn which forces into cultivation land of inferior quality, not only deprives the particular portions of labour and capital thus turned upon the soil of their most beneficial employment, but, by increasing the natural price of corn, lowers universally the productive powers of labour and capital, and gives a general check to the prosperity of the country.'[5]

§ 5. *Later history of the Theory that Increasing Density of Population is connected with Diminishing Returns to Industry*

The later history of the subject has to do mainly with the gradual substitution of a pseudo-scientific law of a 'tendency' to diminishing returns for the rough general rule of diminishing returns rashly deduced from experience during the great war.

[1] *Works*, p. 475. [2] *Hansard*, vol. vii, p. 392 ff, May 7, 1822.

[3] 'Among the most able of the publications on the impolicy of restricting the importation of corn may be classed Major Torrens's *Essay on the External Corn Trade*. His arguments appear to me to be unanswered, and to be unanswerable.' - Ricardo, *Works*, p. 164, note.

[4] *Essay on the Corn Trade*, 3rd ed., 1829, Preface, p. ix.

[5] *Ibid.*, 1st ed., pp. 73, 74.

In the *Essay on the Corn Trade*, Torrens had scarcely committed himself to the theory that the diminution of returns is a general rule, but in his later work, the *Essay on the Production of Wealth*[1] (1821), he teaches it without hesitation.[2] James Mill again and again speaks of an actual diminution of returns as if it were not only a general rule, but an invariable rule, except in cases where colonists from civilized countries 'have the power of cultivating without limit the most productive species of land'.[3] To inventions and discoveries he gives no attention.

M'Culloch states the general rule in his usual clear and emphatic tone. In the earlier periods of a nation's progress, he tells us, 'when population is comparatively limited, it being only necessary to cultivate the best lands, industry is comparatively productive'.[4]

> 'In manufactures the worst machinery is first set in motion, and every day its powers are improved by new inventions; and it is rendered capable of yielding a greater amount of produce with the same expense. . . .
>
> 'In agriculture, on the contrary, the best machines, that is, the *best soils*, are first brought under cultivation, and recourse is afterwards had to inferior soils, requiring a greater expenditure of capital and labour to produce the same supplies. The improvements in the construction of farming implements and meliorations in agricultural management, which occasionally occur in the progress of society, really reduce the price of raw produce, and, by making less capital yield the same supplies, have a tendency to reduce rent. But the fall of price, which is permanent in manufactures, is only *temporary in agriculture*.'[5]
>
> 'From the operation of fixed and permanent causes, the increasing sterility of the soil must, in the long run, overmatch the increasing power of machinery and the improvements of agriculture.'[6]

The belief that the increase of population, in spite of all improvements, in the long run necessitates the employment of a larger and ever larger proportion of the labour of the world in the production of the prime necessaries of life, practically implies that as population increases, mankind become poorer and poorer, unless the diminishing productiveness of the labour of the agriculturists is overbalanced by the increasing productiveness of the labour of the remainder of the community, which is unlikely to be the case, since the remainder of the community must be a diminishing proportion of the whole.

At last, in two lectures delivered at Oxford in 1828, Senior ventured to protest against this gloomy view. Population, he asserted, does not actually increase with such harmful rapidity:

[1] *With an appendix in which the principles of political economy are applied to the actual circumstances of this country.*

[2] Pp. 115 ff, far too long-winded to quote.

[3] *Elements*, esp. 1st ed., p. 41; 3rd ed., p. 55. See the sections on rent, wages, and profits, *passim*.

[4] *Principles*, 1825, p. 205.

[5] *Ibid.*, pp. 277, 278.

[6] *Ibid.*, p. 383.

> 'The evil', he said, 'of a redundant population, or to speak more intelligibly, of a population too numerous to be adequately and regularly supplied with necessaries, is likely to diminish in the progress of improvement. . . .
>
> 'But I must admit that this is not the received opinion. The popular doctrine certainly is that population has a tendency to increase beyond the means of subsistence, or in other words, that whatever be the existing means of subsistence, population has a tendency fully to come up with them, and even to struggle to pass beyond them, and is kept back principally by the vice and misery which that struggle occasions. I admit that population has the power (considered abstractedly) so to increase, and I admit that under the influence of unwise institutions that power may be exercised, and the amount of subsistence bear a smaller proportion than before to the number of people, and that vice and misery, more or less intense and diffused, according to the circumstances of each case, must be the result. What I deny is, that under wise institutions there is any *tendency* to this state of things. I believe the tendency to be just the reverse.'[1]

He sent the lectures to Malthus, and politely[2] invited him to assent to this new doctrine. Malthus declined. As to the past, he said, 'when you state as a fact, that food *has* generally increased faster than population, I am unable to go along with you'.[3] As to the future, he said it was obvious that some retardation of the growth of population is inevitable, and he questioned whether 'we are entitled from past experience to expect that this will take place without some diminution of corn wages and some increased difficulty of maintaining a family'.[4] But he showed some desire to escape from the exact question at issue:

> 'The main part of the question with me', he wrote, 'relates to the cause of the continued poverty and misery of the labouring classes of society in all old states. This surely cannot be attributed to the tendency of food to increase faster than population. It may be to the tendency of population to increase faster than food.'[5]

[1] *Two Lectures on Population delivered before the University of Oxford in Easter term* 1828, *to which is added a correspondence between the author and the Rev. T. R. Malthus*, 1829, pp. 35, 36.

[2] Mr Bonar (*Malthus and his Work*, pp. 3, 4), says that Senior 'confessed with penitence that he had trusted more to his ears than to his eyes for a knowledge of Malthusian doctrine, and had written a learned criticism not of the opinion of Mr Malthus, but of that which "the multitudes who have followed, and the few who have endeavoured to oppose" Mr Malthus, have assumed to be his opinion'. If Malthus's opinion was really different from what the multitudes who followed him and the few who opposed him imagined it to be, it is difficult to see why Senior should have been penitent for having criticized much the most important of the two opinions. But, as Senior very well knew, Malthus's opinion was not different from that which his followers ascribed to him. Senior's apology for having attributed to him the opinion of his followers which, as he says, is inconsistent with a passage in the *Essay on Population*, is merely a polite method of asking Malthus to explain his own inconsistency.

[3] Correspondence in Senior, *Lectures on Population*, p. 66.

[4] *Ibid.*, p. 70. [5] *Ibid.*, p. 72.

And Senior was perhaps justified in declaring that the controversy had ended in agreement.

This discussion, with its absurd metaphors about 'population pressing against food',[2] and being 'ready to start off',[1] was a complete anachronism in leaving the question of diminishing returns and going back to the old vague comparisons of the increase of population and the increase of food. The first writer of eminence who definitely attacked the belief that the returns to agricultural industry have generally diminished, and continue to diminish, in consequence of the increase of population, was Dr Chalmers.

One of the most plausible reasons for believing in the general rule of diminishing returns is the argument that the very fact that cultivation is extended to land inferior in point of situation or fertility to that already in use, shows that the productiveness of agricultural industry has declined. Labour on the new land, it is said, is of course less productive than labour on the old, and therefore the returns to the least productive agricultural industry must have diminished. Ricardo himself argued thus. 'The lands', he says, 'which are now taken into cultivation are much inferior to the lands in cultivation three centuries ago, and therefore the difficulty of production is increased.'[3] But this is a fallacy. Labour on the new land is not so productive now as labour on the old land is now, but before a decline in the productiveness of industry or diminution of returns can be proved, it must be shown that labour on the new land is less productive than labour on the old land was at an antecedent period. Malthus had seen this and pointed it out in the later editions of his *Essay*,[4] and West also had explained it in his pamphlet on the *Price of Corn and Wages of Labour*[5] (1826), but as Malthus looked on the case as a merely temporary phenomenon, and West thought it had not actually occurred, it was reserved for Dr Chalmers to promulgate the more cheerful theory. He did so in his usual turgid style. At the very beginning of his *Political Economy in connexion with the moral state and moral prospects of society* (1832), after remarking that a commanding position 'has been recently gained in Political Economy', in respect especially of 'that department where the theory of wealth comes into contant with the theory of population, and where the two, therefore, might be examined in connexion', he proceeds:

> 'The doctrine or discovery to which we refer, is that promulgated some years ago, and both [*sic*] at the same time by Sir Edward West

[1] *Ibid.*, p. 76. [2] *Ibid.*, p. 61.
[3] *Principles*, 1st ed., pp. 289, 290; *Works*, p. 130. The statement, it may be as well to say, is in a subordinate clause, beginning with 'although'. It is treated as if it were a matter of common knowledge.
[4] 5th ed., 1817, vol. ii, pp. 435, 436; 8th ed., p. 340.
[5] Pp. 45, 46.

and Mr Malthus. It respects the land last entered upon for the purpose of cultivation, and [*sic*] which yields no rent. . . . The imagination is that the land of greatest fertility was first occupied. . . . After all the first rate land had been occupied, an increasing population flowed over, as it were, on the second rate land, which, in virtue of its inferior quality, yielded a scantier return for the same labour. . . . In filling up this sketch or *histoire raisonnée* of the conjunct process of culture and population, economists have given in to certain conceptions which require to be modified. They sometimes describe the process as if at each successive descent to an inferior soil the comfort and circumstances of the human race underwent deterioration. . . . Agreeably to this imagination, even economists and calculators have by a reverse process found their way to a golden age at the outset of the world – when men reposed in the lap of abundance; and with no other fatigue than that of a slight and superficial operation on a soil of first rate quality, richly partook in the bounties of nature. . . . At each new stretch of cultivation, a more ungrateful soil has to be encountered, on which it is thought that men are more strenuously worked and more scantily subsisted than before: till, at the extreme limit of this progression, a life of utmost toil and utmost penury is looked to as the inevitable doom that awaits the working classes of society.

'Now, generally speaking, this is not accordant with historical truth.'[1]

The working classes, he points out, have not, as a matter of fact, throughout the various countries of the world undergone a perpetual deterioration in material welfare. 'We should rather say that there had been a general march and elevation in the style of their enjoyments.' 'Men', he says, 'have been at a loss to reconcile the descent of labourers among the inferior soils with the undoubted rise which has taken place in their circumstances or in the average standard of their comfort.'[2] The matter can, however, easily be explained,

'for as the fresh soils that had to be successively entered on became more intractable, the same amount of labour, by the intervention of tools and instruments of husbandry, may have become greatly more effective. The same labour which, by a direct manual operation, could raise a given quantity of subsistence from soil of the first quality, might with our present implements of agriculture raise as much from soil of the last quality that has been entered on.'[3]

Chalmer's demonstration of the fact that the extension of cultivation does not necessarily imply an actual decrease in the productiveness of agricultural industry, and his statement that, speaking generally, a deterioration of the labourer's condition is not an historical fact, seem to have excited no attention. In 1833, Mountifort Longfield, lecturing at Dublin, could still, after considering the effect of improvements, say with truth:

'On the whole, however, it is generally supposed that the march of population is more certain and constant than that of improvement, and

[1] Chap. i, §§ 2–6. [2] Chap. i, §. [3] Chap. i, § 7.

must outstrip it in the long run, and therefore that there must be a constant tendency to decrease in the productive powers of agricultural labour.'[1]

The first protest which made itself heard came from the other side of the Atlantic. Patriotic Americans in the first half of the nineteenth century were not likely to accept without demur the generalizations made in England during the great war. H. C. Carey, the first part of whose *Political Economy* was published at Philadelphia in 1837 and the third in 1840, offered a vigorous opposition to the gloomy Maltho-Ricardian theory. Over-population, he admitted, was possible at some future period, but so far, he said, experience showed increases of population to be always favourable to the productiveness of industry. The wars and pestilences and other positive checks to the growth of population to which Malthus had ascribed a certain beneficence were regarded by Carey as wholly evil.[2] He went too far in his belief in the advantages of a large and growing population, but he was right in denying flatly that the returns to agricultural industry have diminished in the past. Quoting James Mill's statement that 'if capital had increased faster than population' 'wages must have risen', he retorts, 'Wages *have* risen'.[3] 'Any given quantity of labour', he says, 'will now command a much larger quantity of food than at any former time, and the tendency is to a constant increase':

> 'It is entirely impossible to read any book treating of the people of England of past times, without being struck with the extraordinary improvement of the means of living – with the increased facility of obtaining food, clothing, and shelter, and with the improved quality of all – enabling the common labourer now to indulge in numerous luxuries that in former times were unknown to people who might be deemed wealthy.'[4]

To illustrate the actual increase of the productiveness of agricultural industry, he quotes statistics taken from Eden's *History of the Poor*, vol. i, pp. 45–48:

> 'In 1389, in securing the crop of corn from two hundred acres, there were employed 250 reapers and thatchers on one day and 200 on another. On another day in the same year 212 were hired for one day to cut and tie up 13 acres of wheat and one acre of oats. At that time 12 bushels to an acre were considered an average crop, so that 212 persons were employed to harvest 168 bushels of grain, an operation which could be accomplished with ease in our time by half-a-dozen persons.'[5]

J. S. Mill's teaching as to the relation between increase of population and the productiveness of agricultural industry is by no means

[1] *Lectures on Political Economy*, 1834, p. 181.
[2] *Political Economy*, pt. iii, p. 91.
[3] *Ibid.*, pt. iii, pp. 69, 70; James Mill, *Elements*, 1st ed., p. 29; 3rd ed., p. 45.
[4] *Political Economy*, pt. iii, p. 70.
[5] *Political Economy*, pt. i, p. 58.

consistent. He lived into more prosperous times, but he was never able to shake off completely the effects of the gloomy theories of the second decade of the century with which his father had indoctrinated him.

He believed 'the general law of diminishing return from land'[1] to be of immense importance,[2] and devoted a good deal of space to its exposition in the chapter of his *Principles* which he headed 'Of the Law of the Increase of Production from Land'.[3] He begins by saying that it is evident that the quantity of produce capable of being raised on any given piece of land is not indefinite. Had he proceeded to say that it is evident that the quantity of produce which can be raised at any given time from any given piece of land consistently with the attainment of the highest productiveness of industry possible at that time is also not indefinite, it is probably that, 'the law of diminishing returns' would have soon ceased to be a familiar term in economic textbooks. But he was not able to get rid of the pseudo-historical characteristics of the 'law' as taught by his predecessors. After a few remarks on the importance of the subject and the error of believing that its consideration may be postponed to a remote future, he states the law thus:

> 'After a certain, and not very advanced, stage in the progress of agriculture; as soon, in fact, as men have applied themselves to cultivation with any energy, and have brought to it any tolerable tools; from that time it is the law of production from the land that in a given state of agricultural skill and knowledge, by increasing the labour the produce is not increased in an equal degree; doubling the labour does not double the produce; or, to express the same thing in other words, every increase of produce is obtained by a more than proportional increase in the application of labour to the land.'[4]

'In any given state of agricultural skill and knowledge' is really exactly the same as 'at any one time', since agricultural skill and knowledge, like all other skill and knowledge, are never stationary. Taking it in this sense, Mill's law would be a real law if it were not for the necessary proviso that it is only true when a certain stage in the progress of agriculture has been reached, so that there is a period when, to use a common phrase, it 'has not yet come into operation'. This deprives it of that universality which characterizes a real law. The law of gravitation, for instance, is always true and always 'in opera-

[1] *Principles*, Bk. I, ch. xii, § 2, 1st ed., vol. i, p. 216; People's ed., p. 111 *b*.

[2] *Ibid.*, 1st ed., vol. i, p. 212; People's ed., p. 109 *b*. 'This general law of agricultural industry is the most important proposition in political economy. Were the law different, nearly all the phenomena of the production and distribution of wealth would be other than they are.'

[3] Bk. I, ch. xii.

[4] 1st ed., vol. i, p. 212; Bk. I, ch. xii, § 2. The words from 'as soon' to 'from that time' were afterwards omitted; People's ed., p. 109.

tion'; it does not 'begin to operate' only when the stalk of the apple gives way.

Not content with postponing the enforcement of his law to a somewhat vaguely fixed date, Mill proceeds to 'limit' it:

> 'The principle', he says, 'which has now been stated must be received, no doubt, with certain explanations and limitations. Even after the land is so highly cultivated that the mere application of additional labour, or of an additional amount of ordinary dressing, would yield no return proportioned to the expense, it may still happen that the application of a much greater additional labour and capital to improving the soil itself, by draining or permanent manures, would be as liberally remunerated by the produce as any portion of the labour and capital already employed.'[1]

In a case like this, he says, 'the general law of diminishing return from land would have undergone', to a certain extent, 'a temporary supersession'. When population had sufficiently increased, 'the general law would resume its course, and the further augmentation would be obtained at a more than proportionate expense of labour and capital'.

But even this is not all. Even when the law has once come into operation, and while it is not undergoing a temporary supersession, there is an 'agency' 'in habitual antagonism' which is 'capable for a time of making head' against it, and this is 'no other than the progress of civilization', which is explained to mean much what previous writers had called 'improvements':

> 'That the produce of land increases, *cæteris paribus*, in a diminishing ratio to the increase in the labour employed is, as we have said (allowing for occasional and temporary exceptions), the universal law of agricultural industry. This principle, however, has been denied, and experience confidently appealed to in proof that the returns from land are not less but greater, in an advanced, than in an early, stage of cultivation – when much capital, than when little, is applied to agriculture. So much so, indeed, that (it is affirmed) the worst land now in cultivation produces as much food per acre, and even as much to a given amount of labour, as our ancestors contrived to extract from the richest soils in England.
>
> 'It is very possible that this may be true; and even if not true to the letter, to a great extent it certainly is so. Unquestionably a much smaller proportion of the population is now occupied in producing food for the whole, than in the early times of our history. This, however, does not prove that the law of which we have been speaking does not exist, but only that there is some antagonizing principle at work capable for a time of making head against the law. Such an agency there is in habitual antagonism to the law of diminishing return from land . . . It is no other than the progress of civilization.'[2]

[1] Bk. I, ch. xii, § 2, 1st ed., vol. i, p. 215; People's ed., p. 111 *a*.

[2] 1st ed., Bk. I, ch. xii, § 3, vol. i, p. 217. Superseded by a discussion of Carey's views in later editions, People's ed., pp. 111–113.

If we knew nothing of the previous history of the question we should be at a loss to conceive why Mill should be at the trouble of developing a law which

(1) does not come into operation at a very early date in the history of society;
(2) is liable to temporary supersessions; and
(3) has been made head against by an antagonizing principle, namely, the progress of civilization, throughout the whole known history of England.

If the returns to agricultural industry do not diminish either before or after history begins, why construct a law of 'diminishing returns', why treat the whole period over which the history of England extends as 'a time'? The explanation is, of course, that when Mill expounded the law there were 'two antagonizing principles' at work in his mind, on the one hand, his early impressions derived from economists who believed that returns do, as a general rule, diminish; and, on the other hand, a recognition of the fact that as a general rule they increase. In one place he tells us that 'in Europe five hundred years ago, though so thinly peopled in comparison to the present population, it is probable that the worst land under the plough was, from the rude state of agriculture, quite as unproductive as the worst land now cultivated';[1] in another he says that:

> 'In a society which is advancing in wealth, population generally increases faster than agricultural skill, and food consequently tends to become more costly; but there are times when a strong impulse sets in towards agricultural improvement. Such an impulse has shown itself in Great Britain during the last fifteen or twenty years.'[2]

Perusal of Carey's *Principles of Social Science* did not clarify his ideas. Referring to Carey's theory that cultivation begins with the most infertile and proceeds gradually to the most fertile lands, he says:

> 'As far as words go, Mr Carey has a good case against several of the highest authorities in political economy, who certainly did enunciate in too universal a manner the law which they laid down, not remarking that it is not true of the first cultivation in a newly settled country.'[3]

[1] Book IV, chap. iii, § 5, 1st ed., vol. ii, p. 277; People's ed., p. 438 *a*.

[2] Book IV, chap. ii, § 3, 1st ed., vol. ii, pp. 254, 255. With 'twenty or five-and-twenty' substituted for 'fifteen or twenty'; People's ed., p. 426 *b*. Cp. the following dubious passage from Book I, chap. xiii, § 2, 1st ed., vol. i, pp. 229, 230; People's ed., p. 119: 'In England during a long interval preceding the French Revolution population increased slowly; but the progress of improvement, at least in agriculture, would seem to have been still slower. . . . Whether during the same period improvements in manufactures, or diminished cost of imported commodities, made amends for the diminished productiveness of labour on the land is uncertain. But ever since the great mechanical inventions of Watt, Arkwright, and their contemporaries, the return to labour has probably increased as fast as the population; and would have outstripped it, if that very augmentation of return had not called forth an additional portion of the inherent power of multiplication in the human species.'

[3] Book I, chap. xii, § 3; People's ed., p. 112 *a*.

This is scarcely candid, for so far from 'not remarking' that the 'law' is not true of the first cultivation in a newly settled country, Ricardo and West, surely 'the highest authorities' on this particular subject, had taken the first cultivation in a newly settled country as their type and illustration of the working of the law.[1] 'It is not pretended', Mill goes on to say, meaning that he himself does not pretend, 'that the law of diminishing return was operative from the very beginning of society'. 'Mr Carey will hardly assert that in any old country – in England or France, for example – the lands left waste are, or have for centuries been, more naturally fertile than those under tillage'. Carey's own admission that 'the raw products of the soil in an advancing community steadily tend to rise in price',[2] he says, if true, proves of itself that the labour required for raising raw products from the soil 'tends to augment when a greater quantity is demanded'.

> 'I do not', he adds, 'go so far as Mr Carey; I do not assert that the cost of production, and consequently the price, of agricultural production, always and necessarily rises as population increases. It tends to do so, but the tendency may be, and sometimes is, even during long periods, held in check.'[3]

Evidently at the bottom he still adhered to the old doctrine of a general rule of diminishing returns liable to only temporary interruptions or checks. Nor can we wonder at his reluctance to abandon it when we reflect that if he had done so he would have had to find a new way of accounting for the historical fall of profits and also to change most of his views with regard to the whole question of economic progress. As he says himself, 'were the law different, nearly all the phenomena of the production and distribution of wealth would be other than' he supposed them to be.[4]

The pseudo-historical general rule of diminishing returns, the theory that the returns to agricultural industry have actually diminished, and continue to diminish in spite of occasional interruptions, would, if it had been true, have supplied the reason which Malthus failed to discover for believing that subsistence or produce cannot be increased as fast as population would be increased by human fecundity and matrimonial instincts, if unchecked. The newly discovered reason cannot be more neatly expressed than in Mill's words:

> 'It is in vain to say that all mouths which the increase of mankind calls into existence bring with them hands. The new mouths require as much food as the old ones and the hands do not produce as much.'[5]

[1] Above, p. 157; Ricardo, *Works*, p. 371. Malthus says of Europe generally, 'the best land would naturally be the first occupied', *Essay*, 8th ed., p. 369.

[2] Mill's words.

[3] Book I, chap. xii, § 3, People's ed., p. 113 *a*.

[4] Above, p. 175, note 3.

[5] Book I, chap. xiii, § 2, 1st ed., vol. i, p. 227; People's ed., p. 118 *a*.

Malthus himself had never taken the new hands into account at all. He neglected entirely the increment of labour supplied by the increment of population. In comparing the ratios at which population and produce can increase, he did not say that double the present population may conceivably produce double the present produce twenty-five years hence, but four times the present population will not conceivably be able to produce four times the present produce fifty years hence. Instead of this he simply supposed, without any consideration of the proportionate amount of labour, that 'by the best possible policy and great encouragements to agriculture'[1] the produce might be doubled in twenty-five years, and trebled in fifty years, and so on. The general rule of diminishing returns, on the other hand, brings the labour and the produce into close relationship, and asserts that the additional labour is usually less productive than the old because it must either be employed on less fertile land, or in performing less productive operations on the land already in cultivation. And, of course, as the existing produce per head is not enormously greater than what is necessary to support life, a continuous diminution of the productiveness of industry must very soon put a stop to population doubling itself every twenty-five years, or indeed to its increasing with any considerable rapidity.

The pseudo-scientific law of diminishing returns, the doctrine which teaches merely that the returns to industry 'tend' to decrease, or would decrease if it were not for the progress of civilization, does not, like the general rule, prove to its believers that population cannot increase with considerable rapidity, but it proves that it is not desirable that population should increase at all. If every increase of population tends to cause a diminution of returns, then whether returns actually diminish or not, they would have been greater if population had not increased. Mill says as much:

> 'After a degree of density has been attained sufficient to allow the principal benefits of combination of labour, all further increase tends in itself to mischief so far as regards the average condition of the people.'[2]

The 'progress of improvement', which must 'be understood in a wide sense', has a counteracting effect,

> 'But though improvement may, during a certain space of time, keep up with or even surpass the actual increase of population, it assuredly never comes up to the rate of increase of which population is capable;[3] and nothing could have prevented a general deterioration in the condition of the human race, were it not that population has in fact been

[1] *Essay*, 8th ed., p. 5.

[2] Book I, chap. xiii, § 2, 1st ed., vol. i, p. 228; People's ed., p. 118 *b*.

[3] The meaning of this is somewhat obscure. Is it that improvement never doubles itself every twenty-five years?

restrained. Had it been restrained still more, and the same improvements taken place, there would have been a larger dividend than there now is for the nation or the species at large.'[1]

If a reader desires to know what degree of density of population Mill meant to indicate by that which is 'sufficient to allow the principal benefits of combination of labour', he may turn to Book IV, chap. vi, § 2. There Mill says:

> 'The density of population necessary to enable mankind to obtain, in the greatest degree, all the advantages both of co-operation and of social intercourse has, in all the most populous countries, been attained.'[2]

He looks on the degree of density which is required for the maximum productivness of industry as something fixed once for all, at one hundred, or two hundred, or some other number to the square mile. This is, of course, an eminently unscientific and unhistorical way of regarding the question. The conditions under which men live, the extent of their knowledge, and their ability to profit by their knowledge, change from century to century, from year to year, and even from day to day, and almost every change affects in one way or another the 'density of population necessary to enable mankind to obtain in the greatest degree all the advantages both of co-operation and of social intercourse'. There is no reason whatever to suppose that the average Englishman would be better off now if the population of England had remained stationary at the point it had reached when Mill wrote his *Principles of Political Economy*. No doubt if it had been so restrained, 'and the same improvements taken place, there would', as he alleges, 'have been a larger dividend than there now is'; but that the same improvements could have taken place is perfectly inconceivable.

[1] Book I, chap. xiii, § 2, 1st ed., vol. i, p. 230; People's ed., p. 119 *b*.
[2] 1st ed., vol. ii, p. 311; People's ed., p. 454 *b*.

CHAPTER VI

THE IDEA OF DISTRIBUTION

§ 1. *Early History of the Term, and its Identification with Division into Wages, Profit, and Rent*

In tracing the history of the term 'production', used as the title of a department of political economy, we necessarily anticipated to some extent the corresponding history of the term 'distribution'.[1] The earliest English instance we were able to record of its use was furnished by an almost forgotten work, D. Boileau's *Introduction to the Study of Political Economy, or elementary view of the manner in which the Wealth of Nations is produced, increased, distributed, and consumed,* published in 1811, of which the Third Book is entitled 'Of the Distribution of the Wealth of Nations'. But though this may have been the first English appearance of the substantive in a prominent position as an almost technical term, the use of the verb is to be traced back to the title of Adam Smith's Book I, 'Of the causes of improvement in the productive powers of labour, and of the order according to which its produce is naturally distributed among the different ranks of the people'. Before Adam Smith, English economists did not talk of 'distribution' or of the manner in which wealth or produce is 'distributed'. In France, however, Turgot's *Réflexions sur la formation et la distribution des richesses* had been printed in the *Ephémérides du citoyen* six years before the publication of the *Wealth of Nations.*[2]

Looking at the ordinary non-economic use of the term, we can imagine an essay on the distribution of produce relating to either of two different questions, first, 'In what manner or by what means is the produce parcelled out among those who receive it?' or secondly, 'In what proportions is the produce divided among those who share it, and what determines these proportions?' Turgot, when he used the phrase, seems to have been thinking altogether of the first of these two questions. He does not attempt to show what causes variations in the proportions received by different classes or individuals, but only endeavours to explain the various methods of obtaining an income. In sections XX to XXX, he shows how an owner of land may draw an income from it in five different ways, having it cultivated (1) by labourers

[1] Above, pp. 32–35.

[2] The *Réflexions* were written in 1766, and first printed in the *Ephémérides* for November and December 1769 and January 1770. These numbers, however, were not actually published till January, February, and April 1770. See G. Schelle, *Pourquoi les 'Réflexions' de Turgot ne sont-elles pas exactement connues?* in the *Journal des Economistes* for July 1888, pp. 3-5.

in his own service, (2) by slaves, (3) by villeins, (4) by métayers, (5) by rent-paying farmers, and the next section begins:

> 'Il y a un autre moyen d'être riche sans travailler et sans posséder des terres, dont je n'ai pas encore parlé. Il est nécessaire d'en expliquer l'origine et la liaison avec le reste du système de la distribution des richesses dans la société dont je viens de crayonner l'ébauche.'[1]

But there seems no reason to suppose, and it is highly improbable, that Adam Smith was acquainted with Turgot's *Réflexions*. He did not acquire his use of the word 'distribute' from Turgot, but directly from the source from which Turgot himself had obtained it – the Table or system of Quesnay. Quesnay often uses the word in the ordinary sense of dividing into separate parcels and conveying to various destinations. He speaks of a '*mauvaise distribution des hommes et des richesses*',[2] and of '*une plus grande distribution et circulation*' of the precious metals,[3] and in describing a primitive society with community of goods he says: '*il n'y a d'autre distribution de biens que celle que les hommes peuvent obtenir par la recherche des productions qui leur sont nécessaires pour subsister*'.[4] But he also used the word as the name of the transactions which he imagined were carried out between the productive class, the landowners, and the sterile class, and which he endeavoured to portray in his Economical Table. The *Analyse du Tableau économique*, which appeared in the *Journal de l'agriculture* in 1766, had for its second title, *Analyse de la formule arithmétique du Tableau économique de la distribution des dépenses annuelles d'une nation agricole*,[5] and in it Quesnay, after describing what he calls *l'ordre régulier*[6] of the transactions between the three classes, says:

> 'On ne pourrait rien soustraire à cette distribution de dépenses au désavantage de l'agriculture, ni rien soustraire des reprises du cultivateur par quelque exaction ou par quelques entraves dans le commerce, qu'il n'arrivât du déperissement dans la reproduction annuelle des richesses de la nation et une diminution de population facile à démontrer par le calcul. Ainsi, *c'est par l'ordre de la distribution des dépenses, selon qu'elles reviennent ou qu'elles sont soustraites à la* classe productive, *selon qu'elles augmentent ses avances, ou qu'elles les diminuent, selon qu'elles soutiennent ou qu'elles font baisser le prix des productions, qu'on peut calculer les effets de la bonne ou mauvaise conduite d'une nation.*'[7]

An English version of Mirabeau's account of the *Tableau* opens with the words:

> 'It was first necessary to ascertain whence the income arises, in what

[1] *Œuvres*, ed. Daire, vol. i, p. 22.
[2] *Œuvres*, ed. Oncken, p. 189.
[3] *Ibid.*, p. 301.
[4] *Ibid.*, p. 647.
[5] *Œuvres*, ed. Oncken, p. 305.
[6] *Ibid.*, pp. 314, 319.
[7] *Ibid.*, pp. 319, 320.

> manner it is distributed among the different classes of society, in what places it vanishes, and in what it is reproduced.'[1]

It also speaks of 'the distributive order in which the immediate productions of the earth are consumed by the several classes'.[2] These quotations leave little room for doubt as to the parentage of Adam Smith's phrase, 'the order according to which' the produce of labour 'is naturally distributed among the different ranks of the people'.

A reader who was making his first acquaintance with the *Wealth of Nations* would naturally be led by the title of the First Book to expect to find it fall into two parts, the first dealing with the productive powers of labour, and the second with the manner in which its produce is distributed. His expectation would, however, be weakened when he looked through the titles of the chapters, and found that while Chapters i to iii deal with the division of labour, and Chapters viii to x with wages, profits, and rent, the intermediate chapters deal with money and prices. If there is any transition from 'production' to 'distribution', he would infer, it must be a gradual one, for the chapters on money and prices cannot belong altogether either to production or distribution. On examining the matter more closely he would find that the ostensible train of thought running through the Book is as follows: Division of labour is effected by means of exchanges, and therefore a discussion of it naturally leads to the consideration of the manner in which exchanges are facilitated by the use of money,[3] and to remarks on the prices of commodities, or 'the rules which men naturally observe in exchanging them either for money or for one another';[4] prices are resolvable into their component parts of wages, profit, and rent, and therefore suggest a discussion of the causes which make wages, profit, and rent high or low.[5] The peculiarity of this is that it seems to leave no important place for the consideration of 'the order according to which' the produce of labour 'is naturally distributed among the different ranks of the people'. Adam Smith's theory of distribution, instead of being made one of the main subjects of the Book, is inserted in the middle of the chapter on prices as a mere appendage or corollary of his doctrine of prices. After explaining that the price of every commodity resolves itself into wages, profit, and rent, or into wages and profit, or into wages and rent, or into wages alone, he says:

> 'As the price or exchangeable value of every particular commodity, taken separately, resolves itself into some one or other or all of those

[1] *The Economical Table, an attempt towards ascertaining and exhibiting the source, progress, and employment of riches, with explanations by the Friend of Mankind, the celebrated Marquis de Mirabeau; translated from the French*, 1766, p. 23.

[2] *Ibid.*, p. 37.

[3] Beginning of chapter iv.

[4] End of chapter iv; p. 13 *a*.

[5] End of chapter vii.

three parts; so that of all the commodities which compose the whole annual produce of the labour of every country, taken complexly, must resolve itself into the same three parts, and be parcelled out among different inhabitants of the country either as the wages of their labour, the profits of their stock, or the rent of their land; the whole of what is annually either collected or produced by the labour of every society, or, what comes to the same thing, the whole price of it, is in this manner originally distributed among some of its different members. Wages, profit, and rent are the three original sources of all revenue, as well as of all exchangeable value.'[1]

If this passage had been immediately followed by the chapters on wages, profits, and rent, distribution might certainly have ranked as a main topic of the Book. But it is actually followed by a chapter on the 'natural and market price of commodities', which is succeeded by the chapters on wages, profit, and rent, not because it is interesting to know how the produce is distributed between labourers, capitalists, and landlords, but because wages and profit are causes, and rent an effect, of the prices of commodities:

'When the price of any commodity is neither more nor less than what is sufficient to pay the rent of the land, the wages of the labour, and the profits of the stock employed in raising, preparing, and bringing it to market, according to their natural rates, the commodity is then sold for what may be called its natural price.[2] . . .

'This natural price itself varies with the natural rate of each of its component parts, of wages, profit, and rent; and in every society this rate varies according to their riches or poverty, their advancing, stationary, or declining condition. I shall in the four following chapters endeavour to explain, as fully and distinctly as I can, the causes of those different variations.

'First, I shall endeavour to explain what are the circumstances which naturally determine the rate of wages. . . .

'Secondly, I shall endeavour to show what are the circumstances which naturally determine the rate of profit. . . .

'Though pecuniary wages and profit are very different in the different employments of labour and stock, yet a certain proportion seems commonly to take place between both the pecuniary wages in all the different employments of labour, and the pecuniary profits in all the different employmentx of stock. . . . I shall in the third place endeavour to explain all the different circumstances which regulate this proportion.

'In the fourth and last place, I shall endeavour to show what are the circumstances which regulate the rent of land, and which either raise or lower the real price of all the different substances which it produces.'[3]

To account for distribution occupying so subordinate a place in the body of the Book, and so prominent a one in the title, we may perhaps be allowed to conjecture that in all probability the Book existed in a fairly complete form before Adam Smith became acquainted with

[1] Bk. i, chap. vi, p. 24 *a*. [2] Bk. I, chap. vii, p. 25 *a*.
[3] Bk. I, chap. vi, p. 29 *a*.

the physiocratic doctrine. When this happened, he may very well have thought that his theory of prices and his observations on wages, profit, and rent made a very good theory of what the physiocrats called 'distribution', and thus have been led to affix the present title of the Book, and to interpolate the passage about the whole produce being parcelled out and distributed as wages, profit, and rent.

Whatever may have been the cause of Adam Smith's choosing for his First Book a title which did not really describe its contents, the effect has been to identify 'distribution' in English economic treatises with a discussion of the causes which affect wages, profit, and rent.

It was, however, a long time before this result was fully brought about. In the article on Political Economy in the fourth edition of the *Encyclopædia Britannica*, the chapter, 'Of the manner in which wealth is produced and distributed', contains eight sections headed as follows: (1) 'The Division of Labour', (2) 'Machinery', (3) 'Of the different Employments of Labour and Stock', (4) 'Agriculture', (5) 'Manufactures', (6) 'Commerce', (7) 'The Retail Trade', (8) 'On the coincidence between Public and Private Interest'. Boileau, writing in 1811, manages to deal with wages, profit, and rent, in his Book I, on the 'Nature and Origin of the Wealth of Nations', and fills up his short Book III, 'Of the Distribution of the Wealth of Nations', with remarks on 'Circulation' and money. But J.-B. Say, who, as we have seen,[1] divided his *Traité* into three Books dealing with Production, Distribution, and Consumption, followed in his first two Books the order of subjects adopted in Book I of the *Wealth of Nations* rather closely, with the result that the bulk of his Book on 'Distribution' is concerned with wages, profits, and rents. The discussion on value with which it begins he regards very rightly as only an indispensable preliminary to the explanation of distribution. He says:

> 'Avant de montrer comment et dans quelles proportions s'opère entre les membres de la société, la distribution de la chose produite, c'est-à-dire, de la VALEUR des produits, il faut connaître les bases sur lesquelles se fixe leur valeur. Je ferai remarquer ensuite par quel mécanisme et dans quelles proportions elle se répand chez les différents membres de la société, pour former leur REVENU.'[2]

The next great step towards confining 'distribution' to a dissertation on wages, profits, and rent was taken by Ricardo, when he declared in his Preface that 'to determine the laws which regulate' the 'distribution' 'of the whole produce of the earth' between labourers, capitalists, and landlords, 'is the principal problem in political economy', and James Mill completed the process in his *Elements*, by dealing with nothing but wages, profits, and rents under the head of 'Distribution', and relegating Exchange or 'Interchange', as he pre-

[1] Above, p. 35.

[2] 2nd ed., 1814, vol. ii, p. 2.

ferred to call it, to a subsequent chapter. Since then, every reader of experience would expect to find wages, profit, and rent the chief, if not the sole, topics dealt with under the head of 'Distribution' in an English economic text-book.

§ 2. *The Meaning of Wages, Profit, and Rent*

The proposition that the total produce or income of a nation's labour is 'distributed' into wages, profit, and rent, is of course not exactly identical with the proposition that total wages, profit, and rent together make up the whole produce, since, in the absence of a statement to the contrary, a part of wages, profit, and rent might lie outside of the produce. In the chapter 'Of Money' in Book II, Adam Smith incidentally notices that rent, in the ordinary sense of the term, often includes something besides ultimate produce or income:

> 'The gross rent', he says, 'of a private estate comprehends whatever is paid by the farmer; the net rent what remains to the landlord after deducting the expense of management, of repairs, and all other necessary charges; or what, without hurting his estate, he can afford to place in his stock reserved for immediate consumption, or to spend upon his table, equipage, the ornaments of his house and furniture, his private enjoyments and amusements. His real wealth is in proportion, not to his gross, but to his net rent.'[1]

A similar distinction, though one not so practically important, exists between gross wages and net wages, between the whole of wages in the ordinary sense of the word, and that part of wages which constitutes clear income to the recipient. Most wages in the popular sense are liable to some deductions, such as the expense of tools or particular clothes, and even the higher ground rents which are paid by the working classes in towns must be deducted from their gross wages before their net wages or real income can be found.[2] Profit, by itself, is such a vague term, that it is difficult to say whether, after of course deducting all losses, aggregate profits would include anything other than income or not. There is no doubt, however, that Adam Smith and his followers never intended anything to be included in wages, profits, and rents except true income. The proposition that the produce or income is divided into wages, profits, and rents has always been taken to mean the same as the equation:

Total produce or income = wages + profits + rents.

Wages, profits, and rents must consequently be always understood as net wages, net profits, and net rents.

Everything that is not income being thus excluded from wages,

[1] Bk. II, chap. ii, p. 124 *a*.

[2] See on this subject Giffen, *Essays in Finance*, 2nd series, pp. 381, 382, and *The Gross and Net Gain of Rising Wages* in the *Contemporary Review* for December 1889, pp. 832, 833.

profits, and rents, the next question is how to include the whole of the income under the three terms, and where to draw the line between the different parts. In ordinary language in Adam Smith's time, as at present, the term wages was applied to amounts received by the less well-paid classes of workers from persons who undertake to accept their work at fixed rates agreed on before the labour is executed. Profit was a vague word applicable to almost any kind of gain, if some expense or risk of loss must be incurred in order to secure it. Rent denoted the periodical payments made to the owners of land, houses, and other immovable objects by the tenants who enjoy the use of them.

It must always be remembered, however, that in Adam Smith the wages, profit, and rent into which the whole income is said to be distributed are the wages of labour, the profit of stock, and the rent of land. The 'wages of labour' seems a more comprehensive term than 'wages', and it is easy to extend it so as to include under it the 'salaries' and 'fees' paid to certain classes of workers, and also the amounts earned by certain other classes who 'work on their own account' that is to say, who produce something without first contracting with an employer as to the price to be paid. The 'profit of stock' is a less vague term than profit, and evidently means not all kinds of gains in securing which an expense or risk is incurred, but those only which are obtained owing to the possession of stock or capital. The 'rent of land' does not include the rent of immovable objects other than land, and that kind of rent is therefore placed under the head of profit of stock. Wages, in short, become the whole income derived by individuals from the performance of labour, rent the whole income derived from the possession of land, and profits the whole income derived from the possession of other kinds of property.

This view of the division between the three components of income, however, was not always accepted in the cases where a single individual combines in his own person the functions of labourer and capitalist, or of capitalist and landlord. Adam Smith, indeed, says expressly, that it is confounding wages with profit to call the whole gain of an active farmer or independent workman 'profit';

> 'Common farmers seldom employ any overseer to direct the general operations of the farm. They generally, too, work a good deal with their own hands as ploughmen, harrowers, etc. What remains of the crop, after paying the rent, therefore, should not only replace to them their stock employed in cultivation, together with its ordinary profits, but pay them the wages which are due to them, both as labourers and overseers. Whatever remains, however, after paying the rent and keeping up the stock, is called profit. But wages evidently make a part of it. The farmer by saving these wages must necessarily gain them. Wages, therefore, are in this case confounded with profit.

'An independent manufacturer, who has stock enough both to purchase materials, and to maintain himself till he can carry his work to market, should gain both the wages of a journeyman who works under a master, and the profit which that master makes by the sale of the journeyman's work. His whole gains, however, are commonly called profit, and wages are, in this case too, confounded with profit.'[1]

He also tells us that 'the apparent difference' between 'the profits of different trades is generally a deception arising from our not always distinguishing what ought to be regarded as wages from what ought to be considered as profit',[2] and that the very high 'apparent profit' made by small shopkeepers is 'real wages disguised in the garb of profit'.[3] Obviously he thought that, for scientific purposes, the term wages should be taken to include the whole of the remuneration of labour, in spite of the fact that some of it is performed by persons who may be ranked as capitalists. The early nineteenth-century economists did not dispute this, but ignored the necessity of having an opinion on the subject. They talked of wages as if the term included all remuneration of labour, but they thought of no labour except that which earns wages in the common narrow acceptation of the word, and their theories of wages are consequently inapplicable to a large portion of the phenomena which they profess to explain. J. S. Mill recognised this in his *Essays*. After assenting cordially to Adam Smith's division of what is commonly called profit into remuneration for the use of capital and remuneration for labour, he says it would be a mistake to suppose that the remuneration of employer's labour 'is regulated by entirely the same principles as other wages'. In support of this proposition, he brings forward two reasons. The first is borrowed from the rather unfortunate passage in which Adam Smith endeavours to show that 'the profits of stock' are not 'only a different name for the wages of a particular sort of labour, the labour of inspection and direction'.[4] The remuneration of the employer's labour, or wages of superintendence, Mill says:

'is wages, but wages paid by a commission on the capital employed. If the general rate of profit is 10 per cent, and the rate of interest 5 per cent, the wages of superintendence will be 5 per cent; and though one borrower employ a capital of £100,000 another no more than £100, the labour of both will be rewarded with the same percentage, though in the one case this symbol will represent an income of £5, in the other case of £5,000.'[5]

Now, doubtless, if two men, the one with £100,000 of capital and the other with £100, were to engage in exactly similar transactions, their 'profits' would be at the same rate per cent, and occasionally

[1] Bk. I, chap. vi, p. 24 *b*. [2] Bk. I, chap. x, p. 50 *b*. [3] *Ibid*., p. 51 *a*.
[4] Bk. I, chap. vi, p. 22 *b*. See above, pp. 68, 69; and below, p. 200.
[5] *Essays*, pp. 107, 108.

something of the kind may happen. But the general rule is that men with £100,000 of capital are engaged in quite different transactions from men with £100, and that the wages of superintendence earned by the small capitalists who manage their own capital are immensely larger in proportion to their capital than those earned by the large capitalists. If Mill did not know this from personal observation, he might have learnt it from Adam Smith, who says, evidently taking his example from Kirkcaldy:

> 'In a small seaport town a little grocer will make forty or fifty per cent upon a stock of a single hundred pounds, while a considerable wholesale merchant in the same place will scarce make eight or ten per cent upon a stock of ten thousand.'[1]

There is no basis whatever for the idea that there is any such thing as a rate of wages of superintendence in the same sense as there is a rate of interest. Mill's second reason for thinking that wages of superintendence are not regulated entirely by the same principles as other wages is that 'they are not paid in advance out of capital like the wages of all other labourers, but merge in the profit, and are not realized until the production is completed', which fact, he says, 'takes them entirely out of the ordinary law of wages'.[2] This is quite true if we understand by 'the ordinary law of wages' what Mill understood by it, and it would have been an excellent reason for endeavouring to make a more complete and satisfactory law of wages. Before Mill wrote his *Principles* Senior had pointed out that the remuneration of capitalists' labour 'generally bears a smaller proportion to the capital employed as that capital increases in value', and remarked that while few persons employing £100,000 in England would not be satisfied with 10 per cent per annum, small fruit-sellers with a capital of a few shillings expect over 7,000 per cent.[3] But in the *Principles*, though Mill admits that 'the portion of the gross profit which forms the remuneration for the labour and skill of the dealer or producer is very different in different employments', and actually quotes the case of the grocer spoken of by Adam Smith,[4] he continues to treat of an imaginary rate of profit which includes wages of superintendence, and makes no attempt to bring these wages under the 'ordinary law of wages'.

When a man is both landlord and farmer, Adam Smith says he 'should gain both the rent of the landlord and the profit of the farmer'.[5] By this he seems to mean that his income, though all called 'profit' in common language, should be divided by the economist into two parts—profit and rent. But in the chapter 'Of the Rent of Land',

[1] Book I, chap. x, p. 51 *a*. [2] *Essays*, p. 108.
[3] *Political Economy*, 8vo ed., p. 203.
[4] Book II, ch. xv, § 3, 1st ed., vol. i, pp. 482, 483; People's ed., pp. 247, 248.
[5] Book I, ch. vi, p. 24 *b*.

though he admits that it 'may be partly the case on some occasions', that what is called the rent of an acre of land in ordinary language consists of 'profit or interest for the stock laid out by the landlord on its improvement,'[1] it did not occur to him to exclude the profit on improvements from the rent of land proper.

Ricardo endeavoured to do so. In a note to the *Essay on the Influence of a Low Price of Corn*, he says:

> 'By rent I always mean the remuneration given to the landlord for the use of the original and inherent power of the land. If either the landlord expends capital on his own land, or the capital of a preceding tenant is left upon it at the expiration of his lease, he may obtain what is indeed called a larger rent, but a portion of this is evidently paid for the use of capital. The other portion only is paid for the use of the original power of the land.'[2]

So, too, in the *Principles*, in the chapter 'On Rent' he says:

> 'Rent is that portion of the produce of the earth which is paid to the landlord for the use of the original and indestructible powers of the soil. It is often, however, confounded with the interest and profit of capital, and in popular language the term is applied to whatever is annually paid by a farmer to his landlord. If of two adjoining farms of the same extent and of the same natural fertility one had all the conveniences of farming buildings and were, besides, properly drained and manured, and advantageously divided by hedges, fences, and walls, while the other had none of these advantages, more remuneration would naturally be paid for the use of one than for the use of the other; yet in both cases this remuneration would be called rent.'[3]

Like most people who have not had the advantage of a literary education, Ricardo was apt to think that a word ought to have whatever sense he found convenient to put upon it; and so he implies that though the whole of the remuneration paid for the better provided land would be called rent, it is not rent. He goes on to point out, among other things, that the sums paid to the owners of mines for permission to work them are not paid for the use of the original and indestructible powers of the soil, but for minerals removed, and concludes:

> In the future pages of this work, then, whenever I speak of the rent of land, I wish to be understood as speaking of that compensation which is paid to the owner of land for the use of its original and indestructible powers.'[4]

But even before the printing of his work was completed he had modified his views. In a note at the end of the chapter on Poor Rates

[1] Book I, ch. xi, p. 66 *b*.

[2] *Works*, p. 375.

[3] 1st ed., pp. 49, 50; 3rd ed. in *Works*, p. 34.

[4] 1st ed., p. 52; 3rd ed. in *Works*, p. 35. Yet so strong is the power of custom in language that he gives the very next chapter the heading of 'On the Rent of Mines', and says in it: 'Mines as well as land generally pay a rent to their owner.' – 1st ed., p. 77; 3rd ed. in *Works*, p. 45.

he admits that rent or 'real rent' may include, on some occasions, the profit on capial invested in improvements. Part of the capital invested by landowners on their land 'is inseparably amalgamated with the land, and tends to increase its powers', so that 'the remuneration paid to the landlord for its use is strictly of the nature of rent, and is subject to all the laws of rent'. It is only the remainder of the capital which does not 'obtain for the landlord any permanent addition to his real rent', as it consists of 'buildings and other perishable improvements' which 'require to be constantly renewed'.[1]

James Mill abides by Ricardo's first position. Land once brought into cultivation, he explains, is more valuable than uncleared land. Rather than clear the fresh land, a man will pay an equivalent for the cost of clearing, but this 'is not a payment for the power of the soil, but simply for the capital bestowed upon the soil. It is not rent; it is interest'.[2] M'Culloch defines rent as payment 'for the use of the *natural and inherent* powers of the soil',[3] and illustrates this in a way which suggests that he had never read Ricardo's second thoughts on the subject in the note to the chapter on Poor Rates. J. S. Mill, on the other hand, follows Ricardo's second opinion, including in rent the return due to 'capital actually sunk in improvements, and not requiring periodical renewal, but spent, once for all, in giving the land a permanent increase of productiveness'.[4]

Senior had gone much further, and desired to include under the term 'rent' a very large proportion not only of what every one calls profits but also of what every one calls wages. Instead of inquiring in what sense the words were actually used, and what classification would be at once convenient and in reasonable consonance with their ordinary sense, he somehow jumped to the conclusion that 'wages and profit are to be considered as the rewards of peculiar sacrifices', and therefore that every kind of income which is not the reward of sacrifice must be rent:

> 'If', he says, 'wages and profit are to be considered as the reward of peculiar sacrifices, the former the remuneration for labour, and the latter for abstinence from immediate enjoyment, it is clear that under the term "rent" must be included all that is obtained without any sacrifice; or, which is the same thing, beyond the remuneration for that sacrifice; all that nature or fortune bestows either without any exertion on the part of the recipient or in addition to the average remuneration for the exercise of industry or the employment of capital.'[5]

[1] 1st ed., p. 362, note; 3rd ed. in *Works*, p. 158, note.

[2] *Elements*, 1st ed., p. 15; 3rd ed., p. 31.

[3] *Principles*, 1st ed., p. 266. The italics are, of course, M'Culloch's.

[4] *Principles*, Book II, ch. xvi, § 5, 1st ed., vol. i, p. 505; People's ed., p. 260 *a*. From the fact that Mill uses the phrase 'it appears to me', we may infer that he had forgotten that Ricardo had adopted this view.

[5] *Political Economy*, 8vo ed., pp. 91, 92.

It does not seem to have occurred to him that some one might deny that wages and profit 'are to be considered as the rewards of peculiar sacrifices'. He simply takes this for granted, and makes no attempt to prove it. Later on in his work he says he has defined rent as 'the revenue spontaneously offered by nature or accident', and profit as the reward of abstinence, and then puts the question

> 'Whether the payments received from his tenants by the present owner of a Lincolnshire estate reclaimed by the Romans from the sea are to be termed not rent but profit on the capital which was expended fifteen centuries ago? The answer is, that for all useful purposes the distinction of profit from rent ceases as soon as the capital from which a given revenue arises has become, whether by gift or by inheritence, the property of a person to whose abstinence and exertions it did not owe its creation. The revenue arising from a dock, or a wharf, or a canal is profit in the hands of the *original constructor*. It is the reward of *his* abstinence in having employed capital for the purposes of production, instead of for those of enjoyment. But in the hands of his heir it has all the attributes of rent. It is to him the gift of fortune, not the result of a sacrifice.'

It is evidently assumed here that the original constructor himself saved the capital he invested in the dock, canal, or wharf, since if his heir were now to sell the wharf, and with the proceeds become himself the 'original constructor' of another wharf, it does not seem that he would 'abstain' any more than if he continued to hold the first wharf.

> 'It may be said, indeed,' Senior continues, 'that such a revenue is the reward of the owner's abstinence in not selling the dock or the canal, and spending its price in enjoyment. But the same remark applies to every species of transferable property. Every estate may be sold, and the purchase-money wasted. If the last basis of classification were adopted, the greater part of what every political economist has termed rent must be called profit.'[1]

That is to say, Senior has made up his mind so firmly that profit is the reward of abstinence and nothing else, that he argues that if we call the income of the owner of an inherited wharf 'profit', we must be driven to what he evidently regards as the undesirable consequence of saying that landlords receive no rent but only profit. He forgets entirely that no one but himself wishes to identify profit and the reward of abstinence, and, still more curiously, he fails to see that his own classification leads to the undesirable consequence of reckoning as rent 'the greater part of what every political economist has termed' profit. His examples of inherited property – a dock, a wharf, and a canal, all belong to the class of immovable objects to which the term rent is peculiarly appropriated in the ordinary language of everyday life. But it cannot seriously be maintained that the heir of a cargo of oranges exercises any more abstinence in not, when he sells them,

[1] *Ibid.*, p. 129.

'spending the price in enjoyment', than the owner of the inherited wharf. The income derived from all inherited wealth is to its present possessors 'the gift of fortune, not the result of a sacrifice'. Consequently, it should all, according to Senior, be classed as rent, not profit.[1] Now in modern civilized and wealthy communities, inherited property is far greater than the property which has been acquired by the saving of living persons.

Oblivious of this, Senior proceeds immediately to classify as rent the 'extraordinary remuneration' for 'extraordinary powers of body or mind':

> 'It originates', he says, 'in the bounty of nature; so far it seems to be rent. It is to be obtained only on the condition of undergoing labour; so far it seems to be wages. It might be termed with equal correctness, rent which can be received only by a labourer, or wages which can be received only by the proprietor of a natural agent. But as it is clearly a surplus, the labour having been previously paid for by average wages, and that surplus the spontaneous gift of nature, we have thought it most convenient to term it rent.'[2]

And even yet he has not finished. Having by this time apparently entirely forgotten his distinction between inherited and non-inherited property, he goes on to say:

> 'And for the same reason we term *rent* what might with equal correctness be termed fortuitous profit. We mean the surplus advantages which are sometimes derived from the employment of capital, after making full compensation for all the risk that has been encountered, and all the sacrifices which have been made, by the capitalist. Such are the fortuitous profits of the holders of warlike stores on the breaking out of unexpected hostilities.'[3]

After this we can hear, almost without surprise, that incomes earned in consequence of the possession of acquired useful knowledge and ability are to be looked on as profit, and not wages. At last Senior comes to an end:

> 'According to our nomenclature (and indeed according to that of Smith, if the produce of capital is to be termed profit) a very small portion of the earnings of the lawyer or of the physician can be called wages. Forty pounds a year would probably pay all the labour that either of them undergoes in order to make, we will say, £4,000 a year. Of the remaining £3,960, probably £3,000 may in each case be considered as rent, as the result of extraordinary talent or good fortune. The rest is profit on their respective capitals; capitals partly consisting of knowledge and of moral and intellecutal habits acquired by much previous expense and labour, and partly of connexion and reputation acquired during years of probation, while their fees were inadequate to their support.'[4]

[1] Conversely, all property bought by the savings of its purchasers must bring in profit, and not rent, so that when, for example, Ricardo became a land-owner he received no rent.

[2] *Political Economy*, 8vo ed., pp. 129, 130.

[3] *Political Economy*, 8vo ed., p. 130.

[4] *Ibid.*, pp. 133, 134.

It is rather amusing to see that, after having thus made havoc of the old classification, and created a new and totally different one, Senior finds it convenient to use the old one, and only to make an occasional reference to the new. His extraordinary attempt is only interesting as an example to be avoided, and as an anticipation of that desire to call everything rent which is a marked feature of English economics at the present time.[1]

§ 3. *The Origin and Cause of Wages*

When it is settled that the whole revenue of the community is composed of three great parts, wages, profits, and rents, and it has been decided what revenues belong to each of the three parts, the next question seems to be as to the cause of the division of the whole revenue into the three parts. Why are wages, profits, and rents obtained by those who receive them?

No one seems to have thought of formally asking why wages are paid, or why labour is remunerated. It was considered 'natural' that labour should be remunerated, and Adam Smith went so far as to think it natural that labour should be remunerated, not only by a part, but by the whole of the produce:

> 'The produce of labour', he says, 'constitutes the natural recompense or wages of labour.
>
> 'In that original state of things, which precedes both the appropriation of land and the accumulation of stock, the whole produce of labour belongs to the labourer. He has neither landlord nor master to share with him.'[2]

According to this view of the subject the labourer receives a part of the produce because he produces the whole of it, and what needs explanation is not that he gets a part, but that he does not get the whole. Wages are natural and original, while profits and rent are artificial and of later introduction. We are left to inquire how and why profits and rent come to be deducted from 'the natural recompense of labour'.

§ 4. *The Origin and Cause of Profit*

Adam Smith thought it necessary to explain that profits are not merely a species of wages. 'The profits of stock,' he observes, 'it may perhaps be thought, are only a different name for the wages of a particular sort of labour, the labour of inspection and direction. They are, however, altogether different.'[3] Instead of being proportioned to 'the quantity, the hardship, or the ingenuity' of the 'supposed labour of inspection and direction', they are proportioned to the value of the stock employed. In some cases scarcely any of the work of inspection

[1] 1893. [2] Bk. I ch. viii, p. 29 *a*. [3] Bk. I, ch. vi, p. 22 *b*.

and direction is done by the owner of the capital, it is all done by 'some principal clerk', who receives wages which 'never bear any regular proportion to the capital of which he oversees the management', while the owner of the capital, 'though he is thus discharged of almost all labour, still expects that his profits should bear a regular proportion to his capital'. Profits are thus a real deduction from the natural recompense of wages of labour.

They are regarded as somehow the result of the fact that capitalists employ labour:

> 'As soon as stock has accumulated in the hands of particular persons, some of them will naturally employ it in setting to work industrious people, whom they will supply with materials and subsistence, in order to make a profit by the sale of their work, or by what their labour adds to the value of the materials.'[1]

Employers would not employ labour at all if they did not expect some profit, some surplus over and above their expenditure. Nor would they use a great stock rather than a small one unless their profits were to bear some proportion to the extent of their stock. They 'hazard' their stock in the 'adventure', a thing no sensible man will do for nothing. But this does not explain why the profit is actually obtained. There are many things which men will not do for nothing, and which, in consequence, remain undone. The employer-capitalist is not paid because he hazards his stock, but he hazards his stock because he is paid for it. To know why profits are deducted from the natural recompense of labour we must know something more than the reason why capitalist employers would cease to employ if there were no profit on each part of the capital employed. We require to know why the labourers agree to the deduction, why they do not work for themselves, and decline to be employed. Adam Smith seems to think it is because they are necessitous:

> 'It seldom happens that the person who tills the ground has wherewithal to maintain himself till he reaps the harvest. His maintenance is generally advanced to him from the stock of a master, the farmer who employs him, and who would have no interest to employ him unless he was to share in the produce of his labour, or unless his stock was to be replaced to him with a profit. This profit makes a second deduction[2] from the produce of the labour which is employed upon land.
>
> 'The produce of almost all other labour is liable to the like deduction of profit. In all arts and manufactures the greater part of the workmen stand in need of a master to advance them the materials of their work, and their wages and maintenance till it be completed.'[3]

He evidently believes that no one will ever submit to a master unless he is obliged. If a man has enough to provide himself with the

[1] Bk. I, ch. vi, p. 22 *a*.

[2] Rent being the first.

[3] Bk. I, ch. viii, pp. 29 *b*, 30 *a*.

materials of his work and to maintain himself till it be completed, he will immediately set up as an 'independent workman'.

We may say, then, that to Adam Smith profits appeared to be a deduction from the produce of labour, to which the labourer has to submit because he has no means of support, and no materials of production. Dr Bohm-Bawerk believes that Adam Smith also occasionally advanced another theory, to the effect that profits are an addition to the price of the produce of labour, but the passages he quotes scarcely prove the existence of this theory.[1]

It will be observed that Adam Smith's explanation of the nature of profits relates entirely to the profits of persons employing labour. He does not seem to have seriously considered any profits except those which he imagined were obtained upon sums spent in paying wages or in buying materials. In the examples which he gives he allows nothing for interest or profit on the value of the manufactory and its machinery. In his treatment of interest in Book II, Chap. iv, he considers it as paid either out of the profits of an employer, or else 'by alienating or encroaching upon some other source of revenue, such as the property or the rent of land'.[2]

Lauderdale definitely asked the questions, 'What is the nature of the profit of stock? and how does it originate?'[3] He objected to Adam Smith's representation of profit as a deduction from the wages of labour. If Adam Smith were right, he says, profits would be a derivative and not an original source of revenue, 'being only a transfer from the pocket of the labourer into that of the proprietor of stock'.[4] Profit

[1] Adam Smith says that in the original state of things 'the whole produce of labour belongs to the labourer; and the quantity of labour commonly employed in acquiring or producing any commodity is the only circumstance which can regulate the quantity of labour which it ought commonly to purchase, command, or exchange for'. After the original state of things has passed away, however, 'in exchanging the complete manufacture either for money, for labour, or for other goods, over and above what may be sufficient to pay the price of the materials and the wages of the workmen, something must be given for the profits of the undertaker of the work who hazards his stock in this adventure' (Bk. I, ch. vi, p. 22). Dr Böhm-Bawerk says that this plainly means that the capitalist's claim for interest causes a rise in the price of the product, and is paid for out of this rise – *dass der Zinsanspruch des Kapitalisten eine Steigerung des Preises der Produkte bewirkt, und aus ihr befriedigt wird.* (*Kapital und Kapitalzins*, I, p. 83; Smart, English translation, pp. 72, 73.) But Adam Smith does not really commit himself to any comparison of the price of the product in the original state of things with its price in the actual state of things. All that he means is that in the actual state of things there is a part of the produce of labour which does not go to the labourer, and so is 'over and above' the price of the materials and the wages of the workmen. The wages no longer equal the full value which is added to the raw materials by the process of manufacture, but this, surely, does not prove any rise in the value of the product. All that can be said is that the value of the produce is higher now compared with the wages necessary to produce it than it was in the original state of things, or, to put the same thing in other words, wages are lower now compared with the whole produce than they were in the original state of things.

[2] Bk. II, ch. iv, p. 155. [3] *Public Wealth*, p. 155. [4] *Ibid.*, p. 158.

arises, he thinks, because the capital which yields the profit supplants labour, or does what human labour could not do. In short, profit exists because capital performs a useful service; the payment of profit is to be put on the same basis as the payment of wages. The owner of capital gets a part of what would have been got by the labourers supplanted or dispensed with. He cannot get more, or the labour would be employed instead of the capital. He often, however, in consequence of competition, gets less. Lauderdale thus illustrates his theory:

> 'Supposing, for example, one man with a loom should be capable of making three pair of stockings a day, and that it should require six knitters to perform the same work with equal elegance in the same time, it is obvious that the proprietor of the loom might demand for making his three pair of stockings the wages of five knitters, and that he would receive them; because the consumer, by dealing with him rather than the knitters, would save in the purchase of the stockings the wages of one knitter. But if, on the contrary, a stocking-loom was only capable of making one pair of stockings in three days (as, from the hypothesis that three pair of stockings could be finished by six knitters in one day, it follows that one knitter would make a pair of stockings in two days) the proprietor of the loom could not dispose of his stockings, because he would be obliged to charge one day's wages more than was paid to the knitters, and the machine, though it executed the stockings in the greatest perfection, would be set aside as useless merely because incapable of supplanting any portion of labour.'[1]

The example shows clearly that the owner of capital receives a profit because his capital is useful. If the machine supplants no labour, and is therefore of 'no use', its owner will receive no profit on it. This is the lower limit. The upper limit, on the other hand, is the amount for which the produce could be obtained without the aid of the capital. If one man working with the loom, and repairing it when repairs are necessary,[2] can do as much as six without the loom, the profit obtained by the owner of the loom may come up to, but cannot exceed the wages of five men; if one man with the loom can do exactly as much as one man without the loom, the loom is absolutely worthless, and will bring in nothing to its owner, even if it be used; if one man working with the loom cannot do as much as one man without the loom, the loom will certainly not be used.

Malthus, like Lauderdale, considers that profits are the remunera-

[1] *Public Wealth*, pp. 165, 166.

[2] Dr Böhm-Bawerk (*Kapital und Kapitalzins*, I, p. 170; Smart, English translation, *Capital and Interest*, p. 146) complains that Lauderdale has said nothing about the depreciation of the machine. From the fact that he says nothing about it, we may conclude that he tacitly assumes, as he is entitled to assume if he chooses, that there is no depreciation, that the one man who works the loom also replaces such parts of it as wear out at his own expense, and during his working hours. The sharp distinction which Dr Böhm-Bawerk draws between the labour of working a machine and the labour of maintaining it in good condition corresponds with nothing in nature, and does not add clearness to the subject.

tion of capital, just as wages are the remuneration of labour. Of the three different conditions which must be fulfilled in order that any commodity should continue to be brought to market,

> 'The second condition to be fulfilled is that the assistance which may have been given to the labourer from the previous accumulation of objects which facilitate future production, should be so remunerated as to continue the application of this assistance to the production of the commodities required. If by means of certain advances to the labourer of machinery, food, and materials previously collected, he can execute eight or ten times as much work as he could without such assistance, the person furnishing them might appear, at first, to be entitled to the difference between the powers of unassisted labour and the powers of labour so assisted. But the prices of commodities do not depend upon the irintrinsic utility, but upon the supply and the demand. The increased powers of labour would naturally produce an increased supply of commodities; their prices would consequently fall; and the remuneration for the capital advanced would soon be reduced to what was necessary, in the existing state of the society, to bring the articles to the production of which they were applied to market. With regard to the labourers employed, as neither their exertions nor their skill would necessarily be much greater than if they had worked unassisted, their remuneration would be nearly the same as before, and would depend entirely upon the exchangeable value of the kind of labour they had contributed, estimated in the usual way by the demand and the supply. It is not, therefore, quite correct to represent, as Adam Smith does, the profits of capital as a deduction from the produce of labour. They are only a fair remuneration for that part of the production contributed by the capitalist, estimated exactly in the same way as the contribution of the labourer.'[1]

This amounts to saying that labour can produce more when it has the use of capital, and that profits are the amount which the owner of the capital receives in exchange for the advantages obtained in production by the use of the capital. It recognizes that the amount received by the capitalists is not the whole amount which is due to the existence of the capital, but only a part of this amount. For instance, if the income of England, without any capital, would be but 1 instead of 100, it does not follow that the whole $\frac{99}{100}$ are profits at present.

The weak point in the explanation of profits given by Lauderdale and Malthus is that, while they show clearly enough that the existence and use of capital is an advantage to production, and that the whole advantage cannot be reaped by the capitalist, they fail to show why the advantage has to be paid for at all, why the 'services' of capital are not like those of the sun, gratuitous.

Ricardo, who knew very well what profits meant in the concrete, was little interested in the abstract question of their nature and origin. He gives no definition of the term, and nowhere formally expresses

[1] *Political Economy*, 1st ed., pp. 80, 81.

any opinion on the subject. It seems clear, however, that with him, Lauderdale's theory had gone for nothing. In reading his works, we find ourselves again starting from Adam Smith's standpoint. Profits again cease to have anything to do with the 'productive power of capital', or the advantage which the use of capital may be in production. But while Adam Smith treated them as a deduction from the natural recompense of labour, Ricardo looks on them rather as a surplus of produce over and above natural wages. The surplus exists, according to him, because the worst land actually under cultivation, or rather the least productive agricultural labour employed, returns more produce than is required to pay wages. It always will exist, because the population or amount of labour employed, and consequently the productiveness of the least productive agricultural labour, depend on the amount of capital, and capital never will be accumulated to such an extent as to reduce the productiveness of the least productive agricultural labour so low that the produce would only suffice to pay the wages. The motive for accumulation will 'diminish with every diminution of profit, and will cease altogether' when the profits are so low as not to afford the farmer and the manufacturer 'an adequate compensation for their trouble, and the risk which they must necessarily encounter in employing their capital productively'.[1]

The justice of profits had scarcely been denied, and the claim of the labourer to the whole produce of labour, which afterwards became, for a time at least, the basis of the socialist movement, had not been very loudly asserted in 1821, but in James Mill's *Elements* some apprehension of the approaching storm may be detected. Ricardo, for free trade purposes, had endeavoured to induce the farmer to stand shoulder to shoulder with the manufacturer and the merchant in their fight against the landlords. James Mill was willing to second his efforts in this direction, but also showed a desire to strengthen the position of the capitalist against the labourer by justifying the existence of profits.

After dividing 'the persons who contribute to production' into the two classes of labourers and capitalists, 'the one the class who bestow the labour, the other the class who furnish the food, the raw material, and the instruments of all sorts, animate or inanimate, simple or complex, which are employed in producing the effect', he declares that each of these classes 'must' have their share of the commodities produced, and that the capitalist 'expects' a share: raw material and tools are provided for the labourer by the capitalist, and 'for making this provision the capitalist, of course, expects a reward'.[2] Here there is obviously some tendency to assimilate, so far as possible, the position of the capitalist with that of the labourer. Later on, James Mill tries not merely to assimilate the effects produced by capital and by

[1] 1st ed., p. 136; 3rd ed. *Works*, p. 68.

[2] 1st ed., pp. 8-11, 24.

labour, but to identify them. The 'quantity in which commodities exchange for one another' depends, according to him, upon cost of production. Now cost of production, he says, appears at first sight to consist 'in capital alone', by which he seems to mean capital and the profit upon the capital, since he immediately proceeds to say:

> 'The capitalist pays the wages of his labourer, buys the raw material, and expects that what he has expended shall be returned to him in the price with the ordinary profits upon the whole of the capital employed. From this view of the subject it would appear that cost of production consists exclusively in the portion of capital expended, together with the profits upon the whole of the capital employed in effecting the production.'[1]

But, he explains, the 'first capital must have been the result of pure labour'; its value must consequently have been 'estimated by labour', and so also must the value of later capitals created by the aid of the first capital; and 'if the value of capital must be determined by labour, it follows upon all suppositions that the value of all commodities must be determined by labour'. He concludes, therefore, that the answer to the question with which he set out, 'What determines the quantity in which commodities exchange for one another?' is nothing but 'Quantity of labour'.[2] He seems to have forgotten that in the apparent cost of production he had included not only the capital expended, but also 'the profits upon the whole of the capital employed'. The explanation of the oversight is that he was led away from a close consideration of the question as to what determines the quantity in which commodities exchange for one another by a desire to refute the theory put forward by Torrens, to the effect that after the labourers and the capitalists become two different classes, 'it is always the amount of capital or quantity of accumulated labour, and not, as before this separation, the sum of accumulated and immediate labour, expended on production, which determines the exchangeable value of commodities'.[3] Now into this controversy the question of profits does not enter. Torrens was talking of the 'natural price' of commodities, and he considered that profits are a surplus created during the process of production, which is not included in 'natural price', though it is included in 'market price'. Market price, he says, will exceed natural price by the customary rate of profit,[4] and after laying this down, he asserts in the coolest manner, 'Things equal in natural price will also, upon the average, be equal in market price'.[5] He assumes, in fact, that profit is an addition of a certain percentage to the 'cost of production', or, as he calls it, 'natural price'. James Mill, in refuting him, insensibly adopted the same assumption. If the cost of produc-

[1] *Ibid.*, p. 70.
[2] *Ibid.*, pp. 72, 73.
[3] *Production of Wealth*, pp. 39, 40.
[4] *Ibid.*, p. 51.
[5] *Ibid.*, p. 55.

tion of A is £100 of 'capital expended', and that of B is £200 of 'capital expended', 1 B will be worth 2 A, so long as an equal percentage is added for profit to the £100 and the £200.

If it be decided, no matter by what illogical arguments, that 'cost of production regulates the exchangeable value of commodities',[1] and that 'the exchangeable value of all commodities is determined by quantity of labour',[2] it is very natural to infer that cost of production must consist of labour alone, that as the remuneration of labour is wages, the whole of the commodity or produce must be resolvable into wages alone, and therefore, that if a part of the produce is profits, profits must be wages. M'Culloch seems to have been the first to draw this inference. He boldly asserted in the *Encyclopædia Britannica* Supplement (1823), that 'the profits of stock are only another name for the *wages of accumulated labour*'.[3] James Mill promptly adopted the idea. The second edition of his *Elements* (1824) contains an addition to the chapter on 'What determines the quantity in which commodities exchange for one another?' In this he says, 'there is one phenomenon which is brought to controvert' the conclusion that quantity of labour determines the proportion in which commodites exchange for one another:

> 'It is said that the exchangeable value of commodities is affected by time, without the intervention of labour; because when profits of stock must be included, so much must be added for every portion of time which the production of one commodity requires beyond that of another. For example, if the same quantity of labour has produced in the same season a cask of wine and twenty sacks of flour, they will exchange against one another at the end of the season; but if the owner of the wine places the wine in his cellar and keeps it for a couple of years, it will be worth more than the twenty sacks of flour, because the profits of stock for the two years must be added to the original price. Here, it is affirmed, there has been no new application of labour, but here there is an addition of value; quantity of labour, therefore, is not the principle by which exhangeable value is regulated.'[4]

To the ordinary mind the objection appears perfectly sound, but James Mill denies that there has been no new application of labour:

> 'To this objection', he says, 'I reply that it is founded upon a misapprehension with respect to the nature of profits. Profits are in reality the measure of quantity of labour; and the only measure of quantity of labour to which, in the case of capital, we can resort. This can be proved by the most rigid analysis.'[5]

The 'rigid analysis' consists in showing that the owner of a machine used for profit gets back the value of the machine in the shape of an annuity 'fixed by the competition of the market, and [*sic*] which is

[1] James Mill, *Elements*, 1st ed., p. 69.
[2] *Ibid.*, p. 73.
[3] Art. *Political Economy*, p. 263.
[4] Pp. 94, 95.
[5] P. 95.

therefore an exact equivalent for the capital sum'. The capital value was settled by the quantity of labour expended on the machine, and so each year's annuity is settled by the quantity of labour expended:

> 'Capital is allowed to be correctly described under the title of hoarded labour. A portion of capital produced by 100 days' labour is 100 days' hoarded labour. But the whole of the 100 days' hoarded labour is not expended when the article constituting the capital is not worn out. A part is expended, and what part?'[1]

Ordinary persons consider that an article is half-worn out when it has suffered half the use that it is capable of sustaining before it is entirely worn out; for example, if a carpet will last six years, it is half worn out when it has been in use for three years. If, then, a carpet were really 'hoarded labour', instead of a woollen fabric used for covering floors, we might say that half the hoarded labour had been consumed at the end of three years. James Mill, however, answers the question what part of the hundred days' hoarded labour is expended very differently:

> 'Of this', he says, 'we have no direct, we have only an indirect measure. If capital paid for by an annuity is paid for at the rate of 10 per cent, one-tenth of the hoarded labour may be correctly considered as expended in one year.'[2]

Now by this he cannot mean that one-tenth of the hundred days' labour expended in making the machine may be correctly considered as expended in one year, for this would lead to an absurd result. Suppose, for example, that the machine is a new cut for a brook, which will last an unlimited time without any repairs. A thousand times ten days is ten thousand days, so at the end of a thousand years ten thousand days' labour would have been expended, according to James Mill, although the machine only cost one hundred days. Suppose again, that the machine is one which will last only six years; then the capitalist will get for six years (in order to obtain his 10 per cent) the value of about twenty-three days' labour per annum, ten for profit and thirteen for depreciation. Six times 23 is 138, so here again the total 'labour expended' amounts to more than the whole labour expended in making the machine. And it is obvious that this is always the case when there are any profits.

Mill's labour expended is, in fact, not the original labour at all, but new labour somehow performed by the machine. If, he says, a commodity were made wholly by a machine which required no attendance and no repairs, its price would entirely consist of profits:

> 'But it would surely be absurd to say that labour had nothing to do in creating the value of such a commodity, since demonstratively it is labour which gives to it the whole of its value; and if it could be got

[1] Pp. 96, 97. [2] P. 97.

> without labour it would have no value at all. It is hoarded labour, indeed, not immediate labour, which has created its value. But as immediate labour creates value in proportion to the quantity of it applied, so also does hoarded labour; nor is there any other principle upon which it can be conceived to do so. If there are two machines of the nature supposed above, the one of which is 100 days' hoarded labour, the other 200, the day's produce of the one will be twice the value of the day's produce of the other. Why? Because twice the quantity of labour has been applied to it. The case is precisely the same when what they call allowance for time is taken into account. If the 100 days' hoarded labour is applied for two days, its produce will be equal in value to one day's produce of the 200 days' hoarded labour. Why? Because 100 days' hoarded labour applied for two days is equal in quantity to 200 days applied for one day.'[1]

M'Culloch, however, was not to be outdone. In his *Principles of Political Economy* (1825) he finds it impossible to see any important distinction between wages and profits. Profits might be called the wages of accumulated labour, and wages might be called the profits of 'the proprietors of the machine called man, exclusive of a sum to replace the wear and tear of the machines, or, which is the same thing, to supply the place of the old and decayed labourers with new ones'.[2] A tree now worth £25 may have been planted a hundred years ago at an expense of one shilling; its value, according to M'Culloch, is entirely due to labour. The original shillingsworth of labour was no doubt a trifling amount, but then, as capital or accumulated labour, was no doubt a trifling amount, but then, as capital or accumulated labour, it has been a whole century at work, and the annual produce has been saved up.[3] Similarly, when certain kinds of wine acquire increased value by being kept, this is simply due to the fact that the capital or accumulated labour embodied in the wine has been at work. Some wines do not improve by keeping; in these the capital has not worked, or rather its labour is misdirected or thrown away.[4] This being so, we may conclude that the reason why the inanimate labourers called capital are able to bring in a remuneration, not to themselves, but to their owners, is simply that they produce something. James Mill, in his third edition (1826), endeavoured to explain the rise in the value of the stored-up wine as follows:

> 'It is no solution to say that profits must be paid; because this only brings us to the question, why must profits be paid? To this there is no answer but one, that they are the remuneration for labour; labour not applied immediately to the commodity in question, but applied to it through the medium of other commodities, the produce of labour. Thus a man has a machine, the produce of 100 days' labour. In apply-

[1] P. 98. [2] P. 319. [3] Pp. 316, 317.

[4] Pp. 314–316. In the 2nd ed. (1830) all this matter is omitted, though M'Culloch still asserts that 'the profits of capital are only another name for the wages of accumulated labour' (p. 355).

ing it the owner undoubtedly applies labour, though in a secondary sense, by applying that which could not have been had but through the medium of labour. This machine, let us suppose, is calculated to last exactly 10 years. One-tenth of the fruits of 100 days' labour is thus expended every year; which is the same thing, in the view of cost and value, as saying that 10 days' labour have been expended. The owner is to be paid for the 100 days' labour which the machine costs him at the rate of so much per annum; that is, by an annuity for ten years equivalent to the original value of the machine. It thus appears that profits are simply remuneration for labour. They may, indeed, without doing any violence to language, hardly even by a metaphor, be denominated wages: the wages of that labour which is applied, not immediately by the hand, but mediately by the instruments which the hand has produced. And if you may measure the amount of immediate labour by the amount of wages, you may measure the amount of secondary labour by that of the return to the capitalist.'[1]

These absurd doctrines show the danger of trying to solve economic problems by analysing the constituents of the value of a commodity. Had James Mill and M'Culloch kept before them the idea that the whole produce or income of a country consists of three shares – wages, profit, and rent, they would never have endeavoured to explain why profits are paid by asserting that profits are wages. No amount of confused reasoning about value can get over the fact that every year a large portion of the income of the community is received by certain persons not as remuneration for labour, nor as rent of land. If profits are remuneration for labour, we must ask, Whose labour? Not that of the capitalists, for *qua* capitalists they do not labour. Not that of the labourers of previous years who created the capital, or some of it, because these were all paid their wages at the time.

Senior was too able a man to try to make profits into wages, but he was desirous of showing that profits, like wages, are the remuneration of something, and hit on the idea that they are the remuneration of the conduct or the sacrifice involved in 'asbtinence'. 'By the word abstinence', he says, 'we wish to express that agent distinct from labour and the agency of nature, the concurrence of which is necessary to the existence of capital, and which stands in the same relation to profit as labour does to wages'.[2] And again: 'The words capital, capitalist, and profit' 'express the instrument, the person who employs or exercises it, and his remuneration; but there is no familiar term to express the act, the conduct, of which profit is the reward, and which bears the same relation to profit which labour does to wages. To this conduct we have already given the name of abstinence'.[3] No suspicion ever seems to have crossed his mind that possibly the conduct of which profit is the 'reward' has no name because it has no existence.

[1] Pp. 102, 103.

[2] *Political Economy*, 8vo ed., p. 59.

[3] *Ibid.*, p. 89.

When he has once got a name for this imaginary conduct, all is plain sailing. If any profits are obviously not the reward of abstinence, all that is required is to say that they are not profits but rent. As we have already seen,[1] Senior avails himself very freely of this expedient, consciously or unconsciously excluding from profits the income from all inherited property. He thus makes abstinence co-extensive with saving. A comical result is that a millionaire who saves £30,000 a year, and spends £10,000 on himself, is more abstinent than a clerk who saves £10 a year and spends £100 on himself. Senior goes very near admitting this when he says that 'among the different classes of the same nation those which are the worst educated are always the most improvident, and consequently the least abstinent'.[2] By the 'worst educated' he means to indicate the class which is also the poorest.

Thus his theory does not really take us beyond the proposition that capital is the result of saving, and that people would not save if no income could be obtained from savings. Granting this to be true, it does not explain why an income can be obtained from savings. The train of thought in Senior's mind evidently was that labour is disagreeable, and is therefore rewarded; abstinence is also disagreeable, and it also is therefore rewarded. He took it for granted that the reason why labour is rewarded is that it is disagreeable. Here he was wrong. Labour is rewarded not because it is disagreeable but because it produces wealth. If every kind of labour were always most agreeable, it would still produce wealth, and still receive at least a portion of this wealth as its reward.

Senior is at least entitled to the credit of having seen that profits had not been satisfactorily explained, and of having made an attempt to supply the want. J. S. Mill, on the other hand, seems to have been totally unaware that anything was lacking. He begins by adopting Senior's explanation of the existence of profit. 'As the wages of the labourer', he says, 'are the remuneration of labour, so the profits of the capitalist are properly, according to Mr Senior's well-chosen expression, the remuneration of abstinence.' Then he throws in a little of his own peculiar and unfounded notion, that all capital is consumed.[3] 'They are what he', that is, the capitalist, 'gains by forbearing to consume his capital for his own uses, and allowing it to be consumed by productive labourers for their uses.' We must say, then, that the owner of a steam-engine gets his profit by forbearing to consume the engine for his own uses, and allowing it to be consumed by productive labourers for their uses. What are we to say as to the profit obtained by a corn merchant who retains corn in his possession from one harvest to near the next, in order to supply the consumption of

[1] Above, pp. 196–199. [2] *Political Economy*, 8vo ed., p. 60.
[3] See above, pp. 104, 105.

landlords or unproductive labourers, it is difficult to imagine. How can he be said to have allowed the corn to be consumed by productive labourers for their uses? 'For this forbearance', Mill continues, 'he' (the capitalist) 'requires a recompense.' Possibly; most of us will require or ask for a recompense on every occasion when there is the least chance of getting one, but why is it that he succeeds in getting it? Instead of asking this question, Mill seems to be struck by the question, 'Does he get a recompense?'

> 'Very often in personal enjoyment he would be a gainer by squandering his capital, the capital amounting to more than the sum of the profits which it will yield during the years he can expect to live. But while he retains it undiminished, he has always the power of consuming it if he wishes or needs; he can bestow it upon others at his death; and in the meantime he derives from it an income which he can, without impoverishment, apply to the satisfaction of his own wants or inclinations.'[1]

Lower down, however, in controverting the opinion that profits depend on prices, or on purchase and sale, he finds it necessary to return to the subject:

> 'The cause of profit is that labour produces more than is required for its support. The reason why agricultural capital yields a profit is because human beings can grow more food than is necessary to feed them while it is being grown, including the time occupied in constructing the tools and making all other needful preparations; from which it is a consequence, that if a capitalist undertakes to feed the labourers on condition of receiving the produce, he has some of it remaining for himself after replacing his advances.... We thus see that profit arises not from the incident of exchange, but from the productive power of labour; and the general profit of the country is always what the productive power of labour makes it, whether any exchange takes place or not. If there were no division of employments there would be no buying or selling, but there would still be profit. If the labourers of the country, collectively, produce twenty per cent more than their wages, profits will be twenty per cent, whatever prices may or may not be.'[2]

In this passage J. S. Mill is evidently looking at the question simply from the Ricardian standpoint. Profits appear to be a mere surplus over and above wages, and a surplus which has nothing whatever to do with any service or usefulness of capital. The clear explanation of Lauderdale, who knew that profits are obtained because the same amount of labour produces more when it has the use of capital than when it has not, and the confused attempts of M'Culloch and James Mill to identify profits with wages, have alike gone for nothing.

§ 5. *The Origin and Cause of Rent*

As we have already seen, Adam Smith made no attempt to confine

[1] *Principles*, Bk. II, ch. xv, § 1; 1st ed., vol. i, p. 477; Peoples ed., p. 245 *a*.
[2] *Ibid.*, Bk. II, ch. xv, § 5; People's ed., p. 252; not in 1st ed.

the meaning of the rent of land to so much of the periodical payments commonly called rent as may be left after deducting all that can be considered due to the investment of capital in the soil. In treating of the nature of rent, he finds it necessary to explain that the whole of rent is not due to the investment of capital. This he proves by adducing the fact that landlords demand a rent even for land which is altogether unimproved. When rent is paid for the opportunity of gathering kelp on the sea-shore, or for fishing round the Shetland Islands, it is paid not only for something unimproved, but for something which 'is altogether incapable of human improvement'. The rent of land is therefore, he concludes, something different from profits; 'it is not at all proportioned to what the landlord may have laid out upon the improvement of the land, or to what he can afford to take', but is 'naturally a monopoly price'.[1]

As to why the landlord gets a monopoly price or more than the ordinary profit on any capital that may have been invested, Adam Smith is unusually obscure. In the chapter on the 'Component parts of the price of commodities', he says:

> 'As soon as the land of any country has all become private property, the landlords, like all other men, love to reap where they never sowed, and demand a rent even for its natural produce. The wood of the forest, the grass of the field, and all the natural fruits of the earth, which when land was in common, cost the labourer only the trouble of gathering them, come, even to him, to have an additional price fixed upon them. He must then pay for the licence to gather them; and must give up to the landlord a portion of what his labour either collects or produces. This portion, or what comes to the same thing, the price of this portion, constitutes the rent of land, and in the price of the greater part of commodities makes a third component part.'[2]

Here the demand of the landlord for a share of the produce seems to have the effect of adding something to what would otherwise be the price of the greater part of commodities, but in the chapter on Rent Adam Smith says, either in explanation or contradiction of this passage, that rent

> 'enters into the composition of the price of commodities in a different way from wages and profit. High or low wages and profit are the causes of high or low price; high or low rent is the effect of it. It is because high or low wages and profit must be paid in order to bring a particular commodity to market that its price is high or low. But it is because its price is high or low, a great deal more, or a very little more, or no more, than what is sufficient to pay those wages and profit, that it affords a high rent, or a low rent, or no rent at all.'[3]

Looking on rent so much more as a part of the price of commodities than as a part of the produce of land, Adam Smith was led into

[1] Bk. I, ch. xi, pp. 66, 67 *a*.
[2] Bk. I, ch. vi, p. 23 *a*.
[3] Bk. I, ch. xi, p. 67 *a*.

an inquiry as to what commodities have rent as a part of their price, instead of as to what sort of land yields rent. The fact that the rent of the land on which any particular kind of produce is grown varies with its fertility and situation, he treats as an obvious commonplace, which needs little or no development.[1]

Food for man, he maintains, always and necessarily affords some rent to the owner of the land on which it is grown. Other sorts of produce sometimes may and sometimes may not. The reasoning by which he tries to prove that food always contains rent in its price, or always yields a rent, is, as might be expected, not of a very convincing kind:

> 'As men,' he says, 'like all other animals, naturally multiply in proportion to the means of their subsistence, food is always more or less in demand. It can always purchase or command a greater or smaller quantity of labour, and somebody can always be found who is willing to do something in order to obtain it.'[2]

Now this statement is quite as true of most other commodities as it is of food. If anything it is rather more true of most other commodities than of food, for, as Adam Smith himself observes, 'the desire of food is limited in every man by the narrow capacity of the human stomach, but the desire of the conveniences and ornaments of building, dress, equipage, and household furniture, seems to have no limit or certain boundary'.[3] Circumstances can be conceived in which the Koh-i-noor diamond would not exchange for a small quantity of bread, but circumstances can not only be conceived, but are constantly occurring, in which a great quantity of food is thrown away because it is unsaleable; because, in fact, no one 'can be found who is willing to do something in order to obtain it'. In ordinary circumstances, metals, clothes, and houses are just as much always more or less in demand as food; they can always purchase or command a greater or smaller quantity of labour, and somebody can always be found who is willing to do something in order to obtain them. Regardless of this, Adam Smith, after a short parenthesis, continues:

> 'But land in almost any situation produces a greater quantity of food than what is sufficient to maintain all the labour necessary for bringing it to market in the most liberal way in which that labour is ever maintained. The surplus, too, is always more than sufficient to replace the stock which employed that labour, together with its profits.'

This is only a verbose method of asserting that land 'in almost any situation' will produce more food than is required for paying the wages of the labourers and the profits of the capitalist who cultivate it. 'Something, therefore,' Adam Smith concludes, 'always remains for a rent to the landlord.' In order to give definiteness to his assertion about land 'in almost any situation', he goes on to observe that:

[1] Pp. 67, 68. [2] P. 67 *b*. [3] P. 75 *b*.

> 'The most desert moors in Norway and Scotland produce some sort of pasture for cattle, of which the milk and the increase are always more than sufficient, not only to maintain all the labour necessary for tending them, and to pay the ordinary profit to the farmer or owner of the herd or flock, but to afford some small rent to the landlord.'[1]

Among the products of land which do not always afford a rent to the landlord, Adam Smith seems to have given the chief place to wool, skins, timber, stone, and minerals. Wool and skins are necessarily produced along with meat, and so, he says, when food consists almost entirely of the flesh of animals, there is such a superabundance of these articles, that they are worth little or nothing, and cannot afford a rent to the landlord.[2] This is a reasonable, but not strictly accurate view. If the landlord already has a rent from the food, the addition of the wool and skins to the produce should afford him some additional rent, even if a very small one. As to timber, stone, and minerals, Adam Smith says that in many parts of Scotland good stone quarries afford no rent, and that in some places the landlord generally gives away timber for building houses 'to whoever takes the trouble of asking it',[3] while coal and other mines, he thinks, are sometimes too barren, and sometimes too far removed from the market to pay more than Wages or profits. There thus appears to be a separate reason why each of the different classes of products other than food do not resemble food in always affording a rent to the landlord. Adam Smith's explanations do not amount to much more than a statement that the value of the produce of labourers who produce food is always more than sufficient to pay their wages, and that this sometimes is, and sometimes is not, the case with the value of the produce of labourers who produce other things.

The second statement is true enough, but the first is not. Adam Smith, indeed, gives away his case by only asserting that land in almost any situation produces a greater quantity of food than is sufficient to pay the wages and profits of cultivators. If there is land in any situation which cannot do this, his conclusion that something always remains for rent is incorrect. That there is such land every one knows. Adam Smith speaks of barren moors in Norway, but there is a lower degree of fertility and proximity to the market than moors in Norway. There are the Sahara and Greenland's icy mountains. Between these most barren and distant regions there are lands of every quality and situation, so that it is reasonable to assume that the worst land used in the production of food is not good enough to yield any appreciable amount of rent, but only good enough to yield the expenses of cultivation and profits on the capital employed, and a mere peppercorn to the landlord if it is cultivated by a tenant and not by

[1] P. 67 *b*. [2] Pp. 74, 75. [3] P. 75 *a*.

an owner. This was evident to James Anderson, the Aberdeenshire farmer whom we have already had occasion to quote.[1] In his *Inquiry into the nature of the Corn Laws with a view to the new Corn Bill for Scotland*, which he published in 1777, he gave a numerical example of the cost of raising a boll of oatmeal on soils of various degrees of fertility, which makes it obvious that it may be profitable to raise food from the land which yields no rent.[2] In his *Observations on the means of exciting a spirit of National Industry*, published in the same year, he explained rent as a premium paid for cultivating the more fertile soils:

> 'In every country there are various soils, which are endued with different degrees of fertility; and hence it must happen that the farmer who cultivates the most fertile of these can afford to bring his corn to market at a much lower price than others who cultivate poorer fields. But if the corn that grows on these fertile spots is not sufficient fully to supply the market alone, the price will naturally be raised in that market to such a height as to indemnify others for the expense of cultivating poorer soils. The farmer, however, who cultivates the rich spots will be able to sell his corn at the same rate in the market with those who occupy poorer fields; he will, therefore, receive much more than the *intrinsic* value for the corn he rears. Many persons will, therefore, be desirous of obtaining possession of these fertile fields, and will be content to give a certain premium for an exclusive privilege to cultivate them; which will be greater or smaller according to the more or less fertility of the soil. It is this premium which constitutes what we now call *rent*, a medium by means of which the expense of cultivating soils of very different degrees of fertility may be reduced to a perfect equality.'[3]

Quarter of a century later he was still teaching the same doctrine. 'Rent', he says in his *Recreations*, 'is in fact nothing else than a simple and ingenious contrivance for equalizing the profits to be drawn from fields of different degrees of fertility, and of local circumstances, which tend to augment or diminish the expense of culture.'[4] His answer to the question, Why is rent paid? may thus be said to be, Rent is paid for all land for which it is paid, because such land is more fertile than the worst land which, at the prices prevailing, it is profitable to cultivate. This answer is incompatible with Adam Smith's way of regarding the subject, but both Adam Smith and Anderson failed to notice the incompatibility, or did not consider it of any importance. The passage from Anderson's *Observations* occurrs in the course of a long attack upon Adam Smith's opinions on the effect of the bounty on the exportation of corn from England, but Anderson did not remark that Adam Smith's theory of rent was incorrect, and Adam Smith, who, as Professor Ingram observes,[5] can scarcely have failed to see

[1] Above, pp. 145, 146.
[2] The passage is quoted below, ch. viii, § 4.
[3] P. 376.
[4] Vol. v, p. 403.
[5] *History of Political Economy*, p. 128.

Anderson's criticism, did not amend his theory. The fact is that Anderson wrote before the time had come for regarding the question why rent is paid as an interesting and even an exciting one.

But in 1814, when every one was thinking of protection, prices, and rents, circumstances were much more favourable. In that year the question was definitely asked in David Buchanan's edition of the *Wealth of Nations*. In a note on a passage in Book I, chap. vi,[1] Buchanan observes:

> 'Dr Smith here states that the landlords, like other men, love to reap where they never sowed, and demand a rent even for the natural produce of their land. They do so. But the question is why this apparently unreasonable demand is so generally complied with. Other men also love to reap where they never sowed, but the landlords alone, it would appear, succeed in so desirable an object.'[2]

Buchanan does not succeed in satisfactorily answering his own question. The price of corn, he thinks, is settled entirely by demand and supply, and the state of demand and supply is always such that the price is sufficient to yield a surplus above the cost of production, but he does not show clearly why this should be so. He seems to have thought that it is because the supply of food is 'limited by the quantity of land which can be taken into cultivation'.[3] Rent is thus made the result of the 'monopoly' of land:

> 'The profit of a monopoly stands on precisely the same foundation as rent. A monopoly does artificially what in the case of rent is done by natural causes. It stints the supply of the market until the price rises above the level of wages and profit.'[4]

As he believed that rent existed in consequence of the scarcity of cultivable land, Buchanan, in refuting the physiocrats' theory that rent is the only taxable revenue, was naturally led to insist on the fact that if it is 'advantageous to those who receive it', it 'must be proportionally injurious to those who pay it'.[5]

This sentence appears to have had a good deal to do with the publication of Malthus's *Nature and Progress of Rent*. Malthus could not agree on the subject of rent, he tells us, either with Adam Smith or the physiocrats, and still less with 'some more modern writers', of whom he names only Say, Sismondi, and Buchanan. These writers appeared to him to 'consider rent as too nearly resembling in its nature and the laws by which it is governed the excess of price above the cost of production, which is the characteristic of a monopoly'.[6] Always favourable to the landed interest, he desired at that critical moment to give and answer to the question, Why is rent paid? which

[1] Quoted above, p. 216.
[2] Vol. i, p. 80, note.
[3] Vol. i, p. 274, note.
[4] Vol. i, p. 99.
[5] Vol. iii, p. 272.
[6] P. 2.

should be less likely to make rents odious in public estimation than Buchanan's answer – Because landlords have a monopoly.

> 'The following tract,' he says in his preface, 'contains the substance of some notes on Rent, which, with others on different subjects relating to political economy, I have collected in the course of my professional duties at the East India College. It has been my intention, at some time or other, to put them in a form of publication; and the very near connexion of the subject of the present inquiry with the topics immediately under discussion has induced me to hasten its appearance at the present moment. It is the duty of those who have any means of contributing to the public stock of knowledge not only to do so, but to do it at the time when it is most likely to be useful. If the nature of the disquisition should appear to the reader hardly to suit the form of a pamphlet, my apology must be, that it was not originally intended for so ephemeral a shape.'

At the outset of the tract itself, he says that rent

> 'has perhaps a particular claim to our attention at the present moment, on account of the discussions which are going on respecting the Corn Laws, and the effects of rent on the price of raw produce and the progress of agricultural improvement.'[1]

The question why rent is paid thus became one of practical politics.

Malthus's answer to the question is threefold. Rent, he says, is paid because (1) the land produces more than enough to maintain its cultivators; (2) the necessaries of life have a peculiar quality of 'being able to create their own demand, or to raise up a number of demanders in proportion to the quantity of necessaries produced';[2] and (3) the most fertile land is comparatively scarce. If any one of these three causes were absent, there would be no rent. First, if the whole land were such that it could not be made to produce more than a sustenance for its cultivators, there could obviously be no surplus produce for rent, however much the land might be monopolized. Secondly, if population did not increase with the increase of food, an increase in the quantity of food produced would cause the price of food to fall to its cost of production, thus again leaving no surplus for rent. Having explained this, Malthus considers himself justified in pronouncing a panegyric upon rent, without waiting for the discussion of his third cause. He inquires rhetorically if rent, far from being a mere 'transfer of value advantageously only to the landlords, and proportionably *injurious* to the consumers', is not, on the contrary,

> 'a clear indication of a most inestimable quality in the soil which

[1] The author of *An inquiry into those principles respecting the nature of demand and the necessity of consumption lately advocated by Mr Malthus*, says, 'When Mr Malthus published his *Essay on Rent*, it seems to have been partly with a view to answer the cry of "No landlords", which then "stood rubric on the walls",' (p. 108). He refers to the propaganda of Thomas Spence, the early forerunner of Mr Henry George.

[2] P. 8.

God has bestowed upon man – the quality of being able to maintain more persons than are necessary to work it. Is it not a part, and we shall see further on that it is an absolutely necessary part, of that surplus produce from the land which has been justly stated to be the source of all power and enjoyment; and without which, in fact, there would be no cities, no military or naval force, no arts, no learning, none of the finer manufactures, none of the conveniences and luxuries of foreign countries, and none of that cultivated and polished society which not only elevates and dignifies individuals, but which extends its beneficial influence through the whole mass of the people.'[1]

But he is not yet, to use a colloquial expression out of the wood, and he proceeds to make an admission, afterwards used against him with fatal effect. As to the third cause of rent, 'the comparative scarcity of the most fertile land', he speaks as follows:

'In the early periods of society, or more remarkably, perhaps, when the knowledge and capital of an old society are employed upon fresh and fertile land, this surplus produce, this bountiful gift of Providence, shows itself chiefly in extraordinary high profits and extraordinary high wages, and appears but little in the shape of rent. While fertile land is in abundance, and may be had by whoever asks for it, nobody, of course, will pay a rent to a landlord. But it is not consistent with the laws of nature, and the limits and quality of the earth, that this state of things should continue. Diversities of soil and situation must necessarily exist in all countries. All land cannot be the most fertile: all situations cannot be the nearest to navigable rivers and markets. But the accumulation of capital beyond the means of employing it on land of the greatest natural fertility and the greatest advantage of situation must necessarily lower profits; while the tendency of population to increase beyond the means of subsistence must, after a certain time, lower the wages of labour.'[2]

Then the value of food will be in excess of its cost of production, including profits, 'and this excess is rent'.

'Nor is it possible that these rents should permanently remain as parts of the profits of stock or of the wages of labour. If such an accumulation were to take place as decidedly to lower the general profits of stock, and consequently the expenses of cultivation, so as to make it answer to cultivate poorer land, the cultivators of the richer land, if they paid no rent, would cease to be mere farmers or persons living upon the profits of agricultural stock. They would unite the characters of farmers and landlords – a union by no means uncommon, but which does not alter in any degree the nature of rent or its essential separation from profits.'[3]

A little further on he repeats that the separation of rent from profits and wages is inevitable, and again launches into panegyric:

'It may be laid down, therefore, as an incontrovertible truth, that as a nation reaches any considerable degree of wealth, and any considerable fulness of population, which, of course, cannot take place without

[1] Pp. 16, 17. [2] P. 17. [3] P. 18.

a great fall both in the profits of stock and the wages of labour, the separation of rents, as a kind of fixture upon lands of a certain quality, is a law as invariable as the action of the principle of gravity. And that rents are neither a mere nominal value, nor a value unnecessarily and injuriously transferred from one set of people to another; but a most real and essential part of the whole value of the national property, and placed by the laws of nature where they are, on the land, by whomsoever possessed, whether the landlord, the crown, or the actual cultivator.'[1]

Ricardo, as a free-trader anxious for cheap corn, naturally objected to Malthus's panegyric on rent. Of Malthus' three causes of rent, the third was the only one which appealed to his mind. The first, the fact that land produces more than enough to maintain its cultivators, only makes rent possible, and does not cause it to exist; 'it is one thing to be able to bear a high rent and another thing actually to pay it. Rent may be lower in a country where lands are exceedingly fertile than in a country where they yield a moderate return'.[2] The second cause, 'that quality peculiar to the necessaries of life of being able to create their own demand, or to raise up a number of demanders in proportion to the quantity of necessaries produced,' Ricardo did not believe in. 'It is not', he says, 'the abundance of necessaries which raises up demanders, but the abundance of demanders which raises up necessaries'.[3] But the third cause, the comparative scarcity of the most fertile land, appeared to him sufficient by itself to account for rent, when taken in conjunction with the natural increase of wealth and population. In the *Essay on the Influence of a Low Price of Corn on the Profits of Stock*, he not only makes Malthus's third and least pleasant cause the only cause of rent, but also treats it in such a way as to make it appear far more unpleasant than it does in Manthus's *Inquiry*. In Malthus's *Inquiry* 'the comparative scarcity of the most fertile land', which is one of the causes of rent, is looked on as if it were a fact of which no one could explain. 'All land cannot be the most fertile, all situations cannot be the nearest to navigable rivers and markets'. The superior fertility of the best land is represented as a 'bountiful gift of Providence',[4] which results in rent. Ricardo, on the contrary, in his *Essay*, takes the most fertile and best-situated land as his starting-point, and leads his readers to deplore the niggardliness of nature in not providing more of it, which niggardliness gives rise, among other things, to rent. The tables are completely turned upon Malthus in the first four sentences of the *Essay*:

'Mr Malthus very correctly defines "the rent of land to be that portion of the value of the whole produce which remains to the owner, after all the outgoings belonging to its cultivation, of whatever kind,

[1] P. 20.
[2] *Principles*, 1st ed., p. 559; 3rd ed. in *Works*, p. 247.
[3] *Ibid.*, 1st ed., p. 560; omitted in 2nd ed. [4] Above, p. 224.

have been paid, including the profits of the capital employed, estimated according to the usual and ordinary rate of the profits of agricultural stock at the time being".

'Whenever, then, the usual and ordinary rate of the profits of agricultural stock, and all the outgoings belonging to the cultivation of land, are together equal to the value of the whole produce, there can be no rent. And when the whole produce is only equal in value to the outgoings necessary to cultivation, there can be neither rent nor profit. In the first settling of a country rich in fertile land, and [*sic*] which may be had by any one who choses to take it, the whole produce, after deducting the outgoings belonging to cultivation, will be the profits of capital, and will belong to the owner of such capital, without any deduction whatever for rent.'[1]

Malthus had always treated rent as a 'surplus' or 'excess'. Ricardo is going to treat it as a 'deduction' from something which belongs entirely to the farmer in the first instance, and would continue to belong entirely to him, if only there were a sufficient supply of fertile and well-situated land. Beginning with the case of an individual cultivating the best land at the first settlement of a country, he gives a series of hypothetical figures, in which rents are represented as arising and growing entirely a the expense of profits.[2] From these hypothetical figures he considers himself justified in concluding that:

'Rent, then, is in all cases a portion of the profits previously obtained on the land. It is never a new creation of revenue, but always part of a revenue already created. Profits of stock fall only because land equally well adapted to produce food cannot be procurred; and the degree of the fall of profits and the rise of rents depends wholly on the increased expense of production. If, therefore, in the progress of countries in wealth and population, new portions of fertile land could be added to such countries, profits would never fall, nor rents rise.'[3]

In the chapter on Rent in his *Principles* Ricardo repeated the arguments of the *Essay on the Influence of a Low Price of Corn*:

'It is only then,' he says, 'because land is of different qualities with respect to its productive powers, and because in the progress of population land of an inferior quality or less advantageously situated is called into cultivation, that rent is ever paid for the use of it.'[4]

Malthus was not convinced by Ricardo's *Essay*, nor by his chapter on Rent, nor even by the last chapter of his *Principles*, that on 'Mr Malthus's opinions on rent'. In his *Political Economy* he reprinted the most of his *Inquiry into the Nature and Progress of Rent*, and added passages in which the views objected to by Ricardo are emphatically restated:

[1] *Works*, p. 371. [2] See below, ch. vii, §§ 3, 4. [3] *Works*, p. 375.

[4] 1st ed., p. 54. In the second edition the passage begins, 'It is only, then, because land is not boundless in quantity and uniform in quality, and because in the progress', etc. (p. 51). The third edition follows the second, substituting 'unlimited' for 'boundless' (in *Works*, p. 36).

> 'In whatever way,' he says, 'the produce of a given portion of land may be actually divided, whether the whole is distributed to the labourers and capitalists or a part is awarded to a landlord, the *power* of such land to yield rent is exactly proportioned to its fertility, or to the general surplus which it can be made to produce beyond what is strictly necessary to support the labour and keep up the capital employed upon it. . . . But if no rent can exist without this surplus, and if the power of particular soils to pay rent be proportioned to this surplus, it follows that this surplus from the land, arising from its fertility, must evidently be considered as the foundation or main cause of all rent.'[1]

He finishes his chapter 'Of the Rent of Land' with the declaration that 'in every point of view, then, in which the subject can be considered, that quality of land which, by the laws of our being, must terminate in rent, appears to be a boon most important to the happiness of mankind'.[2]

The dispute between Malthus and Ricardo on this subject was perhaps one of sentiment rather than substance. Apart from sentiment, it does not really make much difference whether we choose to attribute the existence of rent to the bounty of nature in providing a certain amount of good land or to her niggardliness in not providing more of it. Later writers seem generally to have been too much concerned in investigating the causes which make rents higher at one time than at another to trouble themselves much about the question why there should be any rents at all. J. S. Mill, like Buchanan, ascribes the fact to 'monopoly'.[3]

[1] *Political Economy*, pp. 140, 141. [2] *Ibid.*, p. 239.
[3] *Principles*, Bk. II, ch. xvi, § 1; 1st ed., col. i, p. 496; People's ed., p. 255.

CHAPTER VII

PSEUDO-DISTRIBUTION

§ 1. *Wages per head, Profits per cent, and Rent per acre*

The causes which determine the magnitude of the produce of a nation's labour having been discussed under 'Production', and the nature and origin of the three great divisions into which the produce is 'distributed' having been fully considered, the next step forward would naturally be to endeavour to discover the causes which determine the proportions in which the produce is distributed between the three great divisions. In the equation, produce=wages+profits+rents, produce should now be taken as a given quantity, and the question should be to determine what settles the relative magnitude of the three terms on the other side of the equation.

Now with changes in the relative magnitude of wages, profits, and rents, as the terms must be understood in the equation, increases and decreases or rises and falls of wages, profits, and rent, understood in the ordinary sense, are, of course, by no means identical. In the equation, 'wages' means the total or aggregate of all wages, 'profits' the total or aggregate of all profits, and 'rents' the total or aggregate of all rents paid in a given length of time. If the total or aggregate of annual wages or remuneration of labour paid in the United Kingdom amounts to £1,000,000,000, the total or aggregate of profits to £400,000,000, and the total or aggregate of rent to £100,000,000, then the total ultimate produce or income must be £1,500,000,000, for £1,000,000,000+£400,000,000+£100,000,000=£1,500,000,000. But in ordinary languages, when we speak of increases and decreases of wages, profits, and rent, we mean by wages the amount paid to a single man, by profits the rate of interest or proportion which interest bears to principal, and by rent the rent of a single acre of land. This sense of the terms is obviously wholly inappropriate to the equation. We cannot tell how great the produce or income is by adding together a *per capita* wage, a percentage, and a rent per acre. It is not true that £1,500,000,000=£90 a year+3 per cent+£1 an acre. Increases or decreases of wages, profits, or rent in the one sense do not by any means necessarily correspond with increases or decreases of wages, profits, or rent in the other sense. The aggregate of wages depends on the number of workers as well as on the amount paid to each, the aggregate of profits depends on the amount of capital as well as on the rate of interest, and the aggregate of rent depends on the extent of land paying rent as well as on the amount paid per acre. And the relative or proportionate magnitude of aggregate wages, profits, and rent, which is logically the subject of Distribution, is still more remotely connected with wages *per capita*, profits per cent, and rent per acre than their absolute magnitude. A rise of wages *per capita* may be coincident with a fall in the proportion of produce devoted to wages if either the number of workers has diminished or the total produce has increased. A rise of the rate of interest may be coincident with a fall in the proportion of produce allotted to profits if either the total capital has diminished or the total produce has increased. A fall of rent per acre may be coincident with an increase in the proportion of produce allotted to rent, if either the number of acres paying rent has increased or the total produce has decreased.

But the latter part of Adam Smith's First Book is, as we have already seen,[1] primarily a theory of prices. Its last four chapters treat of wages, profit, and rent, not really because they are divisions of 'produce', but because they are parts of the prices of commodities. The 'natural price' of a commodity is represented as varying with the natural rate of each of its component parts; and the causes which increase or decrease each of these component parts, wages, profits, and rent, are discussed with a view to their effects, not upon the way in which the produce is distributed, but upon the natural price of the commodity produced. Now the variations of 'wages', 'profits', and 'rent' which affect the price of any particular commodity are not variations of aggregate wages, profits, and rent, but variations of the wages of the persons, of the profits of the capital, and of the rent of the land employed in producing it. So long as the land, the capital, and the number of persons employed remain the same, the price of the commodity and the rates of wages per head, profits per cent, and rent per acre must necessarily vary together. Consequently, though Adam Smith had declared that the whole annual produce is distributed into wages, profit, and rent, obviously meaning thereby total wages, profits, and rent, the last four chapters of Book I of the *Wealth of Nations* deal with wages per head, profits per cent, and rent per acre.

Subsequent writers, misled partly by some not unnatural confusions and partly by the fact that wages per head, profits per cent, and rent per acre are practically more interesting subjects than the division of produce between wages, profits, and rents, generally followed in Adam Smith's footsteps without troubling themselves to bring the theory of distribution into proper subordination to the theory of production. In giving a history of their doctrine it will be most convenient, in the

[1] Above, pp. 185–188.

first place, to follow the same procedure, however illogical it may be, and to postpone to a later chapter the consideration of any theories which were held as to distribution proper.

§ 2. *Variations of Wages per head*

Within the last century and a half three great theories have been held as to the causes which determine the magnitude of *per capita* wages. They may be called the Subsistence theory, the Supply and Demand theory, and the Produce theory. The basis of the subsistence theory is the fact that in order to live and labour a man must have something to live on, and the assumption that a wage-earner does not 'naturally' get more than enough to live on; the basis of the supply and demand theory is the erroneous idea that labour is a commodity, the demand for which depends on the amount of fund ready to be laid out upon it; and the basis of the produce theory is the fact that wages or earnings are a part of the produce, and therefore depend on the productiveness of industry and the amount deducted from produce per head for profits and rent. During the period covered by the present work the subsistence theory was gradually giving way to the supply and demand theory. The displacement of the supply and demand theory by the produce theory is a matter of later history.

At the time when the *Wealth of Nations* appeared, the subsistence theory reigned supreme. Though millions have died of starvation, it has always been an accepted maxim that a man must live. The undying fame which the cynic won by his inability to see the necessity shows his state of mind to have been the exception which proves the rule. The application of the maxim to wages is obvious enough. Wherever employment is not of a casual character, wages for work which occupies the whole of a man's time, and is his only means of support, will amount to at least a bare susistence. If they did not the workers would soon disappear.

It is very easy for a person who sees that wages 'must', ordinarily at any rate, amount to at least a bare subsistence, and who is not confronted with actual wages which obviously amount to much more than a bare subsistence, to slip into thinking that wages are ordinarily or naturally a bare subsistence; that is to say, are not only no less, but also no more than a bare subsistence. After reading the passages in which Quesnay shows that he thought it was frequently the case that the French peasants and labourers did not receive enough subsistence to enable them to do their work properly,[1] we are not surprised to find Turgot declaring that competition limits the workman's earnings to a bare subsistence:

[1] See, *e.g.*, *Œuvres*, ed. Oncken, p. 266.

'En tout genre de travail il doit arriver et il arrive en effet que le salaire de l'ouvrier se borne à ce qui lui est nécessaire pour lui procurer sa subsistance.'[1]

In England actual wages differed from the lowest possible wages more obviously than in France, but current discussions rather obscured the fact. The mercantilists approached the subject of wages, not from the point of view of the labourers, but from that of the export merchant. If the great object of a country should be, as they assumed, to sell goods to foreign nations for a large total sum of money, it appears at first sight to be the interest of the country that money wages should be low, at all events in certain branches of production. High wages in any particular branch seem naturally identified with a high price of the product of that branch, and if the price of the product rises, the quantity exported will be so reduced that the total money received for it will be less. It was, of course, a delusion that high wages in any particular branch of production necessarily mean a high price of the product. High wages mean high earnings per day, and not necessarily high earnings per each pound avoirdupois, or each yard of the commodity produced; to put the same thing in other words, high wages depend on the amount of the produce per man, as well as the value of each unit produced.[2] Consequently, the fact that wages are higher in some particular branch of trade in England than they are in that branch of trade in other countries is constantly found not to prevent the export of the commodity produced. The mercantilists of the first half of the eighteenth century, however, could scarcely be expected to recognize what is frequently ignored by their successors in the last decade of the nineteenth. Now the high wages which the mercantilists considered an evil were not so much high real wages as high money wages. Most of them would have had no objection whatever to the labourer receiving large quantities of bread, beef, and beer, provided that he did not get a large quantity of money. They concerned themselves about real wages so little, that they fell into the habit of regarding them as fixed, and remaining constant through all variations in the prices of the commodities on which they are expended. Consequently, it became an axiom that if the price of necessaries is raised by taxes (money) wages will rise, so that the labourer will continue to have the same real wages as before.[3] To the question, Why must the labourer have the same real wages? there came very readily the answer, He must live, of course. Now, if a person argues that taxes on the necessaries of life raise money wages because a man must live, he is very apt to assume without much further

[1] *Réflexions*, § vi. In *Œuvres*, ed. Daire, col. i, p. 10.

[2] Adam Smith explains this in the last paragraph of Bk. I, ch. viii, pp. 39 *b*, 40 *a*.

[3] See *Wealth of Nations*, Bk. iv, ch. ii, p. 204 *b*.

consideration that the converse is true, so that taking off taxes on necessaries will lower money wages.[1] When he has done this, if he is asked for a general theory of wages, he naturally answers that (money) wages depend on the price of subsistence, which, of course, implies that real wages always amount to no less and no more than a bare subsistence.

Adam Smith begins his chapter on wages with a kind of anticipation of the produce theory. 'The produce of labour', he says, 'constitutes the natural recompense or wages of labour'. In the 'original state of things which precedes both the appropriation of land and the accumulation of stock, the whole produce of labour belongs to the labourer', and if this state of things had continued, wages would have risen as labour became more productive. But somehow or other, very unfortunately for the labourer one would think, though the idea does not seem to have struck Adam Smith, the original state of things came to an end. Land was appropriated and stock accumulated 'long before the most considerable improvements were made in the productive powers of labour'.[2]

For the actual state of things Adam Smith is content, so far as ordinary circumstances are concerned, with the prevailing subsistence theory. Wages are settled by a bargain between masters and men, but 'upon all ordinary occasions' the masters 'have the advantage in dispute, and force' the men 'into a compliance with their terms'. They are able to do so because, being fewer in number, and not, like the men, hindered by the law, it is easier for them to combine, and because, though 'in the long run the workman may be as necessary to his master as his master is to him', 'the necessity is not so immediate':

> 'A landlord, a farmer, a master manufacturer, or merchant, though they did not employ a single workman, could generally live a year or two upon the stocks which they have already acquired. Many workmen could not subsist a week, few could subsist a month, and scarce any a year without employment.'[3]

However, the masters cannot force wages down below a certain point:

> 'A man must always live by his work, and his wages must at least be sufficient to maintain him. They must even upon most occasions be somewhat more; otherwise it would be impossible for him to bring up a family, and the race of such workmen could not last beyond the first generation.'[4]

[1] The author of *Considerations on Taxes*, 1765, says, 'But it is asserted "that the necessaries which the manufacturing poor consume being rendered dear by taxes, must inevitably oblige them to raise the price of their labour"; which will, of course, enhance the price of our manufactures, and injure our foreign trade. I wonder not that this opinion should prevail, as every one clearly sees that if a populace can live cheap they can afford to labour cheap; from which it is immediately concluded that they will do so' (pp. 5, 6).

[2] Bk. I, ch. viii, p. 29. [3] Bk. I, ch. viii, p. 30. [4] *Ibid.*, p. 31 *a*.

This statement of the subsistence theory is far from making it invulnerable. If the combination of masters has the power of depressing wages with which it is credited, why should it leave the labourers enough to support a family? Doubtless if it did not, then 'the race of such workmen could not last beyond the first generation'; but why should the masters of the present generation concern themselves about that? Trade rings usually adopt the motto, 'After us the deluge'. The individuals who form a combination of masters at any particular time desire to serve their own personal interests, and there is little ground for ascribing to them the enlightened corporate self-interest which might induce them to provide a stock of labourers for the next generation. That Adam Smith himself felt that his doctrine was rather weak on this point we may infer from the prominence which he gives to the irrelevant fact that wages sufficient to support such a family as is required to keep up the population are the lowest 'consistent with common humanity'.[1]

Observing that, as a matter of fact, wages are often above this rate, Adam Smith decided to restrict his subsistence theory to 'ordinary occasions',[2] or the stationary state. For the advancing and the declining state he puts forward the supply and demand theory. 'Certain circumstances' which, though the plural is used, seem to consist only of 'the increase of the revenue and stock' of the country, 'sometimes give the labourers an advantage, and enable them to raise their wages considerably above' the subsistence-for-a-family rate[3]:

> 'When the landlord, annuitant, or monied man has a greater revenue than what he judges sufficient to maintain his own family, he employs either the whole or a part of the surplus in maintaining one or more menial servants. Increase this surplus, and he will naturally increase the number of those servants.
>
> 'When an independent workman, such as a weaver or shoemaker, has got more stock than what is sufficient to purchase the materials of his own work and to maintain himself till he can dispose of it, he naturally employs one or more journeymen with the surplus, in order to make a profit by their work. Increase the surplus, and he will naturally increase the number of his journeymen.'[4]

So when the revenue and stock increase, 'the funds which are destined for the payment of wages', and, what is much the same thing, 'the demand for those who live by wages', also increase. Then 'the workmen have no occasion to combine in order to raise their wages':

> 'The scarity of hands occasions a competition among masters, who bid against one another in order to get workmen, and thus voluntarily break through the natural combination of masters not to raise wages.'[5]

[1] *Ibid.*, pp. 31 *a*, 32 *b*.
[2] *Ibid.*, p. 30 *a*.
[3] Bk. I, ch. viii, p. 31 *a*.
[4] *Ibid.*, p. 31 *b*.
[5] *Ibid.*, p. 31 *b*.

It is not, Adam Smith is careful to explain at considerable length, the actual greatness of the revenue and stock of a country which causes high wages, but their rapid increase. Even if they are very great, if they have continued the same for a considerable time, the number of labourers would have increased, so that there would be no scarcity of hands:

> 'The hands, on the contrary, would in this case naturally multiply beyond their employment. There would be a constant scarcity of employment, and the labourers would be obliged to bid against one another in order to get it. If in such a country the wages of labour had ever been more than sufficient to maintain the labourer and to enable him to bring up a family, the competition of the labourers and the interest of the masters would soon reduce them to this lowest rate which is consistent with common humanity.'[1]

'In a country where the funds destined for the maintenance of labour were sensibly decaying', the competition of workmen would reduce wages even below this level for a time, until the population was diminished 'to what could easily be maintained by the revenue and stock which remained in it'.[2]

This theory of Adam Smith, though in form it supplements his subsistence theory, in reality supersedes it. The power of the masters to depress wages to the subsistence level by combination, and their 'common humanity', which prevents them killing the goose that laid the golden eggs, by depressing them below that level, both disappear. Everything is settled by the demand and supply of labour, and subsistence appears as nothing more than a condition of the supply being equal to the demand in the stationary state. So little room is left for the subsistence theory that Adam Smith seems, towards the end of his work, to have forgotten that he had ever held it. In dealing with 'taxes upon the wages of labour' in Book v, Chapter ii, he says:

> 'The wages of the inferior classes of workmen, I have endeavoured to show in the First Book, are everywhere necessarily regulated by two different circumstances: the demand for labour, and the ordinary or average price of provisions. The demand for labour, according as it happens to be either increasing, stationary, or declining, or to require an increasing, stationary, or declining population, regulates the subsistence of the labourer, and determines in what degree it shall be either liberal, moderate, or scanty. The ordinary or average price of provisions determines the quantity of money which must be paid to the workman in order to enable him, one year with another, to purchase this liberal, moderate, or scanty subsistence.'[3]

He therefore holds that taxes on wages will raise money wages, not because the labourer must live, but because he must have the real wages to which the demand for labour entitles him.

[1] *Ibid.*, p. 32 *b*. [2] Bk. I, ch. viii, p. 33 *a*. [3] P. 390 *b*.

In order to understand the course which the discussion of the causes which determine wages took at the end of the eighteenth and beginning of the nineteenth century, it is necessary to bear in mind that the practical question of the time with regard to the condition of the wage-earning class was the effect of the Poor Law. Along with the 'theoretical' or general question, What determines wages? there was always present the practical question why the Poor Law did not benefit the labourers.

In the *Essay on the Principle of Population* Malthus made a somewhat crude attempt to show that the expenditure of a poor rate (even if levied exclusively from the rich) could not possibly benefit the poor. Their condition, he said quite truly, depends chiefly on the amount of subsistence produced, and

> 'When subsistence is scarce in proportion to the number of people, it is of little consequence whether the lowest members of the society possess eighteen pence or five shillings.'[1]

He was obliged to admit, however, that the rise in the price of provisions which would result from the lowest members of the society having more money 'might in some degree' cause an increase of the whole produce. But, he alleged, the 'fancied riches' of the larger amount of money received by the labourers would give such a 'spur' to population that 'the increased produce would be to be [*sic*] divided among a more than proportionably increased number of people'. In general he either ignored the increase of produce altogether, or minified it till it appeared not worth considering. 'The food of a country that has long been occupied, if it be increasing, increases slowly and regularly, and cannot be made to answer any sudden demends',[2] so that

> 'The poor laws of England tend to depress the general condition of the poor in these two ways. Their first obvious tendency is to increase population without increasing the food for its support. . . .
>
> 'Secondly, the quantity of provisions consumed in workhouses upon a part of the society that cannot in general be considered as the most valuable part, diminishes the shares that would otherwise belong to more industrious and more worthy members.'[3]

Among the 'palliatives' which he suggested in 1798 was that 'premiums might be given for turning up fresh land, and all possible encouragements held out to agriculture above manufactures, and to tillage above grazing'.[4] By 1800 he had discovered that to make the labourers able to pay a high price for their food was itself an encouragement to agriculture. In his *Investigation of the Cause of the present High Price of Provisions*, written in that year, he traced the high price

[1] 1st ed., pp. 76, 77.
[2] 1st ed., p. 82; 8th ed., p. 303.
[3] 1st ed., pp. 83, 84; 8th ed., p. 303.
[4] 1st ed., p. 96.

of corn chiefly to the efforts of the Poor Law authorities to allow the pauper labourers as much money as would procure the usual quantity of bread, and said that one effect of the high price had been 'to encourage an extraordinary importation, and to animate the farmer, by the powerful motive of self-interest, to make every exertion to obtain as great a crop as possible the next year'.[1] Contradicting the doctrine of the *Essay*, he spoke of the Poor Law as causing a high price, which produced 'economy, importation, and every possible encouragement to future production', and even went so far as to say:

> 'The system of the poor laws, in general, I certainly do most heartily condemn, as I have expressed in another place, but I am inclined to think that their operation in the present scarcity has been advantageous to the country.'[2]

Yet he allowed his argument about the Poor Law not increasing the quantity of food to remain even in the latest edition of the *Essay*, and that, too, although Ricardo had pointed out its erroneousness both in private conversation and correspondence.[3]

He did, however, alter another chapter of the first edition in which he contended that an increase of the income of the poor would not benefit them, because it would not increase the quantity of food produced. Adam Smith, he argued in Chapter xvi, was wrong in representing every increase of the revenue or stock of a country as an increase of the 'funds destined for the maintenance of labour'. The increase of the revenue or stock

> 'will not be a real and effectual fund for the maintenance of an additional number of labourers, unless the whole, or at least a great part, of this increase of the stock or revenue of the society be convertible into a proportional quantity of provisions; and it will not be so convertible where the increase has arisen merely from the produce of labour and not from the produce of land.'[4]

An increase in what is merely the produce of labour and not the produce of land, that is to say, an increase of manufactured produce or manufacturing capital, would, he admitted, cause an increased demand for labour, and

> 'This demand would, of course, raise the price of labour; but if the yearly stock of provisions in the country was not increasing, this rise would soon turn out to be merely nominal, as the price of provisions must necessarily rise with it.'[5]

But would not the increased price of provisions lead to a larger production of provisions?

[1] P. 20. [2] P. 19.

[3] See Ricardo's *Letters to Malthus*, ed. Bonar, p. 107 (2nd Jan. 1816). Ricardo thought Malthus had told him that he had altered the passage.

[4] *Essay*, 1st ed., p. 306; 2nd ed., p. 421.

[5] 1st ed., pp. 307, 308; 2nd ed., p. 421.

'It may be said, perhaps, that such an instance as I have supposed could not occur, because the rise in the price of provisions would immediately turn some additional capital into the channel of agriculture. But this is an event which may take place very slowly, as it should be remarked that a rise in the price of labour had preceded the rise of provisions, and would, therefore, impede the good effects upon agriculture which the increased value of the produce of land might otherwise have occasioned.'[1]

In the fifth edition these passages do not occur, though Malthus still thought it desirable to make disparaging remarks about the effects of the increase of manufacturing capital.[2]

Malthus's disciples never shared his curious habit of regarding the supply of food as fixed in some way independently of the demand for it. They were content with the general theory which they was in his work that the condition of 'the labourer' depends on his habits with regard to propagation and on the extent of the funds destined for his support. Buchanan, in a note to Adam Smith's statement that when the wealth of a country becomes stationary, 'the competition of the labourers and the interest of the masters' reduce wages to the subsistence level, remarks:

'The wages of labour are not necessarily at their lowest rate where wealth and population are stationary. In these circumstances the condition of the labourer depends partly on his own moral habits. If in poverty he is content to propagate his race, poverty will be his lot. But if he will not marry on such hard conditions, the race of labourers will decline, and wages will rise until the labourer agrees, by marrying, to supply the market with labour.'[3]

This practically makes the will of the labourers with regard to propagation the regulator of wages, and Buchanan recognizes the fact. In a summary of Malthus's doctrine he says:

'Where the labourer is content, as in China, to propagate his race at the expense of every comfort, population will increase until poverty and wretchedness become the general condition of the labouring classes. But in a community of a different character, where the habits of the labourer are improved, he will not submit to marry and rear a supply of labour on such hard conditions; and in these circumstances population can never increase so far as to diminish the rate of wages below what is necessary to maintain him in comfort. The labourer may thus be said to have the fixing of his own wages, because when the supply of food is stationary, it will depend on himself at what point to stop the supply of people.'[4]

Here Buchanan is regarding the question from the side of the 'supply of labour', and treating the 'demand for labour' as a given quan-

[1] 1st ed., p. 310; 2nd ed., slightly altered, p. 425.
[2] 5th ed., vol. iii, p. 13–20; 8th ed., pp. 372, 374.
[3] Ed. of the *Wealth of Nations*, vol. i, p. 116.
[4] *Ibid.*, vol. iv (*Observations*), p. 47.

tity. Looking at the matter from the side of demand, and treating the supply as a given quantity, he says:

> 'The price of labour, like that of every commodity which is bought and sold rises or falls with the demand; a great or a small demand being invariably followed by high or low wages. But the demand itself is regulated by certain general causes, and particularly by the state of the national stock; which being the great fund for the employment and support of labour, the demand will vary in proportion as it increases or declines,'[1]

and again,

> 'A general scarcity of work can only be remedied by increasing the funds for the support of industry; and no plan which has not this effect will in the least improve the labourer's condition.'[2]

In Mrs Marcet's *Conversations on Political Economy* (1816), further approach is made towards what is now known as the wage-fund theory, the theory that wages are determined by the relative magnitude of the labouring population and the whole or an ill-defined part of the capital of the country:

> 'CAROLINE. – What is it that determines the rate of wages?
> 'MRS B. – It depends upon the proportion which capital bears to the labouring part of the population of the country.
> 'CAROLINE. – Or in other words, to [*sic*] the proportion which subsistence bears to the number of people to be maintained by it?
> 'MRS B. – Yes.'[3]

Ricardo's *Essay on the Influence of a Low Price of Corn on the Profits of Stock* gives in an embryo form the theory of wages which he afterwards elaborated in his *Principles*. A fall in the real wages of labour, that is to say, a diminution of the amount of necessaries, conveniences, and comforts obtained by the labourer, he tells, us, will raise profits, and the rise of profits resulting from such a fall of real wages will be

> 'more or less permanent according as the price from which wages fall is more or less near that remuneration of labour which is necessary to the actual subsistence of the labourer.
>
> 'The rise or fall of wages is common to all states of society, whether it be the stationary, the advancing, or the retrograde state. In the stationary state it is regulated wholly by the increase or falling off of the population. In the advancing state it depends on whether the capital or the population advance at the more rapid course. In the retrograde state it depends on whether population or capital decreases with the greater rapidity.'[4]

'Experience demonstrates', he goes on to remark, 'that capital and population alternately take the lead, so that nothing can be positively

[1] *Ibid.*, p. 42.
[2] *Ibid.*, p. 63.
[3] Pp. 117, 118; see also p. 130.
[4] *Works*, p. 379.

laid down respecting profits, so far as wages are concerned'. Consequently he found it convenient for the purposes of the *Essay* to assume that 'capital and population advance in the proper proportion so that the real wages of labour continue uniformly the same'.[1] In the main this is obviously the supply and demand or population and capital theory, but a leaning towards the old subsistence theory can be detected in the implied proposition that when wages fall in consequence of capital increasing more slowly than population, the fall will be 'more or less permanent according as the price from which wages fall is more or less near that remuneration of labour which is necessary to the actual subsistence of the labourer'. Belief in the subsistence theory appears still more clearly in the proposition that 'the sole effect of the progress of wealth on prices independently of all improvements, either in agriculture or manufactures, appears to be to raise the price of raw produce and of labour, leaving all other commodities at their original prices, and to lower general profits in consequence of the general rise of wages'.[2] Ricardo has made no effort to prove that the effect of progress is to raise the price of labour or money wages, but takes it for granted that every one knows that what raises the price of raw produce will also raise the price of labour.

We may say, then, that the theory of the *Essay* is that real wages depend on the comparative growth of population and capital, and, or but (for it is not very clear which conjunction we should use), are not affected by the variations in the price of raw produce which are caused by changes in the difficulty of procuring the portion raised with the greatest labour.

Though Ricardo's opinions with regard to wages did not change between 1815 and 1817, it is clear that the form in which he expresses them in the chapter 'On Wages' in the *Principles*, was very much affected by the fact that in the meantime he had read Torren's *Essay on the Corn Trade*. In describing the variations to which 'the component parts of natural price' are liable, Torrens says:

> 'In the first place, there is everywhere a general and ordinary rate of wages, which is determined by the circumstances and habits of the country, and which it is found difficult permanently to alter. . . . The circumstances and habits of living prevalent in England have long determined that women in the labouring classes shall wear their legs and feet covered, and eat wheaten bread with a portion of animal food. Now, long before the rate of wages could be so reduced as to compel women in this part of the United Kingdom to go with their legs and feet uncovered, and to subsist upon potatoes, with, perhaps, a little milk from which the butter had been taken, all the labouring classes would be upon parochial aid, and the land in a great measure depopulated. Thus difficult would it be to effect such an alteration in the

[1] *Works*, p. 372. [2] *Ibid.*, p. 377.

rate of wages as would assimilate the real recompense of labour between the eastern and western parts of the same kingdom.'[1]

. . . .

'The proper way of regarding labour is as a commodity in the market. It therefore has, as well as everything else, its market price and its natural price. The market price of labour is regulated by the proportion which, at any time and any place, may exist between the demand and the supply; its natural price is governed by other laws, and consists in such a quantity of the necessaries and comforts of life, as from the nature of the climate and the habits of the country are necessary to support the labourer, and to enable him to rear such a family as may preserve in the market an undiminished supply of labour.'[2]

There is considerable vagueness about the phrase 'an undiminished supply of labour'. If the population of a country has been stationary las year, 'the supply of labour' will continue undiminished this year if the population or number of labourers remains the same this year as it was last year. But suppose that last year, and in previous years, the population or number of labourers increased 2 per cent. Will the supply of labour then continue 'undiminished' if the population ceases to increase at all? or must it continue to increase at the rate of 2 per cent per annum? Torrens, oblivious of this question, goes on to say:

'That the labourer must, usually, obtain for his work a sufficient quantity of those things which the climate may render necessary to preserve himself, and such a family as may keep up the supply of labour to the demand, in healthful existence, is self-evident.'

Anything less self-evident it is difficult to conceive. Supposing we grant that the labourer 'must' live, though we 'cannot see the necessity', why 'must' he be able to bring up such a family as may keep the supply of labour up to the demand for it? And what is keeping the supply up to the demand? What Torrens is really endeavouring to say seems to be that if the labourer does not get the wages to which he is accustomed, he will adopt a course which will reduce the supply of labour till wages rise to the level to which he is accustomed, for he proceeds:

'and when we consider that things not originally necessary to healthful existence often become so from use, and that men will be deterred from marriage unless they have a prospect of rearing their families in the mode of living to which they have been accustomed, it is obvious that the labourer must obtain for his work, not only what the climate may render necessary, but what the habits of the country, operating as a second nature, may require.'[3]

This natural price of labour varies, Torrens explains, with different climates and different habits of living. The part of the difference which depends upon differences of climate is unchangeable, and though 'it is

[1] Pp. 57, 58. [2] P. 62. [3] P. 63.

certain that a gradual introduction of capital into Ireland, accompanied by such a diffusion of instruction among the people as might give a prudential check to marriage, would raise the natural price of labour to an equality with its price in England',

> 'the part that is determined by the habits of living, and the prudential check which may exist with respect to marriage, can be effected[1] only by those circumstances of prosperity or decay, and by those moral causes of instruction and civilization which are ever gradual in their operation. The natural price of labour, therefore, though it varies under different climates, and with the different stages of national improvement, may, in any given time and place, by regarded as very nearly stationary.
>
> 'While the natural price of labour is thus steady, its market price, as has been already observed, fluctuates perpetually according to the proportion between supply and demand. The price which labour fetches in the market may often be considerably more and often considerably less, than that which from the climate and habits of living is necessary to maintain the labourer and his family. But notwithstanding these occasional variations, the natural and the market price of labour have a mutual influence on each other, and cannot long be separated. When the market price falls below the other, the labourer no longer obtaining the quantity of necessaries which climate and habit render necessary to the healthful existence of himself and family, deaths are increased; while the increasing difficulty of maintaining a family, increasing the prudential check on marriage, births are diminished; and thus, by a double operation, the level between the natural and the market price of labour is restored. On the other hand, if the market price should at any time be raised above the natural, the increased comforts enjoyed by the labourer and his family would diminish deaths, and by giving encouragement to marriage, increase births, until by a double operation, the supply of labour was augmented and its market price brought back to that natural level from which it can never permanently recede.'[2]

Ricardo, as he remarks in a note to the second edition of his *Principles*, was of opinion that 'the whole of this subject is most ably illustrated by Major Torrens'.[3] In the opening paragraphs of his chapter on Wages, he follows Torrens very closely, introducing, however, apparently unconsciously, an important modification:

> 'Labour, like all other things which are purchased and sold, and which may be increased or diminished in quantity, has its natural and its market price. The natural price of labour is that price which is necessary to enable the labourers, one with another, to subsist, and to perpetuate their race without either increase or diminution.
>
> 'The power of the labourer to support himself and the family which may be necessary to keep up the number of labourers, does not depend on the quantity of money which he may receive for wages, but on the

[1] This is not a misprint for 'affected'. Torrens has just before spoken of alterations being affected, and is under the impression that the subject of the verb is 'alterations in the part', instead of 'the part'.

[2] Pp. 64–66.

[3] P. 91; 3rd ed. in *Works*, p. 52.

quantity of food, necessaries, and conveniences become essential to him from habit which that money will purchase. The natural price of labour, therefore, depends on the price of the food, necessaries, and conveniences required for the support of the labourer and his family. With a rise in the price of food and necessaries, the natural price of labour will rise; with the fall in their price, the natural price of labour will fall.'[1]

The natural rate of wages, according to Torrens, 'consists in such a quantity of the necessaries and comforts of life as from the nature of the climate and the habits of the country, are necessary to support the labourer and to enable him to rear such a family as may preserve in the market an undiminished supply of labour'. According to Ricardo, it is 'the quantity of necessaries and conveniences become essential to him from habit', 'which is necessary to enable the labourers, one with another, to subsist and to perpetuate their race without either increase or diminution'. 'To perpetuate their race without either increase or diminution' is a far plainer phrase than 'preserve in the market an undiminished supply of labour'. As soon as Torrens's meaning became clear, his natural wages turned out to be nothing but ordinary or average wages, the wages to which the labourers are accustomed. But Ricardo's natural wages, though they are what has become essential to the labourers from habit, are also something more. They are the wages which will just, and only just, keep the population of labourers stationary. Consequently while, according to Torrens, the natural and the market price of labour 'cannot long be separated',[2] according to Ricardo they must be separated for the whole of the long period during which the population of a country may be increasing. 'However much' he says, 'the market price of labour may deviate from its natural price, it has, like commodities, a tendency to conform to it'; when market wages are greater than natural wages, 'the condition of the labourer is flourishing and happy', and he can 'rear a healthy and numerous family', so 'the number of labourers is increased', and 'wages again fall to their natural price, and indeed from a reaction sometimes fall below it', When market wages are below natural wages, the labourers' condition is 'most wretched'; 'poverty deprives them of those comforts which custom renders absolute necessaries', and 'it is only after their privations have reduced their number, or the demand for labour has increased', that 'the labourer will have the moderate comforts which the natural price of wages will afford', But

'Notwithstanding the tendency of wages to conform to their natural rate, their market rate may, in an improving society, for an indefinite period, be constantly above it; for no sooner may the impulse which an increased capital gives to a new demand for labour be obeyed, than

[1] 1st ed., pp. 90, 91; 3rd ed. in *Works*, p. 50.

[2] Above, p. 245.

another increase of capital may produce the same effect; and thus, if the increase of capital be gradual and constant, the demand for labour may give a continued stimulus to an increase of people.'[1]

So Ricardo's natural wages are not the customary wages to which Torrens supposes the labourer to be obstinately determined to adhere, but the wages which will just induce the labourers to keep up the population to its existing level and no more. Instead of being an average rate above and below which market wages are continually fluctuating, they are a minimum below which market wages cannot continue for any length of time, though they may exceed it for an indefinite period. The gloomy character which has always been attributed to Ricardo's theory of wages owes its origin chiefly to the fact that he taught that though market wages might long continue above this minimum, they have a tendency to conform to it. The tendency was a tendency downwards. He always regarded economic progress as a thing which is started with a certain amount of energy, and then gradually slackens in speed until it stops altogether. Accumulation of capital, he thought, depends on the rate of profit, the rate of profit depends on the productiveness of the least productive agricultural labour, and this declines with the progress of population. So

> 'In the natural advance of society the wages of labour will have a tendency to fall, as far as they are regulated by supply and demand; for the supply of labourers will continue to increase at the same rate, whilst the demand for them will increase at a slower rate. If, for instance, wages were regulated by a yearly increase of capital at the rate of 2 per cent, they would fall when it accumulated only at the rate of 1½ per cent. They would fall still lower when it increased only at the rate of 1 or ½ per cent, and would continued to do so until the capital became stationary, when wages also would become stationary, and be only sufficient to keep up the numbers of the actual population.'[2]

There is, however, no ground for the widespread belief that the theory, as a theory, asserts in any way that the natural rate must necessarily be very low. It does not contain any statement that the natural rate must be a bare subsistence for the labourer and a very small family. For anything it says to the contrary, commodities which are now worth £100 a week might become 'essential, from habit', and necessary to keep up the number of labourers. For, Ricardo explains,

> 'It is not to be understood that the natural price of wages, estimated even in food and ncessaries, is absolutely fixed and constant. It varies at different times in the same country, and very materially differs in different countries. It essentially depends on the habits and customs of the people. An English labourer would consider his wages under their natural rate, and too scanty to support a family, if they enabled him to purchase no other food than potatoes, and to live in no better

[1] 1st ed., p. 93; 3rd ed. in *Works*, p. 51.
[2] 1st ed., pp. 102, 103; 3rd ed. in *Works*, p. 54.

habitation than a mud cabin; yet these moderate demands on nature are often deemed sufficient in countries where "man's life is cheap" and his wants easily satisfied. Many of the conveniences now enjoyed in an English cottage would have been thought luxuries at an earlier period of our history.'[1]

If a change took place in the 'habits and customs of the people', so that they should require £100 a week instead of £1 a week in order to keep up the population, this change would counteract the tendency of wages to fall 'in the natural advance of society'. Population would not increase, and, consequently, the benefit of successive 'improvements' would all be obtained by the labourers. There is in reality nothing at all gloomy in the theory that the wages which will be paid when population ceases to increase are the natural wages to which market wages have a tendency to conform. The population of every country must cease increasing sooner or later, and the wages at present paid in the most rapidly increasing populations must consequently have a tendency to conform to what will be paid when the population ceases to increase. The important question is, What determines the rate which will just keep the population stationary? Ricardo, it is quite clear, supposed the rate to be a very low one,[2] but he does not seem to have given any serious consideration to the question of what determines it. To say that it is determined by 'habits and customs' is no contribution to knowledge.

After having taken the trouble to define and explain 'market' wages and 'natural' wages, Ricardo makes no use of the distinction. He finds the unqualified term 'wages', or 'the price of labour', sufficient for all his purposes. The remainder of his teaching with regard to real wages is of a negative rather than a positive character, as it consists of an eager and strenuous endeavour to show that when the food of the labourer rises in price, either in consequence of increasing difficulty of production or taxation, and also when wages are taxed directly, money wages will rise sufficiently to prevent the labourer's real wages from being affected.

In the chapter on Wages he says that, in spite of the tendency of real wages to fall in the natural advance of society, money wages will rise when necessaries rise in price, because if they did not 'the labourer would be doubly affected, and would soon be totally deprived of subsistence'.[3] Most, if for some unexplained reason not quite all, of the

[1] 1st ed., p. 96; 3rd ed. in *Works*, p. 52.

[2] See, for example, 1st ed., pp. 8, 9; 3rd ed. in *Works*, p. 12. 'In the same country double the quantity of labour may be required to produce a given quantity of food and necessaries at one time that may be necessary at another and a distant time; yet the labourer's reward may possibly be very little diminished. If the labourer's wages at the former period were a certain quantity of food and necessaries, he probably could not have subsisted if that quantity had been reduced.'

[3] 1st ed., p. 103; 3rd ed. in *Works*, pp. 54, 55.

additional expense is borne by the capitalist, who has to pay higher money wages. Ricardo supposes, by way of example, that the labourer's wages are £24 per annum, half of which is expended on wheat, and then gives a kind of scale in which the £24 rises to £24 14*s*, £25 10*s*, £26 8*s*, and £27 8*s* 6*d*, when the price of wheat rises from £4 a quarter to £4 4*s* 8*d*, £4 10*s*, £4 16*s*, and £5 2*s* 10*d*, so as to enable the labourer always to buy three quarters of wheat and twelve pounds' worth of other things. In the chapter 'On Profits' it is assumed as an axiom that money wages will rise in this way, except in one place where Ricardo is seized with sudden misgiving:

> 'It may be said that I have taken it for granted that money wages would rise with a rise in the price of raw produce, but that this is by no means a necessary consequence, as the labourers may be contented with fewer enjoyments. It is true that the wages of labour may previously have been at a high level, and that they may bear some reduction. If so, the fall of profits will be checked; but it is impossible to conceive that the money price of wages should fall or remain stationary with a gradually increasing price of necessaries; and therefore it may be taken for granted that under ordinary circumstances no permanent rise takes place in the price of necessaries without occasioning or having been preceded by a rise in wages.'[1]

It may well be doubted whether an objector clothed in flesh and blood would be satisfied with Ricardo's bold assertion that 'it is impossible to conceive' what he, the objector, had himself conceived. In the chapter on 'Taxes on Raw Produce', Ricardo tries to show that a tax on raw produce and on the necessaries of the labourer would raise not only the price of raw produce and necessaries, but also money wages:

> 'From the effects of the principle of population on the increase of mankind, wages of the lowest kind never continue much above that rate which nature and habit demand for the support of the labourers. This class is never able to bear any considerable portion of taxation; and consequently if they had to pay 8s per quarter in addition for wheat, and in some smaller proportion for other necessaries, they would not be able to subsist on the same wages as before, and to keep up the race of labourers. Wages would inevitably and necessarily rise.'[2]

'Keep up the race of labourers' is probably to be taken in the vague sense of Torrens's 'preserve in the market an undiminished supply of labour', rather than in the definite sense of Ricardo's own 'perpetuate their race without either increase or diminution', but in any case his meaning clearly is that the dearness of wheat would act as a new check on the growth of population if money wages did not rise to compensate the labourer for the rise of the price of necessaries. He

[1] 1st ed., p. 129; 3rd ed. in *Works*, p. 65.
[2] 1st ed., p. 199; 3rd ed. in *Works*, p. 93.

sees that among other things it may 'be objected against such a tax' 'that there would be a considerable interval between the rise in the price of corn and the rise of wages, during which much distress would be experienced by the labourer'. To this objection he answers,

> 'that under different circumstances wages follow the price of raw produce with very different degrees of celerity; that in some cases no effect whatever is produced on wages by a rise of corn; in others the rise of wages precedes the rise of corn; again, in some the effect is slow, and in others the interval must be very short.'

Certainly a rise of wages would have to 'follow' the price of raw produce with considerable 'celerity' in order to 'precede' it:

> 'Those who maintain that it is the price of necessaries which regulates the price of labour, always allowing for the particular state of progression in which the society may be, seem to have conceded too readily that a rise or fall in the price of necessaries will be very slowly succeeded by a rise or fall of wages.'[1]

A high price of provisions, he thinks, may arise from four different causes. The second of these causes, which is the only one that concerns us here, is 'a gradually increasing demand, which may be ultimately attended with an increased cost of production':

> 'When a high price of corn is the effect of an increasing demand it is always preceded by an increase of wages, for demand cannot increase without an increase of means in the people to pay for that which they desire. An accumulation of capital naturally produces an increased competition among the employers of labour, and a consequent rise in its price. The increased wages are not immediately expended on food, but are first made to contribute to the other enjoyments of the labourer. His improved condition, however, induces and enables him to marry, and then the demand for food for the support of his family naturally supersedes that of those other enjoyments on which his wages were temporarily expended. Corn rises, then, because the demand for it increases, because there are those in the society who have improved means of paying for it; and the profits of the farmer will be raised above the general level of profits till the requisite quantity of capital has been employed on its production. Whether, after this has taken place, corn shall again fall to its former price or shall continue permanently higher, will depend on the quality of the land from which the increased quantity of corn has been supplied. If it be obtained from land of the same fertility as that which was last in cultivation, and with no greater cost of labour, the price will fall to its former state; if from poorer land, it will continue permanently higher. The high wages in the first instance proceeded from an increase in the demand for labour: inasmuch as it encouraged marriage and supported children, it produced the effect of increasing the supply of labour. But when the supply is obtained, wages will again fall to their former price if corn has fallen to its former price: to a higher than the former price if the increased supply of corn has been produced from land of an inferior quality.'[2]

[1] 1st ed., pp. 202, 203; 3rd ed. in *Works*, p. 94.
[2] 1st ed., pp. 205, 206; 3rd ed. in *Works*, pp. 95, 96.

Ricardo seems here to have quite abandoned the theory of the chapter on Wages and the chapter on Profits, that money wages will be raised by the rise in the price of provisions in spite of the tendency of wages to fall in the 'natural advance of society', 'as far as they are regulated by supply and demand'.[1] The idea of the passage is that the rise of money wages which 'follows', or rather is connected with, a rise of the price of provisions, can only be produced by 'an accumulation of capital', and that all that the rise of the price of provisions does is to maintain the rise of money wages thus gained. In other words, in order to allow the rise of money wages to take place, wages, 'as far as they are regulated by supply and demand', must rise and not fall. But the new theory is even more unsatisfactory than the old. It depends entirely on the proposition laid down in the first sentence, 'When a high price of corn' – Ricardo really means a rise in the price of corn – 'is the effect of an increasing demand, it is always preceded by an increase of wages, for demand cannot increase without an increase of means in the people to pay for that which they desire'. It is difficult to conceive how a member of the Stock Exchange, to say nothing of an economist, could have committed himself to so baseless an assertion as that contained in the second clause of the sentence. We can scarcely doubt that Ricardo would have admitted that a hard frost increases the demand for water-pipes, without increasing the means of the people to pay for them. It is true, of course, that all that is necessary for his immediate argument is that the demand *for corn* should not be able to increase without an increase of the people's means of paying for it. This, however, is only a little less untrue than the more general proposition. When the population is stationary, the demand for corn is not likely to increase without an increase of the people's means of paying for it. But when the population is increasing, the demand for corn naturally increases without any increase in the people's means, and even when the people's means are decreasing. The demand for corn will surely be increased when there is an increase in the number of persons to be fed if wages are equal to what they were before, and even if they are a little less than before. Ricardo's proposition, therefore, that 'when a high price of corn is the effect of an increasing demand, it is always preceded by an increase of wages', is only true when he starts, so to speak, from a condition of things in which population is stationary. In the next sentence he seems to assume that this is the case. He speaks of 'an accumulation of capital raising wages', whereas when population is increasing, according to

[1] In the chapter 'On Profits', 1st ed., p. 133, 3rd ed. in *Works*, p. 66, he speaks distinctly of 'the rise of wages produced by the rise of necessaries'. To introduce there the idea that the rise of wages is not produced but only maintained by the rise of the price of necessaries would play havoc with the argument of the whole chapter.

his own system, an accumulation of capital more rapid than the increase of population is required in order to raise wages. Too much stress must not, however, be laid upon this, since in the next sentence but one he speaks of the rise of wages inducing and enabling the labourer to marry, whereas even when population is stationary 'the labourer', or some of him, is induced and enabled to marry. As to the connection between a rise in the price of provisions and a rise of money wages when population is already increasing, the passage tells us nothing at all.

When Ricardo wrote the chapter on Taxes on Wages he had referred to Buchanan, and found that he, at any rate, flatly denied that wages vary with the price of provisions, except, perhaps, when the labourer is 'reduced to a bare allowance of necessaries', when he would 'suffer no further abatement of his wages, as he could not on such conditions continue his race'.[1] 'The high price of provisions', Buchanan had urged,

> 'is a certain indication of a deficient supply, and arises in the natural course of things for the purpose of retarding the consumption. A smaller supply of food shared among the same number of consumers will evidently leave a smaller portion to each, and the labourer must bear his share of the common want. To distribute this burden equally, and to prevent the labourer from consuming subsistence so freely as before, the price rises. But wages, it seems, must rise along with it, that he may still use the same quantity of a scarcer commodity; and thus nature is represented as countereacting her own purposes – first raising the price of food to diminish the consumption, and afterwards raising wages to give the labourer the same supply as before.'[2]

To this Ricardo answers that deficient supply is not the sole cause of a high price of provisions. 'We are', he says, 'by no means warranted in concluding, as Mr Buchanan appears to do, that there may not be an abundant supply with a high price'. The natural price of commodities, he continues, is determined by 'facility of production'. Then, apparently failing to distinguish between a large aggregate amount of food and a large amount per head, he remarks:

> 'Although the lands which are now taken into cultivation are much inferior to the lands in cultivation three centuries ago, and therefore the difficulty of production is increased, who can entertain any doubt but that the quantity produced now very far exceeds the quantity then produced? Not only is a high price compatible with an increased supply, but it rarely fails to accompany it. If then, in consequence of taxation or of difficulty of production, the price of provisions be raised, and the quantity be not diminished, the money wages of labour will rise, for, as Mr Buchanan has justly observed, "the wages of labour consist not in money, but in what money purchases, namely,

[1] Ed. of *Wealth of Nations*, vol. iii, p. 338.
[2] *Observations*, pp. 59, 60.

provisions and other necessaries; and the allowance of the labourer out of the common stock will always be in proportion to the supply." '[1]

Of course Buchanan's case is that in consequence of difficulty of production the quantity of provisions *per capita* would be diminished, and the money wages of labour would not rise, so that 'the allowance of the labourer out of the common stock' would be less, although it would still be 'in proportion to the supply'. Nothing that Ricardo has said here is at all incompatible with it. Immediately after this passage, however, Ricardo discloses that his reason, or one of his reasons, for thinking that money wages must rise to the full amount of a 'tax on wages', which he regards much in the same light as 'difficulty of production', is that a certain amount of commodities must be given to the labourers in order to call forth the population which will, in Malthus's vague words, which he quotes with approval, satisfy 'the wants of the society respecting population'[2] – a certain amount of commodities 'will be just sufficient to support the population which at that time the state of the funds for the maintenance of labour requires':

> 'Suppose,' he says, 'the circumstances of the country to be such, that the lowest labourers are not only called upon to continue their race, but to increase it; their wages would have been regulated accordingly. Can they multiply [in the degree required] if a tax takes from them a part of their wages, and reduces them to bare necessaries?'[3]

'Bare necessaries' must presumably be taken to mean necessaries for themselves as bachelors, and not as fathers of numerous families, otherwise it would be clear that they *could* multiply in any phyiscally possible degree, though there might be a question as to whether they *would*. If the tax takes from them a part of their wages without reducing them to bare necessaries thus defined, there seems no reason why the answer 'Yes' should not be returned to the question of the first edition, 'Can they multiply?' The question, 'Can they multiply in the degree required?' must be met by the question, 'Required by what?' Ricardo answers, 'By the state of the funds for the maintenance of labour', but instead of explaining how the funds for the maintenance of labour can be said to 'require' a certain population, he goes on to explain that the imposition of a tax on wages will not alter the amount of these funds.

Ricardo's general position, with regard at any rate to the effects of increasing prices of food upon money wages, is a perfectly logical one. If the real wages of labour are determined directly by the proportion

[1] 1st ed., pp. 289, 290; 3rd ed. in *Works*, pp. 130, 131.
[2] Malthus, *Essay*, 2nd ed., p. 406; 8th ed., p. 301.
[3] 1st ed., p. 293; 2nd ed., p. 265; 3rd ed. in *Works*, p. 132. The words in brackets were added, and 'would be' was substituted for 'would have been' in the third edition.

between labourers and real capital, they obviously ought not to be directly affected by other circumstances, such as increasing difficulty in the production of food. The fact that he fails so completely to prove that money wages must rise so as to leave real wages unaffected when the price of food rises, is due to the fact that real wages are not determined by the proportion between labourers and capital.

Malthus thought that Ricardo had not realized that wages always depend on the prudential habits of the labourers with regard to propagation. As was natural in the author of the *Essay on Population*, he wished these habits to be regarded as the prime regulator of wages, not only when wages are at a low and rather unusual level, but at all times:

> 'Mr Ricardo', he says, 'has defined the natural price of labour to be "that price which is necessary to enable the labourers one with another to subsist, and to perpetuate their race, without either increase or diminution." This price I should really be disposed to call a most unnatural price; because in a natural state of things, that is, without great impediments to the progress of wealth and population, such a price could not generally occur for hundreds of years. But if this price be really rare, and, in an ordinary state of things, at so great a distance in point of time, it must evidently lead to great errors to consider the market prices of labour as only temporary deviations above and below that fixed price to which they will very soon return.'[1]

He himself would define the natural or necessary price of labour as 'that price which in the actual circumstances of the society is necessary to occasion an average supply of labourers sufficient to meet the average demand', and by this rather cloudy phrase he seems to mean nothing more or less than the actual wages which are paid in a year not marked by any exceptional circumstances. He rejects entirely the idea of a rigid level of wages, whether fixed by the amount physically necessary for subsistence or by the amount which unexplainable 'habit' renders indispensable:

> 'The condition of the labouring classes of society must evidently depend partly upon the rate at which the resources of the country and the demand for labour are increasing, and partly on the habits of the people in respect of their food, clothing, and lodging.
>
> 'If the habits of the people were to remain fixed, the power of marrying early, and of supporting a large family, would depend upon the rate at which the resources of the country and the demand for labour were increasing. And if the resources of the country were to remain fixed, the comforts of the lower classes of society would depend upon their habits, or the amount of those necessaries and conveniences without which they would not consent to keep up their numbers.
>
> 'It rarely happens, however, that either of them remain fixed for any great length of time together.'[2]

Unlike Ricardo, Malthus devotes some attention to the causes

[1] *Political Economy*, p. 247. [2] *Political Economy*, p. 248.

which make the habits of the people different at different times and places. 'The question', however, he says, 'involves so many considerations that a satisfactory solution of it is hardly to be expected'.[1] Much depends upon climate and soil, but moral causes, such as despotism, oppression, and ignorance on the one hand, and 'civil and political liberty and education' on the other, occasion differences in the amounts on which the labourer will be ready to bring up a family. Moreover, and here Malthus takes a long step towards the abandonment of the remains of the subsistence theory, the habits of the people are very generally affected by the amount of wages actually received:

> 'When the resources of a country are rapidly increasing and the labourer commands a large portion of necessaries, it is to be expected that if he has the opportunity of exchanging his superfluous food for conveniences and comforts, he will acquire a taste for these conveniences, and his habits will be formed accordingly. On the other hand, it generally happens that when the resources of a country become nearly stationary, such habits, if they ever have existed, are found to give way; and before the population comes to a stop, the standard of comfort is essentially lowered.'[2]

As to the way in which 'rapidly increasing resources' raise wages, Malthus had nothing of much importance to say. The demand for labour, he thinks, is regulated by 'the rate at which the whole value of capital and revenue of the country increases annually; because, the faster the value of the annual produce increases, the greater will be the power of purchasing fresh labour, and the more will be wanted every year'.[3] To Barton's attempt to impugn the doctrine that demand for labour depends on the increase of capital by showing that an increase of fixed capital does not imply an increased demand for labour,[5] Malthus has two answers. First, if the labour displaced by the introduction of the fixed capital cannot be employed elsewhere, the increase of fixed capital 'diminishes the value of the annual produce, and retards the increase of the capital and revenue taken together', so that capital is not increased, and the doctrine remains intact. Secondly, in general 'the use of fixed capital is extremely favourable to the abundance of circulating capital'.[3] This he seems to think is proved when he has shown that the use of fixed capital is favourable to the abundance of produce. He concludes his whole inquiry with these words:

> 'It is of the utmost importance always to bear in mind that a great command over the necessaries of life may be effected in two ways, either by rapidly increasing resources, or by the prudential habits of the labouring classes; and that as rapidly increasing resources are neither in the power of the poor to effect, nor can in the nature of

[1] *Political Economy*, p. 250. [2] *Ibid.*, pp. 248, 249.
[3] *Ibid.*, p. 261. [4] Above, pp. 114, 115.
[5] *Political Economy*, p. 261.

things be permanent, the great resource of the labouring classes for their happiness must be in those prudential habits which, if properly exercised, are capable of securing to the labourer a fair proportion of the necessaries and conveniences of life from the earliest stage to the latest.'[1]

Though James Mill has the reputation of having been the most purely 'abstract' of the 'abstract school', the section of his chapter on Distribution which treats of wages consists for the most part of a discussion of various means of raising wages. The causes which determine the magnitude of *per capita* wages are very cursorily dismissed in the first part of the section under the heading, 'That the rate of wages depends on the proportion between Population and Employment, in other words, Capital'. The dependence of wages on the proportion between population and capital is, it seems, a very simple affair. If the number of labourers increases, while the quantity of capital or of 'requisites for the employment of labour, that is, of food, tools, and material' remains the same, some of the labourers will be 'in danger of being left out of employment'. Each of them is therefore obliged to offer to work for a smaller reward:

> 'If we suppose, on the other hand, that the quantity of capital has increased, while the number of labourers remains the same, the effect will be reversed. The capitalists have a greater quantity than before of the means of employment; of capital, in short, from which they wish to derive advantage. To derive this advantage they must have more labourers than before. These labourers are all employed with other masters: to obtain them they also have but one resource – to offer higher wages. But the masters by whom the labourers are now employed are in the same predicament, and will, of course, offer higher wages to induce them to remain. This competition is unavoidable, and the necessary effect of it is a rise of wages.'[2]

He arrives at this conclusion:

> 'Universally, then, we may affirm, other things remaining the same, that if the ratio which capital and population bear to one another remains the same, wages will remain the same; if the ratio which capital bears to population increases, wages will rise; if the ratio which population bears to capital increases, wages will fall.'[3]

The insertion of the proviso, 'other things remaining the same', is truly astonishing. There is nothing about other things remaining the same in the proposition in italics at the head of the sub-section, and Mill does not make the smallest attempt to explain what happens when other things do not remain the same. Regardless of other things, he proceeds to argue that

> 'If it were the natural tendency of capital to increase faster than population, there would be no difficulty in preserving a prosperous

[1] *Ibid.*, p. 291. The Malthus of 1820 was a far more cheerful person than the Malthus of 1798.

[2] *Elements*, 1st ed., p. 27; 3rd ed., p. 43. [3] 1st ed., p. 28; 3rd ed., p. 44.

condition of the people. If, on the other hand, it were the natural tendency of population to increase faster than capital, the difficulty would be very great. There would be a perpetual tendency in wages to fall. The fall of wages would produce a greater and greater degree of poverty among the people, attended with its inevitable consequences – misery and vice. As poverty and its consequent misery increased, mortality would also increase. Of a numerous family born, a certain number only would, from want of the means of well-being, be reared. By whatever proportion the population tended to increase faster than capital, such a proportion of those who were born would die; the ratio of increase in capital and population would thence remain the same, and wages would cease to fall.'[1]

Though he does not expressly state it, James Mill seems to mean by this that when the natural tendency of population to increase faster than capital has worked in a normal manner, and had time to make itself felt, wages will fall to a level which will only afford the means of rearing a family which is not 'numerous'. 'That population has a tendency to increase faster than capital has, in most places, actually increased, is proved incontestably', he believes, by the fact that 'in almost all countries the condition of the great body of the people is poor and miserable'.[2] If capital had increased faster than population, wages would, he says, have risen (he has never proved that they had not risen), and the labourer would have been 'in a state of affluence'. For fear, however, that someone may attribute the lowness of wages to some obstacle which has prevented capital 'from increasing so fast as it has a tendency to increase', he undertakes the formal 'Proof of the tendency of population to increase rapidly', and the 'Proof that capital has a less tendency than population to increase rapidly'. To prove that population has a tendency to increase rapidly, he explains in terms which some would consider scarcely fitted for the 'school book' which he fondly imagined himself to be writing,[3] that the fecundity of the human race, when fully exercised in favourable circumstances, is much more than sufficient to counterbalance ordinary mortality, so that population has 'such a tendency to increase as would enable it to double itself in a small number of years'.[4] To prove 'that capital has a less tendency than population to increase rapidly', he begins by showing that 'the disposition in mankind to save', is 'so weak in almost all the situations in which human beings have ever been placed', as to make the increase of capital 'slow'.[5] But rapidity or slowness is a question of degree, so that it is not very convincing to say that capital must have a less tendency to increase rapidly than population because the possible increase of population may be described by the term 'rapid', and the increase of capital by the term

[1] *Elements*, 1st ed., pp. 28, 29; 3rd ed., pp. 44, 45.
[2] 1st ed., p. 29; 3rd ed., p. 45.
[3] See his Preface.
[4] 1st ed., pp. 30–34; 3rd ed., pp. 46–50.
[5] 1st ed., p. 35; 3rd ed., p. 51.

'slow'. It is, therefore, rather a relief to the reader to find that 'the proof that it is the tendency of population to increase faster than capital does not depend upon this foundation, strong as it is'. It depends on the fact that

> 'The tendency of population to increase, whatever it may be, greater or less, is at any rate an equable tendency. At what rate soever it has increased at any one time, it may be expected to increase at an equal rate if placed in equally favourable circumstances, at any other time. The case with capital is the reverse. As capital continues to accumulate, the difficulty of increasing it becomes gradually greater and greater, till finally, increase becomes impracticable.'

This is a consequence of the general rule of diminishing returns:

> 'Whether, after land of superior quality has been exhausted, capital is applied to new land of inferior quality, or in successive doses with diminished returns upon the same land, the produce of it is continually diminishing in proportion to its increase. If the return to capital is, however, continually decreasing, the annual fund from which savings are made is continually diminishing. The difficulty of making savings is thus continually augmented, and at last they must totally cease.'[1]

As there is no such thing as a general rule of diminishing returns, we need not stop to inquire whether a diminution of the return not to the whole capital, but to a given quantity or unit of capital, necessarily means a diminution of the whole annual fund from which savings are made.

Proceeding, James Mill argues that 'forcible means employed to make capital increase faster than its natural tendency would not produce desirable effects', and when he has proved this, and alleged that it is not desirable that population should increase beyond that degree of density which affords 'in perfection the benefits of social intercourse and of combined labour', he concludes:

> 'The precise problem, therefore, is to find the means of limiting births to that number which is necessary to keep up the population without increasing it. Were that accomplished while the return to capital from the land was yet high, the reward of the labourer would be ample, and a large surplus would still remain.'[2]

Quite unconsciously reducing his theory to the absurd, he adds that the limitation of the number of births, if limitation were possible, might be carried so far as to 'raise the condition of the labourer to any state of comfort and enjoyment which may be desired'.[3] Any state which may be desired!

In his *Encyclopædia* article, M'Culloch had nothing to say about wages per head, except that 'the labourer cannot work if he is not

[1] *Elements*, pp. 41, 42; 3rd ed., p. 56.
[2] *Elements*, p. 52; 3rd ed., p. 65.
[3] 1st ed., p. 53; 3rd ed., p. 57.

supplied with the means of subsistence'.[1] But in the book into which he expanded his article, he definitely put the supply and demand theory into the arithmetical form appropriate to the wage-fund theory. That wages rise when capital increases faster than population, and fall when population increases faster than capital, had become a commonplace. That the rate of wages depends on the proportion between the labouring population and 'capital', had been laid down in Mrs Marcet's *Conversations*.[2] But it was reserved for M'Culloch to give definiteness and rigidity to Mrs Marcet's doctrine by illustrating it with an arithmetical example:

> 'The capacity of a country to support and employ labourers', he asked his readers to believe, 'is in no degree dependent on advantageousness of situation, richness of soil, or extent of territory. These, undoubtedly, are circumstances of very great importance, and must have a powerful influence in determining the rate at which a people *advances* in the career of wealth and civilization. But it is obviously not on these circumstances, but on the actual amount of the accumulated produce of previous labour, or of capital, devoted to the payment of wages, in the possession of a country at any given period, that its power of supporting and employing labourers must wholly depend. A fertile soil affords the means of rapidly increasing capital; but that is all. Before this soil can be cultivated, capital must be provided for the support of the labourers employed upon it, just as it must be provided for the support of those engaged in manufactures, or in any other department of industry.
>
> 'It is a necessary consequence of this principle that the amount of subsistence falling to each labourer, or the *rate* of wages, must depend on the proportion which the whole capital bears to the whole amount of the labouring population. . . .
>
> 'To illustrate this principle, let us suppose that the capital of a country appropriated to the payment of wages would if reduced to the standard of wheat, form a mass of 10,000,000 quarters: If the number of labourers in that country were *two* millions, it is evident that the wages of each, reducing them all to the same common standard, would be *five* quarters.'[3]

He endeavours to illustrate or support the proposition that 'the well-being and comfort of the labouring classes are especially dependent on the relation which their increase bears to the increase of the capital which is to feed and employ them',[4] by comparing the growth of population and capital and the condition of the people in England and Ireland. The Irish population had increased faster than the English population, and the Irish capital had increased slower than the English capital. The Irish suffered from want and were miserable,

> 'And hence the obvious and undeniable inference, that in the event

[1] *Encyclopædia Britannica*, 4th ed., supplement, vol. vi, pt. i, p. 270 *a*.
[2] Above, p. 242.
[3] *Principles*, 1st ed., 1825, pp. 327, 328; 2nd ed., 1830, pp. 377, 378.
[4] *Ibid.*, 1st ed., pp. 328, 329.

> of the population having increased less rapidly than it has done, there would have been fewer individuals soliciting employment, and that consequently the rate of wages would have been proportionally higher. . . . It is obvious too, that the low and degraded conditions into which the people of Ireland are now sunk is the condition to which every people must be reduced whose numbers continue, for any considerable period, to increase faster than the means of providing for their comfortable and decent subsistence; and such will most assuredly be the case in every old settled country in which the principle of increase is not powerfully counteracted by the operation of moral restraint, or by the exercise of a proper degree of prudence and forethought in the formation of matrimonial connections.'[1]

This is open to the same objection as James Mill's argument that population has a tendency to increase faster than capital, because otherwise wages would have risen. M'Culloch entirely forgets to show that there had been any absolute deterioration in the condition of the Irish labourers, or even any deterioration as compared with the English labourers.

Of an upper limit, above which no reduction of population or increase of capital can raise wages, M'Culloch, like James Mill, says nothing, but he provides a lower limit, below which wages cannot fall, in the shape of a 'natural or necessary rate of wages'. This is 'the cost of producing labour', which, 'like that of producing all other articles brought to market, must be paid by the purchasers'. The cost seems at first to be a quantity of food and other articles sufficient for the support of the labourers and 'their families'.[2]

> 'If they did not obtain this supply, they would be left destitute; and disease and death would continue to thin the population until the reduced number bore such a proportion to the national capital as would enable them to obtain the means of subsistence.'[3]

But it is soon explained that 'moral restraint' may and does keep down the population, so that the natural or necessary rate of wages is higher than what is requisite to furnish a bare subsistence. Moreover, M'Culloch follows Malthus's *Political Economy* by saying that moral restraint may be itself increased by changes of habit which have been brought about by increases of wages caused by increases of capital.

M'Culloch's wage-fund theory was refuted in the very next year by Sir Edward West in his *Price of Corn and Wages of Labour*. Answering the contention of those who asserted that government could not add to the demand for labour, West says:

> 'If the capital for the support of labourers were of a given amount, and that amount were necessarily laid out upon the labouring population in the course of the year, it could make no difference in the de-

[1] *Principles*, p. 334. [2] *Ibid.*, pp. 334, 335. [3] *Ibid.*, p. 336.

mand for labour or amount of wages by whom it were expended; whether by government upon unproductive persons, such as soldiers or sailors; or by individuals upon productive labourers; the whole population would get the whole of this capital within the year, and they could not have more.'[1]

This he does not believe to be the case:

> 'What', he asks, 'was the effect of the immense subscriptions and parish donations and increased allowances, during the periods of scarcity of the last thirty-five years? Is it not admitted that the effect of them was to increase the money means of the labouring poor, and to raise the price of corn to a much higher point than it would otherwise have attained? Does it not follow that a larger or smaller amount of the pecuniary means or pecuniary capital of a country may be expended on the labouring population?'[2]

The demand for labour does not, he concludes, depend solely on the rate of the increase of the wealth or capital of a country. A brisk state of trade may double wages without any increase of capital:

> 'The employer of capital and labour employs, we will say, ten men, who produce the article upon which their labour is expended in two months, and he is enabled to sell it immediately, and thus replace his capital with a profit. Now, suppose these ten men to do double work a day at the same rate of wages for the work; their wages by the day will be doubled; the article will produced in one month, that is, in half the time, with the same profit upon the capital expended, that is, with double profit, for profit being the gain upon capital in a given period, increased rapidity of the returns will have the same effect as increased rate of production.'[3]

West was not alone in refusing to accept the wage-fund theory. Mountifort Longfield, in his Dublin lectures, which were published in 1834, ignores altogether the doctrine that wages depend on the proportion between capital and population. Wages, he says, depend upon the relation between the supply of labourers and the demand for them, and 'the supply consists of the present existing race of labourers'.[4] But instead of saying that the demand for them depends on the magnitude of the country's capital, he says that it 'is caused by the utility or value of the work which they are capable of performing. . . . The wages of the great mass of labourers must be paid out of the produce, or the price of the produce, of their labour'.[5] Leaving 'capital' out of account altogether, he puts forward a produce theory:

> 'The real wages of the labourer, that is, his command of the necessaries and comforts of life, will depend entirely on the rate of profits and on the efficiency of labour in producing those articles on which the wages of labour are usually expended.'[1]

[1] P. 83. [2] P. 85. [3] Pp. 86, 87.

[3] *Lectures on Political Economy, delivered in Trinity and Michaelmas Terms* 1833, by Mountifort Longfield, LL.D., 1834, p. 209.

[4] *Ibid.*, p. 210. [5] *Ibid.*, p. 212.

He makes a great mistake in assuming, on the strength of examples in which fixed capital is omitted, that the deduction per head of labourers for profit is indicated by the rate of profit, and he scarcely attempts to show that increased efficiency in producing articles not bought by labourers does not increase wages, but his theory shows a great advance on that of James Mill, Ricardo, and M'Culloch.

Three years before Longfield's lectures Senior had begun to construct a produce theory. In his *Lectures on the Rate of Wages, delivered before the University of Oxford in Easter Term* 1830,[1] he said that if it were assumed that every labouring family consists of the same number of persons, exerting the same degree of industry, the 'proximate cause' which decides the quantity and quality of the commodities obtained by a labouring family in the course of a year would be obvious:

> 'The quantity and quality of the commodities obtained by each labouring family during a year must depend on the quantity and quality of the commodities directly or indirectly appropriated during the year to the use of the labouring population, compared with the number of labouring families (including under that term all those who depend on their own labour for subsistence); or, to speak more concisely, on the extent of the fund for the maintenance of labourers, compared with the number of labourers to be maintained.'[2]

This proposition at first sight seems to be identical with M'Culloch's proposition that wages depend on the proportion between the number of labourers and the amount of capital 'devoted to the payment of wages'.[3] But in M'Culloch the amount of commodities 'devoted' was determined entirely by previous accumulation, and had nothing to do with the productiveness of industry, whereas Senior not only says nothing about capital and accumulation, but declares in his preface that 'the principal means by which the fund for the maintenance of labourers can be increased is by increasing the productiveness of labour'.[4] In his *Political Economy* he is more exact, and makes the quantity and quality of the commodities appropriated to the use of the labouring population, compared with the number of labouring families, depend, 'in the first place, on the productiveness of labour in the direct or indirect production of the commodities used by the labourer; and in the second place, on the number of persons directly or indirectly employed in the production of things for the use of labourers compared with the whole number of labouring families'.[5] With regard to the proportion between the number of persons who produce things for labourers and the number of labouring families, he says:

[1] Published in the same year. [2] P. 19. [3] Above, p. 263.

[1] P. iv; cf. *Political Economy*, 8vo ed., p. 183. 'The extent of the fund for the maintenance of labour depends mainly on the productiveness of labour.'

[5] 8vo ed., p. 174.

> 'There are three purposes to which labour which might otherwise be employed in supplying the fund for the use of labourers may be diverted; namely, the production of things, first, to be used by the proprietors of natural agents; secondly, to be used by the government; and thirdly, to be used by capitalists; or, to speak more concisely though less correctly, Labour, instead of being employed in the production of Wages, may be employed in the production of Rent, Taxation, or Profit.'[1]

In dealing with the first of these heads, Senior does not seem to remember the point. He ought to explain the causes which determine whether a large or small proportion of labour is diverted from the production of wages to the production of rent. Instead of doing so, he adduces arguments to prove that 'the whole fund for the maintenance of labour is not necessarily diminished in consequence of a considerable portion of the labourers in a country being employed in producing commodities for the use of the proprietors of the natural agents in that country'.[2] In dealing with the second head, Taxation, he begins by stating that taxation for unnecessary and mischievous expenditure is taken from the revenue of the whole people, and that the labourer is interested in the distribution of taxation. After this he seems to imagine that he has somehow got rid of the first two purposes to which labour which might otherwise be employed in supplying the fund for the use of labourers may be diverted, for he proceeds:

> 'Rent, then, being considered as something extrinsic, and Taxation a mode of expenditure, the only remaining deduction from Wages is Profit. And the productiveness of labour being given, the extent of the fund for the maintenance of labour will depend on the proportion which the number of labourers employed in producing things for the use of capitalists bears to that of those employed in producing things for the use of labourers; or, to use a more common expression, on the proportions in which the produce is shared between the capitalist and the labourer. . . .
>
> 'In the absence of rent and of unnecessary or unequally distributed taxation, it is between these two classes that all that is produced is divided; and the question now to be considered is, what decides the proportion of the shares?'[3]

The answer is, he says, 'first, the general rate of profit in the country on the advance of capital for a given period; and secondly, the period which in each particular case has elapsed between the advance of the capital and the receipt of the profit'. What he means by the second of these two factors is not very easy to imagine. How long a period elapses between the advance of the capital of a railway shareholder and the receipt of the profit? So far as can be made out, Senior would say that the profit is received as soon as the railway is constructed; the shareholder lays out £100 in the course of, say, two years, and at

[1] *Political Economy*, 8vo ed., p. 180. [2] *Ibid.*, p. 181. [3] *Ibid.*, p. 185.

the end of that time he has an amount of railway worth £105. But where in Senior's system his subsequent dividends find a place it is impossible to discover. As to the rate of profit he is easier to understand, but equally unsatisfactory. His doctrine is simply that additions to circulating capital unaccompanied by additions to population lower the rate of profit, and additions to population unaccompanied by additions to circulating capital raise it. 'If each were increased or each diminished, but in different proportions, profits would rise or fall according to the relative variations in the supply of wages', which seem to be the same thing as circulating capital, 'and labour'.[1] But additions to capital, 'made in a form requiring no further labour for its reproduction', appear to increase both the rate of profit and wages:

> 'A machine or implement is, in fact, merely a means by which the productiveness of labour is increased. The millions which have been expended in this country in making roads, bridges, and ports have had no tendency to reduce either the rate of profit or the amount of wages.'[2]

'Roads, bridges, and ports' are generally public property, and even in the turnpike days no profits had to be paid on a considerable portion of them. Let us substitute 'factories, railways, and docks', and Senior's extraordinary incapacity to keep to the point in this discussion will be sufficiently evident. He has long ago ostensibly done with the first of the two causes which determine the rate of wages, namely, the productiveness of industry, and ought to be considering what, *given a certain productiveness of industry*, determines how much labour is diverted from producing wages to producing profits. Instead of doing so, he declares simply that the accumulation of fixed capital reduces neither the rate of profit nor the amount of wages. The proportion in which the produce is divided between the labourer and the capitalist depends, he says, on two factors, the rate of profit and the period of advance; for the moment, he is taking the period of advance as given; this being so, the proportion between the labourer's and capitalist's shares must depend entirely on the rate of profit. What conceivable contribution to the problem, than, can it be to say that an increase in the productiveness of industry will raise both the rate of profit and the absolute amount of *per capita* wages?

With all its faults, Senior's theory of wages was a suggestive one, and might have been expected to lead to something valuable when considered and amended by other minds. J. S. Mill, however, paid no attention to it, and simply adhered to the ideas of his boyhood. He begins with the proposition that wages depend chiefly on competition, and, boldly leaping an enormous logical gap, proceeds to infer from this that 'wages, then, depend upon the demand and supply of labour,

[1] *Political Economy*, 8vo ed., p. 190. [2] *Ibid.*, p. 194.

or, as it is often expressed, on the proportion between population and capital'.[1] Population, however, he explains, does not mean population, but 'the number only of the labouring class, or rather of those who work for hire'; and capital does not mean capital, but 'only circulating capital, and not even the whole of that, but the part which is expended in the direct purchase of labour', and to this 'must be added all funds which, without forming a part of capital, are paid in exchange For labour, such as the wages of solidiers, domestic servants, and all other unproductive labourers':

> 'There is, unfortunately, no mode of expressing by one familiar term the aggregate of what may be called the wages fund of a country: and as the wages of productive labour form nearly the whole of that fund, it is usual to overlook the smaller and less important part, and to say that wages depend on population and capital. It will be convenient to employ this expression, remembering, however, to consider it as elliptical, and not as a literal statement of the entire truth.'[2]

By the statement, then, that wages depend on the proportion between population and capital we are to understand that wages depend on the proportion between the number of those who work for hire and the amount of the part of capital which is expended in the direct purchase of labour together with the other funds which are paid inexchange for labour.

To some this has appeared nothing more or less than an arithmetical truism.[3] They see that the funds which, without forming a part of capital, 'are paid in exchange for labour', can only mean amounts which are paid in exchange for labour *in a given period*; for instance, the 'funds' paid in exchange for the labour of solidiers must be a certain number of millions *a year*, and not simply a certain number of millions. Applying the analogy to the interpretation of 'the part of capital which is expended in the direct purchase of labour', they infer that the phrase means 'the amount of capital which is expended in the direct purchase of labour in a given period'. They thus make the whole proposition equivalent to a statement that *per capita* wages for any given period, say a week, depend on the proportion between the number of those who work for hire and the amount of capital and other funds expended during that period in the purchase of labour. Thus understood, the proposition is certainly an arithmetical truism, as it simply amounts to a statement that the average will be what the divisor and the dividend determine. We want to know on what *per capita* wages depend, and we are told they depend on the amount paid in wages in a given period divided by the number of wage-receivers.

[1] *Principles*, Bk. II, ch. xi, § 1, 1st ed., vol. i, p. 401; People's ed., p. 207, with the addition of 'mainly' after 'depend'.
[2] *Principles*, Bk. II, ch. xi, § 1, 1st ed., vol. i, p. 402; People's ed., pp. 207, 208.
[3] *E.g.* Jevons, *Theory of Political Economy*, 2nd ed., p. 290.

But this is not at all what J. S. Mill meant, and not exactly what he said. That it is not what he meant is immediately shown by his assertion that 'there are some facts in apparent contradiction'[1] to the doctrine. Facts would have to be very peculiar in order to be in contradiction to an arithmetical truism. The first is that 'wages are high when trade is good'. It is perfectly evident that this fact is not in apparent contradiction to the statement that wages depend on the proportion between the number of persons who work for hire and the amount of capital and other funds expended in a given period on the purchase of labour. If wages are high when trade is good, then by no process of arithmetic is it possible to escape from the conclusion that when trade is good a large amount of funds must be expended in a given period on the purchase of labour compared with the number of persons who work for hire. When trade is good and wages £100 a year per head instead of £90, the amount expended in wages, compared with the number of persons working for hire, is obviously greater. The second fact 'in apparent contradiction' to the proposition is not exactly a fact, but the 'common notion that high prices make high wages'. Here, again, there is no apparent contradiction. The truth or falsehood of the notion cannot in any way affect the proposition. The third 'fact' is the 'opinion' that wages – 'meaning, of course, money wages' – vary with the price of food. This, Mill thinks, is only partially true; but whether partially or entirely true, it is in no way in apparent contradiction to the fact that *per capita* wages depend on the proportion between the total amount paid in wages in a given period and the number of wage-earners.

It is clear, then, that J. S. Mill did not mean to enunciate the arithmetical truism that *per capita* wages for a given period depend on the amount expended in wages during that period divided by the number of wage-receivers. Turning again to his words, we find that he says nothing about an amount spent *in a given period*, and that he does not speak of the *amount* of capital expended in the direct purchase of labour, but of 'the part' of capital which is expended in the direct purchase of labour. Now if the whole capital of a country was a certain amount *per annum*, or so many millions a year, 'the part' of capital which is expended in the purchase of labour would be an amount *per annum* also. But the whole capital is not an amount *per annum*, but an amount pure and simple, not so many millions a year, but so many millions. And 'the part' of capital which is expended in the purchase of labour is also, in Mill's imagination, an amount pure and simple. It is x millions, not x millions per annum.

It is quite true, of course, that when 'the part of capital which is

[1] Bk. II, ch. xi, § 2, 1st ed., vol. i, p. 402; People's ed., p. 208 *a*.

expended in the direct purchase of labour' is thus interpreted, it is impossible to add together into one 'wages fund' the part of capital which is expended in the purchase of labour and 'all funds which, without forming a part of capital, are paid in exchange for labour, such as the wages of soldiers, domestic servants, and all other unproductive labourers'. The two things are not capable of forming an aggregate. The annual wages of 'productive labourers' can be added to the annual wages of unproductive labourers and form one aggregate, but the annual or the weekly wages of unproductive labourers cannot form an aggregate with a part of the capital of the country. You may add £200,000,000 to £500,000,000, but you cannot add £200,000,000 a year to a capital sum of £500,000,000. You might as well try to give an idea of the magnitude of the Rhone by adding together the number of gallons which flow past Lyons in an hour and the number of gallons contained at a given moment in the Lake of Geneva.

That Mill fell into the error of imagining he could add together into one fund a portion of the capital and a portion of the income of the country will seem less incredible when we notice that he says it is 'usual to overlook' the non-capital funds. His father and Ricardo, to whose guidance he usually trusts, had put forward no theory about wages not 'advanced from capital', and had talked as if there were none. J. S. Mill remembers the existence of such wages, and makes a formal rather than a real attempt to drag them under the theory that wages depend on capital and population. He makes no effort whatever to discover the causes which affect the amount of the 'funds' expended on unproductive labour, but confines his attention to the causes which affect the part of capital expended on the purchase of labour.

In considering Mill's theory of wages, then, the only feasible plan is to ignore his attempt to bring in the wages of 'unproductive' labour, and to adopt, as he himself practically does, the old habit of 'overlooking' that labour and its wages.[1]

We have it laid down, then, that the wages of labour depend on the proportion between the number of those who work for hire and the part of capital which is expended in the direct purchase of labour, and we have made out that the part of capital which is expended in the direct purchase of labour does not mean the amount of capital which is expended in that way in a given period, but a particular part of capital. The question that now presents itself is 'What part?'

It seems to be the part of capital which is imagined to be habitually

[1] Mill himself avowedly overlooks them in Book II, ch. iii, § 1, where he divides the 'industrial community' into landowners, capitalists, and productive labourers, labourers, and says that these three classes 'are considered in political economy as making up the whole community'. – 1st ed., vol. i, p. 279; People's ed., p. 145.

or generally, or as a rule, laid out in paying wages, or, to define it in another way, it is the part of capital which is neither tools nor materials. It is not always employed in paying wages, because some of it may be kept idle in its owner's hands; and this is the explanation of the fact that 'wages are high when trade is good', since when trade is bad a quantity of this part of capital is lying idle in its owners' hands. In what form it then exists is not very clear. Granting that there is such a part of capital – a very liberal assumption – we should now expect to be taught something as to the causes which affect the proportion between this part of capital and the number of wage-receivers. We are told something as to the causes which increase and decrease the number of wage-receivers; they are increased by high wages, and decreased by low wages, decreased by a rise in the standard of comfort, and increased by a fall in the standard of comfort. Now if the standard of comfort depended altogether on extraneous causes, wages would in the long run be determined entirely by those causes, since whatever the amount of capital ready to be devoted to the payment of wages, the number of wage-receivers would in the course of time accommodate itself to it, so that neither more nor less than the wages necessary to produce the standard of comfort would be obtained. But it is admitted that the standard of comfort itself often varies with the amount of wages received. Consequently the causes which affect the magnitude of the part of capital which is expended in wages are of great importance in determining wages. If this part of capital grows, wages will rise, and that may raise the standard of comfort; the number of wage-receivers will then not increase proportionately, and the rise of wages will be permanent. If this part of capital diminishes, wages will fall, and this may depress the standard of comfort; the number of wage-receivers will then not diminish proportionately, and the fall of wages will be permanent. Moreover, whether the effects of an increase of the part of capital expended in the purchase of labour be permanent or not, the causes of the increase ought to be investigated. Mill, however, seems to have nothing whatever to say as to causes which increase or decrease this particular part of capital. In an earlier chapter he had laid down a theory as to the increase of capital in general, and possibly thought that sufficient. But he does not say that the part of capital expended on labour is always the same proportion of the whole, and gives us no reason to suppose that he considered it to be so. The truth is that he has entirely forgotten that he is using 'capital' to mean something else than capital. He has used the expression 'wages depend on population and capital' without 'remembering . . . to consider it as elliptical, and not as a literal statement of the entire truth'.

§ 3. *Variations of Profits per cent*

At the beginning of his chapter on the Profits of Stock, Adam Smith attributes the rise and fall of the rate of profit to the increasing or declining state of the wealth of the society:

> 'The rise and fall in the profits of stock depend upon the same causes with the rise and fall in the wages of labour, the increasing or declining state of the wealth of the society; but those causes affect the one and the other very differently. The increase of stock, which raises wages, tends to lower profit.
>
> 'When the stocks of many rich merchants are turned into the same trade, their mutual competition naturally tends to lower its profit; and when there is a like increase of stock in all the different trades carried on in the same society, the same competition must produce the same effect in them all.'[1]

Bringing facts to bear on this theory, he points out that in England the rate of profit has declined as the country has grown richer, and that it is lower in rich countries, such as England and Holland, than in poorer countries, such as France and Scotland. In case any one should object that if increasing wealth raises wages and lowers profits and decreasing wealth raises profits and lowers wages, it is rather surprising that both wages and profits should be high in North America, he explains the position of new colonies at some length. High profits and high wages, he says, 'are things, perhaps, which scarce ever go together except in the peculiar circumstances of new colonies'. The colonists have a great deal of land and very little stock. They

> 'have more land than they have stock to cultivate. What they have therefore, is applied to the cultivation only of what is most fertile and most favourably situated, the land near the seashore and along the banks of navigable rivers. Such land, too, if frequently purchased at a price below the value even of its natural produce. Stock employed in the purchase and improvement of such lands must yield a very large profit.'[2]

The high profit causes rapid accumulation, and the rapidity of the accumulation causes high wages. But 'when the most fertile and best situated lands have been all occupied, less profit can be made by the cultivation of what is inferior both in soil and situation', so that as the colony increases, profits fall. Wages do not fall along with profits, because the rapidity of accumulation does not slacken, since 'a great stock, though with small profits, generally increases faster than a small stock with great profits'.

Adam Smith then proceeds to admit, in contradiction or qualification of the proposition with which the chapter opens, that there is another cause for rising profits besides the decline of the society's wealth:

[1] Bk. I, ch. ix, p. 40 *a*.

[2] P. 42 *a*.

'The acquisition of new territory or of new branches of trade may sometimes raise the profits of stock, and with them the interest of money, even in a country which is fast advancing in the acquisition of riches. The stock of the country, not being sufficient for the whole accession of business which such acquisitions present to the different people among whom it is divided, is applied to those particular branches only which afford the greatest profit. Part of what had before been employed in other trades is necessarily withdrawn from them, and turned into some of the new and more profitable ones. In all those old trades, therefore, the competition comes to be less than before; the market comes to be less fully supplied with many different sorts of goods. Their price necessarily rises more or less, and yields a greater profit to those who deal in them.'[1]

Declining wealth, or, to be more particular, 'the diminution if the capital stock of the society, or of the funds destined for the maintenance of industry', raises profits, because it both reduces wages and raises prices, so that 'the owners of what stock remains in the society can bring their goods at less expense to market than before, and, less stock being employed in supplying the market than before, they can sell them dearer'.[2]

In rather startling contrast to his proposition that high wages and high profits scarce ever go together, Adam Smith declares that when a country becomes stationary 'both the wages of labour and the profits of stock would probably be very low'. 'The competition for employment would necessarily be so great as to reduce the wages of labour to what was barely sufficient to keep up the number of labourers', while 'as great a quantity of stock would be employed in every particular branch' of business 'as the nature and extent of the trade would admit', so that the competition 'would everywhere be as great, and consequently the ordinary profit as low as possible'.[3]

It would be idle to pretend that this account of the causes which determine the rate of profit is, as a whole, entitled to any very great respect. Why 'must' the stock employed in the cultivation of the cheap and fertile land of a new colony 'yield a very large profit'? How can a diminution in the quantity of all goods in the production of which capital is employed raise their prices? If all producers 'bring less to market', how can they each give each other more in exchange for their various products? What is meant by a rate of profit 'as low as possible'? But the main practical question is, What causes the fall of profits as a country grows richer? and Adam Smith was on strong ground when he answered 'Increasing wealth'. In the chapter 'Of Stock lent at Interest' in Book II, he recapitulates his doctrine on this point in the following terms, which render it somewhat plainer than he had left it in Book I:

[1] Bk. I, ch. ix, p. 42 *b*. [2] P. 43 *a*. [3] P. 43 *b*.

> 'As capitals increase in any country, the profits which can be made by employing them necessarily diminish. It becomes gradually more and more difficult to find within the country a profitable method of employing any new capital. There arises, in consequence, a competition between different capitals, the owner of one endeavouring to get possession of that employment which is occupied by another. But upon most occasions he can hope to jostle that other out of this employment by no other means but by dealing upon more reasonable terms. He must not only sell what he deals in somewhat cheaper, but, in order to get it to sell, he must sometimes too buy it dearer. The demand for productive labour, by the increase of the funds which are destined for maintaining it, grows every day greater and greater. Labourers easily find employment, but the owners of capital find it difficult to get labourers to employ. Their competition raises the wages of labour, and sinks the profits of stock.'[1]

There is much truth in this. People endeavour to invest new capital in the way in which it will bring in the largest periodical return in proportion to the outlay. No one will spend twenty days' immediate labour in a particular way, in order to save himself one day's labour per annum hereafter, when he knows that by another way of spending the twenty days' immediate labour he could save himself two days' labour per annum. No one will spend £100 at once in order to get £5 a year, if he knows of another way of investing it which will give him £10 a year. Consequently, so far as its opportunities and knowledge go, a community makes the most profitable investments first, and if knowledge never increased, it would always become 'gradually more and more difficult to find within the country a profitable method of employing any new capital'. Then 'there arises a competition' which causes the proportion of labour annually saved or income annually gained by means of the new capital to regulate the rate of profit on all the capital. The discovery of new profitable methods of employing large quantities of savings checks the decline, and might, of course, if sufficiently great and rapid, cause a continuous rise.

The Ricardian school, however, misled by their habit of looking on profits as a mere surplus remaining to employers after they have paid wages, totally rejected Adam Smith's explanation of the historical fall of profits, and preferred to attribute it to a cause which has no existence, the supposed diminution in the productiveness of agricultural industry. West, the first, though not the name-father and greatest of the 'Ricardian' school, thought that the slightest consideration would 'detect the fallacy'[2] of Adam Smith's opinion that the general fall of profits is caused by an increase of the capital employed in all trades, just as a fall in one particular trade may be caused by the increase of the capital employed in that trade. Increased competition, West argues, lowers the profits obtained in a particular trade by re-

[1] Bk. II, ch. iv, p. 157 *a*.

[2] *Application of Capital*, p. 20.

ducing the price obtained for the product, but increased competition in all trades could not bring down all prices, since price is only the ratio in which articles exchange, and all articles could not be lower in proportion to each other. Nor, he says, could increased competition lower profits by raising wages, since wages are fixed by 'the greatness of the ratio of the increase'[1] of the capital, and this ratio, 'if the country be equally parsimonious',[2] is determined by the rate of profit, so that a falling rate of profit would act as a check on wages. 'The profits of stock', he says, 'are the net reproduction of stock, which can be diminished in two ways only, namely, either by a diminution of the powers of production, or by an increase of the expense of maintaining those powers; that is, by an increase in the real wages of labour'.[3] Believing that the fall of profits cannot be attributed to the second of these causes, he attributes it entirely to the first.

Eleven years later, in the preface to his pamphlet on the *Price of Corn and Wages of Labour*, he complained that Ricardo had not given his *Essay on the Application of Capital* the credit of the discovery that 'the diminution of the net production or the profits of stock, which is observed to take place in the progress of wealth and improvement, must necessarily be caused by a diminution of the productive powers of labour in agriculture'. The complaint was quite unfounded, as Ricardo had put forward the same theory in his *Essay on the Influence of a Low Price of Corn on the Profits of Stock, showing the Inexpediency of Restrictions on Importation*, which appeared before he had read West's pamphlet on the *Application of Capital*.[4] Ricardo proposed to show the inexpediency of restrictions on importation by proving that a low price of corn means high profits, which, as became a man of finance, he assumed to be a blessing.

Obviously with some reminiscence of Adam Smith's remarks on the highness of profits in new colonies in his mind, he takes as his starting-point an assumed profit of 50 per cent 'in the first settling of a country rich in fertile land, and [*sic*] which may be had by any one who chooses to take it'.[5] He imagines, as an example, an individual cultivating such land with a capital of the value of 200 quarters of wheat, half of which is fixed and half circulating capital, and obtaining a net return, after replacing his fixed and circulating capital, of 100 quarters.

So long as equally fertile and equally well-situated land continued abundant, profits would, he says, only fluctuate. They would rise if wages fell so that a less circulating capital was required to obtain the same produce, or if improvements took place in agriculture which increased the produce obtainable by a given expense. They would fall

[1] *Application of Capital*, p. 23.
[2] *Ibid.*, p. 24.
[3] See above, p. 19.
[4] *Ibid.*, p. 165, note 4.
[5] *Works*, p. 371.

if wages rose or 'a worse system of agriculture were practised'. But he asks his readers to 'suppose that no improvements take place in agriculture, and that capital and population advance in the proper proportion, so that the real wages of labour continue uniformly the same'.[1] Then, premising that profits in trade and agriculture must vary together, as otherwise capital would flow into the most inviting of the two employments, he begins to trace the general course of the rate of profit:

> 'After all the fertile land in the immediate neighbourhood of the first settlers were [*sic*] cultivated, if capital and population increased, more food would be required, and it could only be procured from land not so advantageously situated. Supposing, then, the land to be equally fertile, the necessity of employing more labourers, horses, etc., to carry the produce from the place where it was grown to the place where it was to be consumed, although no alteration were to take place in the wages of labour, would make it necessary that more capital should be permanently employed to obtain the same produce.[2] Suppose this addition to be of the value of 10 quarters of wheat, the whole capital employed on the new land would be 210 to obtain the same return[3] as on the old; and consequently the profits of stock would fall from 50 to 43 per cent, or 90 on 210.[4]
>
> 'On the land first cultivated the return would be the same as before, namely, 50 per cent, or 100 quarters of wheat; but the general profits of stock being regulated by the profits made on the least profitable employment of capital on agriculture, a division of the 100 quarters would take place, 43 per cent, or 86 quarters, would constitute the profit of stock, and 7 per cent, or 14 quarters, would constitute rent. And that such a division must take place is evident, when we consider that the owner of the capital of the value of 210 quarters of wheat would obtain precisely the same profit whether he cultivated the distant land, or paid the first settler 14 quarters for rent.
>
> 'In this stage the profits in [*sic*] all capital employed in trade would fall to 43 per cent.'[5]

Having thus shown, as he thinks, that profits would fall with the growth of wealth and population, even 'if the money price of corn and the wages of labour did not vary in price in the least degree', Ricardo proceeds to argue that *a fortiori* must profits fall in the actual progress of wealth and population, since 'the price of corn and of all other raw produce has been invariably observed to rise as a nation became wealthy and was obliged to have recourse to poorer

[1] *Works*, p. 372.

[2] He means that to obtain a given amount of produce from the new land it would be necessary to employ a larger capital than would be required to obtain that amount of produce from the old land.

[3] The 'return' is here the gross produce, though three lines lower it is the net produce.

[4] The 90 quarters is obtained by assuming that the additional 10 quarters of capital consist entirely of circulating capital, and so (having to be replaced at the end of the year) must be deducted from the 100 quarters of net return shown by the first example.

[5] *Works*, p. 373.

lands for the production of part of its food'.[1] He explains that this rise in the price of raw produce takes place because 'the exchangeable value of all commodities rises as the difficulties of their production increase', and that the difficulty of producing corn does increase in the progress of wealth if there are no improvements. Then he makes a prodigious leap, concluding:

> 'The sole effect, then, of the progress of wealth on prices, independently of all improvements either in agriculture or manufactures, appears to be to raise the price of raw produce and of labour, leaving all other commodites at their original prices, and to lower general profits in consequence of the general rise of wages.'[2]

The true and 'only'[3] cause of the fall of profits having been thus expounded, all that remains for him to do is to render the matter free from doubt by demolishing the common theory that profits are affected by 'the extension of commerce and discovery of new markets where our commodities can be sold dearer, and foreign commodities can be bought cheaper':

> 'Nothing is more common', he says, 'than to hear it asserted that profits on agriculture no more regulate the profits of commerce than that [*sic*] the profits of commerce regulate the profits on agriculture. It is contended that they alternately take the lead; and if the profits of commerce rise, which it is said they do when new markets are discovered, the profits of agriculture will also rise; for it is admitted that if they did not do so, capital would be withdrawn from the land, to be employed in the more profitable trade. But if the principles respecting the progress of rent be correct, it is evident that, with the same population and capital, whilst none of the agricultural capital is withdrawn from the cultivation of the land, agricultural profits cannot rise, nor can rent fall; either, then, it must be contended, which is at variance with all the principles of political economy, that the profits on commercial capital will rise considerably whilst the profits on agricultural capital suffer no alteration, or that, under such circumstances, the profits on commerce will not rise.'[4]

Ricardo considers 'the latter opinion' to be 'the true one'. The high profits obtained in a new market are, he thinks, a very partial and temporary affair; they soon 'sink to the ordinary level':

> 'The effects are precisely similar to those which follow from the use of improved machinery at home.
>
> 'Whilst the use of the machine is confined to one, or a very few, manufacturers, they may obtain unusual profits, because they are enabled to sell their commodities at a price much above the cost of production – but as soon as the machine becomes general to the whole trade, the price of the commodities will sink to the actual cost of production, leaving only the usual and ordinary profits.

[1] *Works*, pp. 375, 376. [2] *Ibid.*, p. 377.

[3] 'Profits of stock fall only because land equally well adapted to produce food cannot be procured.' – *Works*, p. 375.

[4] *Works*, pp. 379, 380.

> 'During the period of capital moving from one employment to another, the profits on that to which capital is flowing will be relatively high, but will continue so no longer than till the requisite capital is obtained.'[1]

His theory that the discovery of new and more profitable markets does not raise profits is not itself nearly so startling as his assumption that profits are not raised by the use of more profitable machinery. Certainly one would imagine that the introduction of a new method of employing capital profitably would tend to raise the rate of profit on capital. Ricardo, however, explains that the discovery of machinery and the extension of commerce, as well as the division of labour in manufactures,

> 'augment the amount of commodities, and contribute very much to the ease and happiness of mankind, but they have no effect on the rate of profits, because they do not augment the produce compared with the cost of production on the land, and it is impossible that all other profits should rise whilst the profits on land are either stationary or retrograde.'[2]

The whole argument depends on the truth of two propositions, of which the first, that agricultural profits cannot rise unless some of the agricultural capital is withdrawn from the cultivation of the land, is expressed in the text; and the other, that none of the agricultural capital will be withdrawn while capital and population remain the same, is to be found in a footnote.[3] The first proposition Ricardo bases only on his own exposition of the effect of the progress of wealth and population on agricultural profits,[4] so that his argument against the common theory begins by assuming the correctness of his own, and thus adds no new strength to his position. The second proposition he defends on the ground that it is impossible to withdraw any of the agricultural capital without diminishing the production of food, and the food is 'necessary' for the population. But it is tolerably obvious that one or both of the propositions must be untrue. When Ricardo argues that 'it is impossible that all other profits should rise whilst the profits on land are either stationary or retrograde', it does not appear to have struck him that it might equally well be argued, that it is impossible that agricultural profits should remain stationary or decline while other profits are rising. The discovery of new profitable methods of using capital which raises profits in any trade must tend to raise profits in all other trades, including agriculture. Either some capital must be withdrawn from agriculture in spite of the food being 'necessary' for the population, or else the whole of the capital must be retained in agriculture by a rise of the profits obtained in agricul-

[1] *Works*, p. 380. [2] *Ibid.*, p. 381. [3] *Ibid.*, p. 380.
[4] 'If the principles respecting the progress of rent be correct', above, p. 283.

ture in spite of Ricardo's theory that those profits cannot rise unless capital is withdrawn. No one will invest in agriculture, however necessary for the population food may be, if he can 'make greater profits elsewhere'.

In the chapter 'On Profits' in the *Principles*, the main proposition which Ricardo seeks to establish is 'that in all countries and at all times profits depend on the quantity of labour requisite to provide necessaries for the labourers on that land, or with that capital, which yields no rent',[1] and a corollary of this proposition, incidentally mentioned, is that:

> 'The natural tendency of profits is to fall; for, in the progress of society and wealth the additional quantity of food required is obtained by the sacrifice of more and more labour. This tendency, this gravitation, as it were, of profits is happily checked at repeated intervals by the improvements in machinery connected with the production of necessaries, as well as by discoveries in the science of agriculture, which enable us to relinquish a portion of labour before required, and therefore to lower the price of the prime necessary of the labourer.'[2]

The chapter has a most difficult appearance in consequence of its author's fondness for attempting to prove general propositions by means of imaginary arithmetical examples of particular cases, but its argument is in reality simple enough.

The first theory of the *Essay*, that profits would fall 'during the progress of the country in wealth and population' even 'if the money price of corn and the wages of labour did not vary in price in the least degree', does not reappear. Ricardo prefers now to rely entirely on the second or *a fortiori* argument of the *Essay*, that increasing difficulty in the production of corn lowers profits by raising wages, wages meaning of course not real wages, the amount of necessaries and conveniences enjoyed by the labourers, but money wages. He thinks he has proved in his earlier chapters that 'the price of corn is regulated by the quantity of labour necessary to produce it with that portion of capital which pays no rent', and also that 'all manufactured commodities rise and fall in price, in proportion as more or less labour becomes necessary for their production'.[3] Accordingly he argues:

> 'Supposing corn and manufactured goods always to sell at the same price, profits would be high or low in proportion as wages were low or high. But suppose corn to rise in price because more labour is necessary to produce it; that cause will not raise the price of manufactured goods in the production of which no additional quantity of labour is required. If then wages continued the same, profits would remain the

[1] 1st ed., p. 143; 3rd ed. in *Works*, p. 70.
[2] 1st ed., p. 133; 3rd ed. in *Works*, p. 66.
[3] 1st ed., p. 116; 3rd ed. in *Works*, p. 60.

same; but if, as is absolutely certain, wages should rise with the rise of corn, then profits would necessarily fall.

'If a manufacturer always sold his goods for the same money, for £1,000 for example, his profits would depend on the price of the labour necessary to manufacture those goods. His profits would be less when wages amounted to £800 than when he paid only £600.'[1]

Some one, Ricardo thinks, may imagine that the case of the farmer will be different, since he gets an increased price for his produce. May not the increase of price lead to his having 'the same rate of profits, although he should have to pay an additional price for wages'?[2] Ricardo answers that the increase of price will be just counterbalanced either by rent or by additional wages. He endeavours to show that this is so by the aid of an arithmetical example. Starting from the case of a farmer raising 180 quarters of wheat at £4, by employing ten men at wages of 6 quarters or £24 each, he inquires what will happen if wealth and population increase so that the price of corn rises, and additional groups of ten men are employed, the first additional group producing only 170 quarters, the second 160, the third 150, and the fourth 140. The price of corn, he says, will rise exactly 'in proportion to the increased difficulty of growing it on land of a worse quality'.[3] By this he means that the price will vary exactly with the number of men required to raise a given quantity on the last land employed, or with the last capital employed. If the last ten men employed raise 180 quarters, and the price is £4, then when cultivation is extended so that the last ten men employed raise only 170, the price will rise to $\frac{18}{17}$ of £4, or £4 4*s* 8*d*. When cultivation is still further extended, so that the last ten men only produce 160 quarters, the price will rise to £4 10*s*. When the last ten men produce only 150 quarters, it will rise to £4 16*s*, and when the last ten men produce only 140 quarters, it will rise to £5 2*s* 10*d*. The obvious arithmetical consequence of this is that the total produce of the last ten men, whatever it be, will always sell for the same amount of money – in this case, £720 – and that if the labourers get more of this amount, the farmer will get less. Assuming that money wages will rise steadily with the price of corn, but only half as fast, Ricardo lays it down that as the price of corn rises from £4 to £4 4*s* 8*d*, £4 10*s*, £4 16*s*, and £5 2*s* 10*d*, the wages of ten men will rise from £240 to £247, £255, £264, and £274 5*s*, and so, as the whole produce of the last ten men is always worth £720, the amount of profit left to their employer must fall from £480 to £473, £465, £456, and 445 £15*s*. Here we have the employer of the last ten men receiving a less absolute amount of profit in consequence of the 'rise

[1] 1st ed., pp. 117, 118; 3rd ed. in *Works*, p. 60.
[2] 1st ed., p. 118; 3rd ed. in *Works*, p. 61.
[3] 1st ed., p. 120; 3rd ed. in *Works*, pp. 61, 62.

of wages', but we know as yet nothing about the rates or percentages of his profit, for the amount of the capitals has not been mentioned. Ricardo now attempts to deal with this question:

> 'Supposing', he says, 'that the original capital of the farmer was £3,000, the profits of his stock, being in the first instance £480, would be at the rate of 16 per cent. When his profits fell to £473, they would be at the rate of 15.7 per cent.
>
> | | | |
> |---|---|---|
> | £465, | . . | 15.5 |
> | £456, | . . | 15.2 |
> | £445, | . . | 14.8 |
>
> But the *rate* of profits will fall still more, because the capital of the farmer, it must be recollected, consists in a great measure of raw produce, such as his hay and corn ricks, his unthrashed wheat and barley, his horses and cows, which would all rise in price in consequence of the rise of produce. His absolute profits would fall from £480 to £445 15s.; but if from the cause which I have just stated, his capital should rise from £3,000 to £3,200, the rate of profits, would when corn was at £5 2s. 10d., be under 14 per cent.'[1]

In thus distinguishing the rate at which the farmer's profits on his original capital 'would be' from the italicized *rate* of his profits, by which he means the rate at which they would be on his actual appreciated capital, Ricardo shows, what is also proved by a table he gives in a note to the passage, that he was thinking too much of the farmer who employs the first ten men, and who, when the price of corn rises, begins to pay a rent, and too little of the no-rent-paying farmer who employs the last ten men, and, therefore, according to the scheme, sets the standard of profits. The absolute amounts of profit – the £473, the £465, the £456, and the £445 15*s* – which the last ten men employed successively bring in to their employer as the price of wheat rises, are not earned on the 'original capital' of 'the farmer', but either on the capital of a new farmer, or on an addition to the capital of the original farmer. The original capital continues to be employed in connexion with the original ten men. The new capitals employed with the new groups of ten men, not only are different capitals, but need not be of the same amount. To establish Ricardo's position, it is necessary to assume that they are of the same amount, or that they increase. Assuming, as he generally does in his calculations, that the amounts remain the same, and accepting his other data, we get the results shown in the following table, when wheat is at £4 16*s* per quarter:

[1] 1st ed., pp. 127, 128; 3rd ed. in *Works*, p. 64.

Men.	Produce.	Rent.	Wages.	Profits.	Capital.	Rate of Profit.
Last ten, .	150 qrs. = £720	. .	£264	£456	£3,000	15·2
Third ten, .	160 qrs. = £768	£48	£264	£456	£3,000	15·2
Second ten,	170 qrs. = £816	£96	£264	£456	£3,000	15·2
Original ten,	180 qrs. = £864	£144	£264	£465	£3,000	15·2
All forty, .	660 qrs.@£3,168	£288	£1,056	£1,824	£12,000	15·2

But it would be perfectly reasonable to assume, in the absence of any definite information on the subject, that to employ the second ten men rather less capital will be required than to employ the first, rather less to employ the third than the second, and so on. On the face of it, supposing all forty to be employed by the same farmer on the same land, it is highly improbable that he will require to double his capital in order to double his men, since much of his fixed capital will not require to be increased in anything like the same proportion. Once allow that this is a possible case, and Ricardo's elaborate theory collapses. Instead of his decreasing absolute amounts of profits, £480, £473, £465, and £456 necessarily meaning a fall in the rate of profits, they are, granting all his assumptions, compatible with a rise.

To employ the first ten men, who produce 180 quarters, requires, let us say with Ricardo, a capital of £3,000, and profit is £480, or 16 per cent. Now let us suppose that to employ the second ten men, who produce 170 quarters, requires, not another £3,000 of capital, but only £2,782. When the price of wheat goes up to £4 4*s* 8*d*, and these ten men are employed, their wages, according to Ricardo, will be £247, and the profits of their employer therefore £473. This £473 is 17 per cent on £2,782, so that the rate of profit, instead of falling, has risen.[1] If to employ the third ten men takes £2,695 of capital, and the profits of their employer are, as Ricardo says they will be, £465, there will be a further rise of the rate of profit to 17¼ per cent, and if to employ the fourth ten men requires a capital of £2,533, and the profits of their employer are, as Ricardo says, £456, there will be yet another rise of the rate of profit to 18 per cent. Instead of the state of things represented in the table above, when wheat is at £4 16*s* per quarter, we should then have the following:

[1] It may perhaps be objected that if a larger rate of profit could be obtained by employing the second ten men, they would have been employed before. This, however, is not the case. They would not have brought in 16 per cent to their employer so long as the price of wheat remained at £4, for their produce would have been worth only £4 × 170 = £680, and their wages would have taken £240 of this, leaving only £440 for their employer, which is 15·8 per cent on £2,782.

Men.	Produce.	Rent.	Wages.	Profits.	Capital.	Rate of Profit.
Last ten, .	150 qrs. = £720	..	£264	£456	£2,533	18
Third ten, .	160 qrs. = £768	£19	£264	£485	£2,695	18
Second ten,	170 qrs. = £816	£51	£264	£501	£2,782	18
Original ten,	180 qrs. = £864	£60	£264	£540	£3,000	18
All forty, .	660 qrs. = £3,168	£130	£1,056	£1,982	£11,010	18

Apart from his arithmetical example, which is thus seen to be far from conclusive, Ricardo does not seem to have had any argument in favour of his theory that the rate of profit depends on the productiveness of the last employed, least productive, or no-rent-paying agricultural industry. Nevertheless this theory was widely accepted for a time. Malthus indeed criticized it in a hostile spirit, both in private correspondence with Ricardo,[1] and in his *Political Economy*, and Ricardo and he imagined there was some serious difference of opinion between them on the subject. Yet when we look back on the controversy after the lapse of seventy or eighty years, we can see that the real dispute between them was less about profits in general, than about profits in England after the war. Malthus quite agreed with Ricardo that profits depend on wages, and must therefore depend on the productiveness of the least productive agricultural industry if Ricardo's assumption of invariable real wages be granted. To prove it, he had no need of Ricardo's elaborate arithmetical example, since he constantly identified the rate of profit or 'profits' with the capitalist's proportion of the produce:

> 'It is merely a truism to say that if the value of commodities be divided between labour and profits, the greater is the share taken by one, the less will be left for the other; or in other words, that profits fall as labour rises, or rise as labour falls.'[2]

What he chiefly complained of was that Ricardo had not allowed nearly sufficient importance to the enormous differences which are actually found between real wages – the necessaries, conveniences, and luxuries obtained by the labourers – at different times and places. Ascribing these differences to differences in 'the proportion which capital bears to labour',[3] he put forward that proportion as something which has more actual influence on the rate of profit than the productiveness of no-rent-paying agricultural industry, and declared that

[1] See *Letters of Ricardo to Malthus*, ed. Bonar, *passim.*
[2] *Political Economy*, p. 310.
[3] *Ibid.*, p. 301.

Adam Smith was far nearer the truth in ascribing the fall of profits to the competition of capital than Ricardo was willing to allow:

> 'The argument against the usual view which has been taken of profits as depending principally upon the competition of capital, is founded upon the physical necessity of a fall of profits in agriculture, arising from the increasing quantity of labour required to procure the same food. . . .
>
> 'Now I am fully disposed to allow the truth of this argument as applied to agricultural profits, and also its natural consequence on all profits. This truth is indeed necessarily involved both in the *Principle of Population* and in the theory of rent, which I published separately in 1815. But I wish to show, theoretically as well as practically, that powerful and certain as this cause is, in its final operation, so much so as to overwhelm every other; yet in the actual state of the world its natural progress is not only extremely slow, but is so frequently counteracted and overcome by other causes, as to leave very great play to the principle of the competition of capital; so that at any one period of some length in the last or following hundred years, it might most safely be asserted, that profits had depended, or would depend, very much more upon the causes which had occasioned a comparatively scanty or abundant supply of capital than upon the natural fertility of the land last taken into cultivation.'[1]

James Mill, in the first edition of his *Elements*, regarded the question as a simple one. Premising that the wages and profits received in no-rent-paying industry regulate the wages and profits received in rent-paying industry, so that, 'in considering what regulates wages and profits, rent may be left altogether out of the question', he observes:

> 'When anything is to be divided wholly between two parties, that which regulates the share of one regulates also, it is very evident, the share of the other; for whatever is withheld from the one the other receives; whatever, therefore, increases the share of the one diminishes that of the other, and vice versa. We might, therefore, with equal propriety, it should seem, affirm that wages determine profits, or that profits determine wages; and, in framing our language, assume whichever we pleased, as the regulator or standard.
>
> 'As we have seen, however, that the proportion of the shares between the capitalist and labourer depends upon the relative abundance of population and capital, and that population, as compared with capital, has a tendency to superabound, the active principle of change is on the side of population, and constitutes a reason for considering population, and consequently wages, as the regulator.
>
> 'Wherefore, as the profits of stock depend upon the share which is received by its owners of the joint produce of labour and stock, profits of stock depend upon wages – rise as wages fall, and fall as wages rise.'[2]

It occurs to him that some one may very naturally object that 'when anything is to be divided wholly between two parties', the amount

[1] *Political Economy*, pp. 316, 317.

[2] 1st ed., pp. 56, 57; 3rd ed., with the substitution of 'As therefore' for 'wherefore', pp. 70, 71.

which each party will get will depend not only on the 'shares' or proportions in which it is divided, but also on the magnitude of the thing divided. 'To speak clearly on this point', he therefore says, 'we must remove an ambiguity which adheres to the word profits', and he then explains that 'profits' may mean either the quantity of commodities 'which the capitalist receives as the return for a certain quantity of food, raw materials, and tools employed', or the rate of profit, that is, the ratio between 'the value of that share of the produce which comes to the capitalist', and 'the value of all the commodities employed as capital in affecting the production'.[1] If the word be used in the first of these senses, he admits that 'profits do depend upon two things; upon the quantity of return as well as the state of wages', since 'when the return to capital from the land is great', a given proportion, such as a half, of the yield to 'the same quantity of food, for example, and of implements of husbandry employed as capital', will be a larger quantity than when the return to capital from the land is small. If, however, the term profits be used in the other sense, profits depend on wages because the value of the labourers' and capitalists' joint share of the produce obtained by the same quantity of capital and labour always remains the same, and 'if the value of that which is divided as wages of labour and profits of stock remains the same, it is obvious and certain that the proportion of that value which goes as profits of stock depends wholly upon that which goes as wages'.[2] This is quite true, but James Mill draws a perfectly erroneous inference from it. 'The rate of profits therefore', he says, 'or the ratio which the value of that which is received by the capitalist bears to the value of the capital, depends wholly upon wages'. Obviously, like Malthus, he has here coolly identified the ratio which the capitalist's portion bears to his capital with the ratio which it bears to the produce divided between the capitalist and labourers. In a later chapter he recognizes that the two ratios are not the same, but does not happen to contemplate a case in which they vary in opposite directions.[3]

As to the consequence of profits 'depending on wages', namely, that they rise and fall according as the productiveness of no-rent-paying agricultural industry rises and falls, and that, consequently, they generally fall, he is in perfect agreement with Ricardo.[4]

M'Culloch saw that the matter was not quite so simple as Ricardo and his henchman supposed. At the beginning of his exposition of 'the circumstances which determine the rate of profit',[5] he says that it is obvious that if the proportion of produce-*minus*-rent which goes

[1] 1st ed., p. 58. [2] *Ibid.*, p. 60.

[3] Ch. iii, section iii, on 'the effect upon exchangeable values of a fluctuation in wages and profits'.

[4] 1st ed., pp. 60–62. [5] *Principles of Political Economy*, 1825, p. 363.

to wages is increased, the proportion which goes to profits must be diminished, but, he explains, 'the *profit* accruing to the capitalists is different and totally distinct from the proportion of the produce of industry falling to their share'.[1] A reader naturally expects him to proceed to say that 'profit', meaning the rate of profit – the ratio of profit to capital – is a different thing from the proportion of produce-*minus*-rent received by the capitalist, that, for instance, profits may be 5 per cent, while the capitalist's proportion of produce-*minus*-rent, or profits-*plus*-wages is 30 per cent. But, though M'Culloch does explain this a few pages further on,it is not at all what he is thinking of for the moment. All that he means is that the entire 'return' to the capital of a farmer, for example, does not consist of wages and profits. A portion of that which, 'in the first instance', falls to the capitalist after he has paid wages, is not part of his profits, but is 'required to replace the quantity he had expended in seed' and 'other outgoings'. The explanation is perfectly unnecessary, because Ricardo, and probably every one else in his time, when they talked of the 'produce' of a farm being divided in a particular way between rent, wages, and profits, meant the net produce which remains after providing for 'seed and other outgoings'. Any other interpretation of the term would inevitably lead to the greatest absurdities. When an economist talks of the 'produce' of a tailor, he does not mean to include the cloth, with the production of which the tailor had nothing to do, but only the putting together of the cloth, or the additional value or utility conferred upon it. A corn-grower's annual 'produce', in the economist's sense of the word, is no more the whole of the corn on his farm immediately after the harvest than a sheep-raiser's annual 'produce' is the whole of the sheep on his farm at the end of the breeding season.

After finishing his explanation of the difference between profits and the capitalists' proportion of the produce of industry, and having observed that profits do not depend on exchanges, M'Culloch says:

> 'Mr Ricardo has endeavoured to show, in one of the most original and ingenious chapters of his work, that the *RATE of profit* depends entirely on the *proportion* in which the produce of industry under deduction of rent is divided between capitalists and labourers; that a rise of profits can never be brought about except *by* a fall of proportional wages, nor a fall of profits except *by* a corresponding rise of proportional wages.'[2]

As against this contention, M'Culloch has little difficulty in framing arithmetical examples in which profits appear to be raised directly by increased productiveness of industry or by diminished necessity for using capital, and remain stationary in consequence of increased productiveness of industry, although the proportion of produce falling

[1] *Principles*, p. 366. [2] *Ibid.*, p. 367.

to wages is increased. It is very doubtful, however, if Ricardo 'endeavoured to show' what M'Culloch attributes to him. What he really 'endeavoured to show' was that the rate of profit depends on the productiveness of the last employed, or no-rent-paying agricultural industry, and it is not of much importance to his theory whether this dependence is brought about only through rises and falls of money wages, or also by the direct influence of variations in the productiveness of industry, as M'Culloch supposes. And in rejecting Adam Smith's theory that the historical fall of profits is caused by the plentifulness of capital, and adopting Ricardo's theory that it is caused by the decreasing productiveness of no-rent-paying agricultural industry, M'Culloch makes no reservations, except by introducing increased taxation as another possible cause:

> 'It is not', he says, 'competition, but is the increase of taxation and the necessity under which society is placed of resorting to soils of a decreasing degree of fertility to obtain supplies of food to feed an increasing population, that are the great causes of that reduction in the rate of profit which uniformly takes place in the progress of society. When the last lands taken into cultivation are fertile, there is a comparatively large amount of produce to be divided between profits and wages; and both profits and *real* wages may, in consequence, be high. But with every successive diminution in the fertility of the soils to which recourse must be had, the quantity of produce obtained by a given quantity of capital and labour must necessarily be diminished. And this diminution will obviously operate to reduce the rate of profit – (1) by lessening the *quantity of produce* to be divided between the capitalist and the labourer, and (2) by increasing the proportion falling to the share of the latter.'[1]

Here the fallacy which, as we have seen, vitiates Ricardo's arithmetical example, lurks in the phrase 'a given quantity of capital and labour'. Just as Ricardo, in his arithmetical example, links the labour of ten men indissolubly with £3,000 of capital, so M'Culloch here links the labour of x men indissolubly with y capital. As soon as it is pointed out that the fact that x men are employed in conjunction with y capital does not prove that $2y$ capital must necessarily be employed with $2x$ men, the phrase 'the quantity of produce obtained by a given quantity of capital and labour' ceases to have any intelligible meaning. If x men with y capital obtain z produce at one time, and $2x$ men with $1\frac{3}{4}y$ capital obtain $1\frac{7}{8}z$ produce at a later time, are we to say that the produce obtained by a given quantity of capital and labour has increased, diminished, or remained stationary? When it is once admitted the amount of capital per man employed may diminish concurrently with a decrease in the productiveness of industry, or increase concurrently with an increase in the productiveness of industry,

[1] *Principles*, p. 376.

it must also be admitted that the rate of profit may rise when the productiveness of industry decreases and the labourers take a larger share of the produce, and may fall when the productiveness of industry increases and the labourers take a smaller share of the produce. Regardless of this, M'Culloch asserts in emphatic italics that '*the decreasing fertility of the soil is at bottom the great and only necessary cause of a fall of profits*'.[1]

After reading M'Culloch, James Mill altered and enlarged his own chapter on profits. He easily brushes away M'Culloch's muddle about 'the seed and other outgoings of the capitalist' by explaining that 'in speaking of the produce which is shared between the capitalist and labourer', he always is to be taken to mean 'such net produce as remains after replacing the capital which has been consumed',[2] and then he endeavours to elucidate more than he had done in his earlier editions the meaning of his proposition that profits 'rise as wages fall, and fall as wages rise'. A variation of wages and profits, he says, may have three apparently different meanings. It may mean (1) a variation in the proportions in which produce-*minus*-rent is divided between wages and profits; or (2) a variation in the absolute amounts of produce received as wages and profits; or (3) a variation in 'the value of what is received under these denominations'.[3] But, he observes, if value be taken to mean value in exchange, the third of these interpretations is identical with the second, while if value be used 'in the sense which Mr Ricardo annexed to the word',[4] it is identical with the first, so that there are in reality only two interpretations. Now if, he argues, we understand a variation of wages and profits in the first sense, as meaning a 'change in the proportions' existing between them, it is obvious that profits rise when wages fall, and fall when wages rise: 'the proposition that profits depend upon wages admits of no qualification'.[5] If, on the other hand, we understand a variation of wages and profits in the second sense, as meaning 'a change in the quantity of commodities', it will not be true that profits fall when wages rise, and rise when wages fall, 'for both may fall and both may rise together. And this is a proposition which no political economist has called in question'. Having thus disposed of the two senses in which the variations of profits is never understood by ordinary persons, James Mill descends to everyday life:

> 'In the common mode of expressing profits', he says, 'the reference that is made is not to the produced commodity, but to the capital employed in producing it; including the wages which it is necessary to advance, and from which the owner expects, of course, to derive the same advantage as from his other advances. Profits are expressed, not in aliquot parts of the produce, but of this capital. It is not so much per

[1] *Principles*, p. 380. [2] *Elements*, 3rd ed., p. 71. [3] *Ibid*., p. 73.
[4] *Ibid*., p. 74. [5] *Ibid*., p. 72.

cent of the produce that a capitalist is said to receive, but so much per cent upon his capital.'[1]

He gives a numerical example in which a capitalist receives £20 of profits, which is 10 per cent on his capital of £200 and 28½ per cent of the total produce of £70, and then makes this oracular comment:

> 'It is only, however, the language which here is different; the thing expressed is precisely the same; and whether the capitalist says he receives 10 per cent upon his capital or 28½ per cent of the produce, he means in both cases the same amount, viz. £20.
>
> 'There are, therefore, in reality but two cases. The one that in which we speak of proportions; the other that in which we speak of quantity of commodities.'[2]

He seems to mean that when we are speaking of the rate of profit in the ordinary sense we understand by the phrase the quantity of commodities, and consequently he is willing to admit that the rate of profit in the ordinary sense does not depend altogether on wages, but also on the productive powers of labour and capital:

> 'If', he says, 'at the same time that the shares of the capitalists are reduced by a rise of wages, there should happen an increase of the productive powers of labour and capital, the reduced shares might consist of as great a quantity of commodities as the previous shares, and of course the exchangeable value, and percentage on the capital, expressed in the language of exchangeable value, would remain the same.'[3]

He omitted altogether the pages of the earlier editions in which he had explained how the 'inevitable' 'diminution of the return to capital employed upon the land' causes the historical decline of profits.[4] It would be rash, however, to conjecture that his belief in that theory was at all shaken. The omission may very probably have been suggested by the feeling that the passage was out of place in a book on the pure theory of the subject.

Senior's theory with regard to the causes which determine the rate of profit, as we have already had occasion to say,[5] is simply that additions to the circulating capital or wage capital of a country, unaccompanied by additions to the population, lower the rate, and additions to the population, unaccompanied by additions to the wage capital, raise the rate. But he puts forward nothing in support of his view except a hypothetical example, in which the most monstrous assumptions are made.[6]

J. S. Mill, taught by so confused and vacillating a tutor as his father, could scarcely be expected, at the age of 23, to contribute much towards the solution of the question as to the causes which determine

[1] *Elements*, 3rd ed., p. 75. [2] *Ibid.*, pp. 75, 76. [3] *Ibid.*, p. 77.
[4] *Ibid.*, 1st ed., pp. 60, 62; 2nd ed., pp. 78–80. [5] Above, pp. 269, 270.
[6] *Political Economy*, 8vo ed., pp. 188–192.

the rate of profit. His Essay on *Profits, and Interest*[1] begins with an elaborate attempt to rehabilitate the theory that 'profits depend on wages'.

For this purpose he tacitly adopts the plan suggested by his father in the third edition of the *Elements*, of taking 'produce' to mean, not the net produce which is divided between wages and profits in a given period, but this amount *plus* the fixed and other capital remaining in hand at the end of the period:[2]

> 'We may', he says, 'consider the capital of a producer as measured by the means which he has of possessing himself of the different essentials of production; namely, labour, and the various articles which labour requires as materials, or of which it avails itself as aids. The ratio between the price which he has to pay for these means of production, and the produce which they enable him to raise, is the *rate* of his *profit*. If he must give for labour and tools four-fifths of what they will produce, the remaining fifth will constitute the profit, and will give him a rate of one in four, or twenty-five per cent on his outlay.'[3]

To understand the verb 'produce' in its usual sense would obviously make the last sentence unintelligible. When a capitalist has £10,000 invested in fixed capital, spends £1,000 in the first year in wages, and makes £2,750 profit, £3,750 is the value of what his labourers 'produce' in the ordinary sense of the word, and his profits (granting the assumption of a year's wage-fund collected before the business is begun and retained in a box till exhausted by fifty-two weekly payments) are 25 per cent. But obviously he cannot be said to have given for 'labour and tools' four-fifths of £3,750, i.e. £3,000. If, however, we adopt James Mill's most misleading suggestion, and say that the 'labour and tools' produced the capital as well as the real produce, their produce would be in this case £3,750 + £10,000, i.e. £13,750; and the capitalist, having paid £10,000 for his 'tools' and £1,000 for his 'labour', would have given for labour and tools four-fifths of their pseudo-produce.

Having thus found that the rate of profit depends on 'the ratio between the price of labour, tools, and materials, and the produce of them',[4] Mills proceeds to eliminate tools and materials by converting them into labour. If they could be had in indefinite quantity without labour,

> 'the whole produce', he says, 'after replacing the wages of labour, would be clear profit to the capitalist. Labour alone is the primary means of production; "the original purchase-money which has been paid of everything". Tools and materials, like other things, have origin-

[1] No. iv in *Essays on some Unsettled Questions of Political Economy*. The comma after 'Profits' occurs both in the contents and in the heading of the essay.

[2] See James Mill's *Elements*, 3rd ed., pp. 80, 81.

[3] *Essays*, pp. 91, 92.

[4] *Ibid.*, p. 93.

> ally cost nothing but labour; and have a value in the market only because wages have been paid for them. The labour employed in making the tools and materials being added to the labour afterwards employed in working up the materials by aid of the tools, the sum-total gives the whole of the labour employed in the production of the completed commodity. In the ultimate analysis, therefore, labour appears to be the only essential of production. To replace capital is to replace nothing but the wages of the labour employed. Consequently, the whole of the surplus after replacing wages is profits. From this it seems to follow that the ratio between the wages of labour and the produce of that labour gives the rate of profit. And thus we arrive at Mr Ricardo's principle that profits depend upon wages; rising as wages fall, and falling as wages rise.'[1]

Clearly there is little but hocus pocus in this argument. Starting from the proposition that the ratio between profits and capital, or the rate of profit, is determined by the ratio between capital and capital *plus* profits, Mill, by successive steps, converts this last ratio into

(1) the ratio between capital (true)+wage-fund and capital (true)+wages+profits.

(2) the ratio between previous wages+wage-fund and previous wages+wages+profits.

(3) the ratio between wages and wages+profits.

'It seems to follows', according to him, that 'the ratio between the wages of labour and the produce of that labour gives the rate of profit'. This means that the rate of profit (ratio between profit and capital) is the ratio between absolute profit and wages.

Now, supposing the rate of profit were really the ratio between the amount of profits and wages, which of course it is not, this would not in the least make us 'arrive' at the 'principle that profits', meaning the rate of profit, 'depend upon wages, rising as wages fall and falling as wages rise'. The ratio between the amount of profits and wages which is supposed to be the rate of profit does not depend only on the magnitude of wages, but also on the magnitude of the amount of profits. Somewhat obscurely recognising this, Mill proceeds to explain that 'wages' are not to be understood as meaning the quantity, but the 'value', in the Ricardian sense, which the labourer receives.[2] This Ricardian value, he says, means the proportion of the fruits of his labour which the labourer receives:

> 'A rise of wages with Mr Ricardo meant an increase in the cost of production of wages; an increase in the number of hours' labour which go to produce the wages of a day's labour; an increase in the *proportion* of the fruits of labour which the labourer receives for his own share; an increase in the ratio between the wages of his labour and the produce of it. . . .
>
> 'The wages . . . on which profits are said to depend are undoubtedly

[1] *Essays*, p. 94. [2] *Ibid.*, p. 95.

proportional wages, namely, the proportional wages of one labourer: that is, the ratio between the wages of one labourer and (not the whole produce of the country, but) the amount of what one labourer can produce; the amount of that portion of the collective produce of the industry of the country which may be considered as corresponding to the labour of one single labourer. Proportional wages, thus understood, may be concisely termed the cost of production of wages; or, more concisely still, the cost of wages, meaning their cost in "the original purchase money" labour.'[1]

When it is said, then, that the rate of profit rises as wages fall and falls as wages rise, we are to understand that the rate of profit rises as the proportion of the produce obtained by the labourer falls, and falls as the proportion of the produce obtained by the labourer rises. This, however, is obviously false, and Mill admits that it is. With the aid of a most preposterous arithmetical example, he arrives at the conclusion that the rate of profit really depends, not on proportional wages, but on proportional wages *plus* something else. But proportional wages were defined to be 'the ratio between the wages of one labourer and the amount of what one labourer can produce', and it is difficult to see how we are to add something to this ratio. We can add 10 per cent to 55 per cent, but to add £10 to 50 per cent seems scarcely a usual operation. Mill, however, unconsciously provided for this difficulty when he introduced, in the passage quoted above, the phrase 'the cost of production of wages' as an equivalent for 'the *proportion* of the fruits of labour which the labourer receives', or 'the ratio between the wages of his labour and the produce of it'. No ordinary person would understand the 'cost of production of wages' to mean a *ratio* between wages and produce, and take a rise in the cost of production of wages as meaning an increase in the proportion of the produce received by the labourer. The term is purely absolute, and does not suggest a ratio or proportion in any way. If the difference between the two things had not been slightly disguised by the insertion between them of 'the number of hours' labour which go to produce the wages of a day's labour',[2] Mill could never have treated them as equivalent expressions. Taking advantage of the ambiguity which he has thus himself created, he begins to treat the cost of wages not as a ratio but as an absolute quantity. Profits, he declares, as well as wages, enter into the cost of production of wages, by which he now means, not the ratio between the wages of one labourer and the amount he can produce, but the absolute cost of the commodities which constitute wages. On this cost of production of wages he finally takes his stand,

[1] *Essays*, pp. 96, 97.

[2] In this phrase the idea of a proportion is latent, as it is assumed that 'a day's labour' is composed of a certain fixed number of hours, so that if, for example, wages rise from the produce of six hours' labour to that of seven, the labourer receives, say, $\frac{7}{10}$ instead of $\frac{6}{10}$ of the produce of his labour.

discarding all ideas of ratios between anything and anything else. It is this cost of production of wages concerning which he finally decides that 'Profits cannot rise unless the cost of production of wages falls exactly as much, nor fall unless it rises':[1]

> 'Mr Ricardo's principle that profits cannot rise unless wages fall', he says, 'is strictly true, if by low wages be meant not merely wages which are the produce of a smaller quantity of labour, but wages which are produced at less cost, reckoning labour and previous profits together.'[2]

As to the causes which increase or decrease the cost of wages, and are therefore the ultimate causes of a fall or rise of the rate of profit, Mill has nothing to add to Ricardo:

> 'The rate of profits', he says, 'tends to *fall* from the following causes: (1) An increase of capital beyond population, producing increased competition for labour; (2) An increase of population, occasioning a demand for an increased quantity of food, which must be produced at a greater cost. The rate of profit tends to *rise* from the following causes: (1) An increase of population beyond capital, producing increased competition for employment; (2) Improvements producing increased cheapness of necessaries and other articles habitually consumed by the labourer.'[3]

He does not commit himself to any statement as to the actual rise or fall of profits. In the chapter 'Of Profits' (Book II, Chapter XV) in the *Principles* he discards most of the elaborate machinery by which in the Essay he sought to show that the rate of profit depends on the comparative magnitude of the amounts of profit and of wages. He seems to take it for granted that this is an almost obvious fact. 'If the labourers of the country', he says, 'collectively produce 20 per cent more than their wages, profits will be 20 per cent, whatever prices may or may not be'.[4] The capitalist's profit consists, he asserts, 'of the excess of the produce above the advances; his *rate* of profit is the ratio which that excess bears to the amount advanced'. These 'advances' or 'expenditure' of the capitalist 'consist' or are 'composed' not only of wages but also of 'materials and implements, including buildings', and yet they are nothing but wages, or at any rate 'repayment of wages':

> 'The fact, however, remains, that in the whole process of production, beginning with the materials and tools, and ending with the finished product, all the advances have consisted of nothing but wages, except that certain of the capitalists concerned have, for the sake of general convenience, had their share of profit paid to them before the operation was completed. Whatever of the ultimate product is not profit is repayment of wages.'[5]

[1] *Essays*, p. 103. [2] *Ibid.*, p. 104. [3] *Ibid.*, p. 106.
[4] People's ed., p. 252 *b*. The section (§ 5) does not occur in the first edition.
[5] 1st ed., vol. i, p. 492; People's ed., p. 253 *b*.

The capital of the country, its buildings, ships and mills being thus converted into wages, the problem becomes simple enough:

> 'It thus appears that the two elements on which, and which alone, the gains[1] of the capitalists depend are, first, the magnitude of the produce, in other words, the productive power of labour;[2] and, secondly, the proportion of that produce obtained by the labourers themselves; the ratio which the remuneration of the labourers bears to the amount they produce. These two things form the data for determining the gross[3] amount divided as profit among all the capitalists of the country; but the *rate* of profit, the percentage on the capital, depends only on the second of the two elements, the labourer's proportional share, and not on the amount to be shared. If the produce of labour were doubled, and the labourers obtained the same proportional share as before, that is, if their remuneration was also doubled, the capitalists, it is true, would gain twice as much; but as they would also have had to advance twice as much, the rate of their profit would be only the same as before.'[4]

'As they would also have had to advance twice as much'! As their capital would have had to be doubled! Why does Mill suppose their advances or capital would have had to be doubled? There seems to be no answer to this question, unless it is that, having converted all the capital into wages, he now treats the whole capital as a wage-fund, and supposes that the whole must have been doubled before the remuneration of the labourers could be doubled, for why doubling the produce of the labourers and their remuneration should double either the quantity or the value of the buildings, ships, and mills existing in the country it is quite impossible to conjecture.

Quite content, however, with his argument, Mill proceeds immediately to 'arrive at the conclusion of Ricardo and others, that the rate of profits depends upon wages; rising as wages fall, and falling as wages rise', only considering it necessary to substitute for 'wages' 'what Ricardo really meant', the 'cost of labour'.[5] The alteration does not really amount to more than an explanation that a rise of wages and a fall of wages are not to be taken in their ordinary sense, but are to mean a rise in the proportion of produce (wages+profits[6]) which goes to wages. In the face of so plain a statement that the rate of profit depends on the labourer's 'proportional share' immediately preceding, it is impossible that the 'cost of labour' can mean anything but the labourer's proportion of the produce. It is, Mill says,

[1] *I.e.* the absolute amount of the gains or income.

[2] Mill apparently assumes that the number of labourers remains fixed, since otherwise the magnitude of the produce would not necessarily vary with the productive power of labour.

[3] 'Gross' here means, as often in Mill, aggregate.

[4] 1st ed., vol. i, p. 492; People's ed., p. 253 *b*.

[5] 1st ed., vol. i, pp. 492, 493; People's ed., p. 253 *b*.

[6] 'Leaving rent out of the question.' – *Principles*, 1st ed., vol. i, p. 491; People's ed., p. 253 *a*.

> 'in the language of mathematics, a function of three variables: the efficiency of labour; the wages of labour (meaning thereby the real reward of the labourer); and the greater or less cost at which the articles composing that real reward can be produced or purchased.'[1]

If there is in this any qualification of the theory that the rate of profit depends on the labourer's proportion of the produce, Mill does not explain it in the chapter on Profits.

So far then the *Principles* show retrogression rather than advance from the position occupied in the *Essays*. In the Essay on Profits and Interest, Mill, though he used the most unwarrantable assumptions and invalid arguments, recognized that it is false to say that the rate of profit depends on the labourer's proportion of the produce. In the chapter 'Of Profits' in the *Principles*, he affirms without qualification the truth of that absurd proposition.

The chapter on the 'Influence of the progress of industry and population on rents, profits, and wages'[2] contains the old doctrine that in the progress of wealth and population the rate of profit tends to fall, because the 'cost of the labourer's subsistence tends on the whole to increase', in consequence of the necessity of employing less productive agricultural industry, and that this tendency is counteracted from time to time by 'agricultural improvement'. Mill appears now to think that the two forces are actually about equally strong, since he confines himself to a statement that agricultural improvement, 'in the manner in which it generally takes place', does not actually raise the rate of profit, and does not say that it does not prevent it from falling.[3]

At last, in the chapter 'Of the tendency of profits to a minimum',[4] he betrays some slight suspicion that something more than a *réchauffé* of the ideas of 1815 is required. He begins to quote E. G. Wakefield, Dr Chalmers, and William Ellis, who had written an article on 'Machinery' in the *Westminster Review* in 1826. The result, however, is not very great. The 'minimum' to which the rate of profit tends, is the rate at which the accumulation of capital would cease, because the profit to be obtained would not afford sufficient motive for further saving. Mill does not commit himself to any opinion as to what the minimum is now or is likely to be in the future, except that it must always be more than *nil* per cent. No matter what the real minimum may be, he says, the rate of profit in the great countries of Europe would soon fall to it, and capital consequently cease to increase, 'if capital continued to increase at its present rate, and no circumstances having a tendency to increase the rate of profit occurred in the meantime'.[5] A little further on, slightly varying the expression, he says that

[1] 1st ed., vol. i, p. 494; People's ed., p. 254 *b*.
[2] Bk. IV, ch. iii.
[3] 1st ed., vol. ii, p. 279; People's ed., p. 439.
[4] Bk. IV, ch. iv.
[5] 1st ed., vol. ii, p. 287; People's ed., p. 443.

'the mere continuance of the present annual increase of capital, if no circumstances occurred to counteract its effect, would suffice in a small number of years' to reduce the rate of profit to the minimum. It is by no means clear why Mill encumbered himself with a minimum, when all that he really wished to say was that the mere increase of capital tends to reduce the rate of profit. His supposition of capital increasing at its present rate till the rate of profit falls to a particular figure, and then suddenly ceasing to increase at all, can scarcely be considered a happy one. It was probably only the clumsy form in which he put the theory that enabled him to conceal from himself its practical identity with the theory of Adam Smith which the Ricardian school had rejected.

To show that the mere increase of capital tends to reduce profits, Mill says that as capital increased, population would either increase or not. If it increased 'in proportion to' the increase of capital, the rate of profit would be lowered, because the 'cost of the labourer's subsistence' would be increased in consequence of the employment of less productive agricultural industry.[1] This, of course, is the old Ricardian theory over again. As to what would happen if population did not increase, he relies on the theory so frequently found in his work, that the capital of the country is a wage-fund and nothing else. If population did not increase, he says,

> 'wages would rise, and a greater capital would be distributed among the same number of labourers. There being no more labour than before, and no improvements to render labour more efficient, there would not be any increase of the produce: and as the capital, however largely increased, would only obtain the same gross[2] return, the whole savings of each year would be exactly so much subtracted from the profits of the next, and of every following year. It is hardly necessary to say that in such circumstances, profits would very soon fall to the point at which further increase of capital would cease.'[3]

It is really amazing that J. S. Mill was allowed to say in edition after edition, that 'there would not be any increase of the produce' in consequence of an increase of the capital of the country unaccompanied by an increase of the population. The increase of the machinery of production of which the capital of the country consists, apart from all inventions and discoveries, is itself an improvement which 'renders labour more efficient'. It could only cease to do so if every one were supplied with a sufficiency of the best known tools and machinery – the best known type of factories, engines, ships, roads, and houses – and there seems no very immediate prospect of this consummation being reached, even if we suppose for the moment, with Mill, that population ceases to increase, and that no discoveries are made. Mill

[1] 1st ed., vol. ii, pp. 289, 290; People's ed., p. 444.

[2] Aggregate.

[3] 1st ed., vol. ii, p. 289; People's ed., p. 444 *a*.

either mixes up the mere increase of fixed capital with the discovery of new kinds of fixed capital, or else he has here, as often elsewhere, forgotten the existence of every sort of capital except his wage-fund capital.

The 'counteracting circumstances which in the existing state of things maintain a tolerably equal struggle against the downward tendency of profits',[1] are, he says, first (not perhaps very logically when the downward tendency is represented as the result of increase of capital), the loss of capital in bad investments; second, inventions which cheapen the articles consumed by labourers, and thus tend to reduce the 'cost of labour'; third, the acquisition of new powers of obtaining cheap necessaries from foreign countries; and fourth, again rather illogically, the exportation of capital.[2]

The non-appearance of the discovery of new methods of utilizing savings among these 'counteracting circumstances', is rendered the more surprising by the fact that Mill wrote not very long after the practicability of steam locomotion had been demonstrated, and at a period when great investments of capital were being made in railways. He does not seem to have thought that the profit to be obtained by these investments had any influence on the general rate of profit. He thought that railways might raise the rate of profits if by cheapening the commodities consumed by labourers they encouraged the propagation of the species, and thus reduced the cost of labour.[3] He appears also to have looked on investments of this kind as a sort of beneficial destruction of capital, and as consequently coming under the head of the first of his causes which counteract the decline of profits.[4] But this is all, and he gives us no reason to suppose that he believed that it would make any difference to the general rate of profit in his time whether railways could be constructed to bring in 50, 10 or 5 per cent. His first edition was published when the evil effects of the railway mania of 1845 and 1846 were still fresh in men's memories, and con-

[1] 1st ed., vol. ii, p. 290; People's ed., p. 444 *b*.

[2] 1st ed., vol. ii, pp. 290–298; People's ed., pp. 444–448.

[3] Bk. IV, ch. v, § 2; 1st ed., vol. ii, p. 304; People's ed., p. 451 *b*.

[4] Dealing with 'periods of overtrading and rash speculation', he says, 'Much capital is sunk which yields either no return or none adequate to the outlay. Factories are built, and machinery erected beyond what the market requires or can keep in employment. Even if they are kept in employment, the capital is no less sunk; it has been converted from circulating into fixed capital, and has ceased to have any influence on wages or profits'. – 1st ed., vol. ii, p. 291; People's ed., p. 445 *a*. That an investment, once made, ceases to influence the general rate of profit is true, since the rate of profit is determined by what can be got for new savings, but it is difficult to see how the existence of a factory which is 'kept in employment' can fail to influence wages, and how the capital invested in it can be 'none the less sunk' than if it has been wasted in building a useless factory – except, of course, on the assumption that wages are governed by a wage fund and nothing else.

sequently, instead of expecting every one to see in railways a new instrument of production, and a new method of utilizing savings, likely to add enormously to the productiveness of industry, and to check the fall of the rate of profit, he thought it necessary to apologize for 'the sinking of great sums in railways', and to urge that 'sums so applied are mostly a mere appropriation of the annual overflowing, which would otherwise have gone abroad, or been thrown away unprofitably, leaving neither a railway nor any other tangible result'.[1]

That Mill was here,as often, far behind his time, is shown by the fact that ten years before he published his *Essays*, and fourteen before he published his *Principles*, the little known Dublin professor, Mountifort Longfield, had approached far nearer to a true appreciation of the causes which determine the rate of profit. Rejecting altogether the Ricardian doctrine that the historical fall of profits is due to the declining productiveness of the last employed agricultural industry, he put forward a theory that the general rate of profit depends upon the labour-saving efficiency of the least efficient capital employed, and took as his type of capital, machinery instead of wage-fund.[2] The owner of a machine which gives assistance to the labourer will, he says,

> 'be paid for the use of it in proportion to its value, and the injury it receives from use, and the time during which it is lent, and not in proportion to its effect in increasing the efficiency of labour. . . . If the owner of one machine could obtain more for its use than the owner of another of equal value and durability, people would purchase, and artificers would then make the former rather than the latter, until the profits of each were reduced to their level. This level must be determined by the less efficient machine, since the sum paid for its use can never exceed the value of the assistance it gives the labourer. . . . Thus, the sum which can be paid for the use of any machine has its greatest limit determined by its efficiency in assisting the operations of the labourer, while its lesser limit is determined by the efficiency of that capital, which, without imprudence, is employed in the least efficient manner.'[3]

As the capital of a country becomes more plentiful in proportion to the population, some of it has to be employed in a less and less efficient manner, and consequently the rate of profit falls.

> 'In every case', he says, 'the profits of capital will be regulated by that portion of it which is obliged to be employed with the least efficiency in assisting labour, since none will be diverted to this employment as long as the owner thereof can derive a greater profit by giving it any other direction.
>
> 'This extends to the profits of capital, that principle of an equality between the supply and the effectual demand, which in all cases regu-

[1] Bk. IV, ch. v, § 2; 1st ed., vol. ii, p. 303; People's ed., p. 450 *b*.

[2] *Lectures on Political Economy, delivered in Michaelmas and Trinity Terms*, 1833. Dublin, 1834, Lecture ix.

[3] *Ibid.*, pp. 187, 188.

lates value. . . . In the case of capital and profits, this equality between the supply and the effective demand is produced by such a rate of profit as is equal to the assistance which is given to labour by that portion of capital which is employed with the least efficiency, which I shall call the last portion of capital brought into operation: and for the reasons already mentioned, the rate of profits cannot be much higher or lower than this.'[1]

'If a spade makes a man's labour twenty times as efficacious as it would be if unassisted by any instrument', it does not follow that the labourer who uses some other person's spade will give anything like $\frac{19}{20}$ of the produce of his labour for the use of it:

'This profit is not paid, because on account of the abundance of capital in the country, much must be employed in cases where, in proportion to its quantity, it is not so capable of multiplying the efficiency of the labourer; and the profits on this portion must regulate the profits of the rest.'[2]

§ 4. *Variations of Rent per acre*

Adam Smith 'concludes' what he justly calls his 'very long chapter' on rent, 'with observing that every improvement in the circumstances of the society tends either directly or indirectly to raise the real rent of land, to increase the real wealth of the landlord'.[3] 'The extension of improvement and cultivation', he says, and 'the rise in the real price of those parts of the rude produce of land, which is first the effect of extended improvement and cultivation, and afterwards the cause of their being further extended, the rise in the price of cattle, for example', tend to raise rent directly. Improvements which tend to reduce the real price of manufactures, and also 'every increase in the real wealth of the society, every increase in the quantity of useful labour employed within it', tend to raise rent indirectly.

For the proof of these propositions we naturally look back to the body of the chapter. But three-fifths of it are occupied with the acknowledged 'Digression concerning the variations in the value of silver', and nearly the whole of the remainder with very discursive remarks which relate chiefly to the differences in the rent paid on different kinds of produce at the same time, and only deal with differences in the rent paid on all kinds of produce at different times incidentally and not very frequently. Moreover, it is noteworthy that Adam Smith

[1] *Lectures*, p. 193. [2] *Ibid.*, p. 195.

[3] Book I, ch. xi, p. 115 *a*. The sentence continues, 'his power of purchasing the labour, or the produce of the labour of other people'. A little further down, however, he says, the 'real rent' will rise when 'the landlord is enabled to purchase a greater quantity of the conveniences, ornaments, or luxuries, which he has occasion for'. The two definitions do not coincide, since the quantity of labour required to produce a given quantity of conveniences, ornaments, or luxuries is not always the same.

seems to mean by the heading 'conclusion of the chapter', which he affixed to the last ten paragraphs, simply 'end of the chapter'. If he had meant by 'conclusion of the chapter' to indicate 'final result of the argument of the chapter', he would not have introduced it by saying, 'I shall conclude this very long chapter with observing'. We must then look chiefly to the 'conclusion' itself for the proof of the propositions contained in it.

In support of his first proposition, that 'the extension of improvement and cultivation' tends to raise rent directly, Adam Smith simply remarks, 'the landlord's share of the produce', that is, the amount of produce received by the landlord, 'necessarily increases with every increase of the produce'. The idea that some one might say that the whole increase of produce would go to wages or profits probably never occurred to him. That the real price of the increased quantity should be less than that of the original quantity he would have thought incompatible with the extension of improvement and cultivation.

His second proposition, that the rise in the real price of certain awkwardly defined parts of the produce tends to raise rent directly, he also considers self-evident, taking it for granted that the quantity of produce received by the landlord will not be diminished: 'the real value of the landlord's share, his real command of the labour of other people', he thinks, 'rises with the real value of the produce'. Going most unnecessarily out of his way, he asserts that the rise of price tends to raise rent 'in a still greater proportion' than the extension of improvement and cultivation, and seems to imagine very confusedly that this can be proved by showing that the landlord will have a larger proportion of the produce.

His third proposition, that reductions in the price of manufactures tend to raise rent indirectly, he endeavours to prove by simply pointing out that the cheaper manufactures are, the more of them a given money or raw produce rent will buy. As he does not imagine there is anything in the cheapening of manufactures which will diminish money rent, it follows, obviously, that cheapening manufactures increases the real wealth of the landlord.

The fourth proposition, that 'every increase in the real wealth of the society, every increase in the quantity of useful labour employed within it, tends indirectly to raise the real rent of land', Adam Smith believes to require very little proof. 'A certain proportion of this labour', he says, 'naturally goes to the land. A greater number of men and cattle are employed in its cultivation, the produce increases with the stock which is thus employed in raising it, and the rent increases with the produce.'

Neither in the article on Political Economy in the *Encyclopædia*

Britannica in 1810, nor in Boileau's treatise in 1811, does there appear to be any feeling that Adam Smith's theory as to the causes of variations of rent is seriously inadequate or erroneous. Buchanan, who looked on the ownership of land as a gigantic natural monopoly, probably thought it a simple matter that when population, and consequently the demand for raw produce, increase, the price and the quantity of raw produce should increase also and raise rent. In a note to Adam Smith's comparison of the price of hides in a barbarous country with their price 'in an improved and manufacturing country,'[1] he says:

> 'The demand of an improved country for every sort of rude produce is so great that it must raise the prices in spite of any regulation to the contrary; and Dr Smith's great error is that he never gives sufficient weight to those natural causes.'[2]

And in a note to Adam Smith's remark that when a greater number of men and cattle are employed in the cultivation of the land, 'the rent increases with the produce',[3] he says simply, 'When the produce increases, there is no doubt that the rent must increase along with it.'[4]

In the tract on the *Nature and Progress of Rent*, Malthus, after examining 'the nature and origin of rent', considers 'the laws by which it is governed, and by which its increase or decrease is regulated':

> 'When capital has accumulated', he says, 'and labour fallen on the most eligible lands of a country, other lands, less favourably circumstanced with respect to fertility or situation, may be occupied with advantage. The expenses of cultivation, including profits, having fallen, poorer land, or land more distant from markets, though yielding at first no rent, may fully repay these expenses, and fully answer to the cultivator. And, again, when either the profits of stock or the wages of labour, or both, have still further fallen, land still poorer, or still less favourably situated, may be taken into cultivation. And, at every step, it is clear that if the price of produce does not fall, the rents of land will rise. And the price of produce will not fall, as long as the industry and ingenuity of the labouring classes, assisted by the capitals of those not employed on the land, can find something to give in exchange to the cultivators and landlords, which will stimulate them to continue undiminished their agricultural exertions, and maintain their increasing excess of produce.'[5]

The main causes which increase the difference between the price of produce and the expenses of cultivation[6] are, he says,

> '1st, such an accumulation of capital as will lower the profits of stock; 2ndly, such an increase of population as will lower the wages of labour; 3rdly, such agricultural improvements, or such increase of

[1] Bk. I, ch. xi, p. 108 *a*.

[2] Buchanan's ed. of *Wealth of Nations*, vol. i, p. 390.

[3] Bk. I, ch. xi, M'Culloch's ed., p. 115 *b*.

[4] Buchanan's ed., vol. i, p. 447.

[5] Pp. 21, 22.

[6] At first he says, 'diminish the expenses of cultivation or reduce the cost of the instruments of production compared with the price of produce', but it soon appears that he is thinking of the difference and not the ratio between the expenses of production and the price of the produce (see p. 25).

exertions, as will diminish the number of labourers necessary to produce a given effect; and 4thly, such an increase in the price of agricultural produce, from increased demand, as without nominally lowering the expense of production, will increase the difference between this expense and the price of produce.'

The operation of the first three causes he considers 'quite obvious'. With regard to the fourth he thinks it necessary to offer 'a few further observations', which are simply a part of his explanation of the recent rise of rent in England disguised in the form of wide general propositions. Increase of demand in surrounding nations for imports of raw produce might, he says, greatly raise the price of raw produce in the exporting country, while the expenses of cultivation would rise 'only slowly and gradually to the same proportion'.

> 'Nor would the effect be essentially different in a country which continued to feed its own people, if, instead of a demand for its raw produce, there was the same increasing demand for its manufactures. These manufactures, if from such a demand the value of their amount in foreign countries was greatly to increase, would bring back a great increase of value in return, which increase of value could not fail to increase the value of the raw produce.'[1]

Observing that it will be objected that the increased difference between the price of raw produce and the expenses of cultivation thus caused will form, not a permanent increase of landlords' rent, but a temporary increase of farmers' profits, he relies on the fact that landlords do not compensate their tenants for improvements:

> 'The increased capital which is employed in consequence of the opportunity of making great temporary profits, can seldom or [n]ever be entirely removed from the land at the expiration of the current leases; and on the renewal of these leases the landlord feels the benefit of it in the increase of his rents.'[2]

It is not necessary, of course, he explains, for a rise of rent, that all four causes should operate at once, but only that by one or some of them the difference between the price of produce and the expenses of production should be increased. During the last twenty years rents had been raised 'by improvements in the modes of agriculture and by the constant rise of prices, followed only slowly by a proportionate rise' of the expenses of production, although profits had been higher.

As a corollary of this theory as to the causes which determine rent, Malthus lays it down that 'no fresh land can be taken into cultivation till rents have risen, or would allow of a rise upon what is already cultivated'.[3] Poor land, he says, is costly to cultivate, and if the price of produce will not pay the cost, it must remain uncultivated. Consequently, in order that cultivation may be extended to poorer land, it is necessary that the difference between the price of produce and the expenses

[1] P. 23. [2] P. 26. [3] P. 27.

of cultivation should increase. Whenever this happens rents rise.

> 'It is equally true', he adds, 'that without the same tendency to a rise of rents, occasioned by the operation of the same causes, it cannot answer to lay out fresh capital in the improvement of old land – at least upon the supposition that each farm is already furnished with as much capital as can be laid out to advantage, according to the actual rate of profits.'[1]

In the *Essay on the Influence of a Low Price of Corn* Ricardo ascribed the increase of rent, measured in corn or 'raw produce', entirely to the fall in the rate of profit, which he supposed to be occasioned by the diminishing productiveness of the successive additions to labour or 'capital' expended on the land. Wages being fixed by extraneous causes, the whole of the surplus of produce over wages is supposed in the first stage of cultivation to belong to profits. When additional capital is expended with a diminished return, and the rate of profit consequently falls, a smaller amount of produce is required to pay the profits of the original capital. The whole surplus over wages, or net return, yielded by the original capital therefore becomes divided into two parts; first, the reduced profits, and, secondly, a rent to the owner of the land on which capital yielding a larger return than is necessary to pay the ordinary rate of profit can be employed. In a numerical example, the statistics of the first four stages of cultivation are supposed to be as follows,[2] both capital and produce being reckoned, not in pounds sterling, but in quarters of corn:

	Capital employed.		Produce, including replacement of capital.			
	Fixed.	Circulating.	Replacement of fixed capital.	Replacement of circulating capital.	Profits.	Rents.
FIRST STAGE. Profits 50 per cent	A 100	A 100	x	100	100	0
SECOND STAGE. Profits 42·85 per cent	A 100	A 100	x	100	85·71	14·28
	B 100	B 110	x	110	90	0
THIRD STAGE. Profits 36·36 per cent	A 100	A 100	x	100	72·72	27·27
	B 100	B 110	x	110	76·36	13·63
	C 100	C 120	x	120	80	0
FOURTH STAGE. Profits 30·43 per cent	A 100	A 100	x	100	60·86	39·13
	B 100	B 110	x	110	63·91	26·08
	C 100	C 120	x	120	66·95	13·04
	D 100	D 130	x	130	70	0

[1] Pp. 28, 29.

[2] *Works*, pp. 371, 373. See also above, pp. 281, 282.

The rent paid in respect of the capital numbered A increases from 0 to 14·28, 27·27, and 39·13, and the total of all rents increases from 0 to 14·28, 40·9, and 78·26. How much the rent of any particular acre increases we are not told, since it is left an open question whether the capitals A, B, C, and D are employed on the same or on different land.

The landlord, Ricardo points out, is benefited 'by the increasing difficulty of procuring food, in consequence of accumulation,' in a double manner. He gets a larger rent, reckoned in raw produce, and raw produce is at a higher price:

> 'Not only is the situation of the landlord improved (by the increasing difficulty of procuring food, in consequence of accumulation) by obtaining an increased quantity of the produce of the land, but also by the increased exchangeable value of that quantity. If his rent be increased from 14 to 28 quarters it would be more than doubled, because he would be able to command more than double the quantity of commodities, in exchange for the 28 quarters. As rents are agreed for and paid in money, he would, under the circumstances supposed, receive more than double of his former money rent. . . .
>
> 'As the revenue of the farmer is realized in raw produce, or in the value of raw produce, he is interested, as well as the landlord, in its high exchangeable value, but a low price of produce may be compensated to him by a great additional quantity.
>
> 'It follows, then, that the interest of the landlord is always opposed to the interest of every other class in the community. His situation is never so prosperous as when food is scarce and dear: whereas, all other persons are greatly benefited by procuring food cheap.'[1]

Edward West, in his pamphlet on the *Application of Capital to Land*, treated of the causes which regulate rent, in the course of an endeavour to convince landowners that the consequences of a great importation of corn would not be so injurious to their interests as they supposed. If, he says, the cost of raising rude produce were always the same, whatever the quantity raised, landlords might well be alarmed at the idea of a great importation, since any considerable fall in the price of rude produce would sweep away all rents as well as all agricultural profits:

> 'But', he urges, 'our principle will show that by a diminution of the capital laid out by the farmer he will be enabled both to reproduce his capital with the common profits of stock on that capital, and also a rent not very much, perhaps, below that which he paid before.
>
> 'It is the diminishing rate of return upon additional portion of capital bestowed upon land that regulates, and almost solely causes, rent.
>
> 'If capital might be expended indefinitely with the same advantage upon land, the produce would, of course, be unlimited, and this would have the same effect upon rent as an unlimited quantity of land convenient for cultivation. In either case the rent would be very small. But

[1] *Works*, pp. 377, 378.

it is the necessity of having recourse to inferior land, and of bestowing capital with diminished advantage on land already in tillage, which increases rent. Thus, if in case of any increased demand for corn, capital could be laid out to the same advantage as before, the growing price of the increased quantity would be the same as before, and competition would, of course, soon reduce the actual price to the growing price, and there could be no increase of rent. But on any increased demand for corn, the capital, I have shown, which is laid out to meet this increased demand is laid out to less advantage. The growing price, therefore, of the additional quantity wanted is increased, and the actual price of that quantity must also be increased. But the corn that is raised at the least expense will, of course, sell for the same price as that raised at the greatest, and consequently the price of all corn is raised by the increased demand. But the farmer gets only the common profits of stock on his growth, which is afforded even on that corn which is raised at the greatest expense; all the additional profit, therefore, on that part of the produce which is raised at a less expense goes to the landlord in the shape of rent.

'Thus, suppose 10 acres of land which will return 20 per cent on a given capital, say £100; 10 acres which will return 19 per cent, and so on, as in the following table:

Acres	Capital	Net Produce
10	100	20
10	100	19
10	100	18 etc.
10	100	11
10	100	10'[1]

The assumption that these eleven 10-acre plots will all be cultivated with an equal capital strikes the reader as rather a bold one. West is evidently supposing them all to be devoted to the growth of corn, and to be cultivated in exactly the same manner:

'Supposing the profits of stock to be 10 per cent, the last 10 acres could not be taken at any rent for the purpose of cultivation, but might be cultivated by the owner of the land, or might afford a rent if left as pasture. The 10 acres which afford 11 per cent would, after paying the profits on the tenant's capital, pay 1 per cent as rent; and as the corn which was raised on the 10 best acres would sell for the same price as that raised on the 10 worst, such land would pay to the landlord £10 as rent, the next 10 acres £9, and so on. Suppose now the price of corn to rise, and the profit on the last 10 acres to be increased in consequence from £10 to £11, it is evident that the 10 acres which before could, in cultivation, just pay the profits of stock, would now afford a rent, and might be brought into cultivation, and that the rent would be raised on all land. For the same reason, if the price of corn were to fall so as to reduce the profit on the last 10 acres 1 per cent, some land would be withdrawn from cultivation, and the rent of that land which remained in cultivation would be lowered. But we know that a rise in the price of corn has the effect not only of drawing fresh land into cultivation, but also of turning fresh capital on land before in cultivation; and that a

[1] Pp. 49–51.

permanent fall in the price would have the effect not only of withdrawing land from tillage, but also the effect of withdrawing part of the capital from land which might be still kept in tillage and cultivated in a less expensive manner. But if you take the 10 acres of land I before mentioned, which return, at the given price, 20 per cent, it would seem impossible for any diminution of price under a diminution of one-half to draw capital from such land; for if the price of corn were to fall so low as even to reduce the profit to 11 per cent, still it might be worth while to lay out the same capital, as it would yield 1 per cent more than capital in any other employment, which 1 per cent would be the rent.'[1]

West's actual words in this last sentence imply that the net returns vary exactly with the price of the produce, but 'any diminution of price under a diminution of one-half' is probably only a blundering form of expression for 'any diminution of price which would reduce the net returns on the best ten acres by less than one-half'. By 'the same capital', he means, of course, 'the same amount of capital'. He proceeds to meet the objection thus:

'This difficulty is explicable on our principle alone. The truth is that any land which returns 20 per cent on £100 must, as I have shown, return more on a lesser capital than £100, and consequently must return more on the first portion of £100 laid out on it than on the latter portion of it, and would consequently produce the return somewhat in this way, the first £10 might reproduce 40 per cent net produce; the second £10 30 per cent, and so on, and the last layer of capital would not produce more than 10 per cent, as the farmer would, of course, lay on as much capital as would reproduce him the common profits of stock, which are supposed to be 10 per cent.

'The rent of the landlord would then still, as before, be all that was made on the whole capital above what the last or least profitable portion of that capital produced; and in the same manner as before, if the price of corn increased so as to make that portion of capital which before produced 10 per cent now produce 11 per cent, another portion of capital would be laid on. And in the same manner, if the price of corn were to fall so as to reduce the profits on the last portion of capital from 10 to 9 per cent, that portion would be withdrawn. In case, then, of any fall in the price of corn, that portion of the capital which before afforded the smallest profit will be withdrawn, and that only will be left which continues to yield an adequate return, and the effect of such reduction of price on rent will be nearly as follows:

'Suppose again the case of land let on the calculation of the price of wheat at 90*s* the quarter, the rent £300 a year, the tenant's capital amounting to £1,000, and his profit on that capital to be £100 a year, the produce is, as before, £1,400. Now, after the reduction of wheat to 60*s*, if the tenant retained the same capital on the land, he would not, as I showed, reproduce even his capital, much less be able to pay any rent.

'But suppose now on this fall of price he diminishes his capital to £800. Since he made on his whole capital of £1,000 before the reduction of price £400, i.e. 40 per cent, he must have made more than 40 per cent upon the first £800, and even after the reduction of price he may

[1] Pp. 51–53.

make 40 per cent on the £800, that is, £320, of which his own share as profit will be £80, leaving to the landlord £240 as rent.

'Thus, upon this supposition, a fall in the price of corn of ⅓ would reduce rents but $^1/_5$.'[1]

Torrens,[2] and very probably other writers, adopted, simultaneously with West and Ricardo, the theory that the necessity of cultivating inferior land to supply an increased demand for food raises rent. It would, indeed, have been very extraordinary if the theory had not been put forward in the early months of 1815. Inferior land had been brought into cultivation during the war, and rents had risen. The corn bill was being advocated in order to prevent the inferior lands from going out of cultivation, and to prevent rents from falling. What more natural than to connect the two phenomena?

It was scarcely possible to deny that rents would rise if increasing demand for food could only be satisfied by the employment of less productive agricultural industry than the least productive employed before. To the protectionists this was an extemely objectionable proposition. One of them, who wrote a history of the precious metals, and afterwards became Comptroller of Corn Returns, was asking 'what reason or justice' there could be in the proposal that 'rents must be lowered';[3] another, a 'farmer's friend', thought it as wicked to suggest a fall of rents as to suggest a repudiation of the national debt: 'Rent', he cried, 'is surely as sacred a property as the funds'.[4] Men imbued with these ideas could not be expected to give an enthusiastic welcome to a proposition which associated rise of rent with diminishing productiveness of agriculture, even if it had not been accompanied by the deduction drawn by Torrens, that keeping up rents by protection 'would be tantamount to laying a tax upon bread for the purpose of pensioning off the landed aristocracy'.[5] But to attack the proposition itself was difficult, and they had to content themselves with scoffing at the idea of 'withdrawing' capital from the land,[6] and with a number of rather irrelevant observations, such as that the lands which had been last taken into cultivation were not the worst.[7]

[1] Pp. 53–55.

[2] *Essay on the External Corn Trade*, pp. 219, 220, *et passim*.

[3] William Jacob, *Considerations on the Protection required by British Agriculture, and on the Influence of the Price of Corn on Exportable Productions*, 1814, pp. 82, 83.

[4] George Webb Hall, *Letters on the Importance of encouraging the Growth of Corn and Wool in the United Kingdom*, 1815, pp. 27, 28.

[5] *Essay on the External Corn Trade*, p. 317.

[1] Jacob, *Letter to Whitbread*, 1815, p. 37.

[2] Arthur Young, *Inquiry into the Rise of Prices in Europe*, 1815, in the *Pamphleteer*, vol. vi, p. 189. 'Were I to name any soils least likely to be abandoned, I should without hesitation instance what are usually reckoned poor soils; that is, the great tracts upon which the best and most effective of modern improvements have taken place: in other words, those on which capitals were, in point of time, the last invested: which is directly contrary to the suppositions of those many writers who have treated on the progressive investment of capital to land.'

That the necessity of employing less productive industry in order to supply an increased demand for food can be a cause of rise of rent consequently became immediately an accepted principle of political economy, and has remained so to the present time. But Ricardo was not content to let the necessity of employing less productive industry merely rank as one of many possible causes of rise of rent. He endeavoured to disprove the existence of any other causes. One of the other causes suggested by Malthus, as we have seen, was a fall of wages. In the *Essay* Ricardo says that a fall of wages could not raise rent, and would only raise profits'.[1] In the *Principles* he explains that wages and profits being together fixed by the amount obtainable on the land which pays no rent, a rise or fall of wages cannot affect rent.[2] Another possible cause suggested by Malthus was improvements in agriculture. This cause also Ricardo dismisses very summarily in the *Essay*. In one note, coupling improvements along with falls of wages, he simply remarks that it appears to him that they will only augment profits.[3] In another note he shows that he was ready to admit that at some distance of time after an improvement rent might rise again as high as it was before:

> 'The low price of corn caused by improvements in agriculture would give a stimulus to population by increasing profits and encouraging accumulation, which would again raise the price of corn and lower profits. But a larger population could be maintained at the same price of corn, the same profits, and the same rents. Improvements in agriculture may then be said to increase profits and to lower for a time rents.'[4]

But an admission that rent may recover its old level in spite of an improvement is by no means equivalent to an admission that it may eventually rise in consequence of an improvement. And so sure did Ricardo feel of his ground that he ventured on the following *reductio ad absurdum* of the protectionist claims as the peroration of his *Essay:*

> 'If the interests of the landlord be of sufficient consequence to determine us not to avail ourselves of all the benefits which would follow from importing corn at a cheap price, they should also influence us in rejecting all improvements in agriculture and in the implements of husbandry, for it is as [*sic*] certain that corn is rendered cheap, rents are lowered, and the ability of the landlord to pay taxes is, for a time at least, as much impaired by such improvements as by the importation of corn. To be consistent, then, let us by the same act arrest improvement and prohibit importation.'[5]

In the *Principles* Ricardo put forward exactly the same theory re-

[1] *Works*, p. 372, note.
[2] 1st ed., pp. 568, 570; 3rd ed. in *Works*, pp. 250, 251.
[3] *Works*, p. 372, note 1.
[4] *Works*, p. 377, note 1.
[5] *Ibid.*, p. 390.

garding effects of improvements as in the *Essay*, and worked it out in greater detail:

> 'If', he says, 'a million quarters of corn be necessary for the support of a given population, and it be raised on land of the qualities of Nos. 1, 2, 3; and if an improvement be afterwards discovered by which it can be raised on No. 1 and 2 without employing No. 3, it is evident that the immediate effect must be a fall of rent; for No. 2 instead of No. 3 will then be cultivated without paying any rent; and the rent of No. 1, instead of being the difference between the produce of No. 3 and No. 1, will be the difference only between No. 2 and 1. With the same population and no more, there can be no demand for any additional quantity of corn; the capital and labour employed on No. 3 will be devoted to the production of other commodities desirable to the community, and can have no effect in raising rent unless the raw material from which they are made cannot be obtained without employing capital less advantageously on the land, in which case No. 3 must again be cultivated.
>
> 'It is undoubtedly true that the fall in the relative price of raw produce in consequence of the improvement in agriculture, or rather in consequence of less labour being bestowed on its production, would naturally lead to increased accumulation; for the profits of stock would be greatly augmented. This accumulation would lead to an increased demand for labour, to higher wages, to an increased population, to a further demand for raw produce, and to an increased cultivation. It is only, however, after the increase in the population that rent would be as high as before; that is to say, after No. 3 was taken into cultivation. A considerable period would have elapsed, attended with a positive diminution of rent.'[1]

Ricardo does not say here whether he is speaking of rent measured in produce – corn rent – or rent measured by the money value of that produce, but as he says at the end of the chapter that he has been considering corn rent and not money rent,[2] we may examine his argument on the assumption first that he means corn rent.

The statement that it is only after No. 3 is again taken into cultivation that corn rent will be as high as before obviously contains the proposition that corn rent will not be as high as before until No. 3 is again taken into cultivation, and it seems also to imply, though not quite necessarily, that as soon as No. 3 is again taken into cultivation corn rent will be as high as before. Now neither of these propositions is always true. In the arithmetical example which Ricardo gives to illustrate his doctrine[3] it happens to be true that when the land thrown out of cultivation is again taken into cultivation corn rent is again as high as before, but this is only so because he supposes in the example

[1] 1st ed., pp. 69, 70; 3rd ed. in *Works*, pp. 41, 42.

[2] He says he has been considering the landlord's 'proportion of the whole produce', but the illustrative note which is appended makes it clear that this only means the absolute amount of rent measured in produce.

[3] 1st ed., pp. 72, 73; 3rd ed. in *Works*, pp. 42, 43.

– what is not very likely to occur – that the improvement adds 'an equal augmentation', that is, an equal absolute amount, to the produce of each of the successive qualities of land or portions of capital employed. Supposing four equal portions of capital to yield produce of

$$100+90+80+70=340,$$

and therefore to pay rents of

$$30+20+10=60,$$

he makes an 'improvement' increase each of the four amounts of produce by 25, so that they become

$$125+115+105+95=440.$$

After the intermediate period 'attended with a positive diminution of rent' has elapsed, and the whole of this produce is required, so that 'No. 4', which had ceased to be employed, is once more called in, the corn rent will be as high as before,

$$30+20+10=60.$$

But if Ricardo had supposed the produce to increase to

$$122+115+108+105=450,$$

the corn rent would be

$$17+10+3=30,$$

not so high as it was originally; and if he had supposed the produce to increase to

$$127{\cdot}7+115+102{\cdot}2+89{\cdot}4=434{\cdot}4,$$

the corn rent would be

$$38{\cdot}3+25{\cdot}5+12{\cdot}7=76{\cdot}6,$$

considerably higher than it was originally, and as the gradations between the beginning of 'No. 1' and the end of 'No. 4' must be actually much more numerous than three, this shows that corn rent would be 'as high as before' at some time before the whole of No. 4 is again called in.

The proposition that 'a considerable period would have elapsed attended with a positive diminution of rent' is no more necessarily true than the proposition which precedes it. If the produce

$$100+90+80+70=340$$

increased, as Ricardo supposes, to

$$125+115+105+95=440,$$

so that the produce of Nos. 1, 2, and 3,

$$125+115+105=345,$$

would be sufficient for the immediate wants of the population, corn rent would fall from a total of 60 to

$$20+10=30.$$

If the produce increased, as in our first example above, to

$$122+115+108+105=450,$$

so that the produce of Nos. 1, 2, and 3,

$$122+115+108=345,$$

would be sufficient, corn rent would fall from 60 to

$$14+7=21.$$

and if the produce increased as in our second example to

$$127{\cdot}7+115+102{\cdot}2+89{\cdot}4=434{\cdot}4,$$

so that the produce of Nos. 1, 2, and 3,

$$127{\cdot}7+115+102{\cdot}2=345$$

would be again sufficient, corn rent would fall from 60 to

$$25+12{\cdot}7=37{\cdot}7.$$

But if the produce increased to

$$140+110+90+77=417,$$

so that the produce of Nos. 1, 2, and 3,

$$140+110+90=340$$

would be sufficient, corn rent would rise from 60 to

$$50+20=70,$$

and no period 'considerable' or inconsiderable, 'would have elapsed attended with a positive diminution of rent'.

To make Ricardo's doctrine true of corn rent, we must suppose what we have no grounds for believing, and what seems *primâ facie* improbable, that improvements always add an equal absolute amount to the produce of each of the successive 'layers' of capital, or at any rate that they never add a larger absolute amount to the produce of the more productive layers, than to that of the less productive layers. That either of these assumptions is in accordance with facts Ricardo does not assert, though he perhaps implies that the first is so in the sentence which immediately precedes his arithmetical example:

> 'If by the introduction of the turnip husbandry, or by the use of a more invigorating manure, I can obtain the same produce with less capital and without disturbing the difference between the productive powers of the successive portions of capital, I shall lower rent; for a different and more productive portion will be that which will form the standard from which every other will be reckoned.'[1]

As he professes to be dealing with improvements in general, and yet does not think it necessary to consider the case of improvements which cannot be effected 'without disturbing the difference between the productive powers of the successive portions of capital', we must suppose that it did not occur to him that there was such a case.[2]

[1] 1st ed., p. 72; 3rd ed. in *Works*, p. 42.

[2] Professor Marshall, in his Note on Ricardo's doctrines as to the incidence of taxes and the influence of improvements in agriculture, says (*Principles of Economics*, 4th ed., bk. VI, ch. ix, p. 720) 'that Ricardo divides improvements in the arts of agriculture into two classes, the first of which consists of those improvements which make it possible to "obtain the same produce with less capital, and without disturbing the difference between the productive powers of the successive

If we examine Ricardo's doctrine with regard to improvements on the assumption that, in spite of what he says at the end of the chapter he was really thinking, not of corn rent, but of money rent, the result is still unsatisfactory, though not in quiet so high a degree. As he supposes the price of corn to vary exactly with the productiveness of the least productive capital of labour[1] employed, an increase of corn rent caused by an improvement will often be more than counterbalanced by a fall in the price of the corn. When all the layers of capital are once more in operation – when No. 3 or No. 4 is again taken into cultivation – the increase of corn rent caused by a *proportionate* addition to the produce of each layer will be exactly counterbalanced by the decrease in the price of corn. If, for instance, as we have already supposed, the produce increases from $100+90+80+70$ to $127{\cdot}7+115+102{\cdot}2+89{\cdot}4$, and the corn rent from 60 to 76·6, the price of corn falls in the proportion of 89·4 to 70, and $\frac{70}{89{\cdot}4}x\times 76{\cdot}6=60x$, so that money rent would be the same as it was originally. And when one or more of the layers of capital has temporarily ceased to be employed, the increase of corn rent caused by a proportionate addition to the produce of each layer is necessarily somewhat more than counterbalanced by the decrease in the price of corn. If, for instance, the produce of the four layers of capital is at first

$$100+96+68+66=330,$$

and each is increased by 25 per cent, so that Nos. 1, 2, and 3, producing

$$125+120+85=330,$$

will be sufficient, corn rent will be increased from

$$34+30+2=66 \text{ to } 40+35=75;$$

but as the price of corn will fall in the proportion of 85 to 66, money rent will fall from $66x$ to $\frac{66}{85}x\times 75=58x$. But an improvement which added a larger percentage to the produce of the more productive layers of capital than to that of the less productive might raise money rent not only before No. 4 was again taken into cultivation, but immediately. In our last example, if the produce of Nos. 1, 2, and 3 increases from

$$100+96+68 \text{ to } 130+125+75=330,$$

portions of capital"; of course neglecting for the purpose of his general argument the fact that any given improvement may be of greater service to one particular piece of land than another'. But Ricardo simply divides improvements into 'those which increase the productive powers of the land, and those which enable us by improving our machinery to obtain its produce with less labour' (3rd ed. in *Works*, p. 42; 1st ed., pp. 70, 71, omitting the words 'by improving our machinery'), and it is not merely improvements which affect qualities of land irregularly that are neglected, but also improvements which affect all qualities regularly but not in such a way as to preserve the existing scale.

[1] 'Less capital, which is the same thing as less labour', 1st ed., p. 74; 3rd ed. in *Works*, p. 43.

the corn rent will increase from 66 to 105, and the money rent will will increase from $66x$ to $\frac{66}{75}x \times 105 = 92\frac{2}{5}x$. Consequently, to make Ricardo's doctrine true of money rent, we must suppose that improvements always add an equal percentage to the produce of each of the successive layers of capital, or, at any rate, that they never add a greater percentage to the produce of the more productive layers than to that of the less productive. In the chapter on 'Mr Malthus's opinions on rent' Ricardo boldly asserts that improvements 'probably' do add equal percentages to the produce of all the different layers:

> 'Nothing can raise rent', he says, 'but a demand for new land of an inferior quality, or some cause which shall occasion an alteration in the relative fertility of the land already under cultivation. Improvements in agriculture and in the division of labour are common to all land; they increase the absolute quantity of raw produce obtained from each, but probably do not much disturb the relative proportions which before existed between them.'[1]

But we can scarcely be expected to accept this curious piece of agricultural history on the mere *ipse dixit* of a retired stockbroker. Ricardo himself appears not to have been aware of it when he wrote his chapter on Rent, for there, as we have seen, he gives an example in which the successive layers receive equal and not proportionate augmentations.

What is perhaps the strangest part of Ricardo's theory with regard to the effect of agricultural improvements on rent still remains to be considered. Immediately after describing in general terms the temporary and permanent effects of improvements,[2] and before explaining and illustrating his view, he says:

> 'But improvements in agriculture are of two kinds: those which increase the productive powers of the land, and those which enable us, by improving our machinery, to obtain its produce with less labour. They both lead to a fall in the price of raw produce; they both affect rent, but they do not affect it equally. If they did not occasion a fall in the price of raw produce they would not be improvements; for it is the essential quality of an improvement to diminish the quantity of labour before required to produce a commodity; and this diminution cannot take place without a fall of its price or relative value.'[3]

Hitherto we have assumed that all improvements belong to the first of the two classes, and, as Ricardo puts it, 'absolutely enable us to obtain the same produce' as before 'from a smaller quantity of land'. It is with regard to this class that he supposes his case to be strongest, since when he says the two kinds of improvements do not

[1] 1st ed., pp. 570, 571; 3rd ed. in *Works*, pp. 251, 252.
[2] Above, pp. 322, 323.
[3] 1st ed., pp. 71, 72; 3rd ed. in *Works*, p. 42. The words 'by improving our machinery' are not in the first edition.

affect rent equally, he apparently means that improvements of the first class lower it more than those of the second class, because they lower both money rent and corn rent.[1] We must now inquire how Ricardo attempts to show that improvements of the second class must diminish rent, at any rate temporarily. The answer is that he does not attempt to show it at all. After finishing his discussion of the first class, he says:

> 'But there are improvements which may lower the relative value of produce without lowering the corn rent, though they will lower the money rent of land. Such improvements do not increase the productive powers of the land, but they enable us to obtain its produce with less labour. They are rather directed to the formation of the capital applied to the land, than to the cultivation of the land itself. Improvements in agricultural implements, such as the plough and the threshing machine, economy in the use of horses employed in husbandry, and a better knowledge of the veterinary art are of this nature. Less capital, which is the same thing as less labour, will be employed on the land; but to obtain the same produce less land cannot be cultivated.'

After this explanation of the nature of the second class of improvements, we naturally expect Ricardo to show how 'they will lower the money rent of land'. Instead of doing so, he takes it for granted, and calmly proceeds:

> 'Whether improvements of this kind, however, affect corn rent, must depend on the question whether the difference between the produce obtained by the employment of different portions of capital be increased, stationary, or diminished. If four portions of capital, 50, 60 70, 80, be employed on the land, giving each the same results, and any improvement in the formation of such capital should enable me to withdraw 5 from each, so that they should be 45, 55, 65, and 75, no alteration would take place in the corn rent';[2]

In his assumption that in this case money rent will fall, and in his statement that no alteration will take place in the corn rent, Ricardo, in spite of the rigorous logic with which he is so often credited, is absolutely and almost obviously wrong. This is a mere question of arithmetic. If the number of quarters of corn produced by each of the four 'portions of capital' be x, then the original corn rent will be of the 80, nil, of the 70, $\frac{10}{80}x$, of the 60, $\frac{20}{80}x$, and of the 50, $\frac{30}{80}x$, in all $\frac{3}{4}x$, and if a quarter is worth £4, money rent will be £3x. After the improvement, the corn which regulates the price can be produced with $\frac{5}{80}$ 'less capital, which is the same thing as less labour', and consequently the price of corn falls from £4 to £3$\frac{3}{4}$, the corn rent rises from

$$\frac{10}{80}x+\frac{20}{80}x+\frac{30}{80}x=\frac{3}{4}x$$
$$\text{to } \frac{10}{75}x+\frac{20}{75}x+\frac{30}{75}x=\frac{4}{5}x,$$

[1] An improvement which affected money rent only might of course lower money rent more than an improvement which affected both money and corn rent, but Ricardo does not think of this.

[2] 1st ed., p. 74; 3rd ed. in *Works*, p. 43.

and the money rent remains £$3\frac{3}{4}\times\frac{4}{5}x=3x$, exactly the same as before. If equal absolute amounts are taken away from the 'four portions of capital', corn rent will always rise, and money rent will always remain the same.[1] Curiously enough, Ricardo himself, in the chapter on Taxes on Raw Produce, recognizes, the converse case, namely, that the addition of an equal absolute amount to each of the four portions will diminish the corn rent and leave the money rent unaltered.[2]

Oblivious of his error as to the effect of the subtraction of an equal absolute amount from each capital, he rashly enters on what he imagines to be an *a fortiori* argument:

> 'but if the improvements were such as to enable me to make the whole saving on that portion of capital which is least productively employed, corn rent would immediately fall, because the difference between the capital most productive and the capital least productive would be diminished; and it is this difference which constitutes rent.'[3]

This is quite true. If, for example, the improvement deducted 20 from the 80 of capital, and nothing from the 70, 60, and 50, the corn rent would be

$$\frac{10}{70}x+\frac{10}{70}x+\frac{20}{70}x=\frac{3}{7}x$$

instead of $\frac{3}{4}x$. But what possible right has Ricardo to put this case of the whole saving being made on that portion of capital which is least productively employed, without putting the converse case of the whole saving being made on that portion which is most productively employed? Obviously none whatever, and when we do put this converse case, we find that both the corn rent and the money rent would immediately rise. If, for example, we deduct 20 from the 50 of capital, and nothing from the 60, 70, and 80, we find the corn rent will be

$$\frac{10}{80}x+\frac{20}{80}x+\frac{50}{80}x=x$$

instead of $\frac{3}{4}x$, and as nothing has happened to alter the value of a quarter of corn, the money rent will be £$4x$ instead of £$3x$.

Ricardo's attempt to show that improvements must temporarily lower rent, whether we apply it to his first or his second class of improvements, and whether we suppose him to mean money rent or corn rent, thus ends in complete and hopeless failure. No general rule

[1] To leave the corn rent the same as before, it would be necessary to deduct from the four portions of capital, not equal amounts, but equal percentages. For example, if each were reduced by 12½ per cent, or one-eighth, the corn rent would be

$$\frac{8\frac{3}{4}}{70}x+\frac{17\frac{1}{2}}{70}x+\frac{26\frac{1}{2}}{70}x=\frac{3}{4}x$$

exactly the same as before, while the money rent would fall from £$3x$ to £$3\frac{3}{4}\times\frac{3}{4}x$ $=$£$2\frac{13}{16}x$.

[2] 1st ed., pp. 196–198; 3rd ed. in *Works*, p. 92.

[3] 3rd ed. in *Works*, pp. 43, 44. This and the two preceding quotations are continuous. The 1st ed., p. 75 reads, 'the largest portion of capital, that portion' for 'that portion of capital'.

can be laid down with regard to the immediate effect of improvements. It will vary with the nature of the improvements and the circumstances of the country and soil to which they are applied.

Even if Ricardo had succeeded in proving that improvements must always lower rent for a time, he would not have attained the object he had in view, namely, to disprove the existence of every possible cause of rise of rent except the necessity of employing less productive industry. Whether improvements should be looked on as a cause of rise of rent or not must depend, not on their temporary, but on their permanent effects; and in the later editions of the *Principles* Ricardo admitted not only, as in the *Essay* and the first edition of the *Principles*, that when a certain length of time has elapsed after an improvement, rent may be again as high as before, but also that it may be higher than before in consequence of the improvement. In the third edition he inserted a note to the chapter on Rent:

> 'I hope I am not understood as undervaluing the importance of all sorts of improvements in agriculture to landlords—their immediate effect is to lower rent; but as they give a great stimulus to population, and, at the same time, enable us to cultivate poorer lands with less labour, they are ultimately of immense advantage to landlords. A period, however, must elapse during which they are positively injurious to him' [*sic*].[1]

In the chapter on Mr Malthus's Opinions on Rent he inserted several new sentences, in one of which he says that 'the improvement in agriculture' will give to the land a capability of bearing at some future period a higher rent, because with the same price of food there will be a great additional quantity'.[2] In the chapter on Rent he had supposed four equal portions of capital to yield a produce of

$$100+90+80+70=340.$$

He had made an improvement increase the four amounts of produce to

$$125+115+105+95=440,$$

and said that when the whole 440 was required, rent would be as high as before. At this stage corn would be, according to his assumptions, still only at $\frac{70}{95}$ of its original price. The condition of things contemplated in the new sentence just quoted is evidently a later stage, when, say, two more portions of capital are employed and the produce is

$$125+115+105+95+85+70=595,$$

and rent, instead of $30+20+10=60$, is

$$55+45+35+25+15=175,$$

the price of corn being the same as before. To allow that this increase of rent could not have happened without the improvement, and yet

[1] 3rd ed. in *Works*, p. 43.

[2] 2nd ed., p. 417; 3rd ed. in *Works*, p. 251.

to maintain that the improvement is a cause of diminution rather than increase of rent is inconsistent, and there is ground for Malthus's complaint that

> 'It is a little singular that Mr Ricardo, who has in general kept his attention so steadily fixed on permanent and final results as even to define the *natural* price of labour to be that price which would maintain a stationary population, although such a price cannot generally occur under moderately good governments and in an ordinary state of things, for hundreds of years, has always, in treating of rent, adopted an opposite course, and referred almost entirely to temporary effects.'[1]

Malthus would have none of Ricardo's theory that rise of rent is to be attributed exclusively to the necessity of employing less productive industry, and reprinted his *Nature and Progress of Rent* in his *Political Economy* with very little alteration. James Mill, on the other hand, says 'rent increases in proportion as the effect of the capital successively bestowed upon the land decreases',[2] and mentions no other cause of increase.

M'Culloch at first adopted Ricardo's theory with his usual thoroughness:

> 'An increase of rent is not,' he says, 'as is very generally supposed, occasioned by improvements in agriculture, or by an increase in the fertility of the soil. It results entirely from the necessity of resorting, as population increases, to soils of a *decreasing* degree of fertility. Rent varies in an inverse proportion to the amount of produce obtained by means of the capital and labour employed in cultivation; that is, *it increases when the profits of agricultural labour diminish, and diminishes when they increase.*'[3]

In the second edition of his *Principles* (1830), however, though he reprinted the last two sentences of this passage,[4] he showed that an improvement which added to the produce of the most productive capital, and not to that of the least productive, might raise rent immediately, and insisted that if an improvement did lower rent for a time, that time would be very short.[5]

In 1831 a vigorous attack on the Ricardian theory was made by Richard Jones.[6] Taking a much broader view of the matter than Ricardo, he surveyed the whole of history, instead of confining his attention to the circumstances of England during the war. It was, consequently, perfectly evident to him that the necessity of employing less productive agricultural industry was neither the only possible nor the most important actual cause of rise of rent, since in the last three hundred years, for example, rents in England had risen enormously, although the least productive agricultural industry employed was no

[1] *Political Economy*, p. 230.
[2] *Elements*, 1st ed., p. 16.
[3] *Principles*, 1st ed., pp. 268, 269.
[4] P. 434.
[5] Pp. 452–455.
[6] *Essay on the Distribution of Wealth*, Part I, *Rent*.

less productive than it had been at the beginning of the period. The obvious cause of the actual rise of rent in England was, he thought, not that the most costly portion of agricultural produce was obtained at greater cost, for this was not the case, but simply that a larger amount of produce was obtained.[1] There are, according to him, three great possible causes of rise of rent, and he puts Ricardo's 'One exclusive cause of every increase'[2] in the third place, regarding it as much the least important. The second cause is 'the increasing efficiency of the capital employed', or what Ricardo called improvements in agriculture. Improvements, he says, increase rent, except when 'the progress of improvement outstrips the progress of population and the growth of produce exceeds the growth of demand (an event rarely to be expected)'.[3] He ridicules Ricardo's supposition of 'a sudden spread of improvement by which, as by the stroke of a magic wand, two-thirds of the land of a country are made to produce as much as the whole did immediately before, while the population continues the same and no more':

> 'It is only necessary to remember the slowly progressive manner in which agricultural improvements are practically discovered, completed, and spread to perceive how very visionary this supposition of Mr Ricardo's really is. If two-thirds of the lands of England should ever produce as much as the whole does now (an event extremely probable), we may be quite sure that it will be by no sudden and magical stride that the improvement will establish itself: that the means of effecting it will be discovered in small portions at a time, perhaps at considerable intervals, and will be adopted into general practice tardily, and, we may almost predict, reluctantly and suspiciously. In the meantime, population and the demand for raw produce will not have been standing still. In the process by which increased supplies of food are produced for an increasing population, we observe no such wide dislocation between the supply and demand, no such sudden starts and jerks as Mr Ricardo is driven to suppose, in order to prove that all improvements in agriculture are unfavourable to the interests of the landlords. As the mass of the people slowly increase, we see the gradual pressure of demand stimulating the agriculturists to improvements, which, by an imperceptible progression of the supply, keep the people fed. While these processes are going on, every increase of produce occasioned by the general application to the old soils of more capital, acting upon them with unequal effect according to the differences of their original fertility, raises rents; and the interests of the landlords are at no moment opposed to improvements.'[4]

The cause of rise of rent which Jones places first is 'increase of produce caused by the use of more capital in cultivation',[5] without any decrease of the productiveness of the least productive industry employed. If we go back once more to Ricardo's supposition of an equal

[1] *Essay*, pp. 282–286. [2] *Ibid.*, p. 213. [3] *Ibid.*, p. 237.
[4] *Ibid.*, pp. 211, 212; referred to on p. 238. [5] *Ibid.*, p. 190.

amount of capital, let us say x, producing on four areas of land

$$100+90+80+70=340 \text{ quaters of corn,}$$

it is evident that if the demand increases to 680 quarters of corn, and this amount could be raised by employing $2x$ on each area without any diminution of returns, so as to produce 200+180+160+140, rent would rise from 30+20+10 to 60+40+20. Such a change is quite possible and probable, although Ricardo, as Jones complains, says 'if capital could be indefinitely employed without a diminished return on the old land there could be no rise of rent'.[1] If, however, we suppose that cultivation is always exactly as extensive as it would be if the cultivators started with a *tabula rasa*, so to speak, the change would not be a possible one unless an 'improvement' had been introduced. For if to produce 680 quarters the most profitable plan is to employ $2x$, producing 200 quarters, on land No. 1, $2x$, producing 180 quarters, on land No. 2, and so on, then the most profitable method of producing only 340 quarters would not be to employ x on land No. 1, x on land No. 2, x on land No. 3, and x on land No. 4, but to employ $2x$ on land No. 1, and $\frac{7}{9}x$ on land No. 2. And if there has been an 'improvement', the case is covered by the admission of Ricardo's second edition that an improvement 'will give to the land a capability of bearing at some future period a higher rent, because with the same price of food there will be a great additional quantity'.[2] As a matter of fact, of course, cultivators do not usually start with a *tabula rasa*, as Ricardo imagines when he talks about 'the first settling of a country'. So it might very well happen that x of capital might be employed on each of Nos. 1, 2, 3, and 4, although looking at the matter *a priori*, and disregarding the facts that lands Nos. 3 and 4 are prepared for cultivation, and that a portion of the population is settled upon them, it might be said to be more 'profitable' to employ $2x$ on No. 1, $\frac{7}{9}x$ on No. 2, and nothing on Nos. 3 and 4.

Senior, writing in 1836, makes no very positive contribution to the theory of the subject, but he attributes the rise of rents in England since 1700 to increase in the productivenss of the land.[3]

In his chapter on the 'Influence of the progress of industry and population on rents, profits, and wages', J. S. Mill gave full weight to the admission in Ricardo's third edition of the fact that improvements 'ultimately' benefit landlords, and appears to have been sometimes, at any rate, ready to admit that the actual historical rise of rent has been caused by improvements, and not by the necessity of employing less productive industry to raise the increased quantity of produce re-

[1] *Essay*, p. 297. Ricardo, *Principles*, 1st ed., p. 57; 3rd ed. in *Works*, p. 37. Ricardo apparently for the moment took 'the old land' to consist of one quality only.

[2] 2nd ed., p. 517; 3rd ed. in *Works*, p. 251; quoted above, p. 331.

[3] *Political Economy*, 8vo ed., p. 139.

quired.[1] But, in spite of M'Culloch, he adhered to the Ricardian theory that an improvement must diminish rent unless or until there is an increase of demand for produce. Dividing improvements into (1) those which 'enable a given quantity of food to be produced at less cost, but not on a smaller surface of land than before', and (2) those which 'enable a given extent of land to yield, not only the same produce with less labour, but a great produce; so that if no greater produce is required, a part of the land already under culture may be dispensed with', he says that, under the circumstances supposed, 'by the former of the two kinds of improvement rent would be diminished. By the second it would be diminished still more'.[2] To show the truth of the proposition, he assumes 'that the demand for food requires the cultivation of three qualities of land, yielding on an equal surface, and at an equal expense, 100, 80, and 60 bushels of wheat'. These will yield corn rents of 40+20=60 bushels, and if the 'equal expense' be £x, they will yield money rents of $\frac{2}{3}$ £x+$\frac{1}{3}$ £x=£x. Mill then supposes an improvement to be made which, 'without enabling more corn to be grown, enables the same corn to be grown with one-fourth less labour', meaning by this that the three equal surfaces of land are to continue yielding 100+80+60 bushels, but that the equal expense is to be reduced on each equal surface from £x to $\frac{3}{4}$ £x. Corn rent will then, he says, remain the same as before, but as the price of wheat will fall one-fourth, the money rent will be reduced from £x to $\frac{3}{4}$ £x. The fact that the corn rent remains the same, however, obviously results simply from the fact that, unlike Ricardo,[3] he has supposed the improvement to deduct an equal percentage from the three expenses of production. If he had supposed the improvement to deduct a larger percentage from the more productive expenses than from the less productive, the corn rent would have risen. And if the differences between the percentages had been large enough, not only corn rent but money rent also might have risen. For example, if by the improvement the expense of raising the 100 bushels was reduced to $\frac{1}{2}$ £x, that of raising the 80 bushels to $\frac{8}{11}$ £x, and that of raising the 60 bushels to $\frac{10}{11}$ £x, the corn rent would rise from 60 to 67+32=99 bushels, and the money rent would rise from £x to $1\frac{1}{2}$ £x.

To show that an improvement of the second kind would diminish rent 'still more', or 'in a still greater ratio', than an improvement of the first kind, Mill supposes 'that the amount of produce which the market requires can be grown not only with a fourth less labour, but

[1] *Principles*, Bk. IV, ch. iii; and see above, pp. 175–182.

[2] *Principles*, Bk. IV, ch. iii, § 4, 1st ed., vol. ii, pp. 270, 271; People's ed., pp. 434, 435.

[3] Ricardo deducted an equal absolute amount from unequal expenses, and consequently a larger percentage from the smaller expenses. See above, pp. 329, 330.

on a fourth less land'. Land, he says, 'equivalent to a fourth of the produce', i.e. land on which a fourth of the produce has been hitherto raised, 'must now be abandoned'. Corn rent will therefore fall from 60 to $133\frac{1}{3}-106\frac{2}{3}=26\frac{2}{3}$, and as the bushel of corn will fall to $\frac{60}{106\frac{2}{3}}$ of its former price, money rent will fall from £x to

$$\frac{26\frac{2}{3}}{60}\times\frac{60}{106\frac{2}{3}}\text{ £}x=\tfrac{1}{4}\text{ £}x.$$

In this example an equal percentage, $33\frac{1}{3}$, is added to each of the three quantities of produce. As Professor Marshall points out,[1] if, instead of 100, 80, and 60, the three quantities had been at first 115, 65, and 60 bushels, the improvement adding $33\frac{1}{3}$ per cent to each would have raised corn rent from 60 bushels to $66\frac{2}{3}$. And, as we have already shown,[2] if a larger percentage were added to the less costly quantities of the produce than to the more costly, cases are easily conceivable where the improvement would raise not only corn rent, but money rent also.

In the chapter 'Of Rent', Mill has nothing to say about the causes which produce variations of rent. The main proposition which he seeks to prove is that 'the rent of land consists of the excess of its return above the return to the worst land in cultivation, or to the capital employed in the least advantageous circumstances'.[3] This is obviously intended to give some information, not as to the rents of the same land at different times, but as to the rents of different pieces of land at the same time, and consequently does not belong to this part of our inquiry.[4]

[1] *Economics of Industry*, 1879, p. 85 note; *Principles*, 4th ed., p. 273.
[2] Above, p. 327.
[3] *Principles*, Bk. II, ch. xvi, summary of §§ 3 and 4 in Contents.
[4] See below, ch. viii, § 4.

CHAPTER VIII

DISTRIBUTION PROPER

§ 1. *Division of the whole Produce between Aggregate Wages, Aggregate Profits, and Aggregate Rents*

Now that we have dealt with the teaching of the economists of the period 1776 to 1848, not only with regard to what was known as production, but also with regard to the causes of variations of wages per head, profits per cent, and rent per acre, we are at last able to proceed to deal with the causes which determine the proportions in which the total produce or income of a community is divided between classes and individuals.

The first question is, 'What determines the proportions in which the produce is divided between the class of labourers, the class of capitalists, and the class of landlords, or, as it is put metaphorically, between Labour, Capital, and Land?'

Before Ricardo wrote, this question seems not to have occurred to any one, and it is only possible to find incidental and very incomplete propositions bearing upon it.

Adam Smith in one place says that 'the extension of improvement and cultivation' causes 'a greater proportion' of the produce of land 'to belong to the landlord',[1] but in another place he says, 'in the progress of improvement, rent, though it increases in proportion to the extent, diminishes in proportion to the produce of the land'.[2] The second of these contradictory statements he founded on observations of the facts; the first he founded on the somewhat shallow theory that when the price of the produce rises, a less proportion than before is necessary to remunerate the producer. Both propositions obviously relate to agricultural produce only, and consequently even if either of them had been proved, it would not have thrown much light on the distribution of the whole produce of labour, unless a certain relation between the total of agricultural produce and the total of other produce could have been shown to exist. With regard to the proportions of the produce obtained by profits and wages, Adam Smith has nothing to say. He always considers 'wages' as wages per labourer, and 'profits' either as an absolute aggregate amount, or as a rate or ratio between interest and principal.

The parliamentary inquiries which took place in the closing years of the great war showed that at that time the landlords proportion of

[1] Bk. I, ch. xi, p. 115 *a*. [2] Bk. II, ch. iii, p. 148 *a*.

the whole agricultural produce was declining.[1] Malthus noticed the fact, and West used it as one of the chief supports of his theory of the decline of profits.[2] No attempt was made, however, to deduce from it any generalizations with regard to the division of the whole income of the community between wages, profits, and rents.

The position of Ricardo with regard to the matter is a very peculiar one. In the Preface to his *Principles* he speaks almost as if he had fully realized the importance of the question, and imagined that he had at any rate contributed something towards a complete answer to it. He says:

> 'The produce of the earth – all that is derived from its surface by the united application of labour, machinery and capital, is divided among three classes of the community; namely, the proprietor of the land, the owner of the stock or capital necessary for its cultivation, and the labourers by whose industry it is cultivated.
>
> 'But in different stages of society the proportions of the whole produce of the earth, which will be allotted to each of these classes under the names of rent, profit, and wages, will be essentially different. . . .
>
> 'To determine the laws which regulate this distribution is the principal problem in Political Economy.'

It must be admitted that the repetitions of the word 'earth' and the introduction of the words 'cultivation' and 'cultivated', certainly show that Ricardo had in his mind the proportions in which agricultural produce is divided rather than the proportions in which the whole produce or income of the community is divided. But throughout his work he always appears to treat a farm as a kind of type of the industry of the whole country, and to suppose that the division of the whole produce can be easily inferred from the distribution on a farm, so that too much importance must not be attached to the observation.

Towards the end of the first chapter of the *Principles* he says:

> 'It is according to the division of the whole produce of the land and labour of the country between the three classes of landlords, capitalists, and labourers, that we are to judge of rent, profit, and wages, and not according to the value at which that produce may be estimated in a medium which is confessedly variable.
>
> 'It is not by the absolute quantity of produce obtained by either class that we can correctly judge of the rate of profit, rent, and wages, but by the quantity of labour required to obtain that produce. By improvements in machinery and agriculture the whole produce may be doubled; but if wages, rent, and profit be also doubled, these three will bear the same proportions to one another, and neither could be said to have relatively varied. But if wages partook not of the whole of this increase; if they, instead of being doubled, were only increased one-half, if rent, instead of being doubled, were only increased three-fourths, and the

[1] *Reports of Lords' Committees on Grain and the Corn Laws*, 1814 (in the House of Commons collection, 1814–15, vol. v, pp. 1035–1335), pp. 26, 46.

[2] Malthus, *Nature and Progress of Rent*, pp. 30, 31; West, *Application of Capital*, pp. 2, 27, 30.

remaining increase went to profit, it would, I apprehend, be correct for me to say that rent and wages had fallen, while profits had risen;'[1]

To say that rent and wages have fallen when you admit yourself that they have 'increased one-half' can scarcely under any circumstances be 'correct'. But underneath Ricardo's blundering method of expressing himself, his meaning so far, at first sight, seems to be plain enough. He seems plainly to wish to indicate that in discussing the distribution of the produce into wages, profit, and rent we ought to concern ourselves with the proportions in which it is divided among the three shares, and not with the total absolute amount of produce which goes to each share. The reason he gives for the procedure he recommends, however, puts rather a different face on the matter:

'for if', he continues, 'we had an invariable standard by which to measure the value of this produce, we should find that a less value had fallen to the class of labourers and landlords, and a greater to the class of capitalists than had been given before. We might find, for example, that though the absolute quantity of commodities had been doubled, they were the produce of precisely the former quantity of labour. Of every hundred hats, coats, and quarters of corn produced, if the

labourers had	25
The landlords	25
And the capitalists	50
	100

and if, after these commodities were doubled in quantity, of every 100

The labourers had only	22
The landlords	22
And the capitalists	56
	100

in that case I should say that wages and rent had fallen and profits risen; though, in consequence of the abundance of commodities, the quantity paid to the labourer and landlord would have increased in the proportion of 25 to 44. Wages are to be estimated by their real value, viz. by the quantity of labour and capital employed in producing them, and not by their nominal value either in coats, hats, money, or corn. Under the circumstances I have just supposed, commodities would have fallen to half their former value; and, if money had not varied, to half their former price also. If then, in this medium which had not varied in value, the wages of the labourer should be found to have fallen, it will not the less be a real fall, because they might furnish him with a greater quantity of cheap commodities than his former wages.'[2]

It becomes evident that what Ricardo really wishes to say is that wages, profits, and rent, or, at all events, wages, 'are to be estimated

[1] 1st ed., pp. 44, 45; 3rd ed. in *Works*, p. 31, beginning 'It is according to the division of the whole produce of the land of any particular farm between the three classes of landlord, capitalist, and labourer'.

[2] 1st ed., pp. 45, 46; 3rd ed. in *Works*, pp. 31, 32.

by their real value, viz. by the quantity of labour and capital employed in producing them'.

But variations in the 'real value' of total wages, total profits, and total rent, when real value means 'the quantity of labour and capital employed in producing them', do not always correspond with variations in the proportions in which the whole produce is divided between total wages, total profits, and total rent. If the aggregate produce of the country were at first 100 million 'hats, coats, and quarters of corn', produced by 8 million men, and divided into 25 million hats, coats, and quarters for wages, 25 for rent, and 50 for profit, and were afterwards to increase to 200 million hats, etc., produced by 15 million men, and divided into 50 million for wages, 30 for rent, and 120 for profits, then the proportion of the whole produce falling to total wages would have remained the same, namely 25 per cent, although the 'real value' of the amount of produce falling to wages would have increased in the ratio of 200 to 375; the proportion of the whole produce falling to total rent would have fallen from 25 per cent to 15 per cent, although the 'value' of total rent would have increased in the ratio of 200 to 225; and the proportion of the whole produce falling to profits would have risen only from 50 to 60 per cent, although the 'value' of total profits would have risen in the ratio of 4 to 9. The produce and 'value' at the two periods would be as follows:

FIRST PERIOD.

Total wages,	25,000,000	hats, etc.,	produced by	2,000,000	labourers
,, rent,	25,000,000	,,	,,	2,000,000	,,
,, profits,	50,000,000	,,	,,	4,000,000	,,
	100,000,000			8,000,000	

SECOND PERIOD.

Total wages,	50,000,000	hats, etc.,	produced by	3,750,000	labourers
,, rent,	30,000,000	,,	,,	2,250,000	,,
,, profits,	120,000,000	,,	,,	9,000,000	,,
	200,000,000			15,000,000	

In Ricardo's numerical example variations in the proportions of produce falling to each of the three shares coincide with variations in the absolute amount of 'real value' falling to each share or quantity of labour employed in producing each share simply because he supposes the total amount of labour to remain stationary. He supposes the increase of produce to be brought about, not by increase of population, by 'by improvements in machinery and agriculture', and the whole increased produce to be the product 'of precisely the former quantity of labour'. Consequently the total 'value' to be divided remains the same, and if any one of the three parts, wages, profit, and rent, gets an increased proportion of the whole produce, it must necessarily get an increased absolute amount of 'value'. When the capitalists get 56 per cent of the produce instead of 50 per cent they also get $56x$ of value instead of $50x$.

When the number of labourers, and consequently the total 'value' of the whole produce, is allowed to change, it is not variations in the total 'value' of each share which will coincide with variations in the proportions of the produce falling to each share, but variations in the total 'value' of each share divided by the number of labourers. A rise in the 'value' of total rent divided by the number of labourers will coincide with a rise in the proportion of the produce falling to rent. A rise in the 'value' of total profits divided by the number of labourers will coincide with a rise in the proportion of the produce falling to profits. A rise in the 'value' of total wages divided by the number of labourers will coincide with a rise in the proportion of the produce falling to wages. Thus, in our example above, the proportion of the produce allotted to rent falls from 25 per cent to 15 per cent when the 'value' of total rent divided by the number of labourers falls from $\cdot 25x$ to $\cdot 15x$; the proportion allotted to profits rises from 50 per cent to 60 per cent, when the 'value' of total profits divided by the number of labourers rises from $\cdot 50x$ to $\cdot 60x$; and the proportion allotted to wages remains at 25 per cent, when the 'value' of total wages divided by the number of labourers remains at $\cdot 25x$.

Now total profits divided by the number of labourers, and total rent divided by the number of labourers, are very unfamiliar conceptions, and it may very safely be said that they never occurred to the mind of Ricardo. But total wages divided by the number of labourers is simply 'wages' in the ordinary sense. When Ricardo says 'wages are to be estimated by their real value, viz. by the quantity of labour and capital employed in producing them', he was using the word in its ordinary sense. The passage quoted occurs in the course of an attempt to explain the difference between the effects of a rise of money wages caused by an alteration in the 'value' of money, and a rise of wages resulting 'from the circumstance of the labourer being more liberally rewarded, or from a difficulty of procuring the necessaries on which wages are expended'. If occasioned by the first cause, Ricardo says, it will raise 'prices', and not affect 'profits'; if occasioned by the second cause it will lower 'profits', and not affect prices:

> 'A rise of wages from an alteration in the value of money produces a general effect on price, and for that reason it produces no real effect whatever on profits. On the contrary, a rise of wages from the circumstance of the labourer being more liberally rewarded, or from a difficulty of procuring the necessaries on which wages are expended, does not [except in some instances] produce the effect of raising price, but has a great effect in lowering profits. In the one case, no greater pro-

> portion of the annual labour of the country is devoted to the support of the labourers; in the other case, a larger portion is so devoted.'[1]

Rent is here left out of account altogether, and the 'profits' mentioned are really nothing but the rate of profit or ratio between interest and principal, so that there is no reason for taking 'wages' in anything but the ordinary sense of wages *per capita*, and, as we have just shown, variations in the proportion of the whole produce falling to wages will really coincide with variations in 'the quantity of labour employed in producing' wages *per capita*. If a quarter of the produce goes to wages in the aggregate, a quarter of both the total and the *per capita* labour expended must be employed in producing wages, and so on.

It may probably be said, then, that Ricardo was led into his dictum that variations of rent and profits should be taken to mean variations in the proportions of the whole produce falling to rent and profits simply by a false analogy arising from the ambiguity of the word 'wages'. He saw that the proportion falling to 'wages' would vary with the quantity of labour employed in producing 'wages', but he failed to notice that these last 'wages' are wages *per capita*, and not wages in the sense appropriate to the equation, Produce=Wages+Profits+Rent. He therefore hastily and rashly concluded that the proportions of produce falling to profits and rent would vary with the quantity of labour employed in producing them, that is to say, with what he chose to call their 'value'.

Now it is to the question of the value of things that Ricardo's book primarily addresses itself, and the consequence of the 'value', as he defines the word, of profits and rent not varying with the proportions of the whole produce falling to profits and rent is that his book would not have dealt with the proportions in which the whole income of the community is divided between Labour, Capital, and Land, even if he had always adhered to his definition of the value of the three shares. If, however, he had adhered to that definition, his book, in treating of the variations in the value of wages *per capita*, would also necessarily have treated of variations in the proportion of the whole produce which falls to total wages.

As a matter of fact, however, he did not adhere to his definition of the value of rent, profits, and wages. If the value of rent, wages, and profits is to be estimated by the quantity of labour employed in producing them, and if money is to be supposed, as Ricardo supposes it for the purpose of his inquiry,[2] to be invariable in value, we should certainly be justified in expecting the rent+wages+profits produced by 20 average labourers to be worth exactly twice as much 'money'

[1] 1st ed., pp. 43, 44; 3rd ed. in *Works*, p. 31. The words in brackets are in the third, but not in the first and second editions.

[2] 3rd ed. in *Works*, pp. 29, 30.

as the rent + wages + profits produced by 10 average labourers, and so on. But in Ricardo's examples of the progress of cultivation, the corn produced when 10 men only are employed is worth £4 × 180 = £720, the corn produced when 20 men are employed is worth $\frac{180}{170}$ of £4 × (180 + 170) = £1,482$\frac{6}{17}$, and the corn produced when 30 men are employed is worth $\frac{180}{160}$ of £4 × (180 + 170 + 160) = £2,295. Instead of doubling the money value of the whole produce – wages + profits + rent – when twice the number of men are employed, Ricardo doubles the money value of the produce-*minus*-rent, that is, the money value of wages + profits only, and adds an additional amount of value for rent, which value is unaccounted for by the increase of labour. Instead of the whole produce of ten average men's labour always remaining of the same value, it is only the profits + wages produced by ten average men's labour which remains always of the same value – in Ricardo's example, £720. Consequently the variations in the value of *per capita* wages, estimated in the invariable standard of value, do not correspond with variations in the proportion of the whole produce which falls to wages. Instead of this they corresond with variations in the produce-*minus*-rent which falls to wages. A rise in the 'value' of wages or a rise of 'money wages' or of the 'price of labour' does not necessarily mean that rent + profits will receive a smaller proportion of the produce, but only that wages will receive a larger, and profits consequently a smaller proportion of that part of the produce which remains after rent is deducted. The following table, constructed from the example which Ricardo gives in his chapters on Rent Wages, and Profits,[1] may serve to make this clear:

Period.	Value of total produce.	Rent.	Profits.	Wages.	Number of men employed.	Money wages per man.	Proportion of whole produce falling to		
							Rent.	Profits.	Wages.
I.	£720	None.	£480	£240	10	£24	Nil.	·66	·333
II.	£1482$\frac{6}{17}$	£42$\frac{6}{17}$	£945$\frac{15}{17}$	£494$\frac{2}{17}$	20	£24$\frac{12}{17}$	·028	·638	·333
III.	£2295	£135	£1395	£765	30	£25$\frac{1}{2}$	·058	·607	·333
IV.	£3168	£288	£1824	£1056	40	£26$\frac{2}{5}$	·090	·575	·333
V.	£4114$\frac{2}{7}$	£514$\frac{2}{7}$	£2228$\frac{4}{7}$	£1371$\frac{3}{7}$	50	£27$\frac{3}{7}$	·125	·541	·333

It will be seen that in the series of figures with which Ricardo illustrated his arguments, wages per man, estimated in the invariable standard, money, gradually rise from £24 to £27$\frac{3}{7}$, while the propor-

[1] See especially 1st ed., pp. 76, 106, 126, 127; 3rd ed., in *Works*, pp. 44, 55, 56, 64. The correct fractions of a pound are substituted for Ricardo's inaccurate shillings and pence.

tion of the whole produce falling to wages remains constant at one-third or 33⅓ per cent.

Nevertheless, if variations in Ricardo's money wages *per capita* correspond with variations in the proportion of produce-*minus*-rent which falls to wages, it is worth while to inquire how he supposed these money wages to be determined, since if we know what determines the division of produce-*minus*-rent into wages and profits we have only to find out what determines the divison of the whole produce between rent on the one side and wages+profits on the other in order to complete the inquiry into what determines the division of the whole produce between the three shares. Ricardo's doctrine as to what determines money wages has, however, been anticipated to some extent in the section on variations of *per capita* wages.[1] In showing how he supposed real wages to be unaffected by a rise in the price of the commodities consumed by the labourers, it was necessary to say that he held that when the price of these commodities rises, money wages rise sufficiently to enable the labourer to buy as much, or almost as much, as before. 'The natural price of labour', by which, of course, he means the money price, money wages, and not real wages, 'depends', he says at the beginning of the chapter on Wages, 'on the price of the food, necessaries, and conveniences required for the support of the labourer and his family. With a rise in the price of food and necessaries, the natural price of labour will rise; with the fall in their price, the natural price of labour will fall'.[2] A little further on, when he has lost sight of his 'market' and 'natural' wages, he says 'wages', meaning money wages, 'are subject to a rise or fall from two causes:

'1st. The supply and demand of labourers.

'2ndly. The price of the commodities on which the wages of labour are expended'.[3]

The first cause, of course, affects real wages as well as money wages, the second affects money wages only, Ricardo's meaning evidently being that, given a certain price of the commodities, money wages will be determined by the supply and demand of labourers, and that, given a certain supply and demand of labourers, money wages will be determined by the price of the commodities. Substituting the proportion of the produce-*minus*-rent falling to wages for the equivalent term, 'money wages', we find then that the proportions in which produce-*minus*-rent is divided between wages and profits are determined by the demand and supply of labourers when a certain price of commodities is given, and by the price of the commodities consumed by the

[1] Above, pp. 242, 243, 245–257.
[2] 1st ed., pp. 90, 91; 3rd ed. in *Works*, p. 50.
[3] 1st ed., p. 97; 3rd ed. in *Works*, p. 53.

labourers when a certain demand and supply of labourers is given. This is the doctrine itself. The corollary which Ricardo deduced from it was that in the progress of society money wages or the proportion of produce-*minus*-rent which falls to wages have a tendency to increase. In the *Essay on the Influence of a Low Price of Corn*, he said that 'the rise or fall of wages', meaning real wages, 'is common to all states of society', and that 'capital and population alternately take the lead', so that 'nothing can be positively laid down respecting profits, as far as wages are concerned'.[1] He therefore took it for granted that the assumption which he makes explicitly at the beginning of the *Essay*, namely, that 'the real wages of labour continue uniformly the same',[2] corresponded with the actual facts when the average of a considerable length of time is taken. Having thus eliminated variations of real wages from the problem, and having assumed that, given certain real wages, money wages will vary with the price of the commodities on which they are expended, he was free to argue, as he does, that in 'the progress of wealth', which raises the price of these commodities, there will be a 'general rise of wages',[3] meaning, of course, money wages. But in the *Principles* he not only says that 'as population increases' the necessaries consumed by the labourer 'will be constantly rising in price', but also 'in the natural advance of society the wages of labour will have a tendency to fall, as far as they are regulated by supply and demand'.[4] He might, therefore, if he had understood the word tendency in the sense afterwards sometimes attributed to it, have said that money wages have a tendency to fall in consequence of the supply exceeding the demand, and also a tendency to rise in consequence of the price of necessaries constantly rising, and have left the matter there. But he had not been converted to the belief that variations of real wages are of an importance in any way comparable with variations in the price of necessaries. So, after explaining his proposition that 'wages will have a tendency to fall so far as they are regulated by supply and demand', he proceeds:

> 'I say that, under these circumstances, wages would fall if they were regulated only by the supply and demand of labourers; but we must not forget that wages are also regulated by the price of the commodities on which they are expended.
>
> 'As population increases, these necessaries will be constantly rising in price, because more labour will be necessary to produce them. If, then, the money wages of labour should fall, whilst every commodity on which the wages of labour were expended rose, the labourer would be doubly affected, and would be soon totally deprived of subsistence. Instead, therefore, of the money wages of labour falling they would rise; but they would not rise sufficiently to enable the labourer to purchase as many comforts and necessaries as he did before the rise in the

[1] *Works*, p. 379. [2] *Ibid.*, p. 372. [3] *Ibid.*, p. 377.
[4] 1st ed., pp. 102, 103; 3rd ed. in *Works*, p. 54.

price of these commodities. If his annual wages were before £24, or six quarters of corn when the price was £4 per quarter, he would probably receive only the value of five quarters when corn rose to £5 per quarter. But five quarters would cost £25; he would therefore receive an addition to his money wages, though with that addition he would be unable to furnish himself with the same quantity of corn which he had before consumed in his family'.[1]

In this example the increase of money wages is brought about by supposing the decrease of corn wages caused by the 'tendency to fall' to be in the proportion of 6 to 5, while the increase in the price of corn is in the larger proportion of 4 to 5. If Ricardo had happened to think it 'probable' that the labourer would receive only the value of $4\frac{4}{5}$ quarters of corn when corn rose to £5 per quarter, money wages would have remained at £24. As he always thought the rise in the price of necessaries the more powerful factor, he believed that in the natural advance of society money wages are constantly rising, and therefore that wages receive a larger and profits a smaller proportion of that part of the produce which is divided between them. In the chapter on Profits this is illustrated by the arithmetical example already quoted, in which ten men's labour always produces £720 for profits-*plus*-wages or produce-*minus*-rent. Whenever wages take a larger proportion of this sum, in consequence of the 'rise of wages produced by the rise of necessaries',[2] a less proportion of it is left for profits. Ricardo even considers it worthy of mention that the proportion falling to wages may increase so rapidly as to actually diminish the aggregate absolute amount of profits reckoned in money:

'If', he says, after giving some hypothetical figures, 'the capital employed were so large as to yield a hundred thousand times £720,[3] or £72,000,000, the aggregate of profits would be £48,000,000 when wheat was at £4 per quarter; and if by employing a larger capital,[4] 105,000 times £720 were obtained when wheat was at £6, or £75,600,000, profits would actually fall from £48,000,000 to £44,100,000, or £105,000 times £420, and wages would rise from £24,000,000 to £31,500,000.'[5]

The conclusion is that

'Although a greater value is produced, a greater proportion of what remains of that value, after paying rent, is consumed by the producers, and it is this, and this alone, which regulates profits. Whilst the land yields abundantly, wages may temporarily rise, and the producers may

[1] 1st ed., pp. 103, 104; 3rd ed. in *Works*, pp. 54, 55.

[2] Above, p. 253, note 2.

[3] That is to say, if the capital were large enough to employ 100,000 times ten men, or one million men.

[4] That is, a capital large enough to employ 1,050,000 men.

[5] 1st ed., p. 141; 3rd ed. in *Works*, p. 69. According to Ricardo's scale, when wheat was at £6 the money wages of the labourer would be £18 to allow him to buy his three quarters of corn, and £12 for other things – in all £30, so that the wages of 1,050,000 men would be, as he says, £31,500,000.

consume more than their accustomed proportion; but the stimulus which will thus be given to population will speedily reduce the labourers to their usual consumption. But when poor lands are taken into cultivation, or when more capital and labour are expended on the old land, with a less return of produce, the effect must be permanent. A greater proportion of that part of the produce which remains to be divided, after paying rent, between the owners of stock and the labourers, will be apportioned to the latter. Each man may, and probably will, have a less absolute quantity; but as more labourers are employed in proportion to the whole produce retained by the farmer, the value of a greater proportion of the whole produce will be absorbed by wages, and consequently the value of a smaller proportion will be devoted to profits. This will necessarily be rendered permanent by the laws of nature, which have limited the productive powers of the land.'[1]

With regard to the causes which determine the proportions in which the whole produce is divided into rent on the one hand, and wages-*plus*-profits on the other, Ricardo has really nothing to say. At the end of the chapter on Rent he remarks:

> 'In speaking of the rent of the landlord, we have rather considered it as the proportion of the whole produce, without any reference to its exchangeable value; but since the same cause, the difficulty of production, raises the exchangeable value of raw produce, and raises also the proportion of raw produce paid to the landlord for rent, it is obvious that the landlord is doubly benefited by difficulty of production. First, he obtains a greater share, and secondly, the commodity in which he is paid is of greater value'.[2]

Then in a footnote he endeavours 'to make this obvious, and to show the degrees in which corn and money rent will vary'. He supposes 'that the labour of ten men will, on land of a certain quality, obtain 180 quarters of wheat', and produces a row of figures showing that as the price of wheat rises in consequence of difficulty of production, the money rent paid by the farmer employing these ten men will rise faster than the corn rent. So when he says that he has rather considered rent as the proportion of the whole produce, all he means is that he has hitherto been reckoning the rent in corn rather than in money. It is not true, for he has just been discussing the effects of his second class of improvements on money rent, but the passage in which he does so is a clumsy insertion, probably written after the last paragraph. In any case, there is not the slightest ground for asserting that Ricardo had considered rent as a proportion of the whole produce in the proper meaning of the word proportion. Throughout the chapter he had considered it as an absolute amount either of corn or money, and even if we supposed that the proportion of produce falling to rent varies with the absolute quantity of labour required to

[1] 1st ed., pp. 141, 142; 3rd ed. in *Works*, p. 70.

[2] 1st ed., pp. 75, 76; 3rd ed. in *Works*, p. 44, reading 'the produce obtained with a given capital on any given farm'.

produce it, which we have shown not to be the case,[1] an increase in the absolute amount of money paid in rent would not necessarily coincide with an increase in the proportion of the produce falling to rent.[2] No additional knowledge can be gained from the note at the end of the chapter. It is, indeed, the case that in the arithmetical example the rent becomes a larger proportion, as well as a larger amount, as the difficulty of production increases. The first ten men are supposed to produce 180 quarters, the second ten men 170, the third ten men 160, and so on in this progression; so that when twenty men are employed, rent will take 10 quarters out of a total produce of 350 quarters; and when thirty men are employed rent will take 30 quarters out of a total produce of 510. Rent thus becomes $\frac{1}{17}$ instead of only $\frac{1}{35}$ of the produce. But this is a mere accident of the figures,[3] and Ricardo does not work out the fractions or percentages, or draw attention to the matter in any way.

To sum up Ricardo's ideas on the subject of the proportions in which the whole produce of the country is divided between rent, wages, and profits, we may say that he seems to have imagined that rent takes a larger proportion in the 'progress of society', so that a smaller proportion is left for wages and profits taken together, and he teaches plainly that wages become a larger and profits a smaller proportion of what is left for the two together. Consequently this belief seems to have been that the proportion of the whole produce falling to rent and the proportion falling to wages increase, while the proportion falling to profits decreases. For the belief that rent becomes a larger proportion he had no grounds except possibly the fact that it happened to do so in certain arbitrarily chosen arithmetical examples. For the theory that wages become a larger proportion of what is left after deducting rent, he depended on the old and erroneous belief that wages rise with a rise in the price of necessaries, and on his still more erroneous belief that the returns to agricultural industry diminish in the progress of society.

No great certainty has yet been attained on the point, but the probability is that exactly the opposite of what Ricardo taught is true – namely, that rent and wages take decreased proportions of the whole produce, and profits an increased proportion.

[1] Above, pp. 342–346.

[2] If the third ten men produced 168 quarters instead of 160, as Ricardo supposes, the rent when 30 men are employed would be 180—168+170—168=12+2=14, which is $\frac{1}{37}$ of the whole produce, as against $\frac{1}{35}$ when only 20 men were employed; but in spite of this diminution in the proportion of produce falling to rent, money rent would rise. The price of corn on Ricardo's assumptions would be $\frac{180}{168}$ of £4 per quarter as against $\frac{180}{170}$ of £4 when only 20 men were employed. The money rent would consequently be $\frac{180}{168}$ of 14 × £4 = £60, instead of £42$\frac{6}{17}$. (Ricardo's £42 7*s* 6*d* is an arithmetical blunder.)

[3] This is shown by the example in the note above.

James Mill opens his chapter on Distribution with a statement that 'the whole of the annual produce of the country' is divided between labourers and capitalists and landlords, and then remarks, 'when the parties are determined among whom the whole of the produce is distributed, it remains to ascertain by what laws the proportions are established according to which the division is made'.[1] After this we should certainly expect him to deal with the proportions in which the produce is divided between rent, profits, and wages. But he seems to have been using the word 'proportions' in a very loose sense, and his exposition of distribution is in reality concerned in the main with absolute amount of rent per acre and wages per head, and with the the rate of profit. It is only here and there that we find anything bearing on the question of proportions. With regard to the proportion of the produce which falls to rent he has nothing to say. Rent is, he says, something altogether extraneous to what may be considered as the return to the productive operations of capital and labour',[2] and therefore he only treats of the proportions in which produce-*minus*-rent or profits+wages is divided between wages and profits. When he comes 'to the question as to what determines the share of the labourer, or the proportion in which the commodity or commodity's worth is divided between him and the capitalist', he says:

> 'Let us begin by supposing that there is any[3] number of capitalists with a certain quantity of food, raw material, and instruments or machinery; that there is also a certain number of labourers; and that the proportion in which the commodities produced is[4] divided between them has fixed itself at some particular point.'[5]

Then assuming, after the manner of his generation, that wages per head depend on the proportion between labourers and capital, he shows that 'wages' – that is, wages per head – 'decline' if the labourers increase without any increase of capital. Apparently it does not strike him that variations of absolute wages per head are not necessarily coincident with variations in the proportion of the produce falling to wages. In the section on Wages he has nothing more to say about the proportion falling to wages, and yet early in the section on Profits, in the first and second editions, he remarks complacently: 'We have seen that the proportion of the shares between the capitalist and labourer depends upon the relative abundance of population and capital'.[6] As he teaches that 'capital has a less tendency than population to increase rapidly',[7] we should in consequence naturally expect him to believe

[1] *Elements*, 1st ed., pp. 11, 12; 2nd ed., pp. 27, 28; 3rd ed., pp. 27, 28.
[2] *Ibid.*, 1st ed., p. 54; 2nd ed., p. 70; 3rd ed., p. 68.
[3] In 2nd and 3rd eds., 'a certain'.
[4] In 2nd and 3rd eds., 'are'.
[5] *Elements*, 1st ed., pp. 25, 26; 2nd ed., p. 42; 3rd ed., p. 42.
[6] *Ibid.*, 1st ed., p. 57; 2nd ed., p. 72. [7] Above, p. 261.

that the proportion which falls to wages must decrease, or at any rate, not increase, in the progress of society, but at the very end of his discussion of Distribution he introduces, without warning, a new kind of 'wages', evidently suggested by Ricardo's money wages. This kind of wages increases, though the ordinary kind falls. When the price of corn rises owing to diminishing returns,

> 'the cost of maintaining labour is increased. A certain quantity of the necessaries of life must be consumed by the labourer, whether they cost little or much. When they cost more than they did before his labour costs more than it did before; though the quantity of commodities which he consumes may remain precisely the same. His wages, therefore, must be considered as rising, though his real reward may not be increased'.[1]

In the third edition he omitted this passage, and substituted the word 'regulation'[2] for 'proportion', in the proposition that 'the proportion of the shares between capitalist and labourer depends upon the relative abundance of population and capital'.

M'Culloch, like James Mill, looked on rent as somehow outside the pale within which the economist moves. It is, he says, 'altogether extrinsic to the cost of production', apparently because 'the circumstance of the landlord's consenting to give it up would not occasion any change in the productiveness of industry, or any reduction in the price of raw produce'.[3] So he does not consider the proportions in which the whole produce is divided between rent, wages, and profits, but only 'the proportion in which the whole produce of industry under deduction of rent is divided between labourers and capitalists'.[4] For Ricardo's 'money wages' (money being invariable in 'value') he substitutes the more suggestive term 'proportional wages',[5] which, as Malthus remarked, is a distinct improvement.[6] It is perfectly obvious to him, and he explains it more plainly than Ricardo or James Mill, that if these wages rise, that is, if each average labourer gets a larger proportion of that part of the produce of his labour which is divided between him and the capitalist who employs him, all the labourers will get a larger proportion of that part of the whole produce which is divided between them and the capitalists, and smaller proportion of that part of the produce will be left for the capitalists.[7] Diminishing returns to agricultural industry will, he says, raise proportional wages, because

> 'it is utterly impossible to go on increasing the cost of raw produce, the principal part of the subsistence of the labourer, by taking inferior land into cultivation, without also increasing his wages. A rise of wages

[1] *Elements*, 1st ed., p. 61; 2nd ed., p. 79.
[2] 3rd ed., p. 71.
[3] *Principles*, p. 364.
[4] *Ibid.*, p. 363.
[5] *Ibid.*, pp. 327, 361, 362.
[6] *Definitions*, p. 114.
[7] *Principles*, pp. 364, 365.

is seldom indeed exactly coincident with a rise in the price of necessaries, but they can never be very far separated. The price of the necessaries of life is, in fact, the cost of producing labour. The labourer cannot work if he is not supplied with the means of subsistence – and although a certain period, of varying extent, according to the circumstances of the country at the time, must generally elapse, when necessaries are rising in price, before wages are proportionately augmented, such an augmentation must certainly be brought about in the end'.[1]

He does not attempt to explain the steps of the process by which the augmentation is brought about.

On this question, as on many others, Senior begins by exciting great hopes of a clear exposition, and then miserably disappoints these hopes:

'Having given', he says, 'a general outline of the three great classes among whom all that is produced is distributed, and of the general laws which regulate the comparative value of different products, we now proceed to consider the general laws which regulate the proportions in which landlords, capitalists, and labourers share in the general distribution, or in other words, which regulate the proportions which rent, profit, and wages bear to one another.'[2]

Immediately afterwards he has two chapters or sections headed 'Causes on which the proportionate amount of rent depends',[3] and 'Proportionate amounts of profit and wages'.[4] The first of these tells us nothing whatever about the matter, except that 'the amount' – not even the 'proportionate amount' – of rent

'is subject to no general rule; it has neither a minimum nor a maximum. It depends on the degree in which nature has endowed certain instruments with peculiar productive powers, and the number of those instruments, compared with the number and wealth of the persons able and willing to hire them'.

The second chapter tells us absolutely nothing about the 'proportionate amounts of profit and wages'. The whole question, however, recurs under the heading of 'Causes which divert labour from the production of commodities for the use of labouring families'. 'Labour' Senior says, 'instead of being employed in the production of wages, may be employed in the production of rent, taxation, or profit',[5] and the proportion of the whole labour devoted to the production of each share may be taken to be the same as the proportion of the whole produce falling to each share. But taxation may be regarded as a 'mode of expenditure', and rent as 'something extrinsic', so that all that remains is to consider 'what decides the proportion of the shares of labourers and capitalists:

[1] *Principles*, pp. 379, 380. [2] *Political Economy*, 8vo ed., p. 128.
[3] *Ibid.*, p. 135. [4] *Ibid.*, p. 139. [5] *Ibid.*, p. 180.

'The facts which decide in what proportions the capitalist and labourer share the common fund appear to be two: first, the general rate of profit in the country on the advance of capital for a given period; and secondly, the period which in each particular case has elapsed between the advance of the capital and the receipt of the profit.'[1]

Senior arrives at this curious result by dint of treating the capital on which profit is obtained as if it consisted entirely of wage-fund, a sum periodically 'advanced' in payment of wages. If this were the case, what he says is so obviously true, that it is curious that he considered it necessary to spend many pages in proving it. If the wage fund x is advanced for a year, and the rate of profit is 10 per cent per annum, the 'common fund' to be divided annually will be equal to $x+\frac{1}{10}x$, and the labourers will receive $\frac{10}{11}$ of the whole, and the capitalists $\frac{1}{11}$. If the wage fund x were advanced for only one-twelfth of a year, and the rate of profit was still 10 per cent, the 'common fund' to be divided monthly would be $x+(\frac{1}{10}x\times\frac{1}{12})$, and the labourers would get $\frac{120}{121}$ of the whole. If the wage-fund were advanced for a year, and the rate of profit were 20 per cent per annum, the 'common fund' to be divided annually would be $x+\frac{1}{5}x$, and the labourers would receive $\frac{5}{6}$ of the whole produce. In the course of his argument, Senior happened to give an arithmetical example, in which an addition to fixed capital causes a larger proportion of the produce to fall to profits, and a smaller to wages,[2] but even this did not suggest to him that his theory was unsatisfactory. Yet it is obvious that as soon as the profit on capital other than wage-fund is taken into account, his proposition becomes meaningless.

J. S. Mill tells us nothing about the proportions in which the whole produce is divided between rent, wages, and profit. About the proportions in which produce-*minus*-rent is divided between profits and wages, he does say something, but as he proceeds on the assumption that the rate of profit and the capitalists' proportion of the produce are the same thing, we have already dealt with his teachings on this subject in dealing with variations of profits per cent.[3] He probably agreed with Ricardo in believing that in the progress of society rent and wages receive a larger, and profits a smaller proportion of the whole produce.

§ 2. *Distribution of Wages among Workers*

Supposing the causes which determine average wages to be known, it will clearly be of the greatest importance to know how the total income derived from labour is divided between the various workers. Why does one worker get more and another less than the average? The chief cause of difference is obviously the difference in industry

[1] P. 185. [2] Pp. 193, 194. [3] Above, pp. 298–309.

and capacity. The lazy man and the fool will not generally earn as much as the industrious and the intelligent. Upon so obvious a fact economists have not thought it necessary to waste their time. More obscure are the causes of differences of earnings between persons of equal industry, and so far as is known, equal original capacity, when engaged in different occupations.

The formal contention of Adam Smith's celebrated chapter 'Of wages and profit in the different employments of labour and stock', is that where there is 'perfect liberty' the differences in the wages earned by equal amounts of labour and the differences in the profits gained by equal amounts of stock are caused by the fact that employments have other advantages and disadvantages besides the income obtained by them, and that it is the whole advantageousness of different employments, not the income obtained from them, that any one would naturally expect to be equal:

> 'The whole of the advantages and disadvantages of the different employments of labour and stock', he says, 'must, in the same neighbourhood, be either perfectly equal or continually tending to equality. If, in the same neighbourhood, there was any employment evidently either more or less advantageous than the rest, so many people would crowd into it in the one case, and so many would desert it in the other, that its advantages would soon return to the level of other employments. This at least would be the case in a society where things were left to follow their natural course, where there was perfect liberty, and where every man was perfectly free both to choose what occupation he thought proper, and to change it as often as he thought proper. Every man's interest would prompt him to seek the advantageous, and to shun the disadvantageous employment.'[1]

Apart from differences of wages and profit caused by 'the policy of Europe, which nowhere leaves things at perfect liberty', he says, the difference of pecuniary wages and profit obtained in different employments of labour and stock arises 'from certain circumstances in the employments themselves, which either really, or at least in the imaginations of men, make up for a small pecuniary gain in some, and counterbalance a great one in others'. Of these, the five principal are, he says, so far as he has been able to observe: (1) the different agreeableness of different employments, (2) the different cost of preparing persons to pursue them, (3) the different constancy of employment in them, (4) the different amount of trustworthiness required in them, and (5) the different probability of success in them.

Interest in the examples with which Adam Smith illustrates these five circumstances has often blinded readers to his entire failure to show that 'perfect liberty' causes the whole advantages and disadvantages of the different employments to be either equal or continually

[1] Bk. I, ch. X, p. 45 *a*.

tending to equality. His fourth circumstance, 'the small or great trust which must be reposed in those who exercise' the different employments obviously has no business to be where he places it. It is no disadvantage to a man to have trust reposed in him, and Adam Smith makes no attempt to show that it is. He simply says that goldsmiths and jewellers earn high wages 'on account of the precious materials with which they are intrusted', and that

> 'We trust our health to the physician; our fortune, and sometimes our life and reputation to the lawyer and attorney. Such confidence could not safely be reposed in people of a very mean or low condition. Their reward must be such, therefore, as may give them that rank in the society which so important a trust requires.'[1]

It is impossible to see any force in the 'must'. In several other cases in the course of the chapter, Adam Smith uses the same word, but in those cases he obviously has in his mind the idea of the opening paragraph of the chapter, that 'if in the same neighbourhood there was any employment, evidently either more or less advantageous than the rest, so many people would crowd into it in the one case, and so many would desert it in the other, that its advantages would soon return to the level of other employments'. But that idea is quite inapplicable here. According to it, the advantages of being a goldsmith or jeweller would soon be reduced by competition, and so many people would become physicians and attorneys that they would cease to obtain 'that rank in the society which so important a trust requires'.

Adam Smith's inclusion of this 'circumstance' thus practically amounts to an admission that 'perfect freedom' to choose an occupation would not necessarily produce equality of advantages and disadvantages in all the different employments. That this 'perfect freedom' does not produce equality of advantages and disadvantages, is known as a matter of fact to every one. We have attained in these days to almost perfect freedom in Adam Smith's sense of the words, with regard to competition in different employments, and yet we have not nearly attained to equality of advantages and disadvantages. Doubtless a man, whenever he has the choice, will prefer an occupation which is agreeable, easy to learn, and regular, and which offers a chance of obtaining great prizes, to one which is disagreeable, difficult to learn and irregular, and which offers no great prizes. But it does not follow, as a matter of fact, that pecuniary earnings only differ sufficiently to counterbalance the differences between the other advantages of the different occupations. Adam Smith says that if a long and expensive education or training was not looked upon by parents as a good investment for their sons, it would not be given, but this does not prove that the earnings of those who have received this

[1] P. 47 *b*.

training only exceed the earnings of others by an amount necessary to replace the sum expended on their training, together with the ordinary profits. That the excess is more than this, is suggested in Adam Smith's own proposition that it must be expected to replace the sum expended together with 'at least' the ordinary profits of an equally valuable capital.[1] If the excess were only just a fair return on the capital expended, we should sometimes find parents in doubt whether to make the investment or not, and sometimes find parents who deliberately thought better not to make the investment. But no one ever did hear of a parent who, having the power and the will to lay by a few hundred pounds for the benefit of his son, deliberately invested the amount in accumulative consols for him, and made him a bricklayer's labourer instead of using it to get him into some better paid employment.

Ricardo mentions the subject of differences of wages in different employments only in order to say that the fact that some kinds of labour are 'more valuable' than others 'needs scarcely to be attended to' in comparing 'the value of the same commodity at different periods of time', since 'it operates equally at both periods':[2]

> 'In speaking', he says, 'of labour as being the foundation of all value, and the relative quantity of labour as determining the relative value of commodities, I must not be supposed to be inattentive to the different qualities of labour and the difficulty of comparing an hour's, or a day's labour, in one employment with the same duration of labour in another. The estimation in which different qualities of labour are held comes soon to be adjusted in the market with sufficient precision for all practical purposes, and depends much on the comparative skill of the labourer and intensity of the labour performed. The scale, when once formed, is liable to little variation. If a day's labour of a working jeweller be more valuable than a day's labour of a common labourer, it has long ago been adjusted and placed in its proper position in the scale of value.'[3]

The meaning of this appears to be that, somehow or other, there is more labour in a day's labour in the better paid employments than in the worse paid. This is the only interpretation which will retain labour as 'the foundation of all value', and it is confirmed by the fact that Ricardo quotes, in a footnote, a passage from Adam Smith in which occurs the sentence, 'There may be more labour in an hour's hard work than in two hours' easy business; or in an hour's application to a trade which it costs ten years' labour to learn, than in a month's industry at an ordinary and obvious employment'.[4] Doubtless there 'may be', but the question is rather '*Is* the labour which

[1] P. 46 *a*. [2] *Principles*, 1st ed., p. 13; 3rd ed. in *Works*, p. 15.
[3] *Ibid.*, 1st ed., pp. 12, 13; 3rd ed. in *Works*, pp. 14, 15.
[4] The passage is in *Wealth of Nations*, p. 14 *a*, Bk. I, ch. v (not ch. x as Ricardo says in all his three editions).

brings in £1 a day eight times as much labour as the labour which brings in 2*s* 6*d*?' Ricardo's view, adopted by Marx,[1] plays a part in the history of Socialism; in the history of Economics it is not important.

Malthus, in his *Political Economy*, says that differences of wages 'are accounted for in the easiest and most natural manner upon the principle of supply and demand':

> 'Superior artists are paid high on account of the scanty supply of such skill, whether occasioned by unusual labour or uncommon genius, or both. Lawyers, as a body, are not well remunerated, because the prevalence of other motives besides mere gain crowds the profession with candidates, and the supply is not regulated by the cost of the education.'[2]

He disapproves of Adam Smith's proposition that 'if one species of labour requires an uncommon degree of dexterity and ingenuity, the *esteem* which men have for such talents will give a value to their produce superior to what would be due to the time employed about it'.[3]

James Mill, true to his principle of excluding, so far as possible, everything of human interest from his work, tells us nothing about the causes of differences of wages. M'Culloch, in the section which he inconsistently heads 'Equality of the wages of labour in different employments',[4] professes to show that 'the discrepancies that actually obtain in the rate of wages are all confined within certain limits – increasing or diminishing it only so far as may be necessary fully to equalize the unfavourable or favourable circumstances attending any employment',[5] but he does little more than quote Adam Smith's five circumstances. As to trustworthiness he merely copies Adam Smith's words, and makes no comment and no attempt to show that trust is a disadvantage which must be counterbalanced by high wages. As to the fifth circumstance – the probability or improbability of success in an employment – he fails to understand Adam Smith's position. Adam Smith said that if any employment were 'evidently' more or less advantageous than the rest, people would either crowd into it or shun it, till its advantages returned to the ordinary level, and he put forward his five circumstances as things 'which either really or at least in the imaginations of men', counterbalance differences of pecuniary wages. He believed that the generally ill-grounded hope of obtaining the great prizes of professions like the law or the army, was a circumstance which 'in the imaginations of men' counterbalanced low pecuniary wages. M'Culloch having omitted the proviso, 'either really or at least

[1] See *Capital* (transl. by S. Moore and E. Aveling, 1887), vol. i, pp. 11, 12.

[2] Pp. 244, 245.

[3] From *Wealth of Nations*, Bk. I, ch. vi, p. 22 *a*.

[4] *Principles*, p. 229.

[5] *Ibid.*, p. 230.

in the imaginations of men', ought to have maintained that the real advantages of such professions are no less than the real advantages of other professions, but instead of doing so he follows Adam Smith in attempting to show that their real advantages are less.

Senior, who says that his 'remarks will be chiefly a commentary on those of Adam Smith',[1] takes Adam Smith's five circumstances one by one, and makes a number of acute and interesting observations on their influence. He does not, however, make any attempt to improve the general theory of the subject. Wakefield seems to have been quite right when he said, in 1843, that Adam Smith's chapter on differences of wages and profits 'is allowed on all hands to be free from error, and to contain, even now, the only complete account of the subject to which it relates'.[2] Dissatisfaction was first expressed by J. S. Mill:

> 'A well-known and very popular chapter of Adam Smith,' he said in his first edition, 'contains the best exposition yet given of this portion of the subject. I cannot indeed think his treatment so complete and exhaustive as it has sometimes been considered; but as far as it goes his analysis is on the whole successful.'[3]

In a later edition he altered 'on the whole successful', to the less favourable 'tolerably successful'.[4] He accepts Adam Smith's views with regard to the first, third, and fifth of the five circumstances, but with regard to the other two – trustworthiness and expense of training – he points out that there is a real inequality of all the advantages and disadvantages of the different employments. The superior wages earned in positions of trust are, he says,

> 'not a compensation for disadvantages inherent in the employment, but an extra advantage; a kind of monopoly price, the effect of not a legal, but of what has been termed a natural monopoly. If all labourers were trustworthy, it would not be necessary to give extra pay to working goldsmiths on account of the trust. The degree of integrity required being supposed to be uncommon, those who can make it appear that they possess it are able to take advantage of the peculiarity, and obtain higher pay in proportion to its rarity.'[5]

As regards the expense necessary in order to acquire proficiency in a skilled employment, he says that Adam Smith's principles account for an excess of earnings in the skilled employment sufficient to repay the expense with interest, but for nothing more, whereas

> 'there is a natural monopoly in favour of skilled labourers against the unskilled which makes the difference of reward exceed, sometimes in a manifold proportion, what is sufficient merely to equalize their advantages. If unskilled labourers had it in their power to compete with

[1] *Political Economy*, 8vo ed., p. 200.
[2] In his edition of the *Wealth of Nations*, vol. i, p. 328.
[3] *Principles*, Bk. II, ch. xiv, § 1, vol. i, p. 453.
[4] People's ed., p. 233 *a*.
[5] *Principles*, Bk. II, ch. xiv, § 2, 1st ed., vol. i, p. 459; People's ed., p. 236 *b*.

skilled by merely taking the trouble of learning the trade, the difference of wages could not exceed what would compensate them for that trouble at the ordinary rate at which labour is remunerated. But the fact that a course of instruction is required of even a low degree of costliness, or that the labourer must be maintained for a considerable time from other sources, suffices everywhere to exclude the great body of the labouring people from the possibility of any such competition.'[1]

Competition is still more restricted, he adds, by the fact that into some employments, 'such as what are called the liberal professions', 'a person of what is considered too low a class of society is not easily admitted, and if admitted does not easily succeed'.

> 'So complete, indeed,' he concludes, 'has hitherto been the separation, so strongly marked the line of demarcation, between the different grades of labourers, as to be almost equivalent to an hereditary distinction of caste.'[2]

He expected these lines of demarcation to be broken through in the near future, owing to 'the changes', which he looked on as 'now so rapidly taking place in usages and ideas', and 'the general relaxation of conventional barriers', together with 'the increased facilities of education which already are, and will be in a much greater degree, brought within the reach of all'.

§ 3. *Distribution of Profits among Capitalists*

The proportions in which the total profits made in a country are divided among the various capitalists must obviously depend chiefly on the proportions in which the total capital is divided among the various capitalists. With ordinary care and judgment, a millionaire will always make a larger income in an average year than a man whose capital is £100. The economists of our period, however, devoted little or no attention to the causes which determine the distribution of the capital of a country among its various holders. They made no comprehensive inquiry into the causes which lead to one man having £1,000,000 and another £100. Even J. S. Mill, when making drastic proposals for preventing the transmission of large fortunes from the dead to the living, offered no generalizations as to the accretion and subdivision of these fortunes.[3] Consequently, the history of the theory of the distribution of profits among capitalists is practically confined to a history of generalizations about the causes which make equal capitals sometimes yield different profits, even when both are managed with average skill and judgment.

[1] *Principles*, 1st ed., vol. i, pp. 460, 461; People's ed., p. 237 *a*, reading 'might' for 'could' in line 6.
[2] *Ibid.*, 1st ed., vol. i, p. 462; People's ed., p. 238 *a*.
[3] *Ibid.*, Bk. II, ch. ii, §§ 3, 4, 1st ed., vol. i, pp. 258–268; People's ed. pp. 135–140.

Adam Smith, in a passage which we have already had occasion to quote,[1] asserts that free competition tends to equalize the real or supposed advantages and disadvantages of all the different employments of capital, as well as those of all the different employments of labour. But of the five circumstances which cause equality of advantages in different employments of labour to be consistent with inequality of pecuniary earnings, he thinks only two have the same effect with regard to the employments of capital and pecuniary profits. 'Of the five circumstances', he says, 'which vary the wages of labour, two only affect the profits of stock: the agreeableness or disagreeableness of the business, and the risk or security with which it is attended'. There is not much difference, he adds, in the agreeableness of different employments of capital, and 'the ordinary profit of stock, though it rises with the risk, does not always seem to rise in proportion to it'.[2] Consequently there is less difference between the average and ordinary rate of profit in the different employments of stock than there is between the average pecuniary wages of different kinds of labour. The enormous apparent difference in the rates of profit 'is generally a deception, arising from our not always distinguishing what ought to be considered as wages from what ought to be considered as profits'. He rather forgets this when he gives the high profits of inn-keeping as an example of pecuniary profits being high in order to compensate for the disagreeableness of an employment of stock. It is surely the part of the inn-keeper's income which 'ought to be considered as wages', that is high in consequence of his being 'exposed to the brutality of every drunkard'.[3] As to the fact, however, that the rate of profit will be somewhat higher in the employments which require the capitalist to submit to some disagreeable or disgraceful incidents there can be no doubt. As to the effect of risk, Adam Smith held that in order to equalize the advantages of different employments of stock, the average of profits in risky employments should exceed the average in safer employments by some definite amount which he considered 'sufficient to compensate the risk', but the magnitude of which he does not succeed in explaining satisfactorily. 'To compensate' the risk, he says, 'completely the common returns ought, over and above the ordinary profits of stock, not only to make up for all occasional losses, but to afford a surplus profit to the adventurers, of the same nature with the profit of insurers'.[4] It is far from clear why this extra profit

[1] Above, pp. 359, 360.

[2] Bk. I, ch. x, p. 50 *b*.

[3] P. 46 *a*. It is doubtful, of course, whether 'in the imagination of men' a publican's business is a disagreeable and discreditable one, as Adam Smith supposed it to be. The supply of publicans is probably not so much diminished by the existence of people who think the business disagreeable and discreditable, as it is increased by the existence of those who think it agreeable and creditable.

[4] Bk. I, ch. x, p. 50 *b*.

should be 'of the same nature with the profit of insurers', and Adam Smith certainly does not prove that either no surplus profit, or an insufficient surplus profit, is obtained by remarking, 'but if the common returns were sufficient for all this, bankruptcies would not be more frequent in these than in other trades'. Obviously, in a very risky kind of business a somewhat higher average rate of profit will not prevent bankruptcy being more frequent than in a safe and steady-going one. As a matter of fact, it is extremely doubtful whether, as a general rule, the ordinary rate of profit, if by this be meant the average rate after taking all losses into account, does rise 'more or less with the risk'. It may very plausibly be contended that on the whole the more speculative investments of capital yield a less return than the safer investments.

Adam Smith's doctrine of the equalizing effects of competition on the profits gained in different employments is so simple and obvious, that it received little or no development during the period with which we are concerned. Even his slight confusion about 'insurer's profit' reappears again and again in the works of subsequent writers. M'Culloch tells us that a gunpowder manufacturer 'must obtain as much profit over and above the profit obtained in the securest businesses, as will suffice to guarantee or *insure* his capital from the extraordinary risk to which it is exposed in a business of such extreme hazard'.[1] Now if gunpowder manufacturers could insure their capital, the gunpowder-making trade would be a secure business, and all that would be required to attract sufficient capitalists to it would be that it should bring in ordinary profits after paying the insurance premiums. But if there are no gunpowder manufacturers' insurance companies willing to take the risk, so that the manufacturer cannot insure his capital, it is quite an open question whether ordinary profits, *plus* such an amount as would suffice to insure the capital if it could be insured, will attract capitalists into the business. Senior put forward a very acute theory to the effect that the human imagination exaggerates the probability both of very great gains and of very great losses, so that the average of profits in employments which (like a lottery) offer the chance of enormous gain without the prospect of ruinous loss, would be lower than the average in the safest employments, while, on the other hand, the average of profits in employments which, like gunpowder-making, offer the chance of ruinous loss without the prospect of enormous gain, would be higher.[2] J. S. Mill says:

> 'In such points as this much depends on the characters of nations, according as they partake more or less of the adventurous, or, as it is called when the intention is to blame it, the gambling spirit. This spirit is much stronger in the United States than in Great Britain; and in

[1] *Principles*, p. 246.

[2] *Political Economy*, 8vo ed., pp. 213–216.

Great Britain than in any country of the Continent. In some Continental countries the tendency is so much the reverse that safe and quiet employments probably yield a less average profit to the capital engaged in them than those which, at the price of greater hazards, offer greater gains.'[1]

§ 4. *Distribution of Rents among Landlords*

Just as the distribution of the capital of a country among the capitalists is the first factor in determining the proportions in which the total profits are divided among the capitalists, so the distribution of the land of a country among the landowners must be the first factor in determining the proportions in which the aggregate rental is divided among the landowners. We ask first how many acres a man possesses, and secondly how much rent does he get from an acre. It is strange how little attention the economists who preceded J. S. Mill devoted to this subject. Malthus, indeed, wrote a section in his *Political Economy* on the effects upon production of the land of a country being held by a small or a numerous body of owners, from which we can gather that he believed that 'over almost all Europe a most unequal and vicious division of landed property was established during the feudal times', and that this had been 'protected and perpetuated' by certain laws which had in some countries 'been rendered comparatively inefficient' 'by the aids of commerce and manufactures',[2] though what exactly this means is not very apparent. He had no doubt that the new French law of succession, compelling nearly equal division among children, would have the effect of subdividing the land, and looked on it as 'a fearful experiment'[3] regarded as a permanent institution, although it might have been useful if it could have been put in operation only for a limited period. But beyond this there is little to be found in the great economists of the time. They probably agreed with Malthus in ascribing the very unequal distribution of landed property to the original division made 'during feudal times', and ever since maintained by the law and custom of primogeniture. They did not attempt to generalize as to the causes which influence the aggregation and subdivision of landed property.

With regard, however, to the second factor which determines the distribution of rent, the different value of different areas of land, there is a very considerable mass of generalization. It is a mass, too, the importance of which has been much exaggerated.

Though Adam Smith's opinions as to the cause or origin of rent appear to have been somewhat confused,[4] he was clear enough as to the causes which enable some land to bear a heavier rent than other

[1] *Principles*, Bk. II, ch. XV, § 4, 1st ed., vol. i, p. 489; People's ed., p. 251 *a*.
[2] P. 429. [3] P. 433. [4] Above, pp. 216–220.

land. The rent of any land was, as a rule, he saw, the surplus of produce left after paying the expenses of cultivation and the ordinary profits upon the capital employed.[1] Land on which this surplus was large would yield a large rent, and land on which it was small would yield a small rent:

> 'The rent of land', he says, 'not only varies with its fertility, whatever be its produce, but with its situation, whatever be its fertility. Land in the neighbourhood of a town gives a greater rent than land equally fertile in a distant part of the country. Though it may cost no more labour to cultivate the one than the other, it must always cost more to bring the produce of the distant land to market. A greater quantity of labour, therefore, must be maintained out of it; and the surplus, from which are drawn both the profit of the farmer and the rent of the landlord, must be diminished. But in remote parts of the country the rate of profits, as has already been shown is, generally higher than in the neighbourhood of a large town. A smaller proportion of the diminished surplus, therefore, must belong to the landlord.'[2]

It is evident that Adam Smith believed that in the absence of local variations in the rate of profit (and we may suppose in the absence of local variations in wages and the cost of all articles necessary for cultivation), the differences between the rent of various acres of land are determined by the differences between their fertility and advantages of situation. Granting certain assumptions, such as that skill and the supply of capital are equally distributed over the country, nothing can be more obvious or more in accordance with common sense.

The branch of the 'Ricardian theory of rent' which relates to the differences between the rent of various acres of land at the same time was perforce based on the same idea. It made the idea more definite by insisting on the possibility of cultivated land yielding no rent, and it attempted to illustrate the matter by numerical examples and mathematical statements which are often misleading. James Anderson anticipated it in the following passage, taken from his *Inquiry into the Nature of the Corn Laws, with a view to the new Corn Bill proposed for Scotland*, which was published at Edinburgh in 1777:

> 'In every country there is a variety of soils, differing considerably from one another in point of fertility. These we shall at present suppose arranged into different classes, which we shall denote by the letters A, B, C, D, E, F, etc., the class A comprehending the soils of the greatest fertility, and the other letters expressing different classes of soils gradually decreasing in fertility as you recede from the first. Now, as the expense of cultivating the least fertile soil is as great, or greater, than that of the most fertile field, it necessarily follows that if and equal quantity of corn, the produce of each field, can be sold at the same price, the profit on cultivating the most fertile soil must be much greater than that of cultivating the others; and as this continues to

[1] Bk. I, ch. xi, p. 66 *a*.

[2] Bk. I, ch. xi, p. 67 *b*.

decrease as the sterility increases, it must at length happen that the expense of cultivating some of the inferior classes will equal the value of the whole produce.

'This being premised, let us suppose that the class F includes all those fields whose produce in oatmeal, if sold at 14*s* per boll, would be just sufficient to pay the expense of cultivating them, without affording any rent at all: that the class E comprehended those fields whose produce, if sold at 13*s* per boll, would free the charges without affording any rent; and that in like manner the classes D, C, B, and A consisted of fields whose produce, if sold respectively at 12, 11, 10, and 9 shillings per boll, would exactly pay the charge of culture without any rent.

'Let us now suppose that all the inhabitants of the country where such fields are placed could be sustained by the produce of the first four classes, viz. A, B, C, and D. It is plain that if the average selling price of oatmeal in that country was 12*s* per boll, those who possess the fields D could just afford to cultivate them, without paying any rent at all; so that if there were no other produce of the fields that could be reared at a smaller expense than corn, the farmer could afford no rent whatever to the proprietor for them. And if so, no rents could be afforded for the fields E and F; nor could the utmost avarice of the proprietor in this case extort a rent for them. In these circumstances, however, it is obvious that the farmer who possessed the fields in the class C could pay the expense of cultivating them, and also afford to the proprietor a rent equal to 1*s* for every boll of their produce; and in like manner, the possessors of the fields B and A could afford a rent equal to 2 and 3 shillings per boll of their produce respectively. Nor would the proprietors of these fields find any difficulty in obtaining these rents; because farmers, finding they could live equally well upon such soils, though paying these rents, as they could upon the fields D, without paying any rent at all, would be equally willing to take the one as the other.'[1]

This passage does not give any formula for determining the rents of different acres of land. The formula which it does give is this:

The rent paid in respect of any particular boll is equal to the difference between the expense of raising the most expensive boll raised and the expense of raising that boll.

We are told that when the most expensive boll costs 12*s* to raise, the rent paid for fields belonging to the class A, on which bolls can

[1] The passage occurs in a long footnote to p. 45 of the *Inquiry*. A part of the note was reprinted by M'Culloch in his edition of the *Wealth of Nations*, p. 453, in his *Literature of Political Economy* (1845), pp. 68–70, and in Overstone's *Select Tracts*, 'Miscellaneous' vol. (1859), pp. 321–325. Anderson's anticipation of particular points in the Ricardian theory (see above, pp. 220, 221) must not be mistaken for an anticipation of the whole theory. As we have already seen (above, pp. 145, 146), he was one of those enthusiastic agriculturists who believe not in diminishing returns, but in indefinitely increasing returns. The longest of M'Culloch's extracts (that in *Select Tracts*) stops just short of a passage which would have shown that Anderson was writing in favour of forcing the inferior soils into cultivation by protectionist measures, in the expectation of making them eventually as productive as the superior. If he had lived to 1815 he would most certainly have been one of Ricardo's most vigorous opponents (see especially *Recreations* for Aug. 1801, vol. v, pp. 403–408).

be raised for 9*s*, will be 3*s* per boll, and the rent paid for fields of class B 2*s* per boll, and for fields of class C 1*s* per boll, but we are not told how many bolls will be raised from an acre of land belonging to the classes A, B, and C. If an equal number of bolls were raised from an acre of A, B, and C, the rents per acre would follow the same scale as the rents per boll, but Anderson does not say that an equal number of bolls are raised on equal areas of A, B, and C, and the supposition is contrary to probability. But if an unequal number of bolls are raised from equal areas of A, B, and C, the rent per acre of A, B, and C will follow a different scale from the rent per boll. If, for example, the produce of A is 16 bolls per acre, that of B 12 bolls, and that of C 8 bolls, the rents per acre will be for A 48*s*, for B 24*s*, and for C 8*s*, while if the produce per acre is on A 5 bolls, on B 8 bolls, and on C 12 bolls, the rents per acre will be for A 12*s*, for B 16*s*, and for C 12*s*. All sorts of scales are obviously possible, whatever the probabilities may be.

In Ricardo rent is never calculated by the acre, but always by the amount of 'capital' by which it is supposed to be produced. This is Anderson's method simply turned round. If Ricardo had been obliged to take Anderson's numerical example, instead of saying that the rent for class A would be 3*s* per boll, for B 2*s* per boll, and for C 1*s* per boll, he would have said that the rent paid in respect of a capital of 12*s* would be $\frac{1}{3}$ boll on class A, $\frac{1}{5}$ boll on class B, and $\frac{1}{11}$ boll on class C. He certainly does not commit himself to the idea that the same amount of capital will be laid out on equal areas of the three classes of land, and the fact that he expressly contemplates the probability of the amount laid out on the better classes increasing at the same time as cultivation is extended to the inferior classes, is almost incompatible with any such assumption having been latent in his mind. Consequently, he does not, any more than Anderson, provide a formula for the determination of the rents of different acres of land. His formula is only

> The rent paid in respect of a particular capital is equal to the difference between the return to that capital and the return to an equal capital employed with the least return for which it is profitable to employ capital.

As he expresses it himself, 'rent is always the difference between the produce obtained by the employment of two equal quantities of capital and labour'.[1] As to the extent of the areas on which the two equal quantities are employed he says nothing.

West, however, had been less prudent. In the numerical example with which he illustrates his theory of diminishing returns, the areas

[1] *Principles*, 1st ed., p. 57; 3rd ed. in *Works*, p. 37.

of land which yield smaller and smaller returns to 'a given capital, say £100', each consist of ten acres.[2] Consequently, unlike Anderson and Ricardo, he arrives at the rent of the different acres, as well as the rent paid in respect of a given produce or a given expense. His first ten acres 'pay to the landlord £10 as rent, the next ten acres £9, and so on'. Now, supposing that equal areas of different qualities of land were actually cultivated with equal 'capitals', the formula for the determination of the rent of different acres of land would be

The rent of any particular acre of land is equal to the excess of its gross produce over that of the least productive acre in cultivation.

This, as an account of existing facts, is obviously absurd, and the reason is that equal areas of different qualities of land are not cultivated with equal capitals. One acre is the hundredth part of the grazing ground of a goat, another is the site of the Bank of England. The capital employed on the first is a few pence, the capital employed on the second is many million pounds. Even in the case of a land devoted to the production of corn, to which West seems to have confined his attention, the supposition of equal capitals being employed on equal areas is inadmissible. Thus, while the formula deduced from the theory of Anderson and Ricardo is correct, but gives us no information with regard to the rent of land, the formula deduced from West's theory gives us information which is incorrect.

James Mill seems to have endeavoured to find a formula which would give the information which West attempted to give without adopting his erroneous assumption that equal areas are cultivated with equal capitals. After explaining the effect of diminishing returns, he says:

> 'We may thus obtain a general expression for Rent. In applying capital either to lands of various degrees of fertility, or in successive doses to the same land, some portions of the capital so employed are attended with a greater produce, some with a less. That which yields the least, yields all that is necessary for reimbursing and rewarding the capitalist. The capitalist will receive no more than this remuneration for any portion of the capital which he employs, because the competition of others will prevent him. All that is yielded above this remuneration the landlord will be able to appropriate. Rent, therefore, is the difference between the return yielded to that portion of the capital which is employed upon the land with the least effect, and that which is yielded to all the other portions employed upon it with a greater effect.
>
> 'Taking for illustration the three stages mentioned above, of ten quarters, eight quarters, and six quarters, we perceive that rent is the difference between six quarters and eight quarters for the capital which yields only eight quarters; the difference between six quarters and ten quarters for the portion of capital which yields ten quarters; and if three doses of capital, one yielding ten, and another eight, and another

[2] See above, pp. 317, 318.

six quarters, are applied to the same portion of land, its rent will be four quarters for dose No. 1, and two quarters for dose No. 2, making together six quarters for the whole.'[1]

There is considerable awkwardness in the wording of the proposition, 'rent is the difference between the return yielded to that portion of the capital which is employed upon the land with the least effect and that which is yielded to all the other portions employed upon it with a greater effect'. James Mill himself was evidently dissatisfied with it, for in his second edition he altered it to 'rent is that part of the return made to the more productive portions of capital, by which it exceeds the return made to the least productive portion',[2] and in his third edition he altered this to, 'rent is the difference between the return made to the more productive portions, and that which is made to the least productive portion, of capital employed upon the land'.[3] His third version is perhaps the least satisfactory of the three, but it is plain that he had a perfectly clear idea of the matter, though he found difficulty in expressing it. He saw that the number of doses applied must be taken into account, and his formula may be said to be:

> The rent of any acre of land is equal to the sum of the differences between the return to each of the various doses of capital applied to it, and the return to the least productive dose applied to it or any other land.

If we understand the terms rent, doses of capital, and returns in the senses in which James Mill understood them, this is correct enough. It may be doubted, however, whether, if Adam Smith had lived to the age of ninety-eight, he would have looked on it as adding very much to his own theory that the rent of any farm is equal to the surplus of produce left after paying the expenses of cultivation and the ordinary profits on the capital employed.

It may, of course, be objected that, under James Mill's formula, land which he agreed with Anderson and Ricardo in regarding as of the second degree of fertility may yield a larger rent per acre than land of the first degree. Their land of the first degree is land which yields the largest return to the first 'dose' of capital, irrespective of its return to subsequent doses. Now on land of the second degree, though the return to the first dose is less, the returns to the subsequent doses may make up for this. For example, if on 30 acres of land No. 1, the first dose of capital, represented by 10 men's labour, yielded 180 quarters, the second dose 170, the third 160, and the fourth 150; while on 30 acres of land No. 2 the first dose yielded 170 quarters, the second 165, the third 162, the fourth 160, the fifth 155, the sixth 152, and the

[1] *Elements*, 1st ed., pp. 17, 18.
[2] *Ibid.*, 2nd ed., p. 33.
[3] *Ibid.*, 3rd ed., p. 33.

seventh 150; then, supposing 150 to be the return to the least productive dose applied, the rent of 30 acres of land No. 1 would be 30+20+10=60, while the rent of No. 2 would be 20+15+12+10+5+2=64. Modern economists have met the objection by abandoning the attempt to arrange lands in a scale of fertility which shall remain valid, whatever be the quantity of produce required.[1]

Subsequent writers were by no means always so careful as James Mill to make it plain that the surplus produce of the later doses of capital, as well as the first, must be brought into account in determining the rents of different acres. M'Culloch rashly says:

> 'When recourse had been had to these inferior lands, the corn rent of those that are superior would plainly be equal to the difference between the amount of the produce obtained from them and the amount of the produce obtained from the worst quality under cultivation.'[2]

The meaning which any ordinary reader, unacquainted with the history of the subject, would attach to these words would be that the corn rent per acre of the superior lands would be equal to the difference between their produce per acre and the produce per acre of the worst quality of land under cultivation. This is obviously untrue, unless we make with West the absurd supposition that all acres are cultivated with equal capitals. The idea which M'Culloch had in his mind was no doubt the Ricardian one, that the rent paid in respect of a given amount of capital employed on the superior lands would be equal to the difference between the amount of the produce obtained by it and the amount of the produce obtained by an equal amount of capital employed on the worst quality of land under cultivation. It was too much, however, to ask readers to supply all this.

J. S. Mill was an even worse offender. For a summary of the third section of his chapter 'Of Rent' he says in his Contents, 'The rent of land consists of the excess of its return above the return to the worst land in cultivation'.[3] This might be taken as merely the ordinary inaccuracy of rapid epitomizing, but the section itself opens thus:

> 'If then, of the land in cultivation, the part which yields least return to the labour and capital employed on it gives only the ordinary profit of capital without leaving anything for rent, a standard is afforded for estimating the amount of rent which will be yielded by all other land. Any land yields just as much more than the ordinary profits of stock, as it yields more than what is returned by the worst land in cultivation. The surplus is what the farmer can afford to pay as rent to the landlord; and since, if he did not so pay it, he would receive more than the

[1] See Marshall, *Principles of Economics*, 4th ed., p. 234, 'A mere increase in the demand for produce may invert the order in which two adjacent pieces of land rank as regards fertility'.

[2] *Principles*, p. 267.

[3] *Ibid.*, heading of Bk. II, ch. xvi, § 3 in Contents.

> ordinary rate of profit, the competition of other capitalists, that competition which equalizes the profits of different capitals, will enable the landlord to appropriate it.'[1]

Obviously if 'any land' is to mean any acre of land, and if the worst land in cultivation is to mean an acre of the worst land in cultivation, we require the assumption that all acres of land are cultivated with equal capitals, in order to make it true that 'any land yields just as much more than the ordinary profits of stock as it yields more than the worst land in cultivation', Hitherto, however, Mill had said nothing about the amount of capital employed. He proceeds:

> 'The rent, therefore, which any land will yield is the excess of its produce beyond what would be returned to the same capital if employed on the worst land in cultivation.'

It would require an enormous straining of words to interpret this to mean 'The rent which an indefinite amount of any land will yield is the excess of its produce beyond what would be returned to the same capital if employed on a not necessarily equal area of the worst land in cultivation', and something of this kind is needed to make it true.

[1] *Principles*, 1st ed., vol. i, pp. 499, 500; People's ed., p. 257 *a*.

CHAPTER IX

GENERAL REVIEW: POLITICS AND ECONOMICS

§ 1. *Unsatisfactory Character of the Theories of Production and Distribution regarded from a purely Scientific Point of View*

When we look back after the lapse of another eventful half-century upon the theories of production and distribution elaborated by English economists between 1776 and 1848, it is not very easy to understand the admiration which was once felt for the progress made during that period.

As we have seen,[1] Adam Smith declared in his 'Introduction and Plan' that the *per capita* amount of a nation's annual produce is regulated, first, by the skill, dexterity, and judgment with which its labour is directed; and, secondly, by the proportion between the number of workers and the number of non-workers. The proposition, though incomplete, shows a perfectly clear conception of what is required in a theory of production. All that later economists were required to do was to add what was omitted, and to trace the immediate causes, as far as possible, to their origin. Instead, however, of grappling with this task, they allowed the subject of production to be split up by the unlucky invention of the three requisites or agents. So in the First Book of Mill's *Principles*, which was long the most systematic treatise on Production extant, we find the first six chapters devoted to a 'general survey of the requisites of production' before 'the second great question in political economy, on what the degree of productiveness of these agents depends',[2] is reached. Then, for two or three chapters, Mill restores unity to the subject by treating the productiveness of all three agents together, without attempting seriously to distinguish variations in the productiveness of capital and the productiveness of land. But even thus, the elevation of capital into an agent of production co-ordinate with labour, and the imagination that it possesses a productiveness of its own, prevent any clear and adequate recognition of the fact that variation in the magnitude of the capital of a community is one of the most important causes of variation in the productiveness of labour. When the degrees of productiveness of three 'agents' are being discussed, it is obviously impossible to represent variation in the magnitude of one of the agents as a cause of variation in the productiveness of another. Similarly, the elevation of land into

[1] Above, p. 36.
[2] Bk. I, ch. vii, § 1; 1st ed., vol. i, p. 119; People's ed., p. 63 *a*.

an agent of production co-ordinate with labour prevents variation in the density of population being treated in its proper place as a cause of variation in the productiveness of labour. Mill is consequently driven to the awkward expedient of bringing these factors into a theory as to 'the increase of production',[1] that is to say, not the increase of the productiveness of industry or of the produce per head, but the increase of the aggregate produce. When 'the degree of productiveness' of labour is given, the aggregate produce obviously depends simply on the amount of labour, but Mill represents it as dependent on three 'laws', the 'law of the increase of labour', the 'law of the increase of capital', and the 'law of the increase of production from land'.[2] Thus he succeeds in dividing the subject of production once more into a collection of observations about labour, capital, and land.

Of these observations, those offered with regard to labour were sensible enough, though very incomplete.[3] The principal of those offered with regard to land may be looked on as a somewhat confused exaggeration of the truth that increase of population may lead to a diminution of the returns to industry.[4] But the observations with regard to capital appear to the modern inquirer a most hopeless farrago of blunders.[5] The nature, origin, and function of the capital of a country were totally misunderstood. It was distinguished from the accumulated stock of the country, with which, in any scientific view of the question, it must be regarded as identical, and was mixed up with periodical working expenses. Its origin was attributed to 'saving', but to saving which is not saving but consuming. Its principal function was supposed to be to support labour. The extraordinary confusion which prevailed in Mill's mind upon the subject is shown by the fact that he spent page after page in the futile endeavour to prove the 'truth that purchasing produce is not employing labour'.[6] Of the plain fact that 'employing labour' or paying wages is simply a method of purchasing produce under a particular kind of contract, he was so completely oblivious that, after floundering from one inaccurate illustration to another, he finally gave an example in which wages are treated as equivalent to alms, the amount of produce which the employer receives in exchange for them being entirely ignored.[7]

[1] *Principles*, Bk. I, ch. x, § 1; 1st ed., vol. i, pp. 186, 187; People's ed., p. 96.
[2] *Ibid.*, Bk. I, titles of chapters x, xi, xii.
[3] Above, ch. iii. [4] Above, ch. v. [5] Above, ch. iv.
[6] *Principles*, Bk. I, ch. v, § 9; 1st ed., vol. i, p. 99; 'theorem, that to purchase produce is not to employ labour', People's ed., p. 50 *b*.
[7] 'Suppose', he says, 'that a rich individual, A, expends a certain amount daily in wages or alms, which, as soon as received, is expended and consumed in the form of coarse food by the receivers. A dies, leaving his property to B, who discontinues this item of expenditure, and expends in lieu of it the same sum each day in delicacies for his own table' (People's ed., p. 53; not in 1st ed.). It is quite

The treatment of Distribution in the period under review appears even more unscientific and illogical than the treatment of Production. Adam Smith's rough division of incomes into wages of labour, profits of stock, and rent of land was accepted almost as a matter of course,[1] no regard being paid to the much more important division into incomes derived from the performance of labour, and incomes derived from the possession of property. Erroneous ideas as to the functions of 'capital' prevented the attainment of any clear comprehension of the origin and cause of the different forms of income.[2] The inquiry as to the causes which affect the distribution of the total income between the three shares of wages, profits, and rents was so confusedly conceived that, instead of an exposition of the circumstances which result in variations in the proportions in which a given total is divided between the three shares, we find an exposition of the circumstances which were supposed to determine the absolute magnitude of wages per head of labourers, the rate of profit per cent of capital, and the absolute magnitude of rent per acre.[3] Anything more unsatisfactory than this exposition itself would be difficult to conceive.[4] The 'law of wages' – 'wages depend on the ratio between population and capital'[5] – however obvious it may have appeared a hundred, or even fifty, years ago, is now palpably absurd. The 'law of profits' – 'profits depend on the cost of labour'[6] – is entirely baseless if it be intelligible. On what circumstances rent per acre was supposed to depend it is difficult to say. Ricardo had begun by alleging that it depends solely on the difficulty of procuring the last portion of agricultural produce required, rising when, owing to an increase of population or a deterioration of agricultural methods, the difficulty increases, and falling when, owing to a decrease of population or improvements in agriculture, the difficulty decreases.[7] When this view was found untenable, nothing definite was put in its place. J. S. Mill speaks of the 'law of rent'[8] immediately after speaking of the law of wages, and immediately before speaking of the law of profits, which

forgotten that if A paid wages, he would get something in return for them, and that this something may very well have been 'delicacies for his own table', either produced by the labourers he employed, or bought with the proceeds of the sale of the things produced by them. As a recent writer has observed, if wages and alms were exactly alike, 'philanthropy would become very cheap indeed' (H. M. Thompson, *The Theory of Wages and its Application to the Eight Hours Question and other Labour Problems*, 1892, p. 29).

[1] Above, p. 188.

[2] Above, ch. vi, §§ 3, 4, 5.

[3] *Ibid.*, ch. vii, § 1, ch. viii, § 1.

[4] *Ibid.*, ch. vii, §§ 2, 3, 4.

[5] J. S. Mill, *Principles*, Bk. III, ch. xxvi, § 1; 1st ed., vol. ii, p. 232; People's ed., p. 416 *b*.

[6] *Ibid.*, § 3, 1st ed., vol. ii, p. 237; People's ed., p. 419 *b*.

[7] Above, pp. 315, 316, 321–331.

[8] *Principles*, Bk. III, ch. xxvi, § 2; 1st ed., vol. ii, p. 235; People's ed., p. 418 *a*.

have just been quoted, but then, instead of producing an analogous law, and so telling us something about the causes of the rise and fall of rent, he merely asserts that 'rent is the extra return made to agricultural capital when employed with peculiar advantages', which is not a law at all, but only a bad definition.

Before J. S. Mill wrote, the economists had nothing to say about the distribution of rent among landlords and the distribution of profits among capitalists, and what little they had to say about the distribution of wages among labourers generally took the form of a somewhat indiscriminating eulogy of Adam Smith's illogical attempt to prove the equal advantageousness of all occupations. Mill paid more attention to these subjects, but even he had no idea of representing the explanation of the causes which determine the division of the community's income among its individual members as what it obviously should be, the ultimate aim of all discussions on the subject of Distribution.

Judged, then, by what we may, perhaps, using the term in a sense which has very often, though not very accurately, been given to it, call the 'abstract method', the theories of production and distribution arrived at in the first half of the nineteenth century must be visited with almost unqualified condemnation. But if we try them by the historical method, and inquire how far they met the practical needs of their time, they must obtain a much more favourable verdict.

§ 2. *Practical Character of the Theories of Production and Distribution and their usefulness in regard to the old Poor Law and the Corn Laws*

Among all the delusions which prevail as to the history of English political economy there is none greater than the belief that the economics of the Ricardian school and period were of an almost wholly abstract and unpractical character.

The *Wealth of Nations*, which was the one accepted authority when Malthus and Ricardo began to write, was, in the main, a scientific and not a practical treatise. Adam Smith had mixed with the physiocrats, who were nothing if not practical, and had caught much of their spirit. Consequently, many of the parts of the work in which the influence of the Economical Table is most obvious are far from being characterized by the philosophic calm appropriate to the inquirer who has no practical aims in view.[1] Instead of the cold philospher, we find a patriotic citizen possessed by an ardent, not to say passionate, hatred of the sordid motives and fallacious arguments on which the mercantile system was based. To expect 'that the freedom of trade

[1] See, for example, the concluding paragraphs of Book I, which were evidently written under the influence of the physiocratic system, and contain a vigorous denunciation of merchants and manufacturers.

should ever be entirely restored in Great Britain' he thought 'as absurd as to expect that an Oceana or Utopia should ever be established in it',[1] yet he was evidently determined to do what in him lay to bring about a partial, if not an entire, 'restoration' of freedom of trade. To this extent the *Wealth of Nations* was really a practical treatise, advocating a particular course of policy. But it was much more, and there is no reason to suppose that the origin of the work is to be looked for in its practical aim. Adam Smith was engaged neither in trade nor in politics. He was an ex-professor of moral philsophy. He was a Scotchman who had studied at Oxford. It would indeed have been surprising if such a man had undertaken ten years of study and research in order to help to bring about a partial approach towards the establishment of freedom of trade. There can be no doubt that he actually undertook his task simply with the desire of adding to the bounds of knowledge.

The case of the early nineteenth century economists is entirely different. With them, in the great majority of cases, practical aims were paramount, and the advancement of science secondary.

Malthus discovered his 'Principle of Population' in the course of an attempt to damp his father's hopes of progress. In bringing out the first edition he was inspired, not so much by the desire to publish the existence of the Principle, whatever it may have been, as by the desire to disprove the possibility of any great improvement in the material condition of mankind, and thus to produce acquiescence, if not contentment, with the existing order of things, and prevent the adoption of hasty experiments like the application of 'the forcing manure used to bring about the French revolution', which had 'burst the calyx of humanity, the restraining bond of all society'.[2] He soon exchanged this aim for a still more practical one. In his *Investigation of the cause of the present High Price of Provisions*, published in 1800, he attributed 'the present inability in the country to support its inhabitants' to 'the increase of population', and added:

> 'I own that I cannot but consider the late severe pressures of distress on every deficiency in our crops, as a very strong exemplification of a principle which I endeavoured to explain in an essay published two

[1] Bk. IV, ch. ii, p. 207 *b*.

[2] *Essay*, 1st ed., p. 274. 'Were it of consequence', he says, 'to improve pinks and carnations, though we could have no hope of raising them as large as cabbages, we might undoubtedly expect, by successive efforts, to obtain more beautiful specimens than we at present possess. No person can deny the importance of improving the happiness of the human species. Every, the least, advance in this respect is highly valuable. But an experiment with the human race is not like an experiment upon inanimate objects. The bursting of a flower may be a trifle. Another will soon succeed it. But the bursting of the bonds of society is such a separation of parts as cannot take place without giving the most acute pain to thousands: and a long time may elapse, and much misery be endured, before the wound grows up again' (pp. 274, 275).

> years ago, entitled *An Essay on the Principle of Population, as it affects the future Improvement of Society*. It was considered by many who read it merely as a specious argument, inapplicable to the present state of society; because it contradicted some preconceived opinions on these subjects. Two years' reflection have, however, served strongly to convince me of the truth of the principle there advanced, and of its being the real cause of the continued depression and poverty of the lower classes of society, of the total inadequacy of all the present establishments in their favour to relieve them, and of the periodical returns of such seasons of distress as we have of later experienced.'[1]

Accordingly, he explained, though the first edition of the *Essay* had been out of print for more than a year, he had not yet brought out a second edition, not only because he was 'endeavouring to illustrate the power and universality' of the operation of the principle 'from the best authenticated accounts' 'of the state of other countries', but also because he hoped to be able to make the work 'more worthy of the public attention by applying the principle directly and exclusively to the existing state of society'.[2] The second edition realized his hope by being to a large extent a protest against that indiscriminate encouragement of the propagation of the human species which was afforded both by the public approbation bestowed on improvident marriages and by the more material rewards provided under the Poor Laws. To make the protest effective became the guiding motive of his life. The earnestness of his feeling on this practical matter, and the carefulness with which he had studied it, are to be seen very plainly in his *Letter to Samuel Whitbread, Esq., M.P., on his proposed bill for the Amendment of the Poor Laws* (1807). After reading that pamphlet we can sympathize with the proud words with which, after replying to some of his critics, he ends the fifth edition of the *Essay on Population* (1817). Whether the *Essay* is read with or without the alterations made in the second and later editions, he says, he still trusts that

> 'every reader of candour must acknowledge that the practical design uppermost in the mind of the writer, with whatever want of judgment it may have executed, is to improve the condition and increase the happiness of the lower classes of society.'[3]

It is true that at the outset of the corn law controversy of 1813–15, he appeared for the moment in the character of the impartial economist, desirous merely of furnishing practical politicians with the means of making a decision on the subject, and of giving the general public trustworthy information as to the probable results of each of the two possible decisions. A year after writing it, he said:

> 'The professed object of the *Observations on the Corn Laws*, which I published in the spring of 1814, was to state, with the strictest im-

[1] P. 27. [2] P. 28. [3] Vol. iii, p. 428; 8th ed., p. 526.

partiality, the advantages and disadvantages which, in the actual circumstances of our present situation, were likely to attend the measures under consideration, respecting the trade in corn.

'A fair review of both sides of the question, without any attempt to conceal the peculiar evils, whether temporary or permanent, which might belong to each, appeared to me of use, not only to assist in forming an enlightened decision on the subject, but particularly to prepare the public for the specific consequences which were to be expected from that decision, on whatever side it might be made.'[1]

This is exactly in the style of the modern professor. But Malthus soon threw off the mask, and wrote the *Grounds of an Opinion on the policy of restricting the importation of foreign corn, intended as an appendix to 'Observations on the Corn Laws'*, in the character of an avowed and zealous advocate of restriction.[2] The *Inquiry into the Nature and Progress of Rent and the Principles by which it is regulated*, which he published along with the *Grounds of an Opinion*, has a scientific-looking title, and, as he tells us, contains the substance of some notes on rent which he had collected for purely didactic purposes. But he actually apologizes for the fact that 'the nature of the disquisition' may 'appear to the reader hardly to suit the form of a pamphlet',[3] and the curious slip by which he attributes 'a progressive rise of rents' in general to the extension of 'our' manufacturers and commerce,[4] is a sufficient proof that the professor's notes on rent had undergone considerable manipulation at the hands of the political pamphleteer. His *Political Economy* and *Definitions* add very little to his earlier works. They scarcely attempt to cover new ground, but simply go once more over old controversies.

Ricardo's ruling interests were no less practical than those of Malthus.[5] His career as a writer on economic questions began with the contribution of a series of letters to the *Morning Chronicle* newspaper in September 1809.[6] His object in these was to show that the over-issue of inconvertible bank notes had caused a depreciation of their value, and to insist that the Bank of England should 'gradually decrease the amount of their notes in circulation, until they shall have rendered the remainder of equal value with the coins which they repre-

[1] *Grounds of an Opinion*, p. 1.

[2] See above, p. 161.

[3] 'Advertisement' or Preface.

[4] P. 32. The word 'our' is omitted in *Political Economy*, p. 178, where the paragraph is repeated.

[5] This is, of course, not in contradiction with Ricardo's often quoted remark to Malthus, 'If I am too theoretical (which I really believe is the case), you, I think, are too practical' (*Letters*, p. 96). He is then speaking not of conclusions but of arguments, and deprecating the habit of 'appealing to experience in favour of a particular doctrine'. Had Ricardo foreseen some of the discussions which took place after his death, he would have said, 'If I use the deductive method too exclusively, you, I think, rely too much on the inductive'.

[6] *Three Letters on the Price of Gold*, reprinted Baltimore, 1903, edited by Jacob H. Hollander.

sent'.[1] 'We must keep our eyes', he said, 'steadily fixed on the repeal of the restriction bill'.[2] He republished the substance of the letters in the form of a pamphlet, and when the Bullion Committee were attacked for having adopted his views, he defended them in his *Reply to Mr. Bosanquet's Practical Observations on the Report of the Bullion Committee* (1811). Four years later he published his *Essay on the Influence of a Low Price of Corn*, in opposition to the demand for new restrictions on the corn trade.[3] Early in 1816 he produced his *Proposals for an Economical and Secure Currency with Observations on the Profits of the Bank of England as they regard the public and the proprietors of Bank Stock*. It was in dealing with these practical matters that he formed what, as he tells us, Malthus called his 'peculiar opinions on profits, rents, etc'.[4] We are indebted to the Bullion controversy for the Ricardian theory of value, and to the Corn Law controversy of 1813–15 for the Ricardian theory of rent and distribution in general. Read with the pamphlets which preceded it, Ricardo's *Principles of Political Economy and Taxation* is intelligible enough. Read without them it is the happy hunting-ground of the false interpreter.

The minor lights of the Ricardian period were likewise for the most part pamphleteers and reviewers who wrote because they were interested in the politics of the day. Such certainly were West, Torrens, and M'Culloch. James Mill is the only exception of importance, and even he had begun by writing a pamphlet against Spence's depreciation of the utility of Britain's commerce. The purely scientific and didactic writers of the time were worthies like Boileau and Mrs Marcet, never important, and now almost entirely forgotten.

It would seem at first sight that J. S. Mill, publishing his *Principles* in 1848, ought to have been fairly free from the practical influences which affected the work of Malthus and Ricardo and their contemporaries. The Corn Laws had been repealed in 1846, the old Poor Law had gone in 1834, and cash payments had been resumed in 1819. But though Mill was only forty-two in 1848, he had, owing to his extraordinary precocity, acquired his first impressions of political economy when the Ricardian school was at its zenith. When he was thirteen, in 1819, his father began instructing him 'by a sort of lectures', which he delivered as they walked together:

> 'He expounded each day.' Mill says, 'a portion of the subject, and I gave him next a day a written account of it, which he made me rewrite over and over again until it was clear, precise, and tolerably complete. In this manner I went through the whole extent of the science; and the written outline of it which resulted from my daily *compte rendu* served him afterwards as notes from which to write his *Elements of Political Economy*. After this I read Ricardo, giving an

[1] *Works*, p. 287.
[2] *Ibid.*, p. 290.
[3] Above, pp. 165–167.
[4] *Letters to Malthus*, p. 116.

account daily of what I read, and discussing, in the best manner I could, the collateral points which offered themselves in our progress.

'On Money, as the most intricate part of the subject, he made me read in the same manner Ricardo's admirable pamphlets, written during what was called the Bullion controversy; to these succeeded Adam Smith; and in this reading it was one of my father's main objects to make me apply to Smith's more superficial view of political economy the superior lights of Ricardo, and detect what was falacious in Smith's arguments or erroneous in any of his conclusions.'[1]

About the same time he came under the direct personal influence of Ricardo:

> 'My being an habitual inmate of my father's study made me acquainted with the dearest of his friends, David Ricardo, who by his benevolent countenance and kindliness of manner was very attractive to young persons, and who, after I became a student of political economy, invited me to his house, and to walk with him, in order to converse on the subject.'[2]

His father's method of instructing him in political economy was, he thought, 'excellently calculated to form a thinker', and he was ready to assert that 'it succeeded'.[3] We are, however, scarcely surprised to learn that some years later, 'hearsay information' had made Sterling look on him 'as a "made" or manufactured man, having had a certain impress of opinion stamped on him, which he 'could only reproduce'.[4] Though Sterling found himself mistaken, it seems clear that Mill became somewhat prematurely committed to a set of economic doctrines. At sixteen, he was defending Ricardo and James Mill against Torrens in the *Traveller* newspaper,[5] and his essays on the 'Laws of Interchange between Nations', and on 'Profits and Interest',[6] 'emanated', he tells us, from conversations which took place about the year 1826,[7] though they were not written till 1829 and 1830[8], and were not published till 1844. During the long interval between their composition and their publication, Mill's mind was extremely active, but it does not seem to have been directed towards scientific economics. When a man has been giving study and thought to a subject, he does not take rejected[9] manuscripts which have lain fourteen years in his drawer, and print them 'with a few merely verbal alterations'.[10]

[1] *Autobiography*, p. 28.
[2] *Ibid.*, p. 54.
[3] *Ibid.*, pp. 28, 29.
[4] *Ibid.*, p. 155.
[5] *Autobiography*, pp. 87, 88.
[6] Nos. I and IV of *Essays on some unsettled Questions of Political Economy*.
[7] *Autobiography*, p. 121.
[8] *Essays*, preface; in the *Autobiography*, p. 180, he says, '1830 and 1831', but the preface to the *Essays* is more likely to be correct than the *Autobiography*.
[9] 'When, some years later, I offered them to a publisher, he declined them.' – *Autobiography*, p. 180.
[10] *Essays*, Preface.

Between the publication of the *Essays* and that of the *Principles of Political Economy*, he certainly gave himself no time for the necessary revision of his early impressions. 'The *Political Economy*', he says, 'was far more rapidly executed than the *Logic*, or indeed than anything of importance which' he 'had previously written. It was commenced in the autumn of 1845, and was ready for the press before the end of 1847', and that too, although 'there was an interval of six months during which the work was laid aside'.[1]

Consequently his book, so far as what he calls 'the purely scientific part'[2] of it is concerned, is much less free from the influence of the practical controversies of the Ricardian period than many works which preceded it, and which its popular qualities and apparent completeness caused it to supersede. The 'general tone'[3] and the 'applications' of the 'principles of political economy' to 'social philosophy'[4] were new, but the structure of the theories of production and distribution, though plastered over with a fresh stucco of explanation and limitation, had been built twenty years earlier.

Now for the settlement of the controversies under the influence of which it was created, the system of economics which prevailed after Malthus and Ricardo had written was admirably adapted. Where it was clear and correct, its points against what was practically evil were well and forcibly made; where it was confused and erroneous, its confusions and errors were such as to assist rather than hinder its work; where it was deficient, its deficiencies were not of much practical importance.

For the practical purpose of destroying the abuses of the old Poor Law the theory of production served very well. Its plan of representing 'capital' as the thing which puts industry into motion and supports labour was excellently adapted to inspire distrust of all attempts on the part of the State to employ labour. Its excessive insistence on the disadvantages of increasing population was equally well adapted to bring into discredit the mischievous incitements to matrimony which were offered under the old Poor Law administration.

For the basis of an argument against the Corn Laws it would have been difficult to invent anything more effective than the Ricardian theory of distribution. The divergence of interests with regard to the corn laws was really a divergence of the interests of classes, and not of individuals. It was not a question of 'the classes against the masses', or, in other words, of the rich against the poor, but of the landowning class againt the commercial and manufacturing class. The Ricardian

[1] *Autobiography*, p. 235. The interval was employed in writing articles in the *Morning Chronicle*, advocating the formation of peasant properties on the waste lands of Ireland.

[2] *Autobiography*, p. 246. [3] *Ibid., l.c.* [4] *Principles*, title.

neglect of the problem of distribution between individuals was here perfectly harmless. The confusion of wages per head, profits per cent, and rent per acre with proportions of the produce, was of little importance in view of the fact that variations in wages per head, profits per cent, and rent per acre, when suddenly caused by changes in the corn laws, would, as a matter of fact, correspond with variations in the proportions of the produce allotted to wages, profits, and rent. The doctrine which attributed the rise of rent per acre and the fall of profits per cent to the decreasing productiveness of industry employed at the margin of cultivation was an admirable engine for bringing the manufacturing and commercial class into favour, and exciting odium against legislation in favour of landowners. Much the same may be said of the sharp distinction somewhat falsely drawn between rent and interest, based, as it was, largely on the idea that interest is the reward of a painful or meritorious action. At a later period, when political power had passed in some measure to the wage-earning classes, it would doubtless have been more effective to show that the corn laws diminished real wages, but at the time it simplified the matter to declare the comforts of the labourers a nearly constant quantity, and consequently outside the problem.

§ 3. *Uselessness of the Theories of Production and Distribution in regard to Combination and Socialism*

Partly, no doubt, owing to the very effectiveness of the Maltho-Ricardian political economy, the practical problems with which it was chiefly concerned were soon solved. Since the repeal of the corn laws another great controversy has come, in the popular apprehension, if not always in the opinion of economists, to overshadow all others in economics – the controversy which is carried on in an almost infinite variety of shapes between the supporters of the existing arrangements of society and those who desire that association in one or other of its numerous forms should encroach on the sphere of private property and individual competition in order to improve the condition of the less fortunate members of the community.

However lucky Error may be for a time, Truth keeps the bank, and wins in the long run. Mistakes which were harmless in the discussion of free trade, the poor-law and the resumption of cash payments, have often been extremely pernicious in their influence on the later controversy. The bitter hostility to trade unions, which, at any rate till very recent years, was felt by the 'upper' and 'enlightened' classes, was doubtless chiefly due to dislike of that loss of the more petty delights of power which was involved in the substitution of the relation of buyer and seller of work for the old relation of master and servant, but it was fostered by the 'population and capital' theory of wages, which really made many people believe that associations of wage-earners, however annoying and harmful to employers, must always be powerless to effect any improvement in the general condition of the employed. The exploitation theory of German socialists, which even in England has done much to embitter the higgling of the market – called by some 'industrial war', or 'conflicts of labour and capital' – by representing the fact that 'Labour' does not receive, the whole produce or income of the community, as the result, not of the mere existence of private property, but of some mysterious process whereby 'Capital' cheats 'Labour' out of a part of its legitimate reward, owes its origin to the old subsistence theory of wages, to the confusions about the nature and functions of 'capital', and to a natural reaction against the attempt to explain interest as the reward of some painful or meritorious action. The movement for 'nationalising' land without compensation to present owners, on which Mr Henry George and others have wasted immense energy, would probably never have been heard of, if the Ricardian economists had not represented rent as a sort of vampire which continually engrosses a larger and larger share of the produce, and if they had not failed to classify rent and interest together as two species of one genus. The folly of endeavouring to remedy poverty by advocating the confiscation of land, or by attacking other particular kinds of property, would not so easily have escaped recognition by reasonable individuals in the second half of the nineteenth century, if the economics of the first half had given the distribution of wealth between individuals its proper place, instead of being so exclusively devoted to the distribution of wealth between economic categories such as 'labourers', 'capitalists', and 'landlords'. In that case it would have been much more obvious that the greater extremes of poverty, as well as the greater extremes of riches, are due to the inequality which prevails in the distribution of the aggregate income allotted to each of the three categories, so that just as great riches are due to some individuals having acquired much property, so great poverty is due to some individuals not earning the average wages of labour, and the latter circumstance is no more due to the existence of private property in particular classes of objects than the former.

Besides all this, it seems that for the discussion of changes in a socialist or communist direction, the political economy of the first half of the nineteenth century does not deal with the right subject-matter. Whether any such change should be made or not is generally a question to be decided by the effect which it will have upon the material welfare of the persons concerned. But the subject-matter of the early nineteenth century political economy is not 'wealth' in its original sense of material welfare, but 'wealth' in the secondary sense of material objects possessed of exchange value, or at any rate in the sense of commodities and services possessed of exchange value. That 'wealth' in this sense and material welfare are not the same thing every one recognizes, but the closeness of the connexion between the two is much over-rated. In reality, even as society is at present constituted, the amount of wealth enjoyed by individuals and nations affords very insufficient information about their material welfare. In the first place, according to a well-known rule, each successive increment of 'wealth' produces a smaller amount of material welfare, and consequently a given amount of 'wealth' will produce a greater or smaller amount of material welfare according as it is distributed more or less equally. In the second place, the effort of obtaining the 'wealth' is a factor in the determination of material welfare just as much as the enjoyment of 'wealth'. When the effort is, as often happens, purely pleasurable, the material welfare of the people is increased by it. When, on the other hand, the effort is either excessive, and therefore painful, or accompanied by unpleasant incidents, the material welfare of the people is reduced by it. In the third place, a great quantity of that part of the produce of industry which is created by men and women working, not for money rewards, but from other motives, such as family affection or duty to the community, is for all practical purposes incapable of being valued and set down in the sum-total of commodities and services with exchange value.

But it is just on these very points where the early nineteenth century political economy is so weak that the discussion of socialistic and communistic changes chiefly turns. The aim of socialist and communist aspiration is to increase the material welfare of the race by introducing greater equality in the material goods enjoyed by individuals, by reducing idleness on the one hand, and excessive and irregular effort on the other, and by eventually substituting associated for competitive labour, and abolishing both the institution of private property and the practice of exchange, without which value, in any reasonable sense of the word, cannot exist. As to all this, the economist who confines political economy to the consideration of commodities and services with exchange value is obliged either to keep silence or to resort to the expedient of speaking, not as an economist but as a 'social philospher'.

§ 4. *Changes in the Theories since* 1848

To continue the history of the theories of production and distribution from 1848 down to the present time (1903) even in the briefest possible sketch would be an immense task, largely in consequence of the loss of insularity which English political economy has undergone. In the origin and development of the doctrines dealt with in the present work, France certainly played a great and often underrated part, but the historian could safely neglect the rest of the world. That is no longer possible. During the last half century not only Germany, and at a later date Austria and other European countries, but also America, have entered the lists, and have so profoundly modified English economics that the work of the historian has become much wider and more complicated. Moreover, it seems still true that it is too early to treat of the economics of the second half of the nineteenth century in a historical spirit. It must be left to the next generation, or the next generation but one, to unravel the thread of progress. But the nature of some of the criticisms passed upon the first edition of this book suggests that it may be desirable to add here the shortest possible account of the more important changes which appear to the writer to have taken place in the theories of production and distribution, and to explain how they have affected the attitude of the economist towards the practical economic problems of today.

Whatever definitions of economics may be adopted, it is clear that the conception of its subject has become wider than it was. There is no longer any attempt to imagine a pile of 'wealth' growing and growing, and yet the community no better off. The economist of today recognizes that he has to deal with man in relation to one particular kind of human welfare. The idea that this particular kind of welfare is dependent simply on quantity of goods accumulated or periodically forthcoming, has been rendered untenable by the progress of theory as to the nature and measurement of utility. Ever since Jevons explained the declining utility of successive increments of food it has been impossible for the English economist to rely much on the fact that a loaf is a loaf whether it is crumbled in the hands of a surfeited Dives or devoured by a starving Lazarus. The same loaf is of less use to Dives, and the modern economist must recognize the fact. Hence he is obliged to lay down propositions as to the material welfare of individuals and communities, and cannot, even if he wishes to do so, confine himself to statements about increases of material commodities and services. It would be impossible for any economist of the present day to repeat Malthus's remark that Adam Smith mixes the nature and causes of the wealth of nations with the causes which affect the happiness and comfort of the lower orders of society.

The change has important effects, which are not yet fully worked out, upon the theories of production and distribution. Are we to continue to treat production and distribution as production and distribution of commodities and services, irrespective of the greater or less utility these commodities and services may possess under different conditions? If we do, we require some new department or heading other than 'production' and 'distribution' to be devoted to economic theory on this subject. Or are we, on the other hand, to reckon production as greater or less according as the utility of the commodities and services produced is greater or less? If we take this alternative, we must be prepared for Production swallowing up the Distribution of goods, since the way in which goods are distributed affects their utility. Thus the new 'Production' will include the old 'Distribution', and the new 'Distribution' will be very different from the old, since it will no longer be possible to compare the shares entirely by their value or amount. Of the two alternatives the first involves least break with tradition; and so we often find in the treatises of the present day additional 'books' or 'parts' in which the relationship between goods and utility is dealt with. But there is little agreement as to the title of this new department and the method of arranging it. The uncertainty which prevails on this point is probably one of the most important obstacles to the production of that clearly arranged popular text-book which all teachers demand and none seems able to produce.

The theory of production is still grouped round the requisites or agents of production, but the number of primary or essential requisites is reduced to two by the exclusion of capital, which, as J. S. Mill himself recognized, cannot reasonably be held to be an essential requisite of production, though it doubtless is an essential requisite of high productiveness of industry.

In the doctrine of population, or in other words in the doctrine of the relationship between land and labour, a great change has taken place. It is now clearly recognized that the point at which the returns to industry cease increasing and begin to diminish – the point as it may be called of maximum productiveness – is constantly being shifted by the progress of knowledge and other circumstances, and that the shifting is generally in the direction of increasing the population which is consistent with the maximum productiveness possible at the time. Although the population of the civilized world has enormously increased since 1848, no one would now think of saying, as J. S. Mill said then, 'the density of population necessary to enable mankind to obtain in the greatest degree all the advantages both of co-operation and of social intercourse has, in all the most populous countries, been attained'. We see that while the maximum productiveness point may have been reached in 1848, when the population of England and Wales was $17\frac{1}{2}$ millions, it may not be passed or even attained in 1903, when the population is 33 millions.

The displacement of capital from the triad of productive requisites and its relegation to the same rank as organization, knowledge, mental and muscular power, would not, perhaps, have been of much importance if it had not been represented as the most active element in the triad. As it is, the change is immense. No longer is capital supposed to decide whether industry shall be set in motion or not, and whether it shall flow into this or that channel when it is set in motion. Capital takes its proper place as an inanimate stock of goods and machinery which it is found useful to maintain. The normal amount of industry in the world and in each country of the world is seen to depend not upon the stock of consumable goods and machinery therein, but upon the number of the people and their ability and willingness to work. The power of 'managing' industry is attributed not to the mute and inanimate capital, nor even to the owners of the capital, but to a particular class of workers – the 'entrepreneurs' – and it is clearly seen that even they can only direct industry into particular channels by virtue of their intelligent anticipation of the orders of the consumers, whose demands they have to satisfy on pain of bankruptcy. In the old biograph of production the student was first introduced to an eighteenth-century British farmer standing on a prairie beside a stack of wheat and a table covered with loaves. He raps upon the table, and there enter from nowhere in particular some hungry labourers, who immediately consume the loaves, and are set to work by the farmer's promise to divide the stack among them in the course of a year. The modern economist sees that the stack is only there in consequence of the anticipated demands of the labourers. He recognizes that the inanimate stock of goods does not settle how many men shall be employed; but saving men settle how much stock there shall be, and consuming men settle by their expected demands what forms that stock shall take.

In Distribution, the confusions of the old doctrines are disappearing. The distinction between the landlord 'taking a larger and ever larger proportion of the produce' and 'increasing rents' is no longer frequently overlooked. A fall in the rate of interest is confused with a smaller proportion of produce going to the capitalists only by city editors and that very ignorant person the man in the street. It is comprehended, though not always very clearly, that the earnings of labour may keep on rising and the rate of interest keep on falling, while the proportion of the whole produce going to labour is continually diminishing. Statisticians have scarcely as yet provided a sufficient answer even to broad questions, such as, 'Did earnings of labour form a larger or smaller proportion of the income of the community in 1800 than in 1900?' – but they have at least made it possible to conceive the answer to such a question in numerical form, and when that is done it is impossible to fall into the old confusions any more.

The great questions which used to be treated under 'Distribution', though they are just as much productional as distributional, namely, the questions as to the causes of high and low rent, profit and wages, are far more satisfactorily treated. The Ricardian theory of rent seems to be falling into the background, chiefly, perhaps, because with the growth of urban land rents it has become more evident that the varying number of 'doses of labour and capital' which it is profitable to apply to a particular acre of land is a factor in determining its rent no less important than the yield of each of these doses over and above the return to the 'marginal dose'. For example, it is seen that while the site of a New York skyscraper might very probably yield a larger return as a potato patch than an equal area cultivated in the same manner in Donegal, this surplus is a small matter compared with the extra rent obtainable in consequence of the New York site being a suitable place for the exertions of hundreds of commercial men floor above floor. The Ricardian theory does not profess to give any information about the number of doses yielding more than the marginal dose which it is profitable to apply, and consequently, in telling us that the rent will be equal to the sum of the surplus returns from all the doses which it is profitable to apply, it tells us very little. It is seen, too, that the difference supposed to exist between income derived from the ownership of land and the income derived from the ownership of other things is in fact a difference between income derived from things which cannot be increased or diminished, and things which are liable to diminution by decay and consumption and to increase by human labour. Hence we have Marshall's enlightening conception of the income derived from man-made instruments of production as 'quasi-rent'.

Having by the aid of this conception grouped land and existing forms of capital together, we find it much easier to recognize that the rate of interest is merely the proportion existing at any particular moment between the income and the principal of freshly-created capital, and that this proportion is determined by the advantage to be gained by making the least advantageous or marginal investment – the least profitable investment which (apart from mere miscalculation) it is necessary to make in order to utilize the whole of the capital available. At one time conditions may be such that investments are on the margin which involve the expenditure of £100 or 100 weeks' labour in order to get an additional annual income of £10, or in order to get the same income as before with ten weeks' less labour annually. Then the rate of interest will be 10 per cent. At another time the conditions may be such that all 10 per cent investments have long ago been made, and those investments are on the margin which bring in an additional £5, or save five weeks' labour annually for each £100 or 100 weeks' labour expended. Then the rate of interest will have sunk to 5 per cent. The principal conditions are amount of capital, amount of population, and knowledge of the different means of utilizing capital. The first two are opposing forces: increase of capital pushes the margin further down in the productive scale, while increase of population tends to raise the return from the marginal investment. Increase of knowledge affects the margin in different ways at different times, sometimes raising it by showing new ways of utilising capital at a profit greater than that obtainable on the existing margin, and sometimes lowering it by showing how to dispense with capital in some kinds of production. The historical fall in the rate of interest is easily seen to be the natural result of increase of capital in proportion to population unaccompanied by the discovery of new profitable means of utilising capital sufficient to counterbalance the other force. It is not, as the Ricardians thought, the result of declining productiveness of industry; and the productiveness of industry has not declined.

As to the earnings of labour, we find the economics of 1903 far simpler than those of 1776 or 1848. The modern theory of earnings is that the average earnings per head depend immediately (not indirectly through consequent variations of capital) upon the produce per head and the proportions in which that produce is divided between workers and owners of property. History seems to show that when the proportion taken by owners of property increases, the increase is usually due to the increase of capital. This increase of capital tends to increase the produce per head, so that while the average earnings are tending towards reduction in consequence of a change in distribution, they are tending towards increase in consequence of a change in production. Hence, as a matter of fact, even if, as is probable, the proportion of produce obtained by property has increased, that increase has not been accompanied by a decrease but by an increase in average earnings.

§ 5. *Usefulness of the Existing Theories*

It will perhaps be alleged that the modern theories, though possibly more correct, are not so useful as their predecessors. The politician complains that the modern economist is always sitting on the fence and will not give a plain answer to a practical question. The truth is in reality that the economist refuses to take a side when both sides are wrong, and declines to say Yes or No to a question when both the affirmative and the negative answer would make him admit what he knows to be untrue. Till the politician learns enough to be able to ask a fair question he need not demand a straight answer. To fair questions the modern economist is quite ready to give a straight answer.

Let us examine the attitude of the modern economist towards several great practical problems, beginning with the question of population. It is clear that there is now at work a new force, of which Malthus scarcely thought, tending to make what he called the prudential check much more effective than it was. In consequence we find the population of France stationary, and natality, which is the only source of population, declining in what are considered the most civilized parts of the rest of Europe and America. J. S. Mill, and probably Malthus also, if he overcame scruples about the means, would have hailed the change with delight. What has the modern economist to say? Is the change good or bad? This is a practical question, because the modern state can scarcely avoid discouraging or encouraging natality in various ways. Compulsory education and other restrictions on the earning power of young children discourage it, while free schooling and exemptions of items of the family man's expenditure from taxation encourage it. Hence it is desirable for the government of a state to know whether natality needs encouragement or discouragement.

It must be admitted that the economist cannot decide this question in any particular case. He is sure that population may be too great or too small, but he has no means beyond those possessed by the statesman of judging whether the population of France in 1903 is too small. He may be tolerably sure that 20 millions would be too few for France, but he cannot prove the proposition, and he is not really sure whether the actual population is too small or too great or just about right. But it is surely something to be able to refute the agricultural enthusiasts who believe in an unlimited increase of population, and also the neo-Malthusian fanatics who regard restriction of population as the one thing needful at all places and times. It may also be added that at present there would be little chance of the economist being listened to if he did succeed in discovering some infallible criterion for determining the exact position of the point of maximum productiveness. International jealousies and consequent military considerations, rather than economic motives, will for the present, unhappily, decide whether modern states desire to encourage natality more or less.

With regard to the restrictive policy, called by the sweet name of 'Protection', and its negation, called by the equally attractive name of 'Free Trade', the doctrine of the modern economist is just as ambiguous as that of Adam Smith or Ricardo. Nobody who has once grasped the idea of the human race co-operating in the production of the services and commodities enjoyed and the things saved and added to capital can fall into the absurd confusion involving the conception of the perpetual export of gold from a country with no gold mines which forms the basis of the cruder forms of protectionist fallacy. Once grant that there is no need to fear that the people of each country may purchase from the people of other countries more than they can pay for, and all ordinary popular protectionism falls to the ground,

There only remain the arguments against national specialization in industry, which are for the most part frankly non-economic. So far as they are economic they are sufficiently met by the general demonstration of the effects of the control of self-interest over production. If there is no suggestion that Middlesex and Huntingdonshire or Massachusetts and California get anything but benefit from the specialization brought about by self interest, it is hopeless to argue that Germany and the United States will get anything but benefit from that specialization.

It will perhaps be suggested that at any rate the modern theories have not prevented a revival of protectionism in England. The answer to this is that the supposed revival is somewhat mythical. It is true that a certain considerable amount of protection has been recently secured by English agriculture; but this has only been accomplished by stealth and ruse. The restrictions on the import of cattle and the grain duty would never have been imposed if they had been frankly advocated on protectionist grounds. The fact that they could be imposed at all is chiefly due to the fact that England is now so much more wealthy and imports of agricultural produce are so much greater than in the middle of last century that a considerable bonus can be given to British landlords without the burden on the millions of payers being very much felt. Should the burden once more grow perceptible, it will be cast off again with the same vigour and completeness as in 1846, and the economics of the day will be found to furnish quite sufficiently effective arguments.[1] Even now the current cry for 'efficiency' seems likely to promote the cause of free trade. For the purpose of increasing efficiency in industry there is no greater and more obvious need than the free competition of foreign products and foreign workmen. Under protection the producers have not the same opportunity of copying and improving upon foreign products and foreign methods of production, and they need not, and generally do not, trouble their heads about the matter. A protected 'infant industry' is usually suffocated by its foster-mother. If an article can be made as easily at home as abroad, let it be imported till there is a considerable market for it, and then the home-manufacturer can be profitably started without any protection. Exclude the article and it will take far longer for its manufacture at home to be started. The educative effects of free trade – its effects in producing that kind of knowledge and intelligence which is the greatest need in business, are by no means its least important advantage.

With regard to the effects of combinations of wage-earners upon

[1] This paragraph was written in March, 1903, and sent to the printer two days before the announcement of the abandonment of the grain duty in the Budget of 1903. The author did not expect so early a confirmation of his view.

the earnings of labour, the modern economist gives a plain answer, if his questioners would take the trouble to listen to him. The wage-fund theorists thought combinations could not raise wages, because the fund to be divided was determined by the will of the capitalists, which would not be affected by combinations. This simple view has been abandoned; but it is not true, as is sometimes said, that nothing has been put in its place. Modern doctrine teaches plainly enough that combinations of earners can only raise earnings if they can raise the value or the quantity of the product, and that producers can only raise the value of the product by reducing its quantity. Common observation and careful investigation show that in practice combinations of earners, without power to prevent outsiders from entering the trade, can do little in the direction of raising the value of their product. Where they have raised earnings it has almost always been by increasing the product per head enough to compensate for some loss of value rather than by increasing the value of the product enough to compensate for some loss of quantity.

Lastly, we have to consider the relation of the modern economist towards socialist and communist aspiration. Here the complaints against him are loud and persistent. One side, still imbued with old traditions, is bewildered and annoyed to find that scarcely a single English economist of repute will join in a frontal attack upon socialism in general, while the other side is dissatisfied because nearly every economist, whether of repute or not, is always ready to pick holes in most socialistic proposals.

It is quite true that the economist of today is far less hostile to socialism in general than his predecessors of the classical school. This change is due in great measure to the change in the method of measuring utility. The doctrine of marginal utility stamps as economical many things which could formerly be recommended only on 'sentimental' or non-economic grounds. If socialist aspirations in England ever obtained much strength from Marxian doctrines, that time is past, and it is now chiefly dependent upon the popular belief that greater equality in the distribution of wealth is desirable. Modern economics shows that this belief is correct. Assuming needs to be equal, modern economics certainly teaches that a given amount of produce or income will 'go further' the more equally it is divided. The inequality of the present distribution has no pretension to be in proportion to needs, while the equality striven after in socialist and communist aspiration is always understood sometimes perhaps rather obscurely, to be modified by differences of need.

Hence, so far as distribution alone and taken by itself is concerned, the economist of the present day finds himself in considerable sympathy with socialist aspiration. But having studied the action and reaction of distribution and production upon one another, he cannot isolate changes in distribution and recommend them regardless of their effects upon production. He is not, indeed, obliged to adopt the old view that industry can never at any future time be sufficiently excited without the stimulus of economic self-interest. He sees that as a matter of fact much of the hardest and best labour of the world is done for other than economic rewards, and he can conceive the possibility of arrangements being evolved which would provide similarly effective motives for the industry of a whole people. The assertion that this must always be impossible because human nature always remains the same, does not trouble him when he remembers how many things in our present state would have seemed absolute impossibilities to the mind of William the Conqueror or Queen Boadicea. Nor is he obliged to accept the Malthusian anti-communist argument as fatal to socialist aspiration. It is certainly true that increase of population could not continue at the fastest rate physically possible without disaster of some kind; but there is no reason for supposing that the most thorough communism would encourage or permit such an increase. Even at present it is true that natality is kept down to a considerable extent by non-economic causes, and these causes might very possibly be strengthened in a communist system till they were nearly of the required power. 'Nearly' is all that is necessary, because it seems difficult even for the most enthusiastic individualist to claim that his own system secures more than that.

To the economist the question is one of organization. Could production be as well arranged in a socialist system as with private property and free labour? Would the organization meet the consumer's wants as accurately? Of course there are some people who persuade themselves that the wants of the consumers are only met occasionally and by chance at present. They concentrate their minds on any instances of confusion or waste which they come across, and regard these as normal, and the ordinary working of business as unusual and fortuitous. Instead of seeing the modern civilized world as it is on the whole tolerably well fed, they imagine people are rushing hither and thither, and only occasionally happening to get a meal. Instead of seeing that, after all, nobody goes naked and most are tolerably well clothed, they imagine a shivering population engaged in borrowing and stealing each other's rags. Instead of seeing the millions of fairly comfortable houses mostly spread over a reasonable extent of ground, they think of the whole people as huddled together in damp and insanitary hovels. Instead of seeing the people carried to and fro, by all kinds of means of transport, with regularity and dispatch, they can only see people fighting to get into an over-crowded train or tramcar and being left behind.

But these observers have something amiss in their mental vision. To the healthy eye it is obvious that the existing organization, though not by any means perfect, is at any rate better than any organization which any form of government could have substituted for it in the past or in the present. As regards the past, this will be readily admitted by almost everyone. Nobody thinks that Wessex could have had a socialist organization of production with advantage thirteen hundred years ago. Scarcely any one thinks that Great Britain could have organized production by some conscious effort two hundred years ago. None but fanatics think that Great Britain, or Great Britain and Ireland, or the British Empire, or the civilized world, or the whole world, could with advantage establish socialist arrangements at the present moment. The progress of historical knowledge during the last half-century has quite exploded the old belief in sudden 'revolutions'. The supposed sudden revolutions of the past have been ascertained to be merely salient points in the course of gradual changes extending over centuries. Hence, nobody of ordinary information and intelligence any more expects a 'social revolution', a sudden and complete overturn of the existing order in regard to property and industry and the substitution of complete regulation of industry by some form of territorial government. All that can be expected by the most enthusiastic is gradual change in the direction of such a state of things.

Modern economics contains nothing to show that gradual change may not eventually, in a distant future, evolve some form of conscious organization which at that time will work well and better than the unconscious organization resulting from private property and free labour; but it does not seem in the least necessary for the economist to hold any particular views on the subject beyond the hope that the future may be better than the present. The idea of gradual progress being admitted, he is left at liberty to consider the good and evil of each change which is made or proposed, without supporting a bad change because it appears to tend towards a particular ideal, or condemning a good one because it does not. Hence he is certain to disagree frequently with both socialist and individualist fanatics, who support and oppose changes, not on their merits, but according to the opinion they have formed, often on wholly insufficient grounds, as to their being movements towards or away from their ideal.

TABLE FOR CONVERSION OF REFERENCES TO SMITH'S *WEALTH OF NATIONS*

Pages (with columns distinguished by *a* and *b*) in M'Culloch's edition referred to in footnotes to the present work are given first, and are followed by the pages in Cannan's edition on which the passages quoted, of which there are often more than one in a column of M'Culloch, may be found.

M'C.	Cannan.	M'C.	Cannan.	M'C.	Cannan.
1*a*	i. 1	45*a*	i. 101	147*b*	i. 316
2*b*	i. 5	46*a*	i. 103	148*a*	i. 317
3*b*	i. 7	47*b*	i. 107	148*b*	i. 318
4	i. 9	50*b*	i. 112, 113	149*a*	i. 319
5*a*	i. 11	51*a*	i. 113, 114	149*b*	i. 320
6*a*	i. 13	66*a*	i. 145	150*a*	i. 321
6*b*	i. 15	66*b*	i. 145, 146	150*b*	i. 322, 323
7*b*	i. 17	67*a*	i. 146, 147	152*a*	i. 325
8*a*	i. 18	67*b*	i. 147, 148	153*b*	i. 327
13*a*	i. 30	74–5	i. 162–3	155	i. 332
13*b*	i. 32	75*a*	i. 164	157*a*	i. 335
14*a*	i. 32, 33	75*b*	i. 165	159*b*	i. 340
22*a*	i. 49, 50	86*b*	i. 188	160	i. 341
22*b*	i. 50, 51	87*a*	i. 189	161*a*	i. 342
23*a*	i. 51	108	i. 232	161*b*	i. 343
23*b*	i. 53	115*a*	i. 247	163*b*	i. 347
24*a*	i. 54	115*b*	i. 247	167*a*	i. 353
24*b*	i. 55	118*b*	i. 258	191*b*	i. 404
25*a*	i. 57	119*b*	i. 259, 261	192*a*	i. 406
29*a*	i. 65, 66	120*a*	i. 261	198*b*	i. 419
29*b*	i. 67	120*b*	i. 262	200*b*	i. 423
30*a*	i. 68	121*a*	i. 263	204*b*	i. 430
31*a*	i. 70	121*b*	i. 264	207*a*	i. 435
31*b*	i. 70, 71	122*a*	i. 265	207*b*	i. 435
32*a*	i. 72	122*b*	i. 265, 266	216*a*	i. 453
32*b*	i. 73	123*b*	i. 269	219*b*	i. 459
33*a*	i. 75	124*a*	i. 269, 270	251*a*	ii. 61
36*a*	i. 80	125*a*	i. 272	300*a*	ii. 162
36*b*	i. 81	126*b*	i. 275	305*a*	ii. 173
39*b*	i. 88	127*a*	i. 276	306*a*	ii. 175
40*a*	i. 89	128*a*	i. 278	306*b*	ii. 175
42*a*	i. 94	145*b*	i. 313	307*a*	ii. 176
42*b*	i. 95	146*a*	i. 313	314*b*	ii. 192
43*a*	i. 95	146*b*	i. 314	350*b*	ii. 267
43*b*	i. 96	147*a*	i. 315	390*b*	ii. 348

INDEX